Learning Disabilities in Higher Education and Beyond

International Perspectives

Edited by Susan A. Vogel, Gila Vogel,
Vanda Sharoni, and Orit Dahan

Foreword by Doris J. Johnson

YORK PRESS Baltimore,
Maryland

This book was manufactured in the United States of America.

Typography by Type Shoppe II Productions, Ltd.
Printing and binding by Data Reproductions Corporation
Cover design by Joseph Dieter, Jr.

Library of Congress Cataloging-In-Publication Data
Learning disabilities in higher education and beyond : international perspectives / edited by Susan A. Vogel . . . [et al.] ; with a foreword by Doris J. Johnson.—1st ed.
        p. cm.
Includes bibliographical references (p.   ) and index.
    ISBN 0-912752-74-2
    1. Learning disabled—Education (Higher)—Cross-cultural studies. 2. Learning disabled—Social conditions—Cross-cultural studies. I. Vogel, Susan Ann.
    LC4818.38.L43 2003
    371.92′6—dc21
                        2003014588

Contents

Contributors

Pamela B. Adelman, Ph.D.
Hyde Park Day School
1375 E. 60th Street
Chicago, IL 60637
padelma@midway.uchicago.edu

Alison Aubrejuan, J.D.
Disability Rights Association
449 15th Street, Suite 303
Oakland, CA 94612-2821
general@dralegal.com

Angela Barron-Jeffrey, M.A.
Teaching and Learning Department
Northern Illinois University
De Kalb, IL 60115
abaronjef@niu.edu

Michael Barron-Jeffrey, M.A.
Sinnipsi Centers, Inc.
125 South Fourth Street
Oregon, IL 61061
baronjef@msn.com

MaryLouise Bat-Hayim, M.Ed.
Arts Centre for Academic Writing
York University
Toronto, Ontario, Canada M3J 1P3
mlb@yorku.ca

Andrew Brulle, Ed.D.
Wheaton College
Wheaton, IL 60187
andrew.brulle@wheaton.edu

Phillip Cohn, B.S.
Oxford Health Plan
Wilton, Connecticut

Orit Dahan, M.A.
Beit Berl College
Hod HaSharon, Israel
orit_d@newmail.net

Angela Fawcett, Ph.D.
Department of Psychology
University of Sheffield
Sheffield S10 2TP
United Kingdom
a.fawcett@sheffield.ac.uk

Rosalie P. Fink, Ph.D.
Lesley University
29 Everett Street
Cambridge, MA 02138
rfink@mail.lesley.edu

Jonathan Gillis, J.D.
Bizchut, The Israel Office for Civil
    Rights
Human Rights Center for People
    with Disabilities
Jerusalem, Israel
j.gillis@gsbk-law.co.il

Noel Gregg, Ph.D.
Learning Disabilities Center
334 Milledge Hall
University of Georgia
Athens, Georgia 30602
ngregg@coe.uga.edu

Rosa Hagin, Ph.D.
Department of Psychiatry
School of Medicine
New York University
New York, NY 10016
rhagin200@earthlink.net

Eleanor Higgins, Ph.D.
The Frostig Center
971 N. Altadena Drive
Pasadena, CA 91107
Higgins@frostig.org

Lynda Katz, Ph.D.
Landmark College
River Road South
Putney, Vermont 05346
lkatz@landmark.org

Joshua Konecky
Goldstein, Demchak, Baller, Borgen,
    & Dardarian
300 Lakeside Drive, Suite 1000
Oakland, CA 94612
jgk@gdblegal.com

Lea Kozminsky, Ph.D.
Kaye College of Education
Beer-Sheva, Israel
leako@macam.ac.il

Yona Leyser, Ph.D.
3 Pasternak Street
Ramat Aviv, Tel Aviv
Israel 69205
yleyser@niu.edu

Margaret Morrison, Ed.D.
Athens, Georgia 30602

Marshall Raskind, Ph.D.
The Research Center
The Frostig Center
971 N. Altadena Drive
Pasadena, CA 91107
raskind@frostig.org

Varda Sharoni, Ph.D.
Beit Berl College
Hod HaSharon, Israel
Vsharoni@beiberl.ac.il

Chris Singleton, Ph.D.
University of Hull
Hull HU6 TRX
United Kingdom
c.singleton@psy.hull.ac.uk

Ginny Stacey, Ph.D.
Student Services
Headington Hill Campus
Oxford Brookes University
Headington - Oxford
England OX3 OBP
gstacey@emzie.fsnet.co.uk

Gila Vogel, Ph.D.
Beit Berl College
Hod HaSharon, Israel
gila@beitberl.ac.il

Susan A. Vogel, Ph.D.
Literacy Education Department
College of Education
Northern Illinois University
De Kalb, IL 60115
svogel@niu.edu

Marc Wilchesky, Ph.D.
Support Centre for Students with
    Disabilities
York University
Toronto, Canada
mwilchesky@yorku.ca

Sid Wolinsky, J.D.
Disability Rights Association
449 15th Street, Suite 303
Oakland, CA 94612-2821
general@dralegal.com

Sharon Wyland, M.Ed.
Teaching and Learning Department
College of Education
Northern Illinois University
De Kalb, IL 60115
swyland@niu.com

Foreword

Forty years have passed since the term "learning disability" was first used in the United States. Prior to that time, children with specific learning disabilities received no services or they were placed with other groups of exceptional students. Gradually, laws were passed that mandated a free and appropriate education for all children with special needs. Initially, the services were limited primarily to students in elementary and high schools; however, it was evident, that even with very good special education, many students needed assistance gaining access to postsecondary education, in obtaining support services or accommodations, and in securing appropriate employment.

During the past two decades, numerous clinical and empirical studies have been carried out to identify the characteristics and needs of postsecondary adults with learning disabilities. Laws have been passed, and accommodations or services are now available in many settings. However, colleges and universities often need information about the diagnostic process, eligibility requirements and other matters. In addition, faculties within universities and employers need to understand the needs of adults with special needs. This volume includes a wealth of information for professionals, families, and for the adults themselves.

The book begins with an excellent overview of the laws regarding adults with disabilities, particularly learning disabilities and dyslexia. Anyone who is working with exceptional adults will find these chapters to be excellent resources. The authors provide insights into the ways in which various countries have addressed issues such as college admissions and educational rights. The social and cultural approaches to the handicapped, the contrasts between "legal rights" versus "social rights," and the ways in which countries respond to diversity are particularly interesting. Differences in terminology are evident. For example, the term "Learning Disabilities" is used in many countries, but the focus in the United Kingdom appears to be primarily on dyslexia. Although the chapter on dyslexia is valuable, many college students and adults with LD, have problems other than dyslexia. Hence, if all exceptional college students are to obtain services, their needs in areas such as mathematics, written expression, oral language, and other areas need to be considered.

The second section on assessment and diagnostic models also illustrates various theoretical perspectives. The reader will become familiar with clinical appraisals, the use of aptitude/achievement discrepancies, measurement of cognitive processes, and data pertaining to dyslexia.

The section on Program Models highlights the need for obtaining input from service providers, faculty, and the students themselves. Given the diversity of the LD population, models need to be broad enough to meet the needs of severe dyslexics who cannot read a textbook to those whose only problems are with timed reading comprehension or timed writing fluency. Some students need extensive support, whereas others need only time accommodations. Because of the technological revolution in this country, the review of the types of technology and their effectiveness should be beneficial for practitioners and researchers as well as students with learning disabilities. This section includes a chapter on ADHD, a condition that may be present with or without a learning disability. The author includes a wealth of information regarding prevalence, assessment, and management.

The chapter regarding the attitudes of college faculty in America and Israel highlights the need for studying more than the individual with a disability. Because students will be taking courses from faculty whose knowledge about atypical learners varies, the campus offices for students with disabilities often work with professors to assist individuals who have special needs.

The information regarding support groups includes an excellent overview of selection criteria and a design for a twelve-week program that is well grounded in research with successful adults. However, professionals who are planning such groups should be mindful that even with well planned sessions, some adults prefer individual rather than group discussions.

The section on the social-emotional impact of LD addresses questions that are asked frequently by families and professionals. Because the impact of a disability may change over time, the need for counseling may arise periodically. However, when making referrals, it is wise to consider counselors, social workers, and psychiatrists who understand the nature of the various types of information processing problems in this heterogeneous population.

The chapter on successful adjustment raises several philosophical questions regarding long term goals and planning, if not the meaning of success itself. The structured interview that was given to a relatively heterogeneous group yielded interesting responses that can provide the bases for programming.

Many families, diagnosticians, and educators are interested in possible outcomes of learning disabilities after college. The research findings are, in many respects, quite encouraging. At the same time, the realities of persistent weaknesses and the need for periodic counseling or support across the life span are evident.

The chapter by Fink raises many philosophical questions regarding the identification of dyslexics, approaches to instruction, and outcomes. The interview with high achieving adults illustrates the importance of intrinsic motivation, the use of materials that stimulate curiosity, and the use of interactive approaches to instruction. Even though most of the adults reported that lower level processing weaknesses continued to interfere with some aspects of their decoding and spelling, they make good use of context. The adults from our center report similar strategies. Hence, a balanced approach to reading that incorporates their strengths as well as weaknesses seems most appropriate.

While the intent of this chapter was to discuss high achievers, it is important to remember, the successful dyslexics in all walks of life. Many choose not to pursue careers that involve extensive academic programs and are in occupations that allow them to be productive and maintain a strong sense of self.

Overall, this volume is a fine addition to the body of knowledge regarding learning disabilities in adulthood. The international perspectives will provide researchers and practitioners with information regarding the types of services that foster successful outcomes.

Doris J. Johnson, Ph.D.
Jo Ann and Peter Dolle Professor in
 Learning Disabilities
Department of Communication
Sciences and Disorders
Northwestern University
Evanston, Illinois

Preface

The major purpose of this book is to share the cumulative wealth of experience among professionals in the countries that have been in the forefront in the provision of support services and accommodations for students with LD and to disseminate widely the cutting edge information from some of the leading experts in each of the four countries with mandated college support services. Topics include public policy, assessment, ADHD and learning disabilities, assistive technology, counseling and support groups, faculty attitude and knowledge, and long term outcomes for adults with LD.

UNDERLYING ASSUMPTIONS OF THE BOOK

1. In all four countries, though terminology may differ slightly, there is general consensus regarding the concept of learning disabilities as defined by the National Joint Committee of Learning Disabilities;
2. Dyslexia, as defined by the International Dyslexia Association, is the most common type of LD and, therefore, we are using LD and dyslexia interchangeably;
3. In all four countries, there is general agreement that learning disabilities are a life-long disorder though the manifestations and areas affected may differ based on the demands of the environment and the developmental stage and goals of the adult;
4. Identifying learning disabilities, even if it occurs in adulthood, is a critical first step in determining eligibility for accommodations and support services, in self-understanding, in the development of compensatory strategies, and in requesting accommodations;
5. Learning disability specialists and diagnosticians must be cognizant of the following differences in working with adults as compared to children or adolescents:
   a. Adults requesting services or accommodations in college/university have an immediate and often urgent need;
   b. Adults may need assistance in developing compensatory strategies in order to by-pass the negative impact of their LD, if at all possible, before requesting accommodations;

    c. Learning disabilities must be viewed in a broader context than just its impact on academic skills;

    d. The nature of the relationship between adults with LD and helping professionals is fundamentally different from the relationship between children with LD and professionals.

ORGANIZATION AND CONTEXT: AN OVERVIEW

This book is divided into five parts. Each part begins with a part opener that helps the reader identify the main themes and content of each chapter in that section. The chapters in Part I focus on legal mandates, issues, and concerns that play a crucial role in determining the accommodations and support services that exist for students with learning disabilities in higher education.

The three chapters in Part II, *Screening, Assessment, and Diagnostic Models,* address assessment and diagnosis of learning disabilities; both of critical importance in the provision of support services for students with learning disabilities. The three chapters in this section move from a discussion of theoretical constructs, to the presentation of a general model of diagnosis, to a specific proposal regarding the essential elements of assessment of adults with dyslexia.

Part III, *Support Service Issues in Higher Education,* presents support service issues regarding students with learning disabilities in higher education. The first chapter in this section (Chapter 8) addresses the more general question of who shall determine the nature of these models and services. The authors stress the importance of hearing the personal narratives of all the participants and recommend collaborative research. The next three chapters in this section deal with issues pertaining to ADHD, assistive technology, and faculty attitude and knowledge regarding students with learning disabilities. In chapter 9, the focus is on the support services needed by students with ADHD in higher education after a brief review of issues of identification, requirements for documentation, gender differences, co-morbidity, interventions, and accommodations. In chapter 10, the focus is on the use of assistive technology as support services for post-secondary students with learning disabilities. The range of the technologies currently available, as well as the various models used to deliver the services, are described in addition to current research on the effectiveness of these technologies. The final chapter in this section (chapter 11) focuses on faculty knowledge, attitudes, and practices toward students with LD as they have an impact on the campus environment and student success. Faculty attitudes, as expressed in their willingness to make accommodations in both teaching and examinations, were compared regarding students with learning disabilities enrolled in teacher education versus other fields.

In Part IV, *Social Emotional Impact of Learning Disabilities* there are two chapters. In Chapter 12, a model for a support group for adults with learning disabilities is described based on the research of Paul Gerber and his colleagues. The focus of this support group is to enable the participants to understand and develop strategies pertaining to social and emotional adjustment. Chapter 13 also focuses on successful adults with learning disabilities and described their cognitive and emotional approach to their disability. Sources of support and personal strategies for dealing with their problems are also described. In addition, three different intervention and support programs that were designed on the basis of the findings are described.

Part V consists of three chapters that deal with outcomes for adults with learning disabilities across the life span. Two chapters (14 and 15) describe one of the longest follow-up studies on college-able adults with learning disabilities. In chapter 14, educational attainment, employment, occupational status, job satisfaction and annual salary are reported. Although there are few significant differences between those with and without LD, the adults with LD reported that their learning disability had a negative impact on the job, usually in some aspect of language functioning. In chapter 15, no significant differences were reported on independence, mobility, and leisure activities; however, some adults reported feelings of low self-esteem and lack of self-confidence. Emotional problems were cited as the main way in which their LD affected them including problems with intimate relationships, loneliness, depression, and phobias. In chapter 16, the lives of 60 highly successful adults with dyslexia in the U.S. who achieved high levels of success in diverse professions are described with a special emphasis on reading acquisition and present reading habits. In this final section of the book, it is clear that many adults with learning disabilities can and do achieve high levels of success in spite of their vulnerability.

IN CLOSING

We hope that this book will inspire changes in public policy in other countries so that more adults with LD in higher education can not only be accepted but can graduate as well. The contributors exemplify the need for a multifaceted partnership among lobbyists, attorneys, diagnosticians, LD specialists, counselors, researchers, and adults with LD. The accomplishments of adults with LD as described in the closing section of this volume, provide persuasive evidence that they can achieve if provided with the opportunities, accommodations, and supportive environments.

Susan A. Vogel, Ph.D.

Acknowledgments

We wish to acknowledge our heartfelt appreciation to a number of individuals who contributed to the realization of this volume. First, our sincere thanks to the authors for their commitment to international collaborations exhibited by their willingness to travel to Israel from abroad and within Israel from the farthest corner in the north to the desert in the south. The speakers from outside Israel came from Canada, the United Kingdom, and the United States to share their knowledge and years of experience and to learn from one another. Their presence in Israel was a tremendous affirmation of the efforts of our colleagues in Israel. Second, we are very grateful to our Israeli hosts at Beit Berl College who deserve special commendation for their tireless efforts to make all of the arrangements necessary for a conference of this complexity and to create such a comfortable and aesthetically pleasing setting.

The major work, however, in bringing this book together in its updated and revised format, was carried out by another individual, Elinor Hartwig. We cannot find sufficiently accurate words to express our sincere gratitude to Elinor Hartwig of York Press for her willingness to take on such a project. Her insight, guidance, and careful attention to detail in publishing this book were unparalleled. Her tireless efforts to communicate with authors in four different countries made her work extremely challenging. She did this with grace, efficiency, and equanimity. We are all indebted to her.

Dedication

This book is dedicated to the adults with learning disabilities who disclosed their struggles, challenges, and triumphs so that others could learn how they, too, can achieve their ultimate goals.

PART • I

Legal Mandates, Issues, and Concerns

Each of the four chapters in this section focuses on a different country—the United States, Canada (Province of Ontario mainly), Great Britain, and Israel. We are thus better able to understand the different stages of development that characterize each country with regard to the status of students with learning disabilities in higher education.

In Chapter 1, Sid Wolinsky, Joshua Konecky, and Alison Aubrejuan address the issue of the legal rights of students with learning disabilities in the United States. The authors summarize the rights of students with learning disabilities regarding admission policies and the provision of accommodations guaranteed by the Americans with Disabilities Act of 1990 and raise a number of legal issues. The issues discussed include the ways individuals can meet the legal definitions of having a disability, the reasonable accommodations that must be offered by institutions of higher learning, the type of evidence that must be presented to show that a particular accommodation would interfere with the nature of the academic program and should, therefore, be denied, and the importance of ensuring that eligibility requirements are neither arbitrary nor discriminatory.

The legal culture in the Province of Ontario, Canada (by far the most advanced province with regard to support services for students with LD) is markedly different from that of the United States. In Chapter 2, MaryLouise Bat-Hayim and Marc Wilchesky describe the intricacies and voluntary nature of the system that have arisen in Ontario. They argue that this malleable system enables a larger number of students with special needs to obtain more and better quality services than would have been the case if their rights were legally mandated.

In Chapter 3, Ginny Stacey and Christopher Singleton review the report of the New Working Party (1995) on students with dyslexia in higher education in Great Britain. The report describes the current status of support for students with dyslexia. In terms of legal mandates, the chapter includes information on the impact of the 1995 Disability Discrimination Act and the changes brought about by the Dearing Report (1997) regarding eligibility requirements. Recommendations for institutional and national policy are discussed in this chapter as well.

Support services for students with learning disabilities have begun to emerge in colleges and universities in Israel and the United Kingdom modeled after some programs in the United States and Canada. Initially, the Israeli support services were offered thanks to grants from LESHEM (a private steering group of LD professionals) in spite of the lack of specific legislation protecting the rights of these students as in the United States and in the tradition that encourages diversity as in Ontario. In Chapter 4, Jonathan Gillis describes the development and status of the Equal Rights of People with Disabilities Law of 1998. In addition, recent landmark legislation is described dealing with higher education which may well change the future for thousands of university students with learning disabilities by providing them legal protection and a statement of their rights.

Chapter • 1

The Legal Rights of Students with Learning Disabilities in the United States

Sid Wolinsky, Joshua Konecky, and Alison Aubrejuan[1]

As increasing numbers of bright and skilled people with learning disabilities graduate from high school and enter college and the professional world, a number of legal issues have arisen regarding how they will be accommodated for their disabilities. People with learning disabilities have a rich fabric of statutory rights available for their protection. This includes the Individuals with Disabilities Education Act (IDEA), which provides protections for younger children, the Americans with Disabilities Act of 1990 (ADA) and its predecessor, Section 504 of the Rehabilitation Act of 1973 (Section 504), which protects younger children as well as individuals in the post-secondary context. Of particular importance for this article, the ADA and Section 504 guarantee individuals with learning disabilities the right to reasonable accommodations in higher education and on professional examinations, as well as non-discriminatory procedures for securing these accommodations.

Unfortunately, these rights are not always implemented, and individuals with learning disabilities often encounter a range of barriers to receiving the reasonable accommodations to which they are entitled. It

---

[1]Sid Wolinsky is the litigation director and Alison Aubrejuan is a senior attorney at Disability Rights Advocates (DRA), a non-profit center that deals with the legal rights of men, women, and children with disabilities. One of the firm's specialties is representation of individuals with learning disabilities, particularly in class action litigation. Joshua Konecky is an attorney with Goldstein, Demchak, Baller, Borgen and Dardarian, a class action and public interest law firm based in Oakland, California that also practices disability access law.

is important that educational institutions, testing administrators, learning disability specialists, and individuals with learning disabilities understand the specific mandates of these anti-discrimination laws so that the equal access and opportunity goals of the legislation can be realized.

This article explores several legal issues and disputes that have arisen as individuals with learning disabilities seek equal access to post-secondary education and professional screening, licensing, and competency examinations.

BASIC REQUIREMENTS AND GOALS OF FEDERAL DISABILITY LAW

Elementary and Secondary Education: Identification, Integration, and High Stakes Testing

Although the focus of this article is the legal issues that individuals with learning disabilities encounter in the post-secondary context, it is also important to have an understanding of the legal protections available to children in elementary and secondary schools, as well as of the issues that children with learning disabilities encounter.

The Individuals with Disabilities Education Act (IDEA) requires schools to identify children with disabilities who may need specialized education, and to provide these children with individualized education programs (IEP) tailored to their particular needs.[2] Children with "specific learning disabilities" are explicitly recognized as protected under IDEA. The statute requires that parents be involved in decisions about their children's education, and that children with disabilities be educated in the most integrated setting possible. Unfortunately, many children with disabilities, including learning disabilities, are not receiving the services and protections to which they are entitled. A study released by the National Council on Disability in January 2000 found that every state was out of compliance with IDEA requirements to some degree, and that too often children with disabilities and their families are forced to file complaints to ensure that the law is followed and services are provided.[3]

In 1997, the U.S. Congress amended IDEA in a number of ways, including strengthening the role of parents and urging school districts to use proactive curricular interventions rather than waiting until chil-

---

[2]Children with learning disabilities may also be protected under Section 504. However, there are generally fewer procedural protections for a student who is covered under Section 504 instead of IDEA.

[3]*Back to School on Civil Rights: Advancing the Federal Commitment to Leave No Child Behind*, National Council on Disability (January 25, 2000) at 7.

dren with disabilities fail or are labeled as disabled before providing assistance.[4]

Additionally, in response to the widespread practice of excluding children with disabilities from state and local assessments, Congress amended IDEA to require these entities to include children with disabilities in such assessments, with accommodations as necessary.[5] For those children with disabilities unable to participate in the state or local assessments as a result of their disability, IDEA provides that these children must be provided with an "alternate assessment."

Testing, and the role of alternate assessments, are of particular importance to children with learning disabilities. Increasingly, states and local school districts are relying on testing to hold schools and students accountable, and to make "high stakes" decisions regarding class placement, graduation, and eligibility for honors and scholarships based on tests. In addition, in at least one state, Oregon, it is anticipated that performance on high stakes assessments will be linked to entrance to state colleges and universities.[6]

High stakes testing has become politically popular as a method of improving public education. However, the rights and needs of children with disabilities, including those with learning disabilities, are generally overlooked when these tests are designed and implemented. The validity of these tests are often suspect. For example, these high stakes exams often directly test the area of a child's learning disability, such as

---

[4]20 U.S.C. § 1400(c)(5)(F) (stating that the education of children with disabilities can be made more effective by "providing incentives for whole-school approaches and pre-referral intervention to reduce the need to label children as disabled in order to address their learning needs.").

When passing the ADA, IDEA, and Section 504, Congress authorized the Department of Justice and the Department of Education to promulgate regulations to more specifically define and enforce the basic requirements of the Acts. Many of the specific legal rights and duties discussed in this article arise from these regulations and the judicial interpretations of them. In this article, citations to "C.F.R." refer to regulations, while citations to "U.S.C." refer directly to the statutes. Other citations are to judicial decisions.

[5]20 U.S.C. § 1412(a)(17)(A).

[6]Disability Rights Advocates recently settled a class action lawsuit against the State of Oregon on behalf of students with learning disabilities. The case, *Advocates for Special Kids v. Oregon State Board of Education,* challenged the design and implementation of Oregon's high stakes assessment system as discriminatory. Not only were students with learning disabilities denied accommodations on the assessment, Oregon did not provide the legally mandated alternate assessment for those students who were unable to participate in the general assessment. Under the settlement, Oregon agreed to make extensive changes to the testing system, including the creation of an alternate assessment and the implementation of a reliable accommodations process.

spelling, but there is no evidence that these skills are linked to success in higher education or the professions. Furthermore, these tests are often hastily implemented, and adequate procedures are not put into place for dealing with requests for accommodations or for determining whether a student participates in a general assessment or an alternate assessment.

High stakes tests are particularly problematic for children with learning disabilities because they are often denied accommodations on these tests, and as a result perform poorly and suffer severe emotional consequences. Children whose learning disabilities impair their ability to handwrite, and who have been provided with the accommodation of using a computer or word processor throughout their educational careers, are severely disadvantaged by being forced to handwrite their exams.

Additionally, some children with learning disabilities are unable to participate in these standardized tests, even with accommodations, due to the nature of their learning disabilities. For example, many high stakes tests rely on multiple choice tests, which contain little context for the dyslexic reader to decode the meaning of words. These children require alternate assessments that will allow them to demonstrate fairly their knowledge, skills, and abilities, rather than the effect of their disability. Under IDEA, states and school districts administering assessments were required to provide alternate assessments by July 2000; unfortunately, most states have either failed to develop alternate assessments and/or have limited the assessments they are developing to children with severe cognitive disabilities. Thus, a major area for potential litigation surrounds the design and implementation of high stakes tests and of alternate assessments.

Post-secondary Education

Both the ADA and Section 504 protect the rights of students with learning disabilities in colleges and universities. These statutes generally prohibit discrimination on the basis of disability in both the admissions process and once a student has matriculated. The ADA prohibits discrimination against individuals with disabilities in the "full and equal enjoyment" of the goods and privileges (e.g., academic courses) offered in a place of public accommodation.[7] The ADA also prohibits a "public entity" from excluding an individual from the benefits of its programs,

---

[7]Section 302 of the ADA provides:

No individual shall be discriminated against on the basis of disability in the full and equal enjoyment of the goods, services, facilities, privileges, advantages, or accommodations of any lace of public accommodation by any person who owns, leases (or leases to) or operates a public accommodation.

42 U.S.C. § 12182(a). Public accommodations include "a nursery, elementary, secondary, undergraduate, or postgraduate private school, or other place of education." 42 U.S.C. § 12181.

or otherwise discriminating against an individual, because of the individual's disability.[8] Finally, Section 504 contains the same anti-discrimination mandate for any entity receiving financial assistance from the federal government.[9]

With regard to admissions, Section 504 regulations prohibit schools receiving federal funds from making any "pre-admission inquiry" as to whether an applicant is disabled.[10] Schools are also barred from using any test or criterion for admission that has a disproportionately adverse effect on applicants with disabilities unless the admissions test or criterion has been validated as a predictor of success in the program in question.[11] In addition, admissions tests must be selected and administered so as to best ensure that the test

---

[8]Section 202 of the ADA provides:

No qualified individual with a disability shall, by reason of such disability be excluded from participation in or be denied the benefits of the services, programs, or activities of a public entity, or be subjected to discrimination by any such entity.

42 U.S.C. § 12132. Generally, a public entity means any State or local government, and *any* instrumentality of a State or local government. 42 U.S.C. § 12131. Public entities include State colleges, other public schools, and State licensing boards. *See Bartlett v. New York State Board of Bar Examiners*, 970 F.Supp. 1094, 1118 (S.D.N.Y 1997), aff'd 156 F.3d 321 (2d Cir. 1998), *vacated and remanded on other grounds by* 527 U.S. 1031 (1999). Subsequent citations to this decision refer to portions of the district court's opinion that were unaffected by the appellate decisions.

[9]Section 504 of the Rehabilitation Act of 1973 provides:

No otherwise qualified individual with a disability. . . shall, solely by reason of her or his disability, be excluded from the participation in, be denied the benefit of, or be subjected to discrimination under any program or activity receiving Federal financial assistance. . . .

29 U.S.C. § 794. A program or activity receives federal financial assistance within the meaning of Section 504 if it receives federal funding either directly from the federal government, or indirectly from another entity which extends the benefits of federal funds to it. 29 C.F.R. §§ 794(b)(l)(B); 45 C.F.R. §§ 84.3(f); *Bartlett v. New York State Board of Law Examiners*, 156 F.3d 321, 330 (2d Cir. 1998)(New York State Board of Law Examiners received federal financial assistance within the meaning of the Rehabilitation Act because two other state entities, elected to receive federal funds and then extended that assistance to the Board in the form of vouchers for bar applicants with disabilities), *vacated and remanded on other grounds by* 527 U.S. 1031 (1999).

Although certain of the above provisions apply directly to private entities, others to public entities, and still others to entities receiving federal financial assistance, the courts generally interpret all of them collectively to promote uniformity and the comprehensive enforcement of civil rights for individuals with disabilities. *See. e.g.*, 42 U.S.C. § 12117; 28 C.F.R. § 35.103; *Does 1-5 v. Chandler*, 83 F.3d 1150, 1152 (9th Cir. 1996); *Guckenberger v. Boston University*, 974 F.Supp. 106, 133 (D.Mass. 1997). This means that a provision which on its face governs only a private entity is in practice interpreted by the courts to apply equally to a public entity or a recipient of federal financial assistance, and visa versa.

[10]34 C.F.R. § 104.42(b)(4). However, as discussed *infra*, some testing entities "flag" the test scores of admissions tests when those tests are taken with accommodations. Universities are notified by this flagging practice that an applicant's score may overestimate the applicant's knowledge and skills because the applicant received accommodations for a disability.

[11]34 C.F.R. § 104.42(b)(2); 34 C.F.R. § 104.42(b)(2).

results reflect the applicants' aptitude or achievement, rather than their impairments.[12]

Once a student has been admitted, these laws require educational institutions to make "reasonable accommodations" when necessary to allow qualified people to participate in and benefit from educational programs. A "reasonable accommodation" is a change in the status quo that is necessary to ensure that non-essential aspects of the status quo do not exclude or discriminate against individuals with disabilities.[13] Reasonable accommodations could include a modified course load, the provision of taped texts and note takers, and extended time on examinations. The Congressional goal behind the requirement for reasonable accommodations is to eradicate all forms of discrimination against people with disabilities and to ensure that individuals with disabilities have full and equal access to the benefits offered by society.[14] The ADA and Section 504 recognize that society has traditionally excluded individuals with disabilities from educational, employment, and other opportunities not just because of invidious "affirmative animus," but also because of "stereotypical assumptions not truly indicative of the individual ability of such individuals to participate in, and contribute to, society."

Professional and Licensing Exams

In addition to the general anti-discrimination provisions of the ADA and Section 504, the ADA places a specific legal obligation on those who administer and offer professional examinations to ensure that individuals with disabilities—including learning disabilities—have a full and equal opportunity to demonstrate their skills, knowledge, and competency (or whatever the test is designed to measure). The ADA requires any person or private entity offering examinations related to applications, licensing, certification, or credentialing for secondary or post-secondary education, professional, or trade purposes, to offer the exams in a "place and manner" accessible to persons with disabilities or to offer "alternative accessible arrangements" for individuals with disabilities. This mandate for equal access, and the corresponding prohibition against discrimination, applies to public and private schools, private testing entities, licensing and certification boards, private and public employers, and almost any other person or entity that might administer an examination to a person with a learning disability.[15]

Testing administrators must ensure that the results of the examinations they offer "accurately reflect the applicant's aptitude or achieve-

---

[12]34 C.F.R. § 104.42(b)(2); 34 C.F.R. § 104.42(b)(3).
[13]*Guckenberger*, 974 F.Supp. at 144-45.
[14]Section 309 of the ADA, 42 U.S.C. § 12189.
[15]42 U.S.C. § 12101(a)(7)(ada); *Alexander v. Choate*, 469 U.S. 287, 295–296 (1935) (explaining legislative purpose of Section 504).

ment level or whatever other factor the test purports to measure, rather than reflecting the applicant's [disability]."[17] Furthermore, it is unlawful to "administer a licensing or certification program in a manner that subjects qualified individuals with disabilities to discrimination on the basis of disability."[18] Finally, an entity offering examinations has an affirmative obligation to "make reasonable modifications in policies, practices, or procedures when the modifications are necessary to avoid discrimination on the basis of disability. . . ."[19] These provisions, taken as a whole, require almost any person or entity administering academic, licensing, or other exams to provide "reasonable accommodations" to individuals with learning disabilities as necessary to ensure that the examination measures only the skills and knowledge it is designed to measure, rather than the limitations of the test takers' disabilities.

Despite the obligation to provide accommodations, many testing entities have engaged in a practice that undercuts the nondiscriminatory mandate of the ADA and Section 504: "flagging" test scores to indicate that a test was taken with accommodations, and that the test score may not reflect the test taker's educational ability accurately. Testing entities justify this practice on the ground that they have been unable to certify the comparability of standardized test scores obtained under nonstandard administrations. However, these entities have no basis for asserting that the provision of accommodations has in any way compromised the validity or reliability of the tests.[20]

By providing accommodations only under the condition that the scores be reported in a stigmatizing manner, these entities are effec-

---

[17]28 C.F.R. § 36.309; 34 C.F.R. § 104.42(b)(3).

[18]28 C.F.R. § 35.130(b)(6).

[19]28 C.F.R. § 35.130(b)(6) & (7); see also ADA Title II Technical Assistance Manual II 3.7200 (application of Title II to licensing and certification programs).

[20]On behalf of a variety of individuals with disabilities and disability organizations, Disability Rights Advocates in 1999 filed a lawsuit against the Educational Testing Service (ETS) to challenge its flagging practice. ETS administers hundreds of standardized exams, such as the Graduate Management Admissions Test (GMAT), the Graduate Records Exam (GRE) and the Scholastic Achievement Test (SAT). ETS is perhaps the most influential testing organization in the United States, if not the world. After hard-fought litigation, ETS agreed to stop flagging for the accommodation of extended time on the Graduate Record Examination, the Graduate Management Admission Test, the Test of English as a Foreign Language, and many other standardized admission tests that it administers. When announcing the settlement, the president of ETS explained that "having carefully weighed the expressed concerns of people with disabilities, we decided, in the spirit of furthering opportunity, to end flagging." With regard to the SAT, which is owned by the College Board (not a party to the litigation), an agreement was reached to resolve the issue of flagging by convening a blue ribbon panel of disability and testing experts to make recommendations for the parties and the courts. The agreement stated that the panel was to issue its recommendations for the SAT by March 2002. After ETS made the decision to end flagging, both the National Board of Medical Examiners and the Law School Admission Council have thus far refused to drop the flag, and further litigation against these entities may be necessary.

tively denying people with disabilities the benefits of the accommodations to which they are legally entitled under federal and state anti-discrimination law. The purpose of providing legally required accommodations to disabled individuals is to level the playing field so that the test will in fact measure the individual's ability, rather than reflect his or her disability. Flagging policies thus deliberately undercut the purpose and effect of the accommodations by communicating a stigmatizing message that people with disabilities obtain an unfair advantage when they receive accommodations, and that their scores should therefore be viewed with skepticism.[21]

This practice also raises issues of privacy and discrimination against test takers with disabilities because it reveals an individual's disability status. As a result of flagging policies, people with disabilities are forced to disclose their disabilities, despite privacy interests protected by the ADA and other laws, and are required to explain them to admissions offices, potential employers, and other entities that receive their score reports. Indeed, the two federal cases that addressed flagging held that a person with a disability who is flagged can challenge the policy because, regardless of whether he or she was denied admission because of the flag, the flag causes the independent and separate harm of being identified as a disabled person against one's will.[22]

---

[21]It is well recognized that many admissions offices consider and devalue flagged test scores. *See SUNY Health Science Center at Brooklyn-College of Medicine*, 5 NDLR ¶ 77 (OCR 1993)(finding that medical school had adopted a practice of devaluing the MCAT scores of individuals with disabilities who took the exam with accommodations, thereby subjecting these individuals to discrimination based on their disabilities"); *see also Handbook for the Implementation of Section 504 of the Rehabilitation Act of 1973* at 277 (1981) (prepared by CRC Education and Human Development, Inc. for the Department of Health, Education and Welfare's Office for Civil Rights)(observing that the indication that the test was taken under nonstandardized conditions informs the university of the likelihood that the applicant has a disability).

[21]*Doe v. National Board of Medical Examiners*, 199 F.3d 146 (3rd Cir. 1999); *Breimhorst, et al. v. Educational Testing Service*, Case No. C 99-3387 (N.D.Cal.). In the case against ETS, the federal Court denied the testing agency's attempt to have the case dismissed, reasoning that if testing agencies meet their legal obligations under the ADA, "there would be no reason to flag the test results of disabled test takers who receive accommodations." The Court based its decision in part on the earlier *Doe* opinion, which held that individuals with disabilities can challenge flagging because the practice identifies them as disabled against their will. While the *Doe* opinion denied the plaintiffs' motion for immediate relief through a preliminary injunction, citing a lack of evidence to support a finding of likely success on the merits, it allowed the plaintiff to proceed with the litigation to challenge the flag.

LEGAL ISSUES FOR ESTABLISHING DISABILITY AND THE NEED FOR ACCOMMODATIONS

When Does An Individual with a Learning Disability Have a "Disability" within the Meaning of the ADA and Section 504?

As discussed above, individuals with learning disabilities have the right to reasonable accommodations. However, the ADA and Section 504 do not protect an individual with a learning impairment unless the impairment rises to the level of a "disability" as defined by the statutory and regulatory scheme. One legal issue, which arises for individuals with learning disabilities, is whether their impairments meet the legal definition of disability.

The ADA and Section 504 define "disability" as "a physical or mental impairment that substantially limits one or more of the major life activities of an individual."[23] As a result, to obtain protection under the Acts, a person must demonstrate that she has (1) an "impairment" and that (2) the impairment "substantially limits" (3) a "major life activity."[24]

It is well established that a "specific learning disability" is an "impairment" for purposes of the ADA and Section 504.[25] The courts also recognize that there are a variety of "major life activities" that trigger the protections of the statutes. These activities include reading, learning, writing, working, or any other "basic activities" that the average person in the general population can perform with little or no difficulty."[26] Despite the general agreement on the definitions of "impairment" and "major life activity," disputes still arise when determining if a learning impairment can "substantially limit" a major life activity (and thus be considered a "disability" in the legal sense) if the individual with the impairment is more intelligent or performs better

---

[23]The ADA and Section 504 provide in pertinent part: "the term 'disability' means, with respect to an individual—(A) a physical or mental impairment that substantially limits one or more of the major life activities of such individual; (B) a record of such an impairment; or (C) being regarded as having such an impairment." 42 U.S.C. § 12102(2); 29 U.S.C. § 706(8)(B). This article does not address individuals who have legally recognized "disabilities" by virtue of (B) or (C).

[24]*Price v. National Board of Medical Examiners*, 966 F.Supp. 419,427 (S.D.W.V. 1997); *Bartlett*, 970 F.Supp. at 1116 (citations omitted).

[25]*See. e.g..* 29 U.S.C. § 706(15)(A)(iii); H.R. 101-485(11), 101st Cong. (1990), reprinted in 1990 4 U.S.C.C.A.N. 303, 333-34 (stating that impairments under the ADA include "specific learning disabilities" and that "a major life activity" includes "learning"); 28 C.F.R. § 35.104(1)(1)(B)(ADA Title II); 28 C.F.R. § 36.104(ADA Title III); 29 C.F.R. § 1630.2(h)(2); 34 C.F.R. § 104.3(2)(l)(B)(Section 504); *see also* 42 U.S.C. § 12102(2)(general definition of disability in ADA); 29 U.S.C. § 706(8)(B)(general definition of disability in Rehabilitation Act); *and see Bartlett*, 970 F.Supp. at 1117, 1120-26; *Guckenberger*, 974 F.Supp. at 134; *Price*, 966 F.Supp. at 427.

[26]*Bartlett*, 970 F.Supp. at 1117 (citing 28 C.F.R. § 35.104(l)(iii)(2) & 29 C.F.R. Pt. 1630, App. § 1630.2(i)(1991)).

than the average person in the general population.[27] Recently, an influential federal court recognized that individuals with average reading or other learning related skills can still have significant learning impairments that meet the legal definition of "disability."[28] Previously, the Supreme Court had directed the lower courts to consider the extent to which corrective devices or other mitigating measures impact the functional limitations caused by an impairment.[29] Under this standard, "one has a disability [under the ADA] . . . if, notwithstanding the use of a corrective device, that individual is [still] substantially limited in a major life activity.[30] The precise impact of these rulings on individuals with learning disabilities remains uncertain as of the date this article went to print.

What Accommodations Must a Covered Entity Offer to Individuals Who Have a Legally Recognized Learning Disability?

Once individuals verify that they have legally recognized learning disabilities, they have a federal right to "reasonable accommodations" in their academic courses and on the examinations they are taking.[31] Reasonable accommodations may include the use of readers or note takers, taped texts, a modified course load, extension of test taking time, the use of word processors, computer spell checkers, and private test taking rooms. Any of these accommodations are reasonable (and required by law) in a given case unless (a) the entity demonstrates that

---

[27]In Sections IV and V, *infra*, we discuss the legal issues which arise when testing institutions employ discriminatory practices for determining whether an individual has a learning impairment caused by a learning disability. In this Section, we first discuss the definitional question of whether an impairment, once determined to exist as a factual matter, is sufficiently "substantial" to be regarded as a "disability" under the Acts.

[28]*Bartlett*, 266 F.3d 69, 81 (2nd Cir.2000). The United States Court of Appeals for the Second Circuit (one of the more influential appellate courts in the country) held that a person could be "substantially limited" with respect to reading even if that person had achieved roughly average reading skills on some measures, "if her skills are below average on other measures to an extent that her ability to read is substantially limited."

[29]*Sutton v. United Air Lines*, 527 U.S. 471, 482 (1999); *Murphy v. United Parcel Service*, 527 U.S. 516, 520 (1999).

[30]*Sutton*, 527 U.S. at 488.

[31]In fact, the ADA Regulations use individuals with dyslexia as an illustration for explaining the requirement of reasonable accommodations on examinations. 29 C.F.R. Pt. 1630, App.§ 1630.11.

providing the accommodation would "fundamentally alter" the academic program or test at issue,[32] or (b) if providing the accommodations at issue would result in an undue financial or administrative burden (i.e. significant difficulty or expense).[33] Because the accommodations that people with learning disabilities generally request are inexpensive and relatively easy to administer, the claim of undue financial or administrative burden does not usually arise.

A common legal issue, which arises after individuals establish that they have legally recognized learning disabilities, is whether the accommodations they seek are necessary to allow them an equal opportunity to demonstrate their knowledge, skills, or competency. Determining the necessary accommodation in a particular case often causes controversy because measuring a learning disability is not an exact science, but rather depends upon clinical judgment. Still, there are certain legal principles, which help to define the manner by which an entity must consider clinical documentation of a learning disability when determining the necessary accommodations.

It is generally agreed that the extent to which a requested accommodation is needed must be determined through an assessment of the particular person's individual needs."[34] As an evidentiary matter, the opinion of a qualified clinician treating the applicant may be given "extra weight" in determining the specific amount of additional time required as a reasonable accommodation.[35] Indeed, the federal court in New York recognized that the most accurate diagnosis of a learning disability comes from the clinical judgment of trained learning disability specialists.[36] Similarly, a "Blue Ribbon Panel of Experts," convened during the course of litigation against the California Committee of Bar Examiners, submitted a report that emphasizes to the Bar that the professional judgment of the applicant's evaluator is the key to determining the appropriate accommodation.[37]

---

[32]42 U.S.C. § 12182(b)(2)(A)(ii); 28 C.F.R. § 35.130(b)(6) & (7); 28 C.F.R. § 36.302 & 309(b)(l)(i); 34 C.F.R. § 104.42(b)(3)(i); 29 C.F.R. § 1630.11 (permitting an exam to measure the limitation of the disability only when it is designed to measure the major life function which is affected); *and see Alexander v. Choate,* 469 U.S. at 300; *Guckenberger,* 974 F.Supp. at 145146 (citations omitted); Bartlett. 970 F.Supp. at 1130; *Southeastern Community College v. Davis,* 442 U.S. 397 (1979).

[33]42 U.S.C. § 12182(b)(2)(A)(iii); 28 C.F.R. § 36.303.

[34]*See, e.g., D'Amico v. New York State Bd. of Law Examiners,* 813 F.Supp. 217,221 (W.D.N.Y. 1993); 56 Fed. Reg. at 35704 (Preamble to Section 35.130).

[35]*D'Amico,* 813 F.Supp. at 222; *cf Bartlett,* 970 F.Supp. at 1113-16, 1119-20.

[36]*Bartlett,* 970 F.Supp. 1114, 1116.

[37]This case, *Mueller v. CBE,* challenged (among other things) the Committee's practice of disregarding the recommendations of applicants' clinicians. During the course of the litigation against the California Bar, the parties appointed a "Blue Ribbon Panel of Experts" in learning disabilities and AD/HD to review the Bar's policies and procedures. The Panel issued a report recommending several substantial changes.

The law does not afford post-secondary schools, licensing boards, or other testing entities any special deference for its determinations regarding an individual's disability or need for accommodations.[38] Thus, an expert opinion does not carry more weight merely because it comes from an expert who works for the college, testing entity, or licensing board. To the contrary, legal authority suggests that the ADA and Section 504 prohibit these entities from rejecting the recommendation of a qualified learning disability specialist based upon a different assessment made by someone with less expertise or by someone who has not individually evaluated the applicant.[39]

To the extent that a college or testing entity does not agree with the clinical judgment of a qualified clinician who individually diagnoses an applicant for accommodations, it cannot simply reject the accommodations recommended by the clinician, but has a legal obligation to work cooperatively with the applicant (and the applicant's clinician) to determine the appropriate accommodation.[40]

Similarly, the need for an assessment of an individual's needs to determine reasonable accommodations suggests that blanket policies prohibiting certain types of accommodations may be illegal. For example, educational or testing entities that prohibit the use of a computer or word processor, regardless of an individual's need for such an accommodation, violate the requirement that each individual's needs be accommodated unless the entity can demonstrate that such an accommodation will always pose an undue burden or fundamental alteration.

---

[38]*Bartlett*, 226 F 3d. at 78.

[39]*D'Amico*, 813 F.Supp. at 222 (holding that because the New York State Board of Law Examiners had "no expertise concerning plaintiff's medical condition . . . [it was] in no position to countermand plaintiff's treating physician's opinion as to what is the appropriate accommodation . . . ."); *Bartlett*, 970 F.Supp. at 1114, 1116 (suggesting that a testing entity cannot use test scores alone to second guess the recommendation made by a qualified learning disability consultant who personally assessed the individual); see also *Bartlett*, 2001 WL 930792, at *37 (S.D.N.Y. Aug.15,2001) (Same analysis on remand).

[40]This requirement for cooperation derives from provisions in the ADA which mandate an "interactive process" between the individual seeking the accommodation and the entity providing it. Under this process, a testing entity which does not believe that the accommodation initially requested by the applicant is reasonable, must work with the applicant to obtain additional information to ensure that the accommodation ultimately granted meets the individual's needs. See notes 64–66 and surrounding text, *infra*. In the next section, we discuss the legal issues which arise when there is a breakdown in this interactive process.

The Fundamental Alteration Defense

Often, post-secondary schools and testing entities defend their denials of reasonable accommodations by claiming that the provision of such accommodations would fundamentally alter the nature of the academic program or exam. However, before an entity can reject an accommodation request based upon a "fundamental alteration" defense, it must demonstrate through facts or expert opinion—and not merely unverified presumptions—that providing the accommodation would interfere with the nature of the academic program or the examination's ability to measure the skills and knowledge it is designed to test. Furthermore, even if the entity meets this burden, this defense may not be sufficient if the skills and knowledge used to support the fundamental alteration defense are not essential for the profession or program being guarded by the exam.[41]

Disputes often arise because educational and testing entities and commentators erroneously presume that the provision of an accommodation fundamentally alters the nature of a program or examination even when there is no evidence to support the presumption. For example, a 1998 editorial in *U.S. News and World Report* suggested (without any evidentiary foundation) that the granting of additional time on bar examinations compromises the ability of the exam to measure the competence of the individuals seeking to become attorneys.[42] Yet, at least two State Bars (New York and California) have admitted that their bar exams do not purport to measure reading speed (as opposed to the ability to understand legal concepts, solve analytic problems, and effectively express oneself through language).[43] Given that the overwhelming majority of professional licensing, screening, and competency exams primarily test cognitive and analytic abilities (rather than speed in reading, writing, or spelling), it is usually very difficult to demonstrate that accommodations such as additional time, the use of a word processor, or a private testing room, would fundamentally alter the exam.

---

[41]*Bartlett*, 970 F.Supp. at 1130 (citing *Davis*, 442 U.S. 397). In *Bartlett*, the federal court in New York held that extended time on the bar exam did not fundamentally alter the bar exam both because the bar exam is not designed to measure the ability to read or perform under time constraints and because a competent lawyer does not need to have these particular skills. *Id.* at 1128 ("speed in reading is not tested by the bar examination, nor is speed in reading one of the essential functions of lawyering").

[42]John Leo (October 5, 1998) "Let's lower the bar" *U.S. News & World Report*.

[43]*Bartlett*, 970 F.Supp. at 1128 & 1130; see also Deposition Transcripts in *Mueller v. CBE*, Case No. 97-03309 FMS (PJH)(U.S. District Court, Northern District of California). Relevant portions of the deposition transcripts can be obtained from Disability Rights Advocates, counsel for the plaintiffs in the *Mueller* case.

An Educational or Testing Entity Cannot Impose Documentation or Eligibility Requirements That are Unnecessarily Cumbersome, Expensive, or Invasive to an Individual's Privacy

A common problem facing people with learning disabilities who are seeking reasonable accommodation is the imposition of application requirements that are unnecessarily cumbersome, expensive, or invasive to the person's privacy. The ADA and Section 504 prohibit the use of such requirements because they "screen out or tend to screen out" individuals with disabilities 42 U.S.C. 12182(b)(2)(i).[44]

Eligibility requirements are "policies or criteria that, while not creating a direct bar to individuals with disabilities, diminish an individual's chances of [] participation" in the covered entity's program.[45] Eligibility requirements that people with learning disabilities commonly confront include:

- diagnostic testing requirements that are redundant or otherwise unnecessary;
- requirements that applicants receive particular scores on particular diagnostic tests;
- currency standards that require the diagnostic testing to have occurred within a certain amount of time prior to the application;
- limitations on the clinicians from whom documentation is accepted to verify a learning disability.

Under federal law, requirements such as these are unlawful if (a) they screen out or tend to screen out individuals with disabilities, unless (b) the entity can demonstrate that they are necessary to evaluate the request for accommodations properly.[46]

---

[44]The ADA defines unlawful discrimination to include:

"The imposition or application of eligibility criteria that screen out or tend to screen out an individual with a disability or any class of individuals with disabilities from fully and equally enjoying any goods, services, facilities, privileges, advantages, or accommodations, unless such criteria can be shown to be necessary for the provision of the goods, services, facilities, privileges, advantages, or accommodations being offered."

42U.S.C. § 12182(b)(2)(A). The prohibition against eligibility requirements that screen out or tend to screen out individuals with disabilities appears throughout the regulations and case law. 28 C.F.R. § 35.130(b)(8)(ADA Regulations); 34 C.F.R. § 104.4(b)(4)(Section 504 Regulations); 45 C.F.R. § 84.13 (Section 504); *Guckenberger*, 974 F.Supp. at 134; *and see Emery v. Caravan of Dreams. Inc.*, 879 F.Supp. 640, 643-44 (N.D.Tex. 1995).

[45]*Guckenberger*, 974 F.Supp. at 134-35 (*quoting Doukas v. Metropolitan Life Ins. Co.*, 950 F.Supp. 422,426 (D.N.H. 1996)).

[46]*Guckenberger*, 974 F.Supp. 42 U.S.C. § 12182(b)(2)(i) at 134, 138 (citations omitted); 45 *Id.* at 135 (citing *Coleman v. Zatechka*, 824 F.Supp. 1360, 1368 (D.Neb. 1993)).

Eligibility requirements "screen out or tend to screen out" persons with disabilities if they" preclude or unnecessarily discourage individuals with disabilities from establishing that they are entitled to reasonable accommodation.[47] For example, a requirement that an applicant have particular diagnostic tests scores below the "average range" screens out or precludes persons with learning disabilities who achieve certain average scores despite the presence of a clinically diagnosed learning disability.[48]

An eligibility requirement can violate the ADA and Section 504 even if it does not by definition prohibit individuals from obtaining accommodations. The ADA regulations do not merely prohibit requirements that "screen out" individuals with disabilities, but also those that "tend to screen out" individuals with disabilities. Application criteria "tend to screen out" persons with disabilities if they make it unreasonably difficult, stressful, or intimidating to secure accommodations, even if the applicants through perseverance eventually obtain them.[49] Examples of such criteria are requirements that an applicant submit to excessive testing batteries or unrelated mental status exams. They are unlawful because they are not necessary to verify a learning disability or the need for the accommodation requested, thereby unnecessarily forcing applicants to make financial and other sacrifices, or discourage them from seeking accommodations altogether. Even if the accommodations are ultimately granted, requiring applicants to overcome onerous or intimidating barriers to secure them is discriminatory and unlawful.

Currency Requirements

Many testing and university administrators have established "currency" requirements that make it necessary for applicants to submit documentation based on diagnostic testing that was performed within a certain amount of time prior to the application for accommodations. Currency requirements can impose significant financial burdens and emotional hardships on individuals with disabilities seeking accommodations. Re-testing can be prohibitively expensive and often emotionally traumatic.[50]

The only published federal court decision addressing the question of currency requirements concluded that a three year currency

---

[47]*Id.* at 135 (citing *Coleman v. Zatechka*, 824 F.Supp. 1, at 1368 (D.Neb. 1993).

[48]See, e.g., *Bartlett*, 970 F.Supp. at 1113-16; see also *Bartlett*, 2001 WL 930792, at *37 (S.D.N.Y. Aug. 15, 2001).

[49]*Guckenberger*, 974 F.Supp. at 137-38 (citing *Ellen S. v. Florida Bd. of Bar Examiners*, 859 F.Supp. 1489, 1494 (S.D.Fla. 1994).

[50]*Guckenberger*, 974 F.Supp. at 136.

requirement is unlawful for college students seeking accommodations for their learning disabilities.[51] The court held that the three year currency requirement used by Boston University was unnecessary because learning disabilities do not significantly change after a person reaches adulthood (age 18), and unlawful because the expense and emotional burden of them "screened out or tended to screen out" people with learning disabilities.[52]

The legality of currency requirements of more than three years is very questionable. Currency requirements are more likely to be lawful if they are not presented as rigid rules, but as general guidelines that may, but do not need to be, followed according to the clinical judgment of the applicant's evaluator. For example, the *Guckenberger* court tentatively approved a currency requirement, which called for re-evaluations, but permitted the applicants' clinicians to forego re-testing if in their clinical judgment such re-testing would not be necessary to reevaluate the learning disability.[53] As with the other legal issues that arise in learning disability cases, policies that provide recommended, rather than mandatory, guidelines and permit the clinician to exercise discretion on a case by case basis, are more likely to be lawful than those that impose absolute across-the-board rules.

Criteria for Clinicians Evaluating Applicants

Legal disputes also occur when educational and testing administrators impose unnecessarily restrictive criteria for the clinicians who diagnose applicants and who provide documentary support to verify their learning disabilities. There are a variety of specialists who are qualified to conduct assessments, render diagnoses of learning disabilities, and make recommendations for appropriate accommodations. These include clinical psychologists, school psychologists, neuropsychologists, learning disability specialists, medical doctors, and other professionals. It is unlawful for administrators to establish qualifying criteria that do not permit applicants to rely on specialists who have the necessary training and experience.

In *Guckenberger*, for example, Boston University required applicants to obtain evaluations from either licensed physicians or psychologists.[54] This across-the-board exclusion of specialists with masters

---

[51]A three year re-testing requirement is particularly burdensome in the university setting because it requires those who obtain a diagnosis of their learning disabilities just before matriculating into a four year program to undergo re-testing before graduation.

[52]*Guckenberger*, 974 F.Supp. at 135-36, 138. However, the Court upheld the three-year currency requirement for AD/HD. *Id*. at 139.

[53]*Id*. at 139.

[54]*Id*. at 135.

degrees placed an enormous burden on people who had valid documentation of their disabilities because it required them to spend additional time and money for retesting by a physician or psychologist, even if they had recently received a complete diagnosis by a specialist with the necessary training and experience in learning disabilities, simply because the specialist had a masters degree rather than a Ph.D.[55] The court held that the policy was unlawful because it screened out and tended to screen out individuals with reliably documented learning disabilities.[56]

Legal disputes also occur when application requirements contain unnecessarily intrusive and extensive inquiries of the evaluators. Like any other eligibility criteria, the documentation requirements imposed on evaluators must be reasonable to be lawful under the ADA and Section 504. Clinicians should not need to submit copies of their transcripts, certifications, or degrees. Nor should they be required to elaborate in detail on all their internships, post-doctorate work, and the number of people they have evaluated pre- and post-licensure. Such requirements are unnecessary to verify the qualifications of a learning disability evaluator and can be incredibly burdensome.[57]

IT IS ALSO UNLAWFUL FOR EDUCATIONAL AND TESTING ENTITIES TO USE METHODS OF ADMINISTRATION THAT HAVE THE EFFECT OF DISCRIMINATING AGAINST INDIVIDUALS WITH LEARNING DISABILITIES

The ADA and Section 504 also prohibit "the use of standards or criteria or methods of administration. . . that have the effect of discriminating on the basis of disability."[58] All too often, people with learning disabilities must submit their applications for accommodations to administrators who make their decisions based on misinformation or biases against people with learning disabilities. To add insult to injury, many of these untrained and misinformed decisionmakers operate

---

[55]*Id*. at 136-37.

[56]*Id*. at 137.

[57]For example, the California Committee of Bar Examiners used to require that applicants' evaluators provide the Bar with copies of their transcripts, certifications and degrees as well as descriptions of their internships, post-doctorate work and the number of people evaluated pre- and post-licensure. The Report from the Blue Ribbon Panel of Experts, *see* note 36, *supra*, recommended that the California Bar delete this requirement. Since the Blue Ribbon Report, the California Bar has replaced the onerous documentation requirement with one that simply requests the evaluators to describe their specialized training in the assessment, diagnosis and remediation of learning disabilities and/or AD/HD with the adult population.

[58]42 U.S.C. § 12182(b)(l)(D); *see also* 34 C.F.R. § 104.4(b)(4).

within larger bureaucracies that have failed to establish effective communication channels between the decision-makers, the applicants, and their clinicians. These deficiencies subject individuals with bona fide disabilities to delays, confusion, and the ultimate denial of accommodations. They are unlawful because they result in discrimination against people with learning disabilities.

Decision-Makers Must Have the Necessary Expertise

It is crucial that the people charged with the duty of determining whether to grant or deny accommodation requests have significant training and experience in the assessment and diagnosis of learning disabilities. A testing entity could have excellent procedures, but if the people running the show do not know how to evaluate an application for accommodations, or if they have biases against people with disabilities, the entire system will fall apart.

Educational and testing entities have the obligation to make decisions on requests for accommodations "based on actual risks and not on speculation, stereotypes, or generalizations about disabilities."[59] Congress enacted the ADA and Section 504 to prevent the denial of accommodation requests to people with disabilities because of ignorance and misinformed stereotypes.[60] Thus, the use of bias or uninformed decision-makers in the accommodations review process is an unlawful practice under the ADA and Section 504.[61]

The Requirement of Clinical Judgment

"By its very nature, diagnosing a learning disability requires clinical judgment."[62] The Blue Ribbon Panel of Experts, which recommended changes to the California Bar's policies and criteria, emphasized in its Report that "the professional judgment of the evaluator is the key to a strongly documented diagnosis." A corollary to this rule is that testing and educational administrators cannot reject a request for an accommodation based on particular diagnostic test scores alone.[63] Second guessing the clinical recommendation of a qualified clinician who di-

---

[59]*Guckenberger*, 974 F.Supp. at 141 (quoting H.R.Rep. No. 101-485, pt. II, at 105 (1990), reprinted in 1990 U.S.C.C.A.N. 267, 388).

[60]*Mantolete v. Bolger*, 767 F.2d 1416, 1422 (9th Cir. 1985).

[61]In *Guckenberger*, the Court held that an accommodations process which relied on inexperienced, biased and internally contentious decision-makers violated the ADA and Section 504. *Guckenberger*, 974 F.Supp. at 141. In that case, the unlawful methods of administration caused both the delay and denial of reasonable accommodations. Id.

[62]*Bartlett*, 970 F.Supp. at 1114, 1116.

[63]*See id.* at 1113 ("Test scores alone cannot reliably identify reading disabled individuals").

agnoses the applicant, or rejecting an accommodation request because of diagnostic test scores alone, has the effect of depriving people with learning disabilities of accommodations to which they are legally entitled. As stated by the Blue Ribbon Panel of Experts in the case of the California Bar, "[s]cores are only one small part. . . of a diagnostic profile for LD or AD/HD diagnosis. A diagnosis encompasses a multitude of factors . . . and of course is dependent on the training, interning and years of experience of the clinician or evaluator."

Procedures Must Be Disclosed. Timely and Cooperative

Regulations and case law under the ADA caution against denying requests for reasonable accommodations without first engaging in an "interactive process" with the individuals who are seeking the accommodations.[64]

An "interactive process" is a cooperative interaction between the school or testing administrator, the applicant and qualified experts as needed to ensure that the accommodation ultimately granted is sufficient to enable the applicant to have a full and fair opportunity to demonstrate his or her skills and knowledge when taking the exam.[65] Both the applicant and the entity have an obligation to work with each other in good faith to gather sufficient information to determine the appropriate accommodation.[66]

Schools and testing administrations are in serious risk of violating the ADA and section 504 if they reject a request for reasonable accommodations without first making a good faith effort to work with the applicant and the applicant's clinician to determine the necessary accommodation.[67] For example, the federal court in Boston held that Boston University's procedures violated the ADA because the University failed to clearly develop and disclose them, the students received conflicting, incomplete, or hostile communications from the University when requesting information about their requests, and the entire process was plagued with unnecessary delays.[68] While the precise contours of the rights and responsibilities

---

[64]29 C.F.R. § 1630.2(o)(3) & Pt. 1630 app. § 1630.9. Although the interactive process first emerged in the employment context, it has been applied to the process of requesting accommodations on academic and screening exams. *Guckenberger*, 974 F.Supp. at 141-42 (citations omitted).

[65]*Guckenberger*, 974 F.Supp. at 141-42 (citations omitted).

[66]*See, e.g., Beck v. University of Wisconsin Bd. of Regents*, 75 F.3d 1130. 1135 (7th Cir. 1996).

[67]*Guckenberger*, 974 F.Supp. at 141-42.

[68]*Id.* at 142.

under the interactive process provisions are still in debate,[69] "[t]he Regulations serve[] as a warning . . . that a failure to engage in an interactive process might expose [entities] to liability for failing to make reasonable accommodation."[70]

Testing and Educational Entities Must Establish An Adequate Grievance Procedure

Testing administrators and schools have a legal obligation to provide applicants with an opportunity to appeal denials of accommodation requests to a neutral and informed body, which is independent from the initial decision-maker. Under the Section 504 regulations, a recipient of federal financial assistance, which employs fifteen or more persons "shall adopt grievance procedures that incorporate appropriate due process standards and that provide for the prompt and equitable resolution of complaints alleging [the unlawful denial of an accommodation request]."[71] "Appropriate due process standards" means that appeal rights must be fully disclosed and accessible to applicants, and that applicants have a meaningful opportunity to present their case to a neutral and independent body.[72]

CONCLUSION

There are a number of legal issues that may arise as individuals with learning disabilities seek accommodations in the post-secondary context. The ADA and Section 504 place an affirmative obligation on educational and testing entities to provide necessary accommodations and to modify standard test-taking arrangements as necessary to ensure that their exams accurately measure the skills and knowledge they are designed to measure. It is important to ensure that individuals who exercise their legal right to accommodations are not penalized for doing so by having their scores "flagged" to indicate that their scores are "nonstandard" and may be inflated.

Individuals with learning impairments have a right to reasonable accommodations if their impairments meet the statutory defini-

[69]*See. e.g.. Menigine v. Runvon,* 114 F.3d 415,420 (3d Cir. 1997)(citations omitted); *Tavlor v. Principal Fin. Group,* 93 F.3d 155, 165 (sth Cir. 1996), *cert. denied* 117 S.Ct. 586 (1996); *Beck v. University of Wis. Bd. of Regents,* 75 F.3d 1130, 1135 (7th Cir. 1996); *Willis v: Conopco. Inc.,* 108 F.3d 282, 285 (11th Cir. 1997); *White v. York Int'l Corp.,* 45 F.3d 357, 363 (10th Cir. 1995), cited in *Barnett v U.S. Air., Inc.,* vacated and remanded on other grounds by 535 U.S. 391 (2002) 157 F.3d at 752.
[70]*Barnett,* 157 F.3d at 752
[71]34 C.F.R. § 104.7.
[72]*Guckenberger,* 974 F.Supp. at 143.

tion of "disability." There is still debate concerning the rights of individuals with learning impairments who have developed certain reading skills that are comparable to the average person in the general population. A 1998 federal appellate court decision held that such persons have legally recognized disabilities and a right to reasonable accommodations under the ADA and Section 504. In June 1999, the U.S. Supreme Court vacated the appellate court's decision and directed reconsideration in light of its holding that the determination of whether an individual has a disability should be made with reference to measures that mitigate the impairment. Under the Supreme Court's approach, individuals who undertake remediation for their impairments are still considered "individuals with disabilities" if, notwithstanding the remediation, they are still "substantially impaired in a major life activity."

Reasonable accommodations may include the extension of test taking time, the use of word processors and computer spell checkers, private test taking rooms, or other changes which do not fundamentally alter the nature of a program or the legitimate function of an exam. The determination of the proper accommodation for a particular person depends upon an assessment of the person's "individual needs" under the circumstances. The entity's determinations in this regard do not receive any special deference from the courts, although they will be more favorably considered if made by experts with appropriate qualifications. On the other hand, the clinical judgment of qualified specialists who individually diagnose individuals seeking accommodations should be given great weight by post-secondary entities and the courts.

Finally, educational and testing administrators have a duty to establish informed and non-arbitrary procedures to review requests for reasonable accommodations. This means that application requirements and decision making must meet generally accepted standards in the field, and not result from ignorance, prejudice, or stereotypes concerning the nature and effect of learning disabilities. In fact, most disputes can be resolved (or avoided) if those responsible for administering tests ensure that judgments regarding the skills of people with disabilities—and decisions regarding the testing accommodations they might need to demonstrate these skills—are made by people who have expertise in learning disabilities and who are able to work cooperatively with applicants and their clinicians during the accommodations process.

Chapter • 2

Rights of Students with Learning Disabilities in Higher Education in Ontario: Issues in Law, Practice, and Process

MaryLouise Bat-Hayim and Marc Wilchesky

Although the American, British, and Canadian legal systems arose from a common root, they matured in response to different soils and each branch is now unique. Legislative responses to social problems, such as the Americans with Disabilities Act, may be beneficial in one jurisdiction but may not necessarily be so in another, or could even be detrimental. In Ontario, post-secondary services for persons with learning disabilities (LD) are not mandated, yet they tend to be widespread, collaborative, thorough, and effective. An explanation of how Ontario's voluntary system works requires readers to understand essential elements of the legal culture in which it has developed. Sections II–V of this paper provide a brief introduction to relevant Ontario laws and Canada's negotiated federalism.

Ontario society thrives on difference, and for more than three centuries its legal culture has been developing in a manner that supports diversity. Legal culture refers not only to statutes and due process, but also to the social attitudes and values that determine when, where, and why people turn to the law or government (Sussel 1995). Ontarians have a multi-cultural outlook that encourages educators to develop services that work well for students who are physically, cognitively, linguistically, and culturally diverse. The Province is in the forefront of the movement toward inclusive education for all children (Mandell 1996). Major strategies for inclusion, such as Circle Friends, were developed in Ontario (Bunch 1998). In this climate, students who have been diagnosed with learning disabilities often thrive along with other students with individual needs (Wiener and Siegel 1992). The importance of widespread tolerant public attitudes toward diversity and slowly developed systems of dispute resolution cannot be overestimated in understanding the impact of Ontario's unique legal culture on the educational opportunities for students with disabilities.

The Education Act of Ontario defines and regulates free public special education for students with disabilities in elementary and secondary schools. No specific law mandates services for persons with disabilities in higher education. Nevertheless, all 46 of Ontario's colleges and universities have such services. They are somewhat voluntarily established. The Human Rights Code (hereafter, the Code) in Ontario protects the rights of specific groups to access all aspects of public life. Persons with disabilities are among the groups protected by the Code, and a learning disability is included in the list of potential causes of disability. If a college or university chose not to accommodate the needs of a person with a disability, it could be legally challenged under the Code. Nevertheless, each institution establishes the nature and scope of special services offered there. Section VI of this paper describes outstanding services currently available to students with LD in higher education in Ontario.

It would be misleading to create the impression that Ontario society provides a panacea for persons with disabilities. Ontarians have strong differences of opinion, and at present right-of-center, balance-the-budget political views are prevalent (Walker 1998a, Walker 1998b, Watson 1998). Sections VII and VIII will illustrate how the flux in Ontario's social system currently has an impact on services for adults with learning disabilities. Bill 34 (1996) limits the rights of persons over 21 years old to attend full service high school programs. It has a negative impact on the educational opportunities for adult students with disabilities from less advantaged circumstances (McEwan et al. 1997). By contrast, a 1997 proactive budget directive established the Learning Opportunities Task Force (LOTF). Its primary mandates are to research best practice services for post-secondary students with learning disabilities, and to grant seed funding to further develop best practice services for students with learning differences at Ontario's colleges and universities (Sinclair 1998).

In these uncertain circumstances, some Ontarians believe a specific law regulating the removal of social barriers to the full inclusion of persons with disabilities in both employment and higher education is needed. The Ontarians with Disabilities Act Committee (ODA), for example, advocates legislative solutions. This paper, however, argues that Ontario's existing Human Rights processes, part of a malleable legal culture that facilitates individual negotiation of competing rights, may in fact provide a larger number of students who have special needs more obtainable rights and better quality services than mandated services typically have.

THE EVOLUTION OF ONTARIO'S LEGAL CULTURE

Ontario's legal culture developed as a result of collaboration in a complex multilingual, multi-cultural society. For readers who are not familiar with the Canadian implementation of federalism, this section provides a brief introduction to important elements of our legal culture. They include the Canadian Charter of Rights and Freedoms (1982); the dynamics of federal-provincial authority in Canada (1791–1998); two relevant Ontario laws (the Education Act and the Human Rights Code); the concept of parliamentary supremacy; Canadian systems of dispute resolution (Dickinson and Mackay 1989; Ogloff and Meyers 1991; Sussel 1995); and Ontario's tradition of toleration, consensus, and philanthropy.

Figure 1 provides a chronology of significant dates and documents in the evolution of the Canadian Constitution. The newest

1570—Iroquois Conferderacy: Establishing a basis of treaty government
1599—Samuel de Champlain's first voyage to America
1656—Baruch Spinoza was banished from Amsterdam on the rabbi's orders
1663—Sovereigh Council of Quebec: Establishing resident civil government
1763—Royal proclamation: Transferring Canada to British rule
1774—The Quebec Act: Guaranteeing the religious and linguistic rights of the French
1776—The Delaration of Independence was signed in the United States
1791—The Constitutional Act: Dividing Canada into two provinces
1810—Napoleon Bonaparte established the first free secondary schools in France
1840—The Union Act: Attempting but failing to make English law and language supreme

1842—Britain took control of Hong Kong
1861—1865—The U.S. Civil War
1867—The British North America Act: Creating a federation of four provinces
1931—Statute of Westminister: Making Canada an independent nation rather than a British colony
1947—Canadian citizenship established
1948—Israel became a nation
1949—The Supreme Court of Canada rather than the Judicial Committee of the Privy Council in London became the final court of appeal
1981—Israel annexed the Golan Heights
1982—The Constitution Act: Patriating the highest law of the land and containing a constitutional amending formula and the Canadian Charter of Rights and Freedoms

Figure 1.   Chronology of dates and documents.

addition, the Charter of Rights and Freedoms (the Charter), is part of the Constitution Act of 1982, so it is less than 20 years old. However, the legislative roots of the Charter lie in a long tradition of treaty governance in which respect for the separate powers of distinct authorities has been a cornerstone of Canada's success (Cruxton and Wilson 1978; Ogloff and Meyers 1991). In the more than four centuries since the Aboriginals, the French, and the English began to coexist, there have been and still are strong differences of opinion among various groups in a vast and populated land, but remarkably few issues have ever prompted Canadians to abandon negotiation and to resort to physical conflict. Accepted processes of dispute resolution have tended to be flexible in order to balance competing rights, but slow and weighted in favor of government authorities, both allowing and expecting them to maintain order among groups (Black-Branch 1993; Cruxton and Wilson 1978; MacLellan 1996; Ogloff and Meyers 1991; Zuker 1988). The principle of non-interference by one government agency in affairs under the control of another underlies Canada's co-operative federal system.

The distribution of powers between the federal and provincial governments in Canada is guided by the terms of the Confederation Act of 1867, which provided for a reluctant union among Canada East (Quebec), Canada West (Ontario), New Brunswick, and Nova Scotia. Other provinces that had participated in the four years of negotiations needed to prepare the 1867 Act took as long as 80 years to voluntarily join the union that it created. Canada's founding fathers were disturbed by the tendency of their southern neighbors to resolve conflicts by force. They took great care to avoid a structure that would generate similar patterns. They held a strong belief that a well educated population was the key to a non-violent system. Egerton Ryerson's initiatives in the 1820s spurred the development of high quality free public secondary schools in Ontario (Cruxton and Wilson 1978). John Ralston Saul's observation that all of Canada's Anglophone prime ministers have been graduates of public education emphasizes Ontario's tradition of supporting and valuing high quality public education for all its citizens (Watson 1998). The Canadian Confederation is perhaps the world's most slowly, deliberately, and peacefully planned union of distinct states. It relies on a well educated population to make it work.

Sussel credits A.V. Dicey with first articulating the two basic principles of rule by parliament in 1867. First, parliament has the right to make or unmake any law; and secondly, no person or body may constitutionally set aside the legislation of a parliament (Sussel 1995). Until 1982, these two basic precepts of parliamentary supremacy were limited in Canada only by the division of powers between the distinct levels of government. Education was a provincial concern, so federal law had no jurisdiction over any educational matter.

Since 1982, when the Charter was accepted by the provinces, individual Canadians have had some protection from inappropriate acts of provincial educational authorities, but the protection is subject to "such reasonable limits prescribed by law as can be demonstrably justified in a free and democratic society" (Statute 1982). The civil rights of an individual Canadian may be curtailed by government authority if the restriction is seen as necessary to balance competing rights or to maintain social goals. The Charter's qualifying language provides scope for the Canadian judiciary to continue to support the decisions of legislative authorities in a historically Canadian manner. There is, however, debate in the literature about the extent to which the charter will affect Canada's tradition of non-interference by one government agency in the affairs of another. Some legal experts versed in special education predicted that the Charter's primary effect would be to have provinces look more closely at their own statutes in respect to civil rights issues (MacKay and Sutherland 1990; Ogloff and Meyers 1991). Others (Sussel 1995; Taylor 1990; Watkinson 1991) expected the judiciary to begin to take a more active role in determining social policy following the model provided by U.S. constitutional arguments.

Since 1982 a legal challenge regarding the violation of Charter rights by an educational authority in any Canadian province could be heard by a federal court, which would sit as the Supreme Court of the province. But this can only happen if many preconditions are met, not the least of which is that all avenues of dispute resolution existing within the province's legislation have been exhausted. Thus, in 1998, each province still constructed its own criteria for education, with little federal input or supervision (Sussel 1995).

EDUCATIONAL RIGHTS

Due to the structure of Canadian federalism, the rights of persons with disabilities to educational services varies substantially from province to province. The work of Smith and Lusthaus (1994) illustrated the wide variation in the total number of special education rights that students in different provinces have. Ontario is one of the most progressive jurisdictions in Canada with regard to the educational rights of students with disabilities. Any cross-Canada comparisons of such rights is frustrated by issues resulting from the uniqueness of each province's legislation, programs, and definitional terminology (Smith and Lusthaus 1994).

The provision of special education services to adults with learning disabilities in Ontario is guided by both the Education Act and the Code, yet neither law describes specific characteristics of the services that institutions of higher education should provide. The Education Act only regulates education up to the secondary level, but Section 8 of it establishes a model of delivering service to students with special needs which most colleges and universities follow. The primary function of the Human Rights Code is to guarantee members of protected groups (those identified by their race, color, creed, sex, age, or handicap) equal treatment in the provision of "goods, services, facilities, accommodation, contracts, employment, and membership in associations" (Statute 1995). It specifically identifies individuals with learning disabilities within the larger group—handicapped persons—and establishes principles of dispute resolution that guide the internal polices at Ontario's colleges and universities.

HUMAN RIGHTS CODE AND COMMISSION

The Human Rights Code became an Ontario law in the 1960s, but the benefit that it provides members of the target groups, including those with LD, became much greater when the duty to accommodate their special needs was added in the 1980s. To facilitate the full integration of the target groups in Ontario society, the duty to accommodate is incumbent on every citizen, and on private and public entities that offer services to the Ontario public. Nevertheless, if an "entity responsible for accommodation" can demonstrate that a "requested accommodation" would create an "undue hardship in terms of cost, sources of funding and safety requirements" (Statute 1995), an exemption from the duty to accommodate will be granted. In 1989, the Ontario Human Rights Commission (OHRC) published *Guidelines for Assessing Accommodation Requirements for Persons with Disabilities*. This document defines "the Commission's goal of creating a discrimination-free environment through the encouragement of voluntary compliance with the Code," and is intended to help "the general public understand and apply concepts of accommodation and undue hardship" (OHRC 1989). In Ontario, all citizens, not just government agencies, are held accountable to know and uphold the provisions of the Code (Bujara 1998; OHRC 1989; Statute 1995; Zuker 1990). The excerpts in figure 2 from *Teaching Human Rights in Ontario* illustrate the stress that Ontario places on educating all its citizens to know and uphold human rights principles that encourage equity and diversity to flourish (OHRC 1996).

A climate of understanding and mutual respect will not grow on its own initiative. Making that goal a reality calls for constant and careful nurturing and encouragement through a combination of strong legislation, active community programs and, above all, education.

Living in a country which increasingly reflects the human diversity of the global village, and whose prosperity depends on the harmony and unity of its mosaic, no student should graduate from an Ontario school without achieving the following learning objectives.

1. increase their awareness of the OHR Code and the work of the Commission;
2. identify the grounds and social areas covered by the Code,
3. be able to explain what constitutes discrimination;
4. be able to explain how the Code protects individuals and groups from discrimination and harassment; and
5. know their rights and responsibilities under the law, how to protect those rights and how to help others who experience discrimination or harassment.

Rosemary Brown, P.C.
Chief Commissioner
Ontario Human Rights Commission

Figure 2.   Excerpts from the Preface of *Teaching Human Rights in Ontario.*

Human Rights tribunals, established under the Code, have developed principles of dispute resolution that are widely applied in Ontario. Following a complaint, a Human Rights counselor will investigate allegations and try to facilitate mediation of differences. In each case, there will be a determination of what is an "essential" duty, a "sufficient" accommodation, and "undue" hardship. If a case goes forward to a tribunal, there is no hierarchical principle to resolve cases of conflicting rights. The principle of "minimal harm" to our social goals prevails over claims to individual rights (Bujara 1998; Zuker 1990).

In practice, the vast majority of disputes that have been mediated and cases that have been litigated by the OHRC relate to individuals claiming discrimination or harassment on grounds of race, sex, or sexual orientation (Recorder 1980–95). Nevertheless, there have been a few key decisions relating to persons with LD that set important precedents for adults with learning disabilities in Ontario (Recorder 1996). In the 1996 Gill decision, the Public Service Board was required to re-administer its entrance testing for a dyslexic applicant, not because it had not accommodated (it had provided extra time), but because it had not consulted with the applicant about the accommodations that he required. In the Boehm case, the OHRC required an employer to pay compensation to an individual with a learning disability who had been subjected to ridicule from his supervisor in what was described as a "poisoned work environment." One effect of such decisions is that they put pressure on all parties to negotiate fairly during the preliminary stage of mediation (Bujara 1998; Tieman 1998). Negotiation and mediation services help to explain the scarcity of Ontario cases in the *Canadian Human Rights Recorder*, a publication that records all cases of human rights litigation in Canada.

By contrast, OHRC cases that have been decided in favor of individuals with LD who have challenged a Board of Education (comparable to school districts), the Ministry of Education (comparable to a department of education), a college, or a university are virtually nonexistent. In 18 years (1980–1997), the *Canadian Human Rights Recorder* listed 19 challenges of provincial educational institutions. Only two of these cases originated in Ontario, approximately one per decade. Both the Ontario cases were decided in favor of the educational authorities (Recorder 1996). Just as the federal courts will not hear cases if the internal systems of dispute resolution in a province have not been exhausted, the OHRC will not hear cases if the internal systems of resolution within an educational institution have not been exhausted. All colleges and universities have internal procedures for dispute resolution, and most disagreements regarding the rights of students with disabilities are resolved in-house.

Two important guidelines have been established by OHRC decision. (a) A person with a disability cannot be judged incapable of performing "essential duties" before an effort has been made to accommodate his or her needs; (b) a person with a disability must be consulted to determine what accommodations she or he requires. These principles of dispute resolution challenge the medical model of disability. They emanate from an understanding of disability as a social response to difference (Crow 1995) and acknowledge the government's responsibility to moderate attitudes that are not in keeping with Ontario's social goals. Under the Code, it is an offense even to announce an intention to discriminate against another on a prohibited ground (Statute 1995). The OHRC also does not condone restrictions of individual rights based on hypothetical expert testimony (Bujara 1998).

ROLE OF THE EDUCATION ACT

In 1980, the Education Act was amended by Bill 82 to include a section that guaranteed students with disabilities appropriate public special education (Section 8 of the Education Act of Ontario). However, Ontario retained firm administrative control of special education services in two ways. One is a process of grant funding and the other is legislative. Section 8 set up a collaborative process for identifying and educationally placing students with special needs, called the Identification, Placement and Review Committee (IPRC). If differences of opinion arise, parents, or students, if they are more than 18 years old, have the right to appeal issues of identification or placement through a complex series of tribunals (Wiener and Siegel 1992; Zuker, 1988). However, they have no right to appeal issues relating to the program (Statute 1996). That right is retained for the professional educators.

The Ontario judiciary tends to support administrative policy and not to interfere in politically decided matters. The 1985 decision of the Supreme Court of Ontario upholding a distinction between the parental right to appeal identification and a board's right to control a program illustrates this pattern. In dismissing a parental request for a "total communication" program, Justice Eberle stated:

> Since the Muskoka plan was satisfactory to the Minister (of Education), it is not for the court to meddle with the details of implementation of government policies nor the rate of progress of their implementation. Those are administrative, financial and policy matters primarily. Equally, I do not think it is for the court to attempt to take over the control of such matters even though our American brothers have done so in some instances. I am not at all tempted by their example. It is my firm view that matters of that kind are for elected officials and not for judges (Zuker 1988, p. 102).

With regard to the concept of what constituted appropriate placement, Justice Eberle's argument encapsulates the Canadian principle of balancing competing needs:

> The idea of "appropriate" special education programs, and the appropriateness of the placement of the pupil, surely involves the idea of suitability, and is not to be confused with a placement which amounts to perfection the language used (in Section 8) is a far cry from language which would for example require a placement which fulfils the needs of the pupil . It is essential to consider which programmes and services are available and perhaps even the degree of availability. To recommend the placement of a child to a non-existent programme seems to me absurd (Zuker 1988, p. 110–111).

Summarizing the effects of the Dolmage decision, Judge Marvin Zuker, a frequent lecturer at the Ontario Institute for Students in Education and author of *The Legal Context of Education*, concluded that Judge Eberle's ruling established that "what is appropriate placement and whether the needs of an exceptional pupil are met by a placement will be professionally and not legally determined" in Ontario (Zuker 1988, p.111).

Those who have challenged the Ministry of Education legally are frequently bitterly frustrated (Taylor 1990). In the first five years after Bill 82 was passed, some parents seeking to have private special education services funded by the province tried to take their cases directly to Ontario courts. Because they did not exhaust the internal processes of dispute resolution established by the Education Act, their cases were dismissed (Haswell 1998). If one takes the point of view that legal challenges are a desirable method of securing educational rights, the appeal processes set up at Ontario's educational institutions seem to be regressive obstructions to civil rights. However, the early stages of these processes require thorough fact finding and well documented individual case review. They allow for the negotiation of competing rights, and result in the resolution of most issues of a program during the preliminary stage of mediation (Flatters and Oppenheim 1990; Rooke 1991).

In our experience at York University over the past twelve years, having served approximately 600 students with LD, we can recall no disagreement about educational accommodations ever going beyond the Associate Dean level to the higher authorities within York's administration. When both parties to a dispute understand the Ontario system, neither side expects to win a decision outright, and all expect the costs in terms of time and resources to be very high. The system of dispute resolution, involving multiple levels of review and stringent requirements at each stage, thus favors mediation (Flatters and Oppenheim 1990; Zuker 1988). Both the Education Act and the Code sanction such procedures. The flurry of educational court cases that some writers (Sussel 1995) anticipated would follow the passing of Bill 82 and the Charter of Rights and Freedoms really has not developed at Ontario colleges and universities.

TYPICAL SERVICES IN ONTARIO COLLEGES AND UNIVERSITIES

Carleton University's Educational Equity Policy (Carleton 1998) and its online explanation of its Mediation Service (Carleton 1996) are good examples of an Ontario university's proactive policies. Note in figure 3 how the language protects the rights and the dignity of those requiring special services. Carleton publicly accepts the responsibility of training its faculty and staff on human rights issues as these relate to curriculum and to pedagogy, and acknowledges its duty to seek out and change those aspects of the university's local culture that are inconsistent with equity.

Carleton University seeks to identify University policies, programs, and services that need to be changed, enhanced, or created, subject to the availability of resources, in order to:

a) increase the access, retention and graduation of groups of students who have traditionally been under-represented, and under-served and
b) provide a supportive and welcoming learning environment for all students.

In suport of its commitment to achieve and maintain a hospitable campus climate for all students, faculty, and staff, the University undertakes to provide education and training on human rights issus as these relate, inter alia, to curriculum and to pedagogy.

Approved by Senate: 29 October 1993

Figure 3. Highlights of Carleton University's Educational Equity Policy.

In its effort to encourage equity, Ontario provides all its colleges and universities with transfer payments that are designated for special needs student services. Individual institutions have autonomy in deciding how the funds are spent. The enrollment, demographic, and cultural priorities at a college or university influence the emphasis that it places on policies to assist students from the various groups identified by the Code.

A policy of York University, in the heart of multicultural Toronto, is to encourage the admission of students from groups that traditionally have had low access to higher education. The student body is culturally, racially, linguistically, and socio-economically diverse. In a tolerant province, York's campus culture stands out for its commitment to equity. In this climate, and due to the humanitarian goals of its founder, York University's Learning Disabilities Programme (LDP) is at the forefront of post-secondary special education services in Ontario.

The LDP was started in 1985, at the initiative of Harold Minden, a professor/philanthropist, who lobbied for grants to fund what he considered to be a missing component in the education of students with learning disabilities. The range of services that LDP has developed in response to students' needs now includes learning skills assessment, career counseling, case management, individual tutoring, study skills instruction, and exam accommodations, as well as personal and/or group counseling designed to improve self-esteem, manage test anxiety, and encourage time and stress management. The department also sponsors, in conjunction with the Department of Languages, Literature, and Linguistics, a full-credit, critical skills course designed to support the full inclusion of students with LD in other university courses. Dr. Minden envisioned that the LDP would become a center of excellence and act as a model for other universities in Ontario. In many ways, his dream has been realized.

Ontario's colleges and universities share techniques for meeting the needs of students with disabilities in several ways. Several Ontario institutions of higher education now follow York's model and conduct their own learning skills assessment to provide current data for effective accommodation recommendation. In the late 1980s, a voluntary association formed consisting of special needs service-providers from all universities in Ontario. The Inter-University Disabilities Issues Association (IDIA) meets approximately five times a year to discuss issues of common concern. Topics for discussion include policy and problems of implementing strategies. The group also provides feedback to the Ministry of Education and Training regarding many of the legislative and policy initiatives aimed at enhancing the provision of educational support services to students with disabilities in university. A parallel association, the College Committee on Disability Issues (CCDI), comprises the special needs service providers at the community college level and serves a similar function to IDIA. The elected executive committees of these associations communicate regularly about their respective activities, and periodically joint professional development programs are established.

Additionally, Ontario provides eligible students who have disabilities access to technology bursaries of up to $2000. When these funds are combined with funds available through federal grants, an eligible student is able to access up to $7000 a year. The distribution of these funds is at the discretion of the special needs counselors of the college or university. Figure 4 shows the assistive technology that York's LDP typically recommends for a student with LD.

Although special needs counselors in Ontario do not all have as strong administrative support as the Carleton and York programs have, they all establish criteria for identification, determine reasonable accommodations (within the context of their available supports), recommend that professors cooperate with the suggested accommodation, and mediate disputes if they occur (Zuker 1988). Such processes protect a college or university from censure by the OHRC and the Ontario public, who expect their public institutions to operate in a fair manner.

Ontario's voluntary process meshes well in a climate tolerant of diversity. Two advantages of allowing each institution to control its

Home Computer:	32 MB RAM
	4 GB har driv
	233 MHZ cpu
	15–17" monitor @ $400
	56K fax mdem
	24x CD-Rom drive
	Color Printer
Other:	Dragon Dictate (requires 133 MHZ and 32 MB RAM)
	DD, Naturall Speaking
	Text Reders: Textease or Texthelp
	Zoom Text
Note:	Laptops (circa $3000) considered on a case by case basis
	E-mate ($1059) requires a home computer
	Grapics equipment for Fine Arts considered case by case

Figure 4.   York's Recommended Technology Specifications 99

own special services policy seem to be that (1) as the service providers find ways to be more effective within the confines of their own budgets, creative problem solving is encouraged, and (2) faculty backlash, against imposed accommodations, is rare.

LEARNING OPPORTUNITIES TASK FORCE

The strong response by Ontario colleges and universities to the Learning Opportunities Task Force (LOTF) indicates a widespread high-level desire to provide well for students with unique needs. In 1997, the Province initiated a $30 million dollar competition among its colleges and universities to develop new "best practice" services for students with learning differences. The LOTF conducted a survey of existing services in Ontario, researched best practice in post-secondary education, and reviewed the bids submitted by 34 of Ontario's 46 colleges and universities. Eight proposals were accepted. In September 1998, Ontario began to provide amounts ranging from $300,000 to $1.5 million (over four years) to assist the selected colleges and universities in setting up new "best practices" services (Sinclair 1998).

The LOTF grants were available only to institutions that proposed to create new services for persons formally diagnosed with LD, but LOTF's printed materials used the term "learning differences" rather than "learning disabilities." By providing grants to assist individuals in adjusting to their differences, Ontario has taken another precedent-setting step toward a social model of disability and away from a medical model.

The Canadian expectation that our governments have the duty to balance competing social needs was clearly reflected in the LOTF decisions. Dr. Bette Stephenson, a highly respected educational and influential political leader (who introduced Bill 82 in 1980 when she was Minister of Education) directed LOTF to award the largest grant to a consortium of Francophone colleges. In terms of services for student with differences, French language institutions have lagged significantly behind Anglophone ones. Francophones are one of the smaller minorities in Ontario, but their educational and linguistic rights have been guaranteed by treaty since 1774 (MacLellan 1996). Even staff at institutions whose bids were rejected have praised Dr. Stephenson's decision to provide the Francophone colleges the largest grant (Morris 1998).

> It has frequently been observed that the extent of a democracy in a society can be best assessed by the way that society treats its minorities. Viewed by this measure, Canadian society since 1982 has been rather successful in broadening the scope and quality of its democratic life—a trend that is clearly illustrated in the constitutional and legislative provisions relating to Canadians with disabilities (Sussel 1995, pp. 64–65).

CURRENT POLITICAL REALITIES

The Progressive Conservative government in power in Ontario at the time of writing, under the leadership of Mike Harris, has a strong right-of-center bias. The Canadian tradition of parliamentary supremacy allows it broad scope to effect immediate social change. Ontario's current social turmoil is evinced in the Province's willingness to override referendum results and amalgamate traditionally distinct municipal governments, as well as in its radical changes to educational policy. The Harris government's decisions have resulted in the longest-ever strikes by Ontario's teachers and university faculties. The budget of the OHRC, welfare benefits, and daycare services have been deeply cut. In the context of such major reductions of government services, subtle changes to educational access for students with LD (primarily affecting those from lower socio-economic backgrounds) are likely to go undetected for several years. In the meantime, as these measures improve the appearance of the Province's balance sheet, they reduce the social mobility of a certain class of students with disabilities.

In the forward to *Canada's Legal Revolution: Public Education, the Charter, and Human Rights*, Greg M. Dickinson, eminent lawyer and professor of education at the University of Western Ontario, summarized the current problem for Ontario educators who support equity policies:

> I predict that increasingly, in the 1990s and beyond, this question will be asked: How much rights can we afford? Welfare rights—of which education rights are a big part—may be in for the battle of their lives. There are internal, and financial, or economic, cultures—just as there is a legal culture. With evidence of growing support for right-of-center political philosophies that are critical of group rights and affirmative action, and with taxpayer revolts being a plainer threat than ever, a reassertion of conservative values and a financial revolution of sorts may well affect the permanence of the legal-educational revolution (Sussel 1995)

Officials at the Ontario Ministry of Education claim that music, art, and drama have not been cut, but in reality the Ministry's new curriculum has fewer art credits. Art, music, and drama teachers are being reassigned to core subjects, and extracurricular art programs are threatened because regular teaching loads in high schools have been increased from 6/8 to 7/8 periods per day. Walter Pitman, a prominent educator, chairman of the Ontario Arts Council, formerly president of Ryerson University, and chairman of the Ontario Institute for Students in Education, has publicly stated that in focusing only on business skills, "the Harris government has got it all wrong" (Walker 1998b). Pitman believes that the arts will be a unifying factor in learning horizontally in the 21st century and he is willing to encourage other educators to oppose Harris' regressive educational policies (Walker 1998b).

In Canada today, rule by parliamentary supremacy is limited not only by the division of powers in the Confederation Act of 1867, but also by the Charter of Rights and Freedoms. The Charter gives the courts the power to invalidate provincial legislation that conflicts with human rights guarantees. Legal challenges to actions by a government are now possible. Groups (including the Ontarians with Disabilities Act Committee, the Court Challenges Program, and the Legal Education and Action Fund for Women) have formed to pursue judicial and legislative solutions to the Harris crisis, but in Ontario, a court challenge is likely to be a very protracted process. A more effective course of action for those concerned about social justice for postsecondary students with LD is likely to be political action. By joining with other groups who are negatively affected by the Harris agenda and by appealing to Ontarians' equity consciousness, it is reasonable to hope that the government will be pressured to rescind recent discriminatory policies.

A broadly based coalition of individuals and community organizations has formed to pressure the Harris government to pass an Ontarians with Disabilities Act as an effective new law that would achieve a barrier-free Ontario for persons with disabilities. The extent of public support for such initiatives can be seen by the fact that Lou Harris Polling donated its professional services to design and conduct an opinion survey on public attitudes to the need for legislation requiring the removal and prevention of barriers before persons with disabilities. A highlight is that 84% of the 523 Ontarians in the random sample said that legislation to remove barriers would benefit society as a whole (ODA 1997). Many Ontarians believe that the long-term social costs of failing to educate adequately a substantial portion of the population will far outweigh the short-term savings sought by the incumbent provincial government, and that these groups will unite in common political action.

CONCLUSION: FAITH IN A LEGAL CULTURE

Dickinson could be right that "education rights may be in for the battle of their lives" (Sussel 1995). Yet Ontario is fortunate that to date most of the services for students with learning disabilities at the postsecondary level have evolved not so much in response to a "legislated hammer" as in deference to a tradition of respecting and valuing the diversity of individuals. At the present time, people working within the social services that have been cut are aware of inequitable effects of recent changes to both the Education Act and the OHRC. Nevertheless, government rhetoric blurs the differences in the minds of many citizens. Within a few years, with the concerted effort of knowledgeable professionals, the general public will understand the inequitable impact of these policies. It is highly unlikely that they will be tolerated.

The Canadian founding fathers' desire to foster a "cultural mosaic" has produced a society in which cultural difference is not only tolerated but celebrated. When European, African, or Asian World Cup soccer teams win a game, throngs of Torontonians waving the flag of their "ancestral homelands" celebrate in the streets; these connections survive even to the third and fourth generations. Ontario's appreciation of diversity is consistent with an approach to disability, which recognizes that many individuals may need accommodations to realize their full potential, so that society can benefit from their talents, skills, and unique perspectives. Within this paradigm, accommodations are provided because they are in the best interests of all concerned, not solely because a law mandates that it be so. The fact is that most disagreements about post-secondary services for students with disabilities are resolved within a college's or a university's own mediation process. Very few cases have required the assistance of OHRC mediation services. This record suggests that the Ontario tradition of negotiation and reasoned compromise has served both the students and post-secondary institutions well.

Parliamentary legislation is enacted subject to the wishes of the political party in control at any given moment, but social attitudes cannot quickly be altered through legislation. In the final analysis, if employers or educators want to make life difficult for any individual, they can usually find ways to circumvent any law. We believe that a legal culture based on a tradition of fostering equity and achieving social justice through negotiation is more powerful than law. This is not to suggest that court challenges to inequitable legislation and legislation prohibiting discrimination on the basis of disability are not important. However, the success of Ontario's cooperative model suggests that it may be unwise to focus solely on legalities (Zuker 1990). It seems at least as important to work toward the development of public attitudes that recognize disability not as weakness, but as diversity, difference that adds value both within an educational institution and in the community at large.

REFERENCES

Black-Branch, J. L. 1993. The past, present and future tenses of the Canadian Charter of Rights and Freedoms for Special Education Students: The perceptions of academics and legal practitioners. *Canadian Journal of Special Education* 9(2):134–44.

Bujara, I. 21 June 1998. Recent decisions of the OHRC. Paper presented at the CACUSS'98, Ottawa.

Bunch, G. 1998. Interview: York University Faculty of Education.

Carleton. 1996. *Carleton University Mediation Center.* Carleton University Senate. Available: http://www.carleton.ca/equity/Home_Pages/Med/Med.html#anchor342539.

Carleton. 1998. *Educational Equity Policy.* Carleton University Senate. Available: gopher://ernest.carleton.ca:406/00/root-all/uni-policies/academ-policies/edu-equ-policy.

Crow, L. 1995. Including all of our lives: Renewing the social model of disability. In *Encounters with Strangers*, ed. J. Morris. Toronto: The Women's Press.

Cruxton, J. B., and Wilson, W. D. 1978. *Flashback Canada*. Toronto: Oxford University Press.

Dickinson, G. M., and Mackay, A. W. 1989. *Rights, Freedoms and the Education System in Canada: Cases and Materials.* Toronto: Emond Montgomery.

Flatters, N., and Oppenheim, C. 1990. Mediation: The nexus between law and education constructive dispute resolution in the school system. In *Education & Law: A Plea for Partnership*, ed. W. Foster. Vancouver: Editions Soleil.

Haswell, C. 1998. Interview.

MacKay, A. W., and Sutherland, L. 1990. Making and enforcing school rules in the wake of the Charter of Rights. In *Education & Law: A Plea for Partnership*, ed. W. Foster. Vancouver: Editions Soleil.

MacLellan, D. K. 1996. The legal question of extending public funds to private funds in Ontario: Alder v. Ontario. *Education & Law Journal* 7:61–75.

Mandell, A. L. 1996. A question of rights: The educational placement of children with mental and physical disabilities. *Exceptionality Education Canada* 6 (1):1–14.

McEwan, R., Mombourquette, F., McBride, A., and Dickinson, G. 1997.The erosion of adult education in Ontario. *Education & Law Journal* 8:89–106.

Morris, M. 1998. Interview: Humber College Counseling Services.

ODA. 1997. Results of the Lou Harris Poll. Available: http://www.indie.ca/oda/survey.html May 12, 1997.

Ogloff, J., and Meyers, C. 1991. The Charter of Rights and Freedoms and human rights in education: A delicate balance of competing interest. In *Education & Law: Strengthening the Partnership*, eds. W. Foster and F. Peters. Vancouver: Editions Soleil.

OHRC. 1989. Guidelines for assessing accommodation requirements for persons with disabilities. Queens Printer, Ontario. Available: http: //www.ohrc.on.ca/pub.htm

OHRC. 1996. Teaching human rights in Ontario. Queen's Printer for Ontario. Available: http: //www.ohrc.on.ca/text_only/english/publications/enscptoc.htm

Recorder, C. H. R. (ed.) 1980–95. *Canadian Human Rights Recorder.* (Vol.12–27). Vancouver: Canadian Human Rights Recorder.

Recorder, C. H. R. (ed.) 1996. *Canadian Human Rights Recorder.* (Vol.28). Vancouver: Canadian Human Rights Recorder.

Rooke, J. D. 1991. Dispute resolution through arbitration and mediation. In *Education & Law: Strengthening the Partnership*, eds. W. Foster and F. Peters. Vancouver: Editions Soleil.

Sinclair, H. 1998. Interview: Learning Opportunities Task Force.

Smith, W. K., and Lusthaus, C. 1994. Equal education opportunities for students with disabilities in Canada: The rights to free and appropriate education. *Exceptionality Education Canada* 4 (1):37–73.

Statute. 1982. *Charter of Rights and Freedoms.* Government of Canada.

Statute. 1995. *Human Rights Code.* Queen's Printer for Ontario. Available: http://www.ohrc.on.ca/text_only/english/code/codeeng.htm

Statute. 1996. *Education Act, R.S.O.*, Queen's Printer for Ontario. Toronto: Province of Ontario.

Sussel, T. A. 1995. *Canada's Legal Revolution: Public Education, the Charter, and Human Rights.* Toronto: Emond Montgomery.

Taylor, D. R. 1990. Special education: A legal quagmire. In *Education & Law: A Plea for Partnership*, ed. W. Foster. Vancouver: Editions Soleil.

Tieman, G. 1998. Interview.

Walker, S. 1998a: June 6. The case for making art. *The Toronto Star*, pp. M 1–16.

Walker, S. 1998b: June 6. Pitman says arts are key to success in 21st century. *The Toronto Star*, p. M 16.

Watkinson, A. M. 1991. School rules: Students' rights. In *Education & Law: Strengthening the Partnership*, eds. W. Foster and F. Peters. Vancouver: Editions Soleil.

Watson, C. 1998. Jon Ralston Sol: Public education, democracy and an unconscious civilization. *Education Today* 17–22.

Wiener, J., and Siegel, L. 1992. A Canadian perspective on learning disabilities. *Journal of Learning Disabilities* 25 (6):340–50.

Zuker, M. 1990. Education and the law in Canada: Emerging challenges in the '90's. In *Education & Law: A Plea for Partnership*, ed. W. F. Foster. Vancouver: Editions Soleil.

Zuker, M.A. 1988. *The Legal Context of Education*. Toronto: OISE Press.

Chapter • 3

Dyslexia Support in Higher Education in the United Kingdom

Ginny Stacey and Chris Singleton

Changes in education and employment training have made it very difficult for people to be promoted without possessing formal qualifications from courses, i.e., certificates, degrees, diplomas, etc. European Union directives are threatening to render unemployable people who do not have certain relevant qualifications. The phasing out of apprenticeships has removed a practical style of training. Redundancies and re-deployment mean people need re-training in new areas of knowledge and skill. The complexity of machinery often needs operators to have sound grounding in scientific knowledge. In so many ways, qualifications beyond school level are essential for working and living.

There are many minority groups who need these qualifications and who experience particular difficulties in acquiring them. Persons with dyslexia make up just one of these groups, and their particular difficulty is that their poor abilities in language and sometimes also in numeracy may make language-based learning a problem.

Throughout the 1990s, a series of initiatives was funded by the Higher Education Funding Councils in the U.K. to give students from minority groups wider access to higher education (HE). Many of these projects involved support for students with dyslexia. At conferences held as part of these initiatives, institutions shared progress reports, with the expectation that good practice would pass from one to another. These conferences had a positive effect, but a need was felt for consistency throughout the sector and for regularization of criteria for identification of dyslexia in adults at the higher education level. Therefore, in 1995 a National Working Party was funded to review dyslexia support in the U.K. The report (Singleton et al. 1999) was published in February 1999.

The report discusses the impact of dyslexia on students in higher education and is very positive in its approach to the thinking strengths of dyslexic people. It includes a survey of the situation in 1996, a discussion of the issues and challenges of dyslexia support in higher education, a description of the good practice that has been developed, and more than 100 policy recommendations.

The aim was to produce a report that could be used by any institution offering HE courses for guidance in developing dyslexia support so that practice across the HE sector would have more equality and so that the same good practice need not be re-invented by each individual institution.

This chapter is a review of the work and report of the National Working Party.

THE NATIONAL WORKING PARTY, ITS WORK AND REPORT

The Working Party consisted of a total of 14 professionals, all but two of whom work with students with dyslexia in higher education. Four members of the group were psychologists and seven were professionals providing support or counselling for students with dyslexia. The remaining members were the then-chairperson of the National Federation of Access Centres (a federation of centers providing needs evaluation of technology for people of all disabilities), a representative from the British Dyslexia Association, and a representative from the Adult Dyslexia Organisation. Some of the members have dyslexia. The Working Party was kept reasonably small in the interests of efficiency and economy.

The activities of the Working Party had three components: a survey to gather data, consultations to seek opinions and concerns from outside the Working Party, and discussions and research by members of the Working Party. The consultations included a meeting with Local Education Awards Officers. It is the responsibility of these personnel to assess whether any student with a disability (including dyslexia) should be awarded funds to pay for additional expenses due to the effects of the disability on studying.

The report opens with an Executive summary of only a few pages to give senior management a concise view of the main themes. The introductory chapter briefly discusses wider social issues such as the Disability Discrimination Act (1995) and the Dearing Report

(1997), which was a national inquiry into higher education as a whole. There also is a discussion of some of the controversies surrounding dyslexia and "graduateness" (HEQC 1996), and of the problems of dyslexia. This chapter of the report sets the social context of the work of the National Working Party and concludes by outlining the aims and activities of the Working Party.

The second chapter of the report discusses the nature of dyslexia with particular reference to its neurological bases, cognitive character-istics, and compensating strengths. The flavor of dyslexia is given through personal stories. There is an overview of the impact of dyslexia on the educational experience of dyslexic students in HE.

The third chapter describes how the national survey was con-ducted and reports its responses and results. The data gathered are presented statistically. The fourth chapter deals with the consulta-tions, including the meetings that were held and the way discussions were conducted; it also summarizes points raised by representatives of HE institutions and of local education authorities who attended the meetings.

The remaining chapters of the report address eight major areas concerned with supporting dyslexic students in HE institutions. The major areas were identified as: (1) Institutional and national policy, (2) Staff development and institutional awareness, (3) Admission to higher education, (4) Identification of students with dyslexia, (5) Evaluation of needs and provision of support, (6) Counseling of stu-dents with dyslexia, (7) Examinations and assessment, and (8) Career advice for students with dyslexia. With one exception, each of these chapters contains three sections: (1) Issues, problems, and challenges, (2) Proposals on good practice, and (3) Recommendations on [each area of support]. The exception to this pattern is the chapter about identification of dyslexia in students, i.e., in adults functioning at the level necessary for higher education. The lack of sufficiently good measures or tests for dyslexia at this level means that the good prac-tice that should be described has not yet been sufficiently developed. Therefore in this chapter, the good practice section is replaced by Provisional proposals on dyslexia screening and Guidelines for diag-nostic assessment for dyslexia. The urgent need for thorough work in this area is stressed in the concluding chapter.

The concluding chapter summarizes the report with an over-view; it contains a priority list that should be useful for institutions that are either just beginning to develop dyslexia support or have limited funds available. It looks forward by outlining research, de-velopment, and reforms that are necessary in the provisions for stu-dents with dyslexia. Finally, the benefit to society, as well as to the students, is recognized in that the support provided aims to give skills to people who have unorthodox thinking talents to offer to their future employers.

SOCIAL CLIMATE, THE LAW, AND FUNDING

Both the social climate regarding dyslexia and the disability law have changed significantly in recent years, and more funding has been made available to support students with disabilities.

Within the U.K. school system, specific learning difficulty (or dyslexia) has been recognized as a category of special educational need for many years. The 1981 Education Act created a mechanism whereby children with special educational needs could access additional support from the Local Educational Authority (LEA). The Code of Practice on the Identification and Assessment of Special Educational Needs (DfE 1994) established a new framework within which children with dyslexia could be identified and supported primarily in the school, rather than being the responsibility of the LEA. The Code of Practice has carefully distinguished stages of evaluation of need and support to ensure that each child has help at the right level for his or her disability. As far as higher education is concerned, the existence of more widespread support in the school system means more students come to a university having received support and expecting a similar level while at the university.

Social acceptance of support is also encouraged by the relatively higher profile that dyslexia now has. This profile has been promoted by television and radio programs, by celebrities with dyslexia describing the impact of dyslexia on their lives, and by articles in newspapers and magazines.

In 1995, the Disability Discrimination Act was passed by the British Parliament. Under the law, dyslexia is a disability because it affects "the ability of a person . . . to carry out normal day-to-day activities" by affecting "memory or ability to concentrate, learn or understand" (Disability Discrimination Act 1995 Schedule 1.4). Even if a person has learned to manage the dyslexia using alternative strategies, the dyslexia is still to be regarded as a disability: "An impairment which would be likely to have a substantial adverse effect on . . . the person concerned . . . but for the fact that measures are being taken to treat or correct it, is to be treated as having that effect" (Disability Discrimination Act, 1995 Schedule 1.6).

There are two sections in the Act that particularly affect students in HE. The first requires that institutions publish statements regarding the policy on provisions available to students with dyslexia. The second section says that the disability statement is part of the conditions that govern the funds granted to an institution. Thus, there could be a financial penalty if an institution does not do its best to make adequate provisions for students with disabilities.

Some institutions were well placed to respond since they have developed the facilities offered to disabled students over many years. Other institutions had less well developed facilities. The body of the report of the National Working Party should provide all institutions with guidelines for further development of the dyslexia part of the support for students with disabilities.

No development happens without funds. Since 1990, Disabled Students' Allowances (DSAs) have been available to pay for the expenses incurred on a course due to any recognized disability. Until October 1998, these allowances were means tested, with the unfortunate result that students with disabilities from poor families were given financial help and those from wealthy ones could afford to pay for their help, but those from families in the middle income bracket tended to struggle unnecessarily. Now, as a result of the Dearing Report (1997), these allowances are not means tested so that the majority of disabled students now have their support funded. Those who still do not receive any financial help are part-time students and foreign students, although the Dearing Report recommends that these groups should also be helped. The organization of these allowances may yet undergo further changes, as the students' grant system is in the process of ongoing modification. The DSAs enable students to afford the special support in HE that has been developed through the projects funded by the Higher Education Funding Councils.

The Dearing Report, which covered higher education as a whole, also recommends (1) that training for HE teachers should include disability provision, and (2) that a professional institute should be established to accredit the teacher training. It addresses the problem of whether provisions are seen as individual and targeted at particular students or institutional and developed over the whole institution.

The recent changes in the social climate and the disability law in the U.K. are considerable. They result in much wider availability of support for dyslexic students in HE, and funding mechanisms are improving to enable students to use the support.

SURVEY OF THE HE SECTOR AND RESULTS

The first stage for the Working Party was to find out what support existed already. Therefore, a questionnaire was constructed and sent to all universities and colleges offering higher education courses. The questionnaire needed to be (1) sufficiently comprehensive to elicit the data required, (2) both precise enough to be answered simply and flexible enough to invite extra information, and (3) written in such a way as to maximize response. There was an 83% response rate.

The findings of the survey cover the admissions policy; how dyslexia is identified; the incidence of dyslexia and the spread across subjects; whether any support for students with dyslexia is available; whether there is a specialist staff within each institution; and whether there is any general heightening awareness of dyslexia within the institution. These themes relate to the institution rather than the individual students. For the students themselves, the survey collected data regarding technical support, how the students were helped to obtain funds through the DSA, and what range of examination provisions ("accommodations") were available. The survey also asked about the biggest problem people encountered. The six most frequent were:

1. funding for assessments
2. equipment and support
3. lack of knowledge about dyslexia among staff and students
4. lack of qualified staff to help dyslexic students
5. increasing numbers of students with dyslexia in higher education and the problems of identifying them
6. difficulties obtaining the DSA

The survey confirmed that there is no uniform support throughout the sector, and it illustrated differences in the support available at different institutions. One major use of the report should be the application of recommendations for good practice in support, which all institutions can try to implement.

CONSULTATIONS WITH SUPPORT PERSONNEL

As well as collecting statistics and brief statements on the questionnaire about wider issues, there was a series of consultation meetings in five different cities across England and Scotland. Each meeting was organized along the same pattern.

Delegates were sent pre-consultation documentation that outlined the meeting and invited them to do some preparatory work on the major themes to be discussed. The meetings had two sections. First was an opening session, during which one of the Working Party members outlined the work being undertaken and the methodology being used, and gave a progress report on the data so far analyzed. For the second part, the meeting broke up into discussion groups, each with at least one member of the Working Party. The groups were asked to discuss the following three topics:

1. Identification of dyslexia at the higher education level
2. Evaluation of the learning needs of students with dyslexia in higher education
3. Institutional perspectives on the support for students with dyslexia in higher education

Each area was divided into seven issues for discussion. The order and organization of the discussion was decided by each group. The role of the member of the Working Party was to act as note-taker in order to be able to report the concerns of the delegates back to the Working Party. The second part of the consultation meetings ended with a plenary session when the major points raised in each group were discussed generally.

Using the notes taken by the Working Party members, the discussions were analyzed and divided into the eight sections listed above in the National Working Party, its work and report. The following are some of the points raised: It was generally accepted that everybody should have the opportunity for higher education if doing so is within his or her potential; many students with dyslexia have that potential despite literacy problems. The more open attitude to access to higher education requires acceptance by staff members and their readiness to undertake training. There is a need for research into dyslexia in higher education, both in terms of more suitable identification at this level of functioning and of better understanding of appropriate support mechanisms. The greater acceptance of dyslexia as a syndrome has resulted in more students with dyslexia seeking help openly, which has finance and resource implications for the identification of dyslexia and for the systems of support. There was acknowledgment that what has already been achieved and the developments that are still needed must be embedded in national and institutional policy that has the backing of senior management.

CONSULTATIONS WITH AWARDS OFFICERS

The DSAs (Disabled Students' Allowances) are funded by central government and administered by Local Education Authorities (LEAs). Other funding authorities are involved, such as the NHS Health Bursary Agencies; they usually have allowances that are kept in line with the DSAs. Awards Officers within the LEAs, therefore, have to make decisions about these allowances and their allocation to students with dyslexia.

A consultation meeting was held specifically for Awards Officers after all the other meetings; this meeting followed the pattern of the other meetings with minor variations. It was noted that knowledge of dyslexia is outside the remit of Awards Officers but that they are expected to have full responsibility and accountability for the Disabled Students' Allowances. The process of application for DSAs works well when full documentation about a student exists, including assessments that have been carried out by personnel with recognized qualifications, and with an evaluation of needs produced by an Access Centre or equivalent authority. Other cases can be contentious and the administration becomes excessive and costly. Concerns were raised about (1) the way dyslexia becomes recognized during higher education, (2) the controversies concerning the nature and identification of dyslexia, (3) the variability in the information presented to support a student's application for DSA, and (4) the possibility that some students and institutions could be exploiting the system. The discussions included eventual ownership of technology purchased through the DSA and whether hire of equipment was a feasible alternative. It was also noted that there is a danger of expecting technology to meet all of the needs of a student with dyslexia when considerable teaching and counseling support may also be required.

It was recognized that administration of the DSAs needs to be simplified and standardized. Currently, the DSAs are allocated on an individual basis for each student's particular needs. They are administered in England, Wales, and Northern Ireland by Local Education Authorities. Each Authority has its own procedures for the administration and, as mentioned above, each institution has developed a support system to suit the needs presented by the students. Since there is no single procedure to follow, the amount of administration involved is excessive. Two possible solutions are: (a) to have all the administration carried out by a single central agency as in Scotland, or (b) to top-slice the DSA fund and pay it directly to each institution. If the latter solution were adopted, the funds would need to be ring-fenced so that they were not diverted from support for students with dyslexia and other disabilities.

WHAT IS DYSLEXIA?

One chapter in the report deals with the topic "What is dyslexia?" The chapter's purpose is to give readers with little or no experience with dyslexia an overview of the complexities surrounding the syndrome, a clear but brief account of the current definitions and latest research into origins, and an understanding of how dyslexia affects students in higher education. The chapter briefly discusses the present under-standing of dyslexia in terms of its biological bases and cognitive char-acteristics; it enumerates the impact dyslexia has on education and behavior, and includes a discussion about the positive thinking strengths often encountered in students with dyslexia. Students with dyslexia are so different one from another that trying to make a com-posite picture from the stories of several students leaves an unrealistic image; therefore, this chapter contains several vignettes. The chapter closes by reviewing the difficulties that dyslexic students might encounter at the various stages of university life as listed above in the introduction.

It is important to remember why defining dyslexia is a difficult task. The symptoms vary from one person to another. Persons with dyslexia have talents as well as problems. The problems they en-counter are not static; for example, one moment a person with dyslexia might know how to spell a word, and then a little later he or she might not be able to spell the same word.

Recent research gives evidence of neurological differences be-tween dyslexic and non-dyslexic brains, and differences in brain usage are shown by brain imaging techniques (Frith and Frith 1996; Galaburda 1993; Hynd and Hiemenz 1997). These findings support terminology used in the definitions of dyslexia such as "neurologi-cally based" (The Orton Dyslexia Society, now the International Dyslexia Association 1994) and "constitutional in origin" (British Dyslexia Association 1995). Thus, in the report, dyslexia is recognized as "a difference in cognition and learning" and the focus of attention is "the pattern of strengths and weaknesses."

The cognitive characteristics are currently divided into four cate-gories: (1) A marked inefficiency in the working or short-term mem-ory system (e.g., Beech 1997; McLoughlin, Fitzgibbon, and Young 1994; Rack 1997); (2) Inadequate phonological processing abilities (Beaton, McDougall, and Singleton 1997); (3) Unusual difficulty in au-tomatizing skills (Nicolson and Fawcett 1990, 1994); and (4) A range of problems connected with rapid visual processing (Lovegrove 1994; Willows, Kruk, and Corcos 1993), such as binocular instability (Cornelissen et al. 1994; Evans 1997; Stein 1991) and visual discomfort (see Evans 1997; Evans, Drasdo, and Richards 1996; Wilkins 1995).

The educational and behavioral aspects of dyslexia vary as a per-son moves from school to tertiary education; many of the achieve-ments with basic reading and spelling have reached a certain level of performance and variability. Individual pupils will have worked out idiosyncratic ways of tackling the literacy tasks that they encountered at school. Many pupils will have found friends, parents, or teachers who know how to give just the right help to get over problems. School has become a known system. Higher education is a new system. Students without dyslexia are able to build on their previous attainments. But for students with dyslexia, the new system of higher education often means that they have to rebuild many strategies for literacy tasks and for general organization of their life and work.

Although dyslexia usually has a significant impact on literacy skills, it is important that dyslexia be acknowledged as more than just a literacy problem. There are many tasks in education that are affected by dyslexia—such as memorizing—that tend to be overlooked if dyslexia is only understood in terms of literacy. Also, dyslexia can easily be missed as an underlying cause of difficulties (e.g., in exams) when "compensated dyslexics" have coping strategies that enable them to read and spell adequately (McLoughlin, Fitzgibbon, and Young 1994). The report discusses in more detail the "other difficulties" typically experienced by dyslexic students. These include: numeracy, oral skills, attention span, distractibility, energy levels, social and emotional factors, and organization.

The role of compensating strategies for managing dyslexia is often very important in the lives of students with dyslexia. These often consume time and energy, and, as the Disability Discrimination Act recognizes (see above), the use of such strategies cannot be taken as a sign that dyslexia is cured. The compensating strategies very often utilize the students' innate positive thinking strategies, which to a large extent accounts for the fact that there are a large number of persons with dyslexia who have done well in many professions (Aaron, Phillips, and Larsen 1988). West (1991) discusses the visual-spatial talents that many people with dyslexia have and how certain famous people with dyslexic characteristics have developed distinct talents. Dyslexia affects people of all levels of intelligence. It is important to support the extremely intelligent dyslexic students; it is also important not to expect all students with dyslexia to be high achievers. Perhaps most importantly, we should not miss the fast, visual, experience-based thinker with dyslexia behind the slow, ponderous speech that results from poor word retrieval skills, because given the right educational environment, visual thinking can contribute greatly to success at HE level.

In the report, the experience of dyslexia in higher education is illustrated through six vignettes. The students interviewed represent the wide range of experience among this population. The first student had been identified as having dyslexia reasonably early in childhood, but was given no appropriate help; instead, she was de-skilled by being told certain tasks were too difficult for her. The second was a mature student in his fifties and only recently identified as having dyslexia. He was delighted with the identification because it explained so much, but he was angry about all the wasted years. The third student had a difficult time at school; her parents still reject the idea of dyslexia and she still is unable to use the support available. The fourth was identified early in childhood and had support throughout his school years. He was very positive and optimistic, but worried about the next stage of employment. The fifth was well-compensated, had supportive teachers throughout school and supportive parents. Her dyslexia was not identified until she was in a university. Using the support at the university was not without difficulties, but she was determined to succeed, got a first class degree and went on to get a Ph.D. The last student was identified at school and enjoyed support at school and university.

The experiences of these students are quite different in flavor; their outlooks on life and robustness are obviously dissimilar. Their stories show some of the vast range of situations surrounding students with dyslexia in higher education.

These stories help us understand the importance and justice of supporting students with dyslexia in higher education, but they do not help staff understand the problems experienced by the students with dyslexia. For this reason, the report includes an overview of the impact of dyslexia on students and staff in higher education. This contains summaries of:

1. problems students with dyslexia are likely to have with the admissions process and with their expectations before entry;
2. difficulties with communication and organization they are likely to encounter within the institution's administration systems;
3. the problems encountered during lectures, with reading and writing, and with examinations and course work assessment;
4. the impact of staff attitudes about dyslexia on the way in which students with dyslexia conduct themselves;
5. concerns dyslexic students have when making decisions about employment and whom to ask for references.

IDENTIFICATION OF DYSLEXIA IN STUDENTS

Proper identification of dyslexia is a crucial factor for any support system for students with dyslexia. It is necessary to know that all those wanting support for dyslexia do meet the appropriate criteria. Professional agreement about these criteria is vital, especially about the different manifestations in adulthood. Personnel carrying out identification procedures must be properly trained to work with adults at high levels of compensation and intellegence. Students who are struggling with their courses should be checked for dyslexia. Funding should be available for psychological assessment, so that no dyslexic students go without support because they cannot afford to be assessed.

The Working Party was clear about the role of intelligence in defining dyslexia at HE level. If there is no discrepancy between an adult's language function and other intelligences, many of the support provisions are hard to justify. The aim of the provisions should be to let other abilities be used despite language problems.

The survey showed that 57% of dyslexic students come to university with their dyslexia already identified. The other 43% are identified while at university. Many who are already identified have fairly recent documentation, written for their A-level (matriculation) exams. The content of the documentation varies from very detailed psychological reports with full scores and interpretations to very brief summaries in response to questions on a form requesting provisions for exams. The cost of psychologists' reports has a deleterious influence on whether a student will register as having dyslexia. It is the student's responsibility to pay for these reports, unlike any other disability for which documentation can be obtained from the National Health Services. Thus there is a financial barrier to support for those who come to university with reports that do not match the university's criteria, or for those who are conjectured to have dyslexia while at university. To avoid as much unnecessary expense as possible, many institutions have screening procedures so that only those who are highly likely to be confirmed as having dyslexia are referred to psychologists.

Screening procedures have been developed as part of the ongoing work by professionals in several HE institutions in the U.K. Some screeners use interview-based methods, others use more formal testing procedures, including computerized ones, and others use a combination of methods. The report contains provisional proposals on dyslexia screening because this area of support is not as well developed as many other areas are.

The least developed area with respect to dyslexia support is the formal identification process. Currently, the professionals most likely to carry out formal identification are independent chartered psychologists. They use psychometric tests developed and normed by psychological corporations. Neither the psychologists nor the corporations have the same direct involvement with students with dyslexia as do the support staff at HE institutions. Nor are they likely to be funded through a Higher Education Funding Council project to conduct the research and development necessary to refine these instruments to be more suitable for use at HE level.

The necessary development is the production of normed tests for literacy and for a wide range of intelligences (Williams 1983; Campbell et al. 1996) that adequately probe the performance of students with dyslexia at levels appropriate to HE. Several factors complicate the testing of adults. Many struggle with the literature in their subject, but have seemingly adequate general reading skills when tested. Many have developed unorthodox, reasonably reliable methods for accomplishing language tasks that circumvent problems and give false results in tests (Stacey 1992). Many will use direct personal experience to take a test so that a large number of tests will not present the same challenge to the whole adult population with dyslexia; although the same can be said for the population without dyslexia, the effect is less likely to produce significantly different test scores.

Too many of the tests currently available have been devised to assess literacy skills up to the level of development expected at mid-teens. Advanced language skills are ignored. Some recently developed tests have norms for the country of origin, usually the U.S., and not yet for the U.K. Tests often focus on one language sub-skill at a time, so that a compensated student with dyslexia may apply full mental attention to each sub-skill in the test situation, but may be unable to combine skills in the way necessary for study-via-literacy at HE level. Systematic case studies of adults with dyslexia, students and non-students, are needed to provide a better basis for the development of psychometric tests appropriate for formal identification of dyslexia in adults. In the meantime, identification is possible with extreme care and with recourse to the wealth of experience of the testing personnel.

The report contains a lengthy section titled "Guidelines for Diagnostic Assessment of Dyslexia." This section discusses the people carrying out formal identification, the evidence to be investigated, the purpose of the assessment report, and other important considerations.

The categories of people identifying dyslexia are set out in this section as: (1) chartered psychologists, (2) educational, clinical, and occupational psychologists, (3) experienced and appropriately qualified teachers, and (4) psychologists or persons in related professions with appropriate competence and experience. It is proposed that a body should exist with responsibility for setting the standards for psychometric testing for all these categories. Possibly this could be the British Psychological Society, which has a similar role with respect to psychometric testing for occupation and careers.

The guidelines set out in some detail what evidence should be investigated in the identification procedure in terms of

- evidence of discrepancy
- assessment of literacy skills
- evidence of neurological or cognitive disabilities
- evidence of effects on learning
- other relevant evidence
- evidence that the difficulties are not due to other factors.

There is a discussion about the complications of compensation, degree of dyslexia and day-to-day variations of dyslexia, all of which are relevant to the testing and report writing. The purpose for which an assessment report is required is also relevant to the content and recommendations that it contains. Feedback to the students and issues of confidentiality need to be considered by the assessor.

From the HE institutions' point of view, additional issues to be considered are the uses to which the results are to be put and the cost of psychometric testing.

Once dyslexia has been properly identified, there should be no need for further psychological assessment, although there may be a need for an up-to-date evaluation of current needs in relation to current performance. The issue is primarily a question of who pays. In the U.K., the DSA can be used to fund an evaluation of needs but not the costs of the identification process. Hence the HE institution needs to consider whether there is doubt concerning previous identification of dyslexia or whether it really requires up-to-date evidence about current functioning of the student's literacy skills. For the 43% of students first identified as dyslexic in HE, the institution should consider the costs of testing and make arrangements so that there is no financial injustice in the support available to students with dyslexia simply because some cannot afford the psychometric testing for identification of dyslexia.

INSTITUTIONAL AND NATIONAL POLICY

Higher education institutions are autonomous, yet they have a system of external examining to maintain equality of standards across the sector. This equality will be altered for students with dyslexia if the level and kinds of provisions the institutions offer vary across the sector. Thus, it is important to have national standards of provisions. This will only come about if there is a national policy that applies to all institutions. The Dearing Report (1997) stated that "universities would be wise to develop a more considered stance on disability over time."

Similarly, within an institution, the aim is to have equality of standards between faculties. This aim will only be achieved when senior management backs the provisions for disabled students. Policies should be formulated that are binding on all faculties, with clearly stated exceptions if necessary, covering all aspects of provisions for students with disabilities. For dyslexia, these policies need to cover who makes the identification, any criteria the documentation must meet, what provisions are available for exams and course assessment and any marking regulations, what support is available, and who provides it.

Senior management needs to be confident that academic standards are maintained and that equality of opportunity is offered to all students. Resources for the support should be available in terms of personnel, premises, and equipment, and the support procedures need to be regularly monitored. The Working Party report contains a clear set of recommendations on policies required within institutions.

STAFF DEVELOPMENT AND INSTITUTIONAL AWARENESS

Students with dyslexia present a challenge to academic staff and support staff because their learning style is usually different from that used or assumed by staff. The trend toward modular programs in many institutions means that dialogue between staff and students is fragmented, and a holistic picture of a student's achievements and problems is hard for staff members to acquire. In this system, a student may never feel thoroughly at ease with a member of the staff and therefore may be reluctant to ask necessary questions. The student may also lack confidence because no member of the staff has a real opportunity to ascertain what he or she can do well.

Some work can be done with the staff, through staff awareness workshops and campaigns. Such methods have the advantage of promoting discussion between staff, providing an opportunity to air reservations or debate problems. Some work can be done with individual staff members, often initiated by problems encountered by one particular student. Solving those problems often increases the support for the other students with dyslexia in that faculty because of raised awareness of the issues.

Staff in all faculties and departments need to appreciate the talents and weaknesses of students with dyslexia and learn how to work with them. For instance, if a student with dyslexia comes to a reception desk for information, it is unhelpful to send him or her to a notice board to find the information. A request for information could happen anywhere; therefore, all staff members need to be aware of supportive communication methods for students with dyslexia. This includes not only academic (teaching) staff but also admissions staff, librarians, computer staff, site and estates staff, exams office staff, student administration, student services, counselor, and careers advisors.

Improving communications for students with dyslexia, if well done, should improve communication with students who are not dyslexic as well.

Most importantly, all staff members need to realize that the nature of dyslexia is such that these students have other innate intelligences that are of a higher level than the language that is the carrier medium. When differences in styles of thinking can be accommodated, successful learning can be promoted in students with dyslexia.

ADMISSION TO HIGHER EDUCATION

At the national level, admission to higher education for students with dyslexia is part of the widening access policy of the government, funding councils, and the Dearing Report (1997).

The national survey of the Working Party showed that most institutions admit students with dyslexia to all courses. A few said that teaching-related and medically related courses did not accept students with dyslexia. The relevant chapter in the report looks at the implications that this exclusion raises for the Disability Discrimination Act. It discusses the importance of dyslexic student-teacher role models for pupils and the competence of employees with dyslexia who use their compensating coping strategies to handle the effects of dyslexia in the workplace. When a policy of excluding students with dyslexia is thought necessary, it should be openly stated and justified. Not all students are willing to acknowledge their dyslexia before entry because they are worried about discrimination.

In order to make informed decisions during the admissions process, both students and staff need proper information. Students need to know what support is available, and what evidence of dyslexia needs to be produced in order to access that support. They need to know the policy of the institution as well as the attitudes of the staff toward dyslexia, and whether there is encouragement "to go it alone" if they so choose. Staff members need to understand the problems dyslexia generates both during the admissions process and the course of study; they need to know about the alternative strengths and the differences among students with dyslexia.

The proposals on good practice in the report cover:

1. Equal opportunities issues, with the belief stated that dyslexia should not be a barrier to entry to any profession.
2. Guidance on support discusses the information needed by students, information needed by admissions staff and tutors, and the necessity of contact with personnel dealing with dyslexia support.

3. Liaison within the institution to ensure that required support is obtained and that documentary evidence of dyslexia is properly considered.

4. Admissions route: there will be different needs and problems for dyslexic students entering higher education via different routes; for example, straight from school, colleges offering further education, access courses for many mature students. Staff need to know about these needs and problems, and take them into account.

EVALUATION OF NEEDS AND PROVISION OF SUPPORT

The chapter "What is dyslexia?" in the Working Party's report lists other problems of dyslexia than those associated with reading and writing. Evaluation of needs must be based on an understanding of the full breadth of the impact of dyslexia on a student's life and study preferences. Institutions must consider who will carry out the evaluation, what procedures will be used, the purpose of those procedures, how the evaluation will be funded, and what facilities will be made available.

The needs of students with dyslexia range from help acquiring the new skills necessary for university study, possible regular one-to-one support from a dyslexia specialist, information technology equipment, and exams and course work provision. There also needs to be some response to the psychologists' frequent recommendation of giving "sympathetic consideration to infelicities in the use of language." From time to time, students may also need help navigating the institution's systems, including the library.

One of the complications of dyslexia is that the condition is not static. It is impossible to evaluate the needs of a student throughout the college career. Review and flexibility of response will both be required in evaluating needs. It is important to consider the skills required for success in the course, as well as whether the student possesses these skills, has alternative strategies, or needs separate teaching to acquire appropriate skills and/or strategies.

Funding is an issue in the U.K. because support for disabilities can be paid for by the Disabled Students Allowances (DSAs) on an individual basis. However, not all support is supplied on such a basis; for example, library provisions are organized on an institutional rather than individual basis.

In the report, the kinds of support that students with dyslexia may need are listed as:

1. to be taught self management techniques
2. specialist tuition to improve skills and essential sub-skills
3. use of appropriate technology, including technology support

4. other types of help such as readers and scribes, if justified by the level of disability
5. proofreaders
6. referrals to specialists (such as optometrists with expertise in the visual correlates of dyslexia)
7. sessions with counselors
8. information on support networks

The report contains considerable detail about each kind of support.

EXAMINATIONS AND ASSESSMENT OF WORK

The support for students with dyslexia should properly be regarded as an equal opportunities issue. These are students who are capable of studying through alternative thinking processes, but whose language skills do not reliably match these alternative processes. The whole system of education uses language as the principal carrier of information and main means of communication, and is not about to undergo radical re-styling to accommodate unorthodox thinkers. Provisions for examinations and assessment of course work are part of the process of reducing the barriers erected by education's dependence on language.

Academic staff and management need to be convinced that academic standards are maintained, and that the knowledge and skills to be learned on a course are indeed being learned, demonstrated, and assessed. Students—those without dyslexia as well as those with dyslexia—need to be aware of the equal opportunities issues associated with the examination provisions: students with dyslexia should know they are not being patronized; those without dyslexia should know that they are not at a disadvantage.

The *Proposals on good practice* in this chapter starts by making the point that course material is the outcome of the course, not the carrier language. It looks at the time scale for setting up provisions. It contains suggestions on how examination papers are set. It discusses individual and group provisions, the dynamics of extra time, and the use of word processors. Marking policies are varied across the HE sector. There are guidelines so that institutions can draw up policies that are consistent but which still reflect the different patterns of examinations throughout the year that are use in different institutions.

COUNSELING

Counseling for students with dyslexia is understood to be different from support work, although sometimes the same person carries out both functions. Support work is not expected to deal with personal issues at the level more properly discussed in counseling sessions. Counseling needs to be properly supervised so that only the student's issues are dealt with.

There are several particular times when students with dyslexia may need counseling, for example:

1. The students who are first identified at university often have to re-think much of their lives. The identification may suddenly put many past incidents into a new light. There is often anger because no one noticed before or nothing was done to help.

2. Some mature students find coming back into an educational situation re-awakens old memories of failure at school, and the confidence that developed in the intervening years can evaporate quickly.

3. Some fairly competent students with dyslexia miss the familiar patterns of school, friends, and family, and lose their way in the new surroundings of higher education. They may not expect their dyslexia to have such a profound effect, and can become depressed as past problems that had seemed solved occur yet again.

4. Some students with dyslexia need to learn stress management or to be counseled through fears about examinations or giving presentations, or even fears that arise in dealing with the library.

Some of the problem situations may be similar for students without dyslexia, but the impact— because of the dyslexia—will be different.

All student counselors should be aware of the outward signs of dyslexia. They should also know the wide ranging impact that dyslexia has on the whole life of the student with dyslexia; for example, difficulty talking easily in social situations may arise from difficulty in working with spoken words because of the short-term memory problems of dyslexia. Counselors should also be aware of the different learning styles that many students with dyslexia have.

CAREERS ADVICE

The advice on careers for dyslexic students is summarized by the following quote:

> Dyslexic people are not intellectually deficient, they are not odd and they are by no means inadequate workers. They may have to organize

their lives differently from others, but that does not mean that they do not perform as well. Indeed, in many instances, it will be found that the problems they meet are little different from those met by everyone else—but they are exaggerated and made more obvious (Hales 1995).

With this view in mind, career advice should help students with dyslexia choose jobs that use their talents rather than ones that avoid their weaknesses. Students should be helped to be realistic about both their strengths and weaknesses, and about what adjustments they will need to make in order to perform as well as anyone else. It is often beneficial for students with dyslexia to think carefully about their career preferences early on in their courses.

Students with dyslexia will need help writing curriculum vitae and preparing for job interviews. Students will need to consider whether to mention the dyslexia.

The question of mentioning dyslexia in references is addressed. The fact that a student has dyslexia is confidential and should not be put in a reference without the student's consent. The issues need to be discussed thoroughly, probably by the tutor writing the reference, the student, the dyslexia support person, and a careers advisor.

RECOMMENDATIONS

Each chapter dealing with the eight major areas of support for students with dyslexia has a section of specific recommendations. The most important of these recommendations for HEIs are included in the executive summary, as follows.

1. Institutional and national policy [13 recommendations].

    Dyslexia should be explicitly recognized by all HEIs both as a disability and as a special educational need (5.3 Recommendation 1).

    Each institution should have a clear general policy setting out regulations, procedures and guidelines, as appropriate, for the identification and support of students with dyslexia. The general policy should make reference to, but not necessarily provide detail in every respect of, all the following basic areas of concern: staff development and awareness, admissions, identification, evaluation of needs, provision of learning support (including technological support), counselling, examinations and assessments, and careers advice (5.3 Recommendation 2).

2. Staff development and awareness [10 recommendations].

All appropriate staff of each HEI should become aware of the institution's policy on dyslexia, of the needs of students with dyslexia, and of the support that is available within the institution (6.3 Recommendation 1). There should be a member of the academic staff within each faculty and/or sub-faculty unit (e.g., school or department) with explicit responsibility for students with dyslexia within that area (6.3 Recommendation 2).

There should be a program of staff development and awareness within the institution that (a) relates explicitly to provision for students with dyslexia; (b) should be referred to in the institution's general policy on provision for students with dyslexia; and (c) has been constructed with the advice of a professional with understanding and experience of dyslexia support (6.3 Recommendation 4).

3. Admission to higher education [14 recommendations].

    Each HEI should maintain and publish an admissions policy that does not discriminate against students with dyslexia, except in those subjects and areas of study for which a clear, explicit, and published justification is given by the institution (7.3 Recommendation 1).

    When dealing with the admission of students with dyslexia, admissions tutors or officers should endeavour to understand the educational problems and needs of students with dyslexia (7.3 Recommendation 3a).

4. Identification of students with dyslexia [15 recommendations].

    All HEIs should formulate a clear policy on identification of dyslexia which embodies the National Working Party's Guidelines on diagnostic assessment of dyslexia (8.4 Recommendation 1).

    When considering applications for Disabled Students' Allowances from students with dyslexia, all LEAs should expect such applications to be accompanied by reports of diagnostic assessments that conform to the Guidelines on diagnostic assessment of dyslexia given in this report (8.4 Recommendation 5).

5. Evaluation of all the needs and support provisions [16 recommendations].

    All HEIs should have a policy and set of procedures for evaluation of the learning and support needs of students with dyslexia (9.3 Recommendation 3a).

All HEIs should have, either on the staff or otherwise available to students, at least one tutor with training and/or experience in supporting students with dyslexia and all students with dyslexia should be made aware of that tutor (9.3 Recommendation 4a).

6. Counselling [6 recommendations].

Every HEI should have at least one student counsellor available who has specific knowledge and/or experience of dyslexia counselling (10.3 Recommendation 1).

7. Examinations and assessment [16 recommendations].

Every HEI should have a written policy on the examination and assessment of students with dyslexia ("the examinations policy") (11.3 Recommendation 1).

The examinations policy should: (a) acknowledge that academic standards are paramount and that special arrangements in examinations and assessments are for the purpose of creating a level playing field for these disabled students; and (b) be compiled having due regard to the Working Party's proposals on good practice given in Section 11.2 of this report. (11.3 Recommendations 2a and 2b).

8. Careers Advice [11 recommendations].

At least one careers adviser in every HEI should have explicit knowledge and/or experience of dyslexia as it relates to the employment of graduates (12.3 Recommendation 1).

CONCLUSIONS AND FURTHER RESEARCH

The report concludes with an overview of the Working Party's aims and a summary of its main findings. The aims were to survey the current position in the U.K., to consult with other professionals, and then to produce guidelines and proposals on good practice. The ultimate aim was to enable the higher education sector to work toward fair support provision for students with dyslexia that will be equal across all institutions. A priority list for developing support is given.

Future research and development that needs to be addressed at this time includes a systematic study of the effects of dyslexia on adults, students and non-students. Identification procedures also need to be upgraded to match the symptoms and characteristics of dyslexia in adults. There is discussion about how a national policy could be developed so that many of the present problems could be sensibly resolved.

In the context of the conference at Beit Berl, it is obvious that many of the issues raised by speakers from other countries are similar to those faced by institutions in the U.K. The areas of research and development are common to many countries. The same difficulties are present when some people refuse to accept dyslexia as a genuine syndrome. As we all work together pooling our knowledge and ideas, and listening to adults with dyslexia, gradually most of the rest of the world will come to understand dyslexia and accept it. The report of the National Working Party on Dyslexia in Higher Education is one contribution to this change in attitude and knowledge.

REFERENCES

Aaron, P. G., Phillips, S., and Larsen, S. 1988. Specific learning disability in historically famous persons. *Journal of Learning Disabilities* 21:523–45.

Beaton, A., McDougall, S., and Singleton, C. H. eds. 1997. Dyslexia in literate adults. (Special issue of the *Journal of Research in Reading*, 20:1). Oxford: Blackwell.

Beech, J. R. 1997. Assessment of memory and reading. In *The Psychological Assessment of Reading*, eds. J. Beech and C. H. Singleton. London: Routledge.

British Dyslexia Association 1995. *The Dyslexia Handbook*. Reading, Berks: BDA.

Campbell, L., Campbell, B., and Dickinson, D. 1999. *Teaching and Learning through Multiple Intellegences 2nd ed.* Boston: Allyn and Bacon.

Cornelissen, P., Bradley, L., Fowler, S., and Stein, J. 1994. What children see affects how they spell. *Developmental Medicine and Child Neurology* 36:716–27.

Dearing, R. (Chair) 1997. *Higher Education in the Learning Society. Report of the Committee of Inquiry into Higher Education.* London: Department for Education and Employment.

DfE. 1994. *Code of Practice for the Identification and Assessment of Special Educational Needs.* London: Department for Education.

Evans, B. J. W. 1997. Assessment of visual problems in reading. In *The Psychological Assessment of Reading*, eds. J. Beech and C. H. Singleton. London: Routledge.

Evans, B. J. W., Drasdo, N., and Richards, I. L. 1996. Dyslexia: The link with visual deficits. *Ophthalmic and Physiological Optics* 16:3–10.

Hales, G. 1995. Stress Factors in the Work Place. In *Dyslexia and Stress*, eds. T. R. Miles and V. Varma. London: Whurr.

Frith, C., and Frith, U. 1996. A biological marker for dyslexia. *Nature* 382:19–20.

Galaburda, A. M. ed. 1993. *Dyslexia and Development: Neurobiological Aspects of Extra-ordinary Brains.* Cambridge, MA: Harvard University Press.

HEQC 1996. What are Graduates? Clarifying the Attributes of Graduateness— A Paper to Stimulate Discussion. London: Higher Education Quality Council.

Hynd, G. W., and Hiemenz, J. R. 1997. Dyslexia and gyral morphology variation. In *Dyslexia: Biology, Cognition and Intervention*, eds. C. Hulme and M. Snowling. London: Whurr.

Lovegrove, W. 1994. Visual deficits in dyslexia: Evidence and implications. In *Dyslexia in Children: Multidisciplinary Perspectives*, eds. A. J. Fawcett and R. I. Nicolson. New York: Harvester Wheatsheaf.

McLoughlin, D., Fitzgibbon, G., and Young, V. 1994. *Adult Dyslexia: Assessment, Counselling and Training.* London: Whurr.

Nicolson, R. I., and Fawcett, A. J. 1990. Automaticity: A new framework for dyslexia research. *Cognition* 30:159–82.

Nicolson, R. I., and Fawcett, A. J. 1994. Comparison of deficits in cognitive and motor skills in children with dyslexia. *Annals of Dyslexia* 44:147–64.

Orton Dyslexia Society. 1994. A new definition of dyslexia. *Annals of Dyslexia.* Fall.

Rack, J. 1997. Issues in the assessment of developmental dyslexia in adults: Theoretical and applied perspectives. *Journal of Research in Reading* 20:66–76.

Singleton, C. H., Cottrell, S. ni G., Gilroy, D., Goodwin, V., Hetherington, J., Jameson, M., Laycock, D., McLoughlin, D., Peer, L., Pumfrey, P. D., Reid, G., Stacey, G., Waterfield J., and Zdzienski D. 1999. *Dyslexia in Higher Education: Policy, Provision and Practice.* Hull: University of Hull.

Stacey, G. 1992. A Taste of Dyslexia (video). Oxford: Oxfordshire Dyslexia Association.

Stein, J. F. 1991. Vision and language. In *Dyslexia: Integrating Theory and Practice*, eds. M. Snowling and M. Thomson. London: Whurr.

West, T. G. 1991. *In the Mind's Eye.* New York: Prometheus Books.

Wilkins, A. 1995. *Visual Stress.* Oxford: Oxford University Press.

Williams, L. V. 1983. *Teaching for the Two Sided Mind.* New York: Simon and Schuster, Inc.

Willows, D. M., Kruk, R. S., and Corcos, E. eds. 1993. *Visual Processes in Reading and Reading Disabilities.* London: Lawrence Erlbuam Associates.

Chapter • 4

The Equal Rights for People with Disabilities Law 5758–1998[1]: Advent of a Social Revolution in Israel

Jonathan Gillis

This chapter concerns disability law and adults with learning disabilities. However, the area of disability law in the field of learning disabilities is not extensive. I have therefore extended the theme, to describe Israel's new Equal Rights for People with Disabilities Law undoubtedly the most important development in disability law in Israel in recent times. I will give an account of how this law came into being and discuss its current and potential impact, and discuss also the current bill to amend and extend the law. There recently have been some legislative developments in the field of the rights of students with learning disabilities and I shall look at these as well.

The Equal Rights for People with Disabilities Law was initiated by Bizchut, the Israel Human Rights Center for People with Disabilities. The factors behind the initiation of the law are closely related to the very factors that brought Bizchut into being and it is therefore worth alluding to these briefly here. (The Hebrew word *bizchut* means literally "by right" the point being that people with disabilities are entitled to their legal rights by right, not through charity or the goodwill of others.) Arguing that the person with disabilities has *the right* to equality is not empty rhetoric. It means that the person with disabilities has the same right as anyone else to participate fully and equally in the life of the

---

[1]The Equal Rights for People with Disabilities Law 5758–1998 (Laws of the State of Israel 5758, p. 152 [Hebrew]) passed by the Knesset on 27 Shvat 5758 (23.2.1998).

community, and that through legislation, litigation, or any other means he or she must be enabled to exercise that right.

Bizchut came into being in 1992 precisely because such a view was not reflected in the law, or in the basic attitudes of officialdom; nor was it shared by society as a whole. People with disabilities account for over 10% of Israel's population, yet in almost every aspect of Israeli economic, social, political, and cultural life they are either excluded completely or severely marginalized. They are prevented from realizing their full potential and from participating, wholly or as much as they are entitled, in everyday life.

In its first years Bizchut also encountered great difficulties in securing the rights of people with disabilities in the courts; such legislation as did exist was piecemeal, too specific, or not enforced. For example, the Equal Opportunities in the Workplace Law of 1988 prohibits discrimination in the workplace on various grounds, but these grounds do not include disability. This partly accounts for the massive unemployment among people with disabilities. A 1997 survey of the service for the blind in the Ministry of Labor and Welfare found that 72% of blind people were unemployed. A similar rate of unemployment was found among people with severe disabilities or mental retardation. Among the deaf, a survey in 1992 found that between 18% and 22% in the 30 to 64 age range was unemployed, two and a half times the national unemployment rate.

Other examples of highly specific laws are the Allowances for the Deaf Law 1992, and the Prohibition of Discrimination against Blind People Accompanied by Guide Dogs Law 1993. The Special Education Law of 1988 was, for a long time, improperly enforced. Even now, though the situation is much improved, implementation of the law is not evenly spread across the population: the Arab sector of the population fares particularly poorly here. Against this background Bizchut has embarked on a campaign of empowerment in this sector of the population.

In the area of physical access to buildings, the provisions that do exist in the Building and Planning Law of 1965 are woefully inadequate, and even the provisions that exist are not properly enforced. As a result, most schools, universities, and colleges (like many cinemas, theaters, shops, and restaurants) are inaccessible to people in wheelchairs.

BACKGROUND TO THE LAW

In such a situation, reliance on the occasional judgments of the High Court of Justice in the area of equality, or the recent Basic Law:

Individual Dignity and Liberty, was inadequate to overcome the grievous lack of equality suffered by people with disabilities. Redress might have to come eventually through the courts, but the path-breaking that would provide the courts with the wherewithal for such redress had to come from the legislature.

The principal factor behind the drafting of the proposed law was Bizchut's observation of developments in other countries around the world, where a crop of comprehensive pieces of legislation regarding equal rights for people with disabilities was being introduced. These include: in the U.S., the Americans with Disabilities Act of 1990 (ADA); in Canada, Article 15 of the Canadian Charter of Rights and Freedoms and the Employment Equity Act of 1995; in Britain, the Disability Discrimination Act of 1995; in Australia, the Disability Discrimination Act of 1992; and similar provisions in Sweden, Finland, Japan, and Jordan.

First, Bizchut approached all the disability organizations in Israel for their input on the idea of such a law, and was overwhelmed by the response in terms of ideas, needs, and content. Bizchut then looked at the laws in other countries and noticed two distinct trends. In the Anglo-Saxon countries, the new disabilities law was couched in language prohibiting discrimination and pointing out the need to make reasonable accommodations. In Scandinavian countries, by contrast, emphasis was placed on integration into the community and provision of individual assistance in the community. Thus, a split emerged between what was essentially a human rights based approach on the one hand, and welfare state legislation on the other. What Bizchut sought to do was to combine these: to set out the basic principles of equality and non-discrimination as well as to provide a solution to specific needs.

The draft law that resulted began with outlining basic principles and then went on to deal with disability rights in all spheres of life: employment, public transport, access, education, living in the community, health, and so on. The final section provided for setting up a disabilities commission to oversee implementation of the law.

In June 1995, at a special session of the Knesset Constitution and Law Committee headed at the time by M. K. Dedi Zuker, Bizchut presented the draft law, after which it was presented to the Knesset for its preliminary reading, with the signatures of 11 Knesset members. Note that these parliamentarians represented nearly every section of the Israeli political spectrum: right, left, religious, and secular.

The bill passed its preliminary reading, and then, in March 1996, its first reading. By a strange coincidence, that same day the Israeli Supreme Court handed down its judgment in the case of Shahar Botzer versus the Maccabim Reut municipality and the Ministry of

Education. This case, brought by Bizchut, concerned a 12-year-old boy confined to a wheelchair, whose school building was inaccessible. Specifically at issue, in those days before The Equal Rights for People with Disabilities Law, were the Regulations under the Planning and Building Law 1965. These contained a section on accessibility that required such buildings as Shahar Botzer's school to make at least one floor accessible to the disabled and to provide toilet facilities for the disabled. In Shahar's school, however, the facilities were not located on the one accessible floor. In addition, most of the other school facilities were inaccessible to Shahar: his own classroom, the staff room, the school library, and the school laboratories. Shahar was suing, inter alia, for a chair lift between floors. Ultimately this was a case about equality and human dignity.

In finding for the petitioner, President of the Supreme Court Aharon Barak broke new ground in the treatment of disability issues:

> At the most abstract level it may be said that the purpose of this provision in the law (Building and Planning Law) is to enable the integration of a disabled person in society. Its purpose is to enable a disabled person to participate fully in society. It is intended to achieve the central value of equality in all that pertains to the disabled. It is designed to grant to the disabled person equality of opportunity. It purports to allow the disabled person independence and non-dependence. It comes to protect the dignity and freedom of the disabled person by ensuring equality of participation in society in all areas of life.
>
> In the past, the dominant view was that a disabled person was different and that it was therefore necessary for him to be cared for away from the community ("separate but equal"). Today the prevailing view is that a disabled person is to be integrated in society and to be guaranteed equality of opportunity ("integrated and equal"). The modern view is that separation deepens the lack of equality and perpetuates discrimination. A disabled person is a person with equal rights. He/she is not outside society or on its periphery. He is a regular member of the society in which he lives. The purpose of these arrangements is not to favor him/her in his isolation, but rather to include him—at times through affirmative action—in the regular fabric of the life of the community. (HCJ 7081/93)[2]

After the 1996 elections, the Ministers of Justice and of Labor and Social Affairs appointed a Public Commission chaired by Dr Yisrael Katz (formerly Minister of Labor and Social Affairs and also Director of the National Insurance Institute) to examine the need for comprehensive legislation in the area of equal rights for people with disabilities. The appointment of such a Public Commission in fact proved a

---

[2]HCJ 7081/93 Botzer, Bizchut et al. v. Maccabim-Reut Local Authority and the Minister of Education. Supreme Court Judgments Vol. 50 (1) p. 19.

very necessary step. The Commission included representatives from organizations working to advance the rights of people with disabilities (including Bizchut), academics in the field, and experts from the relevant government ministries. It examined scores of witnesses, including people with disabilities, professionals in the field, and academics, and received hundreds of written representations from people with disabilities throughout the country. It also examined the position of people with disabilities in various legislative regimes throughout the world and to this end received expert testimony from a host of leading academics and judicial experts abroad. It published its report within eight months, in July 1997. The report recommended comprehensive legislation on disability rights in all areas of life: education, housing, transport, employment, and so on. In essence, with some modifications, the report fully endorsed the Equal Rights for People with Disabilities bill, and thus gave it a crucial, official, non-partisan seal of approval.

The bill then passed to its Knesset committee stage to be prepared for its second and third readings in the Knesset. In a letter to Shaul Yahalom, the new chairman of the Constitution and Law Committee, the Finance Minister called on him to delay the bill and not promote it in parliamentary committee. Yahalom's response was to intensify the committee's work on the bill. In February 1998, however, Yahalom was on the verge of an appointment to the cabinet after the untimely death of Zevulun Hammer. By this stage, the committee had completed its work on only four sections of the bill: basic principles, employment, public transport, and the establishment of the disabilities commission. Sections outstanding (then) were: living in the community, access, and education.

The Committee split the bill into two and presented the first part (those sections it had already completed) for its second and third readings as the Equal Rights for People with Disabilities Law. The readings were scheduled for February 23, 1998. The government declared itself against the bill, saying the time was not appropriate. On the day of the second and third readings, the Finance Minister threatened to resign if the law was passed. A few compromises were indeed reached with the government, notably the removal of intercity buses from the requirement for public transport accommodations and deletion of the provision of state-sponsored incentives in the section on employment. Eventually, however, after intensive lobbying, the law was passed.

THE LAW

The law as passed provides the basis for a legal, social, and cultural revolution in the status of people with disabilities in Israel. It is a slow revolution, however. The passing of the law itself is only the beginning. The legal provisions have to be implemented and enforced, and regulations have to be put into place. Beyond that, the Knesset, the courts, government departments, and an Israeli public unaccustomed to dealing with the implications of equality in this field, all need to become acclimated to a new legal situation.

The principles underlying the law and which inform all of the various sections are set out in the four sections that make up Chapter One of the law:

1. The rights of people with disabilities and the commitment of Israeli society to such rights are based on the recognition of the principle of equality and the value of human beings created in the Divine image.

2. The purpose of this Law is to protect the dignity and freedom of people with disabilities, to enshrine their right to equal and active participation in society in all the major spheres of life, and, furthermore, to provide an appropriate response to the special needs of people with disabilities, in such a way as to enable them to live with maximum independence, in privacy and in dignity, realizing their potential to the full.

3. Action taken in order to correct prior or present discrimination against people with disabilities, or to promote the equality of people with disabilities, does not constitute discrimination.

4. People with disabilities have the right to make decisions that pertain to their lives according to their wishes and preferences; this right shall be exercised in conformity with the law. (The Equal Rights for People with Disabilities Law 5758–1998)[3]

The language of this opening part of the law has a constitutional flavor. Though the law itself has none of the constitutional status accorded to Israel's Basic Laws, its purpose—a situation in which equality in the context of persons with disabilities has actual meaning and where they are the arbiters of their own destinies—may be said to be to seek to constitute a new legal reality in Israel, and this broad aim is reflected in the law's provisions. The law is a frame, with broad provisions, relying on regulations and programs to be put into effect. Chapters such as those on employment and transport mandate the rel-

---

[3]The Equal Rights for People with Disabilities Law 5758–1998 (Laws of the State of Israel 5758, p. 152 [Hebrew]) passed by the Knesset on 27 Shvat 5758 (23.2.1998).

evant government Ministries to prepare regulations and programs for the practical implementation of the law's general provisions.

Thus clause 16, for example, states:

> 16 (a) The Minister of Labor and Social Affairs shall initiate, develop, and prepare programs concerning the following -
>
> (1) employment and rehabilitation for people with disabilities, with preference being given to the integration of people with disabilities in regular places of work;
>
> (2) the establishment of systems for the determination of suitable employment for people with disabilities, in order to secure the integration of people with disabilities in the field of employment;
>
> (3) the provision of advice and professional guidance to employers and employees regarding the integration of people with disabilities in employment.
>
> (b) The Minister of Labor and Social Affairs shall present to the Labor and Social Affairs committee of the Knesset an annual report concerning programs stated in subsection (a).[4]

And in addition to such programs are the regulations, on which the law relies for its effect. The process of enacting such regulations has been slower than anticipated. In the period since the law came into effect on January 1, 1999, notwithstanding the demands of the law to the contrary, none of the mandated regulations have yet come into force. In June 2000, Bizchut petitioned the Supreme Court against the Ministries of Transport and Finance, over the two year delay in the issuing of regulations for making buses accessible to people with disabilities, as mandated by the law. The Court called the parties back in January 2001, and the Ministry of Transport stated that its draft regulations would be immediately submitted to the Knesset. The regulations were indeed submitted but were found to be inadequate, leaving much work to be done in Knesset committee. The Constitution and Law Committee has now set up its own subcommittee to complete this work. A similar fate has befallen the work on the remainder of the original bill. This last, in a slightly extended form, had to be resubmitted for its First Reading as an amendment to the Equal Rights law, with the following chapters: Access; Living in the Community and Personal Assistance; Leisure; Education; The Legal System and the Courts; and Special Needs. It passed its First Reading on December 29, 2000. In July 2001, the law's long overdue regulations calling for State support for accommodations in the workplace were introduced to the

---

[4]The Equal Rights for People with Disabilities Law 5758–1998 (Laws of the State of Israel 5758, p. 152 [Hebrew]) passed by the Knesset on 27 Shvat 5758 (23.2.1998).

Knesset Labor and Welfare Committee. The regulations were subsequently approved by the committee; however, the Finance Minister refused to sign them, thus effectively blocking the regulations' entry into force. The objection of the Finance Minister lay in his refusal to recognize the need for accommodations that were not actually physical. This would exclude such accommodations as providing interpreters or other methods for making aurally delivered materials available to people with hearing impairments.

The lesson from all the above is clear: equal rights legislation takes a long time to come into being, and an even longer time to take real effect.

But some progress has been made. The law called for the establishment of a Commission for the Equal Rights for People with Disabilities, whose function was to act as a form of ombudsman, providing a means for enforcing the principles enshrined in the law from within a State-funded statutory body, as well as representing, through the members of its advisory body (most of whom are people with disabilities), an embodiment of the principle that people with disabilities should control their own destinies. The models for such a Commission, like other aspects of the Equal Rights Law, were Commissions already in existence in other Western countries. The first Commissioner, Ariela Auphir (a former executive director and legal advisor of Bizchut) was appointed by the government in May 2000, with the Commission formally beginning its work in September 2000.

The Commission, as an instrument of social change, carries enormous potential. It is worth noting, however, that its position as part of the establishment while ostensibly promoting the interests of those presently being represented by nongovernmental organizations (NGOs), places it in a delicate situation. On the one hand it must work within, and with the cooperation of, the establishment which provides its funding. On the other hand, its ostensible constituency are people with disabilities, represented by the various non-governmental disability groups (including Bizchut). These were the groups that lobbied hard for the Commission's creation and they expect the Commission to serve their interests. At times, however, such interests will not necessarily coincide with its own. The Commission will thus be compelled at times to perform a complex balancing act—to preserve its legitimacy as the champion of the rights of the disabled, while gaining the trust and cooperation of the Government. These are early days.

In addition to the Commission, the passing of the law has brought other significant developments, some of which are worth mentioning briefly here. In its petition to the Supreme Court in June 2000 against the Ministry of Transport over the regulations for the accessibility of public transport, Bizchut also enjoined as respondents the Dan Bus Company, which, despite the explicit provisions of the Equal Rights Law, had imported a new fleet of "low floor" buses that turned out to be inaccessible to people with disabilities. Through the Court's intervention, the Ministry of Transport, Dan and also the Egged Bus Company undertook to strive to make their existing buses accessible and not to import new buses that were not accessible. The first accessible buses, containing manual ramps, are now in use in Egged bus lines in Jerusalem and Haifa.

Another knock-on effect of the Equal Rights Law came as a result of another Bizchut petition to the Supreme Court—this time in May 1999, immediately prior to the general elections—over the inaccessibility of polling stations to people with mobility impairments. Again, as a result of the Court's intervention, the Elections Law was amended, new voting procedures were put in place, and thousands of people with disabilities were enabled to exercise their democratic right.

EDUCATION - THE EQUAL RIGHTS BILL AND OTHER LEGISLATION

The chapter on education in the Equal Rights bill begins in the same manner as all its other chapters, by affirming a basic right for the person with disabilities—a right upon which the rest of the chapter expands, as follows:

> A person with disabilities is entitled to education, training and learning according to his age and in accordance with the special needs resulting from his disability, with preference being given to including such person in a mainstream educational framework. (Knesset Draft Laws)[5]

The language of this section contrasts sharply with the language used in the Special Education Law 1988. Section 2 of that law reads:

> The purpose of special education is to promote and develop the capacities and ability of the child with special needs, to mend and improve his bodily, mental and emotional functioning and his behavior, and to give him knowledge, skill and aptitude, and to endow him with acceptable behavior so as to facilitate his inclusion in society and in the workforce. (The Special Education Law 5748–1998)[6]

The absence of a specific right in the Special Education Law of 1988 and the whiff of paternalism in the language of the above section partially explain some of the difficulties encountered by Bizchut and organizations representing children with special needs in securing full

---

[5]Knesset Draft Laws 2525, 20 Adar 5756 (11.3.1996) p. 628.
[6]The Special Education Law 5748–1998 (Laws of the State of Israel 5748 p. 114).

special educational provision for such children within mainstream education. The Ministry of Education has long resisted an interpretation of the Special Education Law which would regard the law's basket of special education services as the right of the child with special needs within mainstream education rather than in some special education framework. In an attempt to remove such ambiguity, an amendment to the Special Education Law, initiated by Bizchut and parents campaigning for such inclusion, was adopted by the chairman of the Knesset Education Committee, M. K. Zevulun Orlev, and presented to the Knesset in June 2000. The objective of such an amendment anticipates the general objective of the Equal Rights Bill—to state explicitly the right of a child with special needs to the services of special education in whatever educational framework the child happens to be in. This amendment was passed into law by the Knesset on November 13, 2002. Three months previously the Supreme Court produced a ground-breaking judgment on this very issue in a case brought by YETED (an organization representing young people with Down syndrome) and 50 others against the Minister of Education (HCJ 2599/2000). The amendment, and previously the Bagatz judgment, mark a shift in the approach of the judiciary and the legislature in Israel-particularly remarkable at a time of recession and budget cuts.

The ambit of the Special Education Law of 1988 still does not include adults with special needs nor does it include people with learning disabilities—children or adults. The mechanisms for recognizing such learning disabilities and making the requisite accommodations, in both the school system and universities, has for long been woefully inadequate. A move to change this began in July 2001 with a new bill to provide for students with special needs, which was presented to the Knesset and passed its First Reading. It is moot whether legislation is the appropriate response in this case, or indeed in any other case in view of our earlier comments. At the very least, however, it might be argued that proposed legislation can focus attention on a specific need and set in motion forces for social change in the long run. This particular bill was originally directed at both children and adults with learning disabilities, but its references to students in higher education have, in the meantime, been dropped.

The chapter on education in the Equal Rights Bill would cover both children and adults, and both learning disabilities and special needs, as well as other forms of disability. The passage of this chapter through the Knesset, however, is unlikely to be straightforward. Previous attempts over recent years have met with resistance, particularly from Ministry of Finance bureaucrats anxious to prevent provisions being passed into law which might require considerable funding. Thus provisions in the bill mandating the Minister of Education and the Council for Higher Education to institute programs for securing the accessibility of all educational institutions were blocked once and eventually dropped. They reappear again in the current bill and, hopefully, this time, may get through. The chapter's other provisions, requiring accommodations to be made in modes of acceptance to educational institutions, in examinations and in educational resources, face a similar struggle. Thus the experience of the past few years has taught those involved in disability issues to adopt a cautious approach to the business of disability rights legislation. If, or when, such bills do get passed into law, it is important to see such laws at first for what they are—as no more than pages in the statute book, their passing marking only the beginning of the real work that lies ahead.

PART • II

Assessment and Diagnostic Models

The three chapters in this section move from a discussion of theoretical constructs, to the presentation of a general model of diagnosis, to a specific proposal regarding the essential elements of assessment of adults with dyslexia.

In Chapter 5, Rosa Hagin presents the components of an in-depth assessment of adults with suspected learning disabilities. The essential elements include a detailed history, assessment of reading, writing, mathematics, and cognitive functioning, and motivational and emotional factors. Dr. Hagin proposes that the major diagnostic question the professional should ask is "How can I help you?" The author also discusses the necessary components of effective reporting of the data by the clinician.

Noel Gregg (Chapter 6) provides an in-depth consideration of several diagnostic issues. These include the selection criteria used in diagnosis and the role of clinical judgment of the professional. Gregg proposes making use of sophisticated statistical analyses available today to develop and test models of selection criteria.

In Chapter 7, Angela Fawcett proposes a two-stage process for diagnosing dyslexia. The initial stage is a low-cost screening process, to be followed by a more thorough testing procedure for those judged to be at risk. The screening measure she developed with colleagues was developed and tested successfully with adults in the United Kingdom and are presented in this chapter. The author presents the strategies to use the test results to develop an individually tailored support program.

Chapter • 5

Diagnosing Adults with Learning Disabilities:
Essential Components

Rosa A. Hagin

Diagnosing learning disabilities in adults in higher education is not a simple task. The diagnostic report must be broad, yet it must be specific and realistic. It must draw upon the history of the disorder, taking into account developmental processes of the individual, yet it must be current. Even though learning disabilities are life-long conditions, most agencies require recent evaluations, usually less than three-to-five years old. Diagnosis must be comprehensive, yet it must also be parsimonious with regard to the time of the individuals involved. Clinicians must be encouraging and generous with their clients, yet they must be stingy in their judgments. Accommodations should be recommended only for those clients who need them, and not for any student who experiences a "sudden attack of learning disability" a few weeks before taking a major examination.

This paper will discuss three aspects of this diagnostic process: (1) some general cautions and concerns, (2) essential elements of diagnosis, and (3) reporting diagnostic data.

SOME CAUTIONS AND CONCERNS

The purpose of diagnosis with any person suspected of having a learning disability is to find out what is wrong and to outline what can be done to correct the problems. In higher education, bright adults with learning disabilities who come in for diagnosis are often well "worked over" by their teachers, family, educational requirements, previous encounters with standardized tests, and their own attempts to compensate for the effects of their learning disabilities. They may come for diagnosis burdened with anger, bitterness, suspicion, withdrawal, and/or depression that come from their struggles to survive academically.

The task of the diagnostician is to tease out among the layers of behavior, emotional overlay, compensations, and defensive operations, the unique problems that make learning difficult for this individual. Diagnosticians need to separate the basic learning problems from the techniques people with learning disabilities have developed (or have been taught to use) in order to survive in the demanding world of academia.

However, this formulation is but the beginning. To complete the process, the diagnostician must also devise effective and realistic intervention plans that will enable these individuals to achieve all that is possible for them to achieve. Simple prescriptive formulas will not suffice. It is pointless for a diagnostician after superficial contact to advise a student that he has a learning disability and that he should "see an educational therapist for remediation" or that he is depressed and should "seek psychotherapy." For students in higher education, diagnosis should provide broad-based assessment, formulated so that they can understand the nature of their problems and the steps they must take for remediation.

Clinicians should also realize how anxiety-producing the diagnostic process may be for many adults with learning disability. It focuses on symptoms that they have often, in the course of their studies, attempted to ignore, deny, avoid, or disguise ("I can't read this because I left my glasses home.") Examiners are urged to approach diagnosis tactfully, to explain procedures throughout the process, to assure the client of the confidentiality of findings, and to make sure the client understands all aspects of the results during informing sessions.

With awareness of other assessment models, I have chosen to recommend a clinical model for several reasons. Clinical evaluation can draw on a balance of formal and informal measures: interview and work samples, as well as with formal clinical measures. The clinical measures, with their known statistical characteristics, are useful in verifying informal observations and in providing data useful in evaluating remedial progress. Formal tests have been subjected to criticisms, the most telling of which is that they do not always provide sufficient information for instructional planning. These shortcomings can be minimized by the skill of the examiner. The effectiveness of diagnosis depends to a very great extent upon the skills and experience of the diagnostician in choosing appropriate measures and in interpreting them intelligently. Who then is qualified for the significant role of diagnostician? In the United States guidelines based on profession and licensing requirements have been advocated. For example, the guidelines established by the Association for Higher Education and Disability recommend that "clinical or educational psychologists, neuropsychologists, educational specialists and medical doctors known to specialize in learning disabilities" be responsible for diagnosis (1996). It seems that solid professional experience, in this case, is more pertinent than the credential, license, or diploma one possesses. Thus adequate professional training in one's own field (education, psychology, or medicine) together with supervised experience in working with adults and study in the field of learning disabilities are appropriate requirements for diagnosticians who deal with adults with learning disabilities in higher education.

ESSENTIAL ELEMENTS OF DIAGNOSIS

Although diagnostic probes in some additional areas may be necessary to meet the unique needs of individuals, four essential components are necessary in the diagnosis of learning disability in most adults in higher education: (1) a detailed educational history, (2) educational status, (3) measures of cognitive functioning, and (4) motivational and emotional factors.

Detailed Educational History

As with any diagnostic study, the examination should begin with a description of the current problem. Any kind of diagnostic work might be expected to raise the level of anxiety of adult clients. Clients will find reassurance in the opportunity to describe the current problems and to demonstrate from current work samples the conditions that cause them to seek assistance.

During this initial interview details of the client's educational history and relevant developmental and medical history should be obtained. Information on the following topics is usually important to understanding the problem:

>occupational goals
>work history
>family structure
>academic accomplishments of close relatives
>language competencies/difficulties
>major illnesses/disabilities

reports of previous evaluations
previous interventions/results
special abilities (e.g. art, music, computer applications, science, mathematics)

In addition, a detailed chronological history of all educational experiences from nursery school to the present is essential information. Especially important are memories of early reading and writing experiences. Memories of early schooling may be recalled painfully. This part of the interview will call upon the examiner's tact and sensitivity in eliciting this vital information.

Young adults are seldom able to recount their history of neonatal development and early milestones that are the usual content of clinical histories. The relevance of such data in most adults is questionable, at any rate. However, if questions arise in specific cases, the diagnostician can always suggest that the client ask parents or siblings for the missing data. The major purpose of this interview is to determine where the client has been and where he or she hopes to go educationally. Thus the diagnostician's final question is a significant one: "How can I help you?"

Educational Status

The next step in broad-based assessment is the determination of the educational status. This process may involve both formal and informal measures of all skill areas. Although some organizational guidelines list specific tests to be used, I believe that the choice of measures is the prerogative of the clinician. Measures should be chosen to answer the questions raised by the client in the initial interview.

For example, if the client mentions difficulty in completing assignments and examinations within appropriate time limits, the examiner should make sure that careful measures of reading rate are included. If a client complains that he has difficulty with confusing words in reading or in spelling correctly in written work, careful assessment of word identification and word attack skills is essential. It is inadequate to administer some hasty measure that produces little more than a numerical score and does not provide information about how the client reads.

Diagnosticians working with adults with learning disabilities should realize that the processes people use in reading may change over the lifespan of the client. Stages of Reading (Chall 1983) highlights the changes in the reading process over the lifespan with the statement that first children learn to read but at later stages, as reading becomes a tool, adults "read to learn."

Clinicians working with adults need to define the reading task in broad terms and avoid conceptualizing learning disabilities as a problem only in single word decoding. Many adults with learning disabilities, after great struggles, have learned how to decode single words. However, they may not be able to decode in the "condition, manner, and duration" (in the words of the regulations for the Americans with Disabilities Act of 1990) that average adults do, because they have not reached the level of automaticity necessary for effective comprehension.

Clients with reading problems usually raise questions about the accuracy of their word attack skills, the effectiveness of their reading comprehension, and their reading rate. At a minimum, it is necessary to assess

- word recognition (i.e., oral reading of unselected words)
- word attack (i.e., oral reading of phonetically regular pseudo-words)
- reading comprehension with regular time limits
- reading comprehension with extended time.

The first two skills can then be compared to assess independent word attack skills. One should not assume that all adults are able to decode accurately, even though they may have a number of words they are able to recognize as sight words. Analysis of their response to phonetically regular pseudowords (which they cannot identify by meaning cues or context) may surprise the examiner. Gaps in their phonetic knowledge can be assessed in terms of correct decoding of consonants, consonant blends, digraphs, long and short vowels, r-. l-, and w-controlled vowels, hard and soft letters, and diphthongs.

Accuracy and rate of comprehension can be determined under timed and extended time conditions. Further analysis of comprehension items can be based on the proportion of correct responses to the various types of questions, such as vocabulary definitions, factual items, translational items that require application of material in the text, and abstract items that require generalization and abstraction of main ideas.

Written language can be assessed informally from samples of formal written work done as part of class assignments and spontaneous writing samples done during the examination. The spontaneous writing sample gives an examiner the opportunity to observe not only a client's skills in the mechanics of spelling, capitalization, punctuation, and grammar, but also the legibility, convenience, and rapidity of handwriting. Formal measures of spelling may also be useful in individual cases.

Mathematics skills available to adults may also be a useful part of this evaluation. Tests of computation should be interpreted judiciously because of the pervasiveness of calculators and computers. Computation skills tend to decay through lack of use. On the other hand, work with applied problems permits the examiner to assess basic mathematics skills, as well as rote memory, spatial orientation, accuracy in using operational signs, errors with rote sequences of measures, time, and coins.

Cognitive Functioning

The third component of a comprehensive diagnosis is the assessment of cognitive functioning. In my years of clinical work, I have found the use of an individual intelligence test, such as the Wechsler Adult Intelligence Scale III (WAIS III), the most effective way of obtaining information on the cognitive abilities of adult clients with learning disabilities. One important caveat is that intelligence tests assume a level of adequacy of educational opportunity that may not have been available to individuals with learning disabilities. The cumulative effect of this lack may be reflected in lower scores on aspects of tests that draw upon educational factors. With the WAIS III, this effect may be apparent in subtests tapping vocabulary, general information, and arithmetic reasoning. The result is that total scores on tests may underestimate the intellectual potential of individuals with learning disabilities.

However, this caution does not invalidate the use of tests of cognitive abilities with adults with learning disabilities. Effective use of these measures can enable a clinician to determine not only weaknesses related to the history of learning problems, but it can also point out strengths that the client may not have been aware of because of the overwhelming nature of the disability.

Results of individual intelligence testing should be viewed broadly through analysis of the data that go beyond IQ scores to determine how a client solves cognitive problems. This analysis can consider the following questions with the WAIS III:

- Do interscale differences highlight strengths in specific aspects such as non-verbal performance skills in contrast to verbal abilities?
- Do the index scores, based on the factorial structure of the WAIS III, indicate statistically significant differences among such components as verbal comprehension items, perceptual-integrative items, working memory items, and processing speed?
- To what extent do statistically significant differences among individual subtest scores show cognitive strengths and weaknesses of the client?

When such clinical services are available, studies of the neuropsychological substrate underlying learning disabilities can be useful. Although formal batteries used in the diagnosis of brain damage are often not productive with bright, relatively intact adults with learning disabilities, eclectic batteries that assess such aspects as motor control, visual recall, auditory memory, rote sequencing, laterality, verbal fluency, and attention can be very useful in clarifying a client's cognitive abilities.

Ultimately, the administration of individual cognitive tests constitute standardized sampling of many kinds of behaviors. Qualitative observations by an experienced examiner can provide cues for understanding the nature of a client's problems and for developing realistic intervention plans.

MOTIVATIONAL AND EMOTIONAL FACTORS

Although motivational and emotional factors are seldom the original causes of learning disability, they must be reckoned with in the diagnosis of adults with learning disabilities. Adults who come for assessment bring not only the learning problems themselves, but also the emotional baggage of years of disappointment, failure, unrealized hopes, self-devaluation, depression, anger, or denial that they have experienced during their school years.

It is the diagnostician's task to separate the original problem from the emotional overlay. The diagnostician needs to understand the effects of expectation of failure and unfocused or unrealistic goals on intervention planning. With some clients whose problems are relatively accessible, extended interviewing will clarify these dynamics. With others, the more conscious methods of personality study, such as questionnaires and incomplete sentences methods, will be useful. Sometimes projective techniques are necessary for an understanding of the emotional needs and defensive operations of some clients.

Motivation can be inferred from clients' overall responses to the diagnostic process, including their initial contacts to arrange appointments, their availability for completion of assessments, and their openness in the planning process. Finally, the quality, specificity, and realism of their answers to the major diagnostic question, "How can I help you?" will hold important clues concerning a client's motivation.

REPORTING DIAGNOSTIC DATA

Reports of diagnostic findings may serve several purposes. Most frequently they meet the needs of individual clients for information and document requests for accommodations under laws like the

Americans with Disabilities Act. Of utmost importance is the diagnostician's responsibility to inform clients, so that they may have a full understanding of the current aspects of their disability and the opportunity to make appropriate intervention plans with the diagnostician. A second purpose is to submit the reports to educational and/or administrative agencies in order to demonstrate the impact of the disability on current functioning so as to document requests for accommodations in education or employment. In either case, data from the diagnostic study need to be integrated in logical, informative, tightly composed reports for these purposes.

Reports should summarize the four major diagnostic components described above in order to document the impact of the learning disability on the client's current functioning. It is not enough to state that the client has a history of a learning disability and has received accommodations in the past (although this information can be important in reporting a complete history); what is essential, is to show specifically how the learning disability currently limits the client's major life activities. For example, the report can show that a client's slow rate of reading requires provision of extended time on examination in order that the client can demonstrate the full extent of his or her knowledge. Or the report can show that a client's inaccurate decoding skills produce errors in spelling that interfere with full written expression on essay-type examinations and that these inaccurate decoding skills make the use of a word processor with spell-checking capacity necessary.

Professional identity of the examiner is a part of the basic information to be provided in the report. Examiners should provide exact information concerning their professional discipline, professional degrees and licenses, and the organization one represents, if it is relevant.

SUMMARY

Effective reports are:

Accurate. They report all data accurately and completely. In reporting scores it is advisable to use percentiles or standard scores, rather than grade scores or such vague terms as "average" or "borderline."

Factual. They are honest, stating directly the purposes of the examination and the client's response patterns. They avoid vague generalizations, such as "scores suggest . . ." or "results are consistent with . . ." They avoid lecturing the reader in general terms such as "people with learning disabilities usually present such behavior . . ." Straightforward descriptions are preferable to exotic diagnoses or technical language used in an attempt to intimidate the reader.

Specific. They use specific diagnostic terms, avoiding cloudy descriptions such as "reading difference" or "learning styles." Recommendations are clearly stated (e.g., "provision for 50% extended time") and should be supported by the results of measures administered during the examination. For example, it seems pointless to recommend extended time accommodations unless the client's reading rate has been examined. Recommendations need to be supported by test data and clinical observations, rather than opinions expressed by the examiner.

Recognizable. Choice of tests should be made by the examiner on the basis of the presenting problems of a client. However, it is advisable to choose mainstream tests, such as those reviewed in the Mental Measurements Yearbooks (1998), because they will be more familiar to people who review the documentation. Well-known measures will generate more confidence in the conclusions reached by the examiner.

Recent. Despite the life-long nature of learning disabilities, most schools, agencies, colleges and universities, require that documentation be recent, usually within three to five years of the request for accommodations. Earlier reports, if they are available, can be useful in verifying the long-term existence of the disability as part of the history. However, unless recent information is presented, reviewers may reject requests for accommodations because older data cannot usually be cited to document the impact of a learning disability on a client's current functioning.

Professional. Finally the language and tone of the examiner's report should be professional in quality. It should ask for consideration, rather than make demands. Rather than exotic terminology and condescending lectures, the report should supply factual information in terms of mature clinical judgment.

REFERENCES

AHEAD. 1996. Ad hoc Committee on Learning Disabilities, Guidelines for documentation of a specific learning disability. Latest Developments.

Americans with Disabilities Act. 1990. 42 USC section 122102 ff.

Buros Institute of Mental Measurements. 1998. *Mental Measurements Yearbook.* Lincoln, Nebraska: University of Nebraska Press.

Chall, J. 1983. *Stages of Reading Development.* New York: McGraw-Hill

Wechsler, D. 1997. *Wechsler Adult Intelligence Scale III.* San Antonio, Texas: The Psychological Corporation.

Chapter • 6

Diagnostic Issues Surrounding Students with Learning Disabilities

Noel Gregg

Measurement tools and selection criteria for operationalizing the standard of disability are critical to accommodations for students either requesting entrance into or currently enrolled at postsecondary institutions. Specifically, major determinations to be made by colleges and universities include (1) who is an individual with a documented learning disability, and (2) whether she or he is "otherwise qualified" to be part of a particular program of academic study. As Gregg and Scott (2000) noted, a considerable amount of effort has gone into arguing about which definition and selection criteria are, from a policy or procedural perspective, most appropriate for students of different types, spans, and severity levels of learning disabilities. They encouraged raising (some of) this debate to a level of sophistication by use of more theory-driven research to support underlying constructs or assumptions inherent in definitions, measurement tools, and selection criteria for the adult population with learning disabilities. The purpose of this chapter is to examine several diagnostic issues surrounding assessment for postsecondary students with learning disabilities.

SELECTION CRITERIA

A student requesting accommodations at a postsecondary institution must provide documentation that supports the need for the particular kinds of academic adjustments sought (State University of New York 1993). Inherent in this documentation will be the selection criteria used by examiners in decision-making resulting in the confirmation of a specific diagnosis. Currently, considerable variability exists in the type of selection criteria used by professionals to document learning disabilities (Brackett and McPhearson 1996; Hoy et al. 1996; McGuire et al. 1996). Leadership has been taken by individual states, testing agencies, and advocacy organizations to provide policies and guidelines to govern the quality of documentation and the selection criteria accepted by institutions (Brinckeroff, Shaw, and McGuire 1993; Gregg et al. 1994). The selection criteria applied by an examiner will determine the number and type of individuals identified (Gregg 1994; Hoy et al. 1996).

The purpose of this chapter is not to provide an in-depth description of the primary selection criteria currently being used by professionals (see Gregg and Scott 2000 for such a review). Rather, the focus is on specific issues surrounding selection criteria—such as the concepts of discrepancy, general ability, and clinical judgment—that influence the decision-making process in determining learning disabilities. As part of this discussion, a review of some of the most promising current theory-driven research in learning disabilities using advanced statistical analyses will be put forth as an alternative to popular procedures applied by many professionals.

Aptitude/Achievement Discrepancy

The concept of discrepancy is the driving force underlying the majority of selection criteria used by professionals in documenting learning disabilities. This is particularly the case with adult populations (Gregg et al. 1999). Many types of discrepancy (i.e., intra-cognitive, intra-achievement, and aptitude/achievement) have been advocated as important to consider in determining learning disabilities. The aptitude/achievement discrepancy, the most frequently applied selection criterion, is fraught with technical and theoretical problems (Gregg and Scott 2000). First, the aptitude/achievement selection criteria assume a "unidirectional influence" of broad cognitive ability (intelligence) on achievement in which intelligence sets the upper limit on expected levels (Berninger 1994, p. 159). Interestingly, Berninger et al. (1992), using Mahalanobis statistics, found that intelligence did not consistently establish the upper limit on achievement—certainly a challenge to the validity of the aptitude/ achievement concept. One of the major difficulties with relying on intelligence to set the upper limit is that in "many cases the disability is reflected in, and consequently diminishes, the intelligence or aptitude score" (Mather 1993, p. 113). Such an over-reliance on the role of intelligence therefore appears to identify more adults with higher cognitive ability and milder achievement disabilities (Hoy et al. 1996).

Reliance on the ability/achievement criteria also assumes that aptitude and achievement (as measured by current standardized instruments) demonstrate very little variance, a misconception of critical importance. For example, 50% of the test items on the Wechsler Adult Intelligence Scale-Revised (Wechsler 1981) are "achievement-like" (Woodcock 1990). In addition, in comparing performance, it is critical for professionals to have examined the composition of processes measured across subtests that comprise the broad or full-scale score of the constructs being used. As Woodcock (1990) noted, aptitude scores are "simply an average of whatever has been chosen by the test author to be included in the battery" (p. 250).

The Woodcock-Johnson-Revised (WJ-R) Cognitive and Achievement Batteries (Woodcock and Johnson 1989a and b), and the new Woodcock-Johnson-III (Woodcock, McGrew, and Mather 2000) are designed around the use of a broad-based scale as well as aptitude, cognitive, and achievement cluster scores to be used for the purpose of identifying discrepancy. Using the WJ-R norm data (age five to adulthood), McGrew and Knopik (1993) examined the relationship between seven cognitive clusters and achievement, finding that cognitive clusters accounted for 50% to 70% of the variance. In addition, they found that across all ages the scholastic aptitude clusters were better predictors of achievement than was the broad cognitive score. This was consistent across various intelligence measures (Kaufman and Kaufman 1993; Wechler 1981).

The WJ-R aptitude score (Scholastic Aptitude Score) and the new WJ-III (Predicted Achievement Score) are indirectly identified in Woodcock's (1990) observation about the composition of broad-based intelligence scores—what you put in is what you get out. For instance, if the composition of the aptitude cluster is determined by factor analysis methods that do not integrate content and measurement theory, potential for misinterpretation of statistical outcomes cloud sound theoretical judgment. The WJ-R Reading Aptitude Cluster contains the subtest Visual matching, Sound Blending, Memory for Sentences, and Oral Vocabulary to predict expected reading performance. However, if an individual demonstrated deficits in phonological awareness, the aptitude cluster would be lowered so that no discrepancy could be identified from overall reading achievement. On the WJ-III, the Predicted Achievement score is also a combination of differentially weighted subtests. The scores are based on actual discrepancy norms. However, the score is to be used as predicting achievement in a curriculum area. It is not a discrepancy score used for learning disabilities eligibility.

Technical validity clearly has been identified as a problem in the use of the aptitude/achievement selection criteria, particularly when examiners do not rely upon co-normed ability achievement measures to account for error (McGrew 1994). In addition, Flanagan, Andrews, and Genshaft (1997) stressed the need for professionals to control for regression to the mean and to examine the meaningfulness of discrepancy (i.e., clinical or statistical) in decision-making. Technical validity is obviously and ethically critical to ensuring more reliable decision-making in professional use of a selection criteria.

Intracognitive discrepancy

The basic assumption of the intracognitive selection criterion is that cognitive processing discrepancies lie at the root of learning disabilities (Mather 1993; Swanson 1991). Using such selection criterion, an examiner would identify the intracognitive discrepancies first and then examine the relationship between aptitude and ability in the individual's profile. Without the intracognitive discrepancies, however, aptitude/ability would be statistically significant but have no clinical application.

The Horn-Cattell Gf-Gc theory (Cattell 1941, 1957; Horn 1991; Horn and Noll 1997) and Carroll's (1997) three-stratum theory provide a framework for a general cognitive ability (CHC) model that appears to be contributing significantly to a better understanding of cognitive abilities. McGrew (1997) proposed a CHC framework that infused new research from both Carroll (1993; 1997) and Horn and Noll (1997). According to McGrew (1997), his new framework provides a "bridge between the theoretical and empirical research on the factors of intelligence and the development and interpretation of psychoeducational assessment batteries" (p. 170).

The significant problem with the intracognitive discrepancy selection criterion rests more with technical than with theoretical issues. First, as with the aptitude/achievement selection criterion, one is still left with the negative feature of univariate regression. Second, a significant amount of overlap exists among cognitive processing measures. As Morris (1996) stated, "the majority of the tests described as measuring a single construct are actually multi-dimensional in nature" (p. 13). With adults, this becomes significantly problematic. The types of cognitive tasks adults normally encounter usually require a significant integration of attention, memory, and executive functioning. Identifying isolated cognitive abilities via such tasks is not always practical or theoretically sound despite statistical factors. For instance, a test that purports to measure attention by using a cancellation format also requires a significant amount of memory, learning, and planning (executive functioning) abilities. Again, discrepancies across isolated cognitive processing subtests will never be able to provide insight into the intra-relationship among these cognitive functions. Discrepancies could be clinically meaningless despite the score differences obtained across tasks—a not-unfamiliar occurrence in the evaluation of adults.

Deviation from Reading Level

Siegel (1989), concerned about the bi-directional influence between intelligence and achievement, felt that deviation on a measure was a more appropriate basis than aptitude/achievement or intracognitive selection criteria for the identification of reading disorders among children. She stressed that intelligence tests do not assess the cognitive processes and abilities that are most closely associated with academic achievement and are not providing needed information for diagnostic or institutional purposes. In examining the role of the aptitude/achievement selection criteria, she found that intelligence scores of students dropped with age, thereby having an impact on the significance of achievement-based discrepancies and resulting in diagnostic reclassification from "dyslexic" to "poor reader" (Siegel and Himel 1998).

Criticism of the deviation from grade level is both theoretical and technical. Technically, such a selection criterion does not take into account intelligence as an index of expected achievement, thus identifying those individuals in the lower part of the bottom half of the achievement distribution. Therefore, the criteria are biased against those individuals at the higher end of ability (Berninger 1994; Gregg 1994). In addition, a deviation cut-off on achievement measures assumes strong predictive and construct validity for, in this case, reading measures. Debate continues as to whether intelligence, listening comprehension (Stanovich 1993), verbal knowledge (Carver 1998), pronunciation (Carver 1998), or cognitive speed (Carver 1998) should be used to measure potential in reading. In addition, opinions differ as to the impact of orthography, as well as phonology, on reading skills (Ehri 1980; Frith 1985; Stanovich and Siegel 1994; Torgesen, Wagner, and Rashotte 1994; Wanger and Torgesen 1998). A significant amount of research would support the claim that spelling measures, rather than reading word attack skills, are some of the best predictors of residual dyslexia among the adult population (Perfetti 1997). Berninger and Abbott (1994) warned against identifying reading disabilities based on a single measure such as pseudoword reading tasks. They pointed out the contributions of orthography as well as phonology to reading development (Ehri 1998; Perfetti 1997).

Theoretically, the deviation from a reading level model does not account for the role of strategy and overall ability in the compensation of reading or the multidimensionality of reading performance in the adult population. Swanson (1991) proposed that often, the problems experienced by individuals with learning disabilities result not so much from a production deficiency, but rather from a failure to perform elaborative processes or strategies. In addition, the deviation from reading level does not account for the impact of intervention on reading ability. If an individual received a phonics-based approach to reading over the years, her or his word recognition skills may not be severely below average. However, her or his rate of reading and performance on reading comprehension measures could be impacted by the residual effects of dyslexia. If a professional relied solely on a deviation cut-off on a word attack measure, these other areas of performance would never be identified. The use of cut-off scores has not been supported in the courts as comprehensive selection criteria for adults with learning disabilities (Bartlett v. New York State Board of Law Examiners, 1997, 1998).

The most significant theoretical problem with this set of selection criteria is its application only to the area of reading. Many students with learning disabilities (e.g., those for whom cognitive processing deficits are more significant in such areas as visual-motor, visual-spatial, or executive functioning) would never be identified because the academic area of underachievement would show up more in the area of mathematics or written expression. To date, generalization of a grade deviation has not been explored by researchers for other content areas such as mathematics or written expression.

Models of Ability

An investigation of the selection criteria used by professionals in diagnosing or documenting learning disabilities leads one to question the artificially created categories of cognition, affect, language, and achievement. As McGrew (1997) stated, "intelligence and achievement distinction is largely an artificial dichotomy used in educational settings" (p. 170). He encouraged professionals to recognize the factorial complexity of many language and achievement measures. Focusing on intelligence scores outside of the context of affective, language, and achievement abilities to losing "sight of what Silvern (1984) characterized as the principle of 'equifinality,' namely that different people can attain the same outcome through different pathways" (Greenspan and Driscoll 1997, p. 132). Service providers working on a daily basis with college students with learning disabilities often relate the personal competencies (character, temperament) that contribute to the success of these individuals. Which affective, conceptual, language, and achievement abilities also appear to contribute toward overall personal competence for the college population with LD? What then is the variance across these constructs?

Intelligence measures have taken on a significant role in defining and selecting who receives services for learning disabilities across both child and adult populations. While investigating agencies serving the adolescent and adult population with learning disabilities, Gregg et al. (1999) found that only 20% of the state Special Education agencies and 14% of the Vocational Rehabilitation agencies explicitly included intelligence within their definitions of learning disabilities. However, 90% of the Special Education and Vocational Rehabilitation agencies' selection criteria identified intelligence as a factor in considering eligibility for services. Definitions and selection criteria used for identifying services for the adult population with LD are inconsistent in policy.

THEORY-BASED MODELS

Theory-Based Models investigated through the use of structural equation modeling (SEM) and confirmatory factor analyses (CFA) are necessary to examine more closely the constructs implied by selection criteria. Because many of the selection criteria constructs so far discussed are largely unobservable variables (such as intelligence, cognitive processes, and reading achievement), such structural models allow for more complex relationships between latent (unobserved) and observed to be hypothesized.

The use of CFA has been applied to questions debated across many disciplines, such as special education, general education, and counseling (Crowley and Fan 1997; Fassinger 1987; Hoyle and Smith 1994). Due to the extensive use of CFA to test hypotheses about theories, Keith (1997) described in detail its application to facilitate a better understanding of the constructs measured by intelligence tests. When using CFA to investigate hypotheses, it is important to keep in mind that even if a theory does appear to "fit the data," that is only partial evidence for the validity of the theory. There may be other models that also fit the data; the search should be for the model that "best fits" the data. As Keith (1997) so aptly stated, "CFA are needed if we are really interested in understanding the constructs we are measuring. Thus, I encourage the comparison of meaningful alternative explanations to a researcher's pet theory through the testing and comparison of alternative factor models" (p. 398). Absent from research examining selection criteria for the adult population has been an empirical investigation of these models through a comparison of "best fit" criteria.

Confirmatory factor analyses is one statistical method; it is a sub-set of what is known as structural equation modeling (SEM). An advantage of SEM is that it allows for an examination of stability of measured constructs, independent of measurement. In addition, multi-sample SEM provides a means to control predictive bias in measurements (Keith 1997). Gregg and Scott (2000) provided a cautionary warning that SEM does not in and of itself point the direction for further theory development. It does, however, provide an opportunity to investigate previously unobserved implications of theories. In particular, it provides a more sophisticated method for investigating the measurement tools and models used in selection criteria.

Constructs Measured

Researchers would be wise to apply CFA in their investigation of the constructs measured by standardized intelligence, cognitive processing, language, and achievement test instruments. First, it will be important to determine whether the "theory" underlying the measures appears to fit the standardization data. For instance, although Keith (1997) found that the KAIT does measure what it purports to measure (theory), he noted that the "RDR [Delayed Rebus Learning] and ADR [Delayed Auditory Comprehension] subtests of the KAIT should be considered additional measures of the abilities measured by the two primarily KAIT scales (Fluid and Crystallized) rather than measures of memory or delayed recall" (p. 385). Such information has significant implications when used clinically and/or in SEM for theory comparison. Unfortunately, particularly with many language and achievement measures, both the standardization population and the number of items proposing to measure constructs are small and often not representative of the population of adults—all have a negative impact on validity and reliability.

Using CFA, the potential to relationships between factors and tests is available using statistical applications that will lead to more sophisticated discussions. Do ability/ability, ability/achievement, and ability/language models measure statistically indistinguishable factors? The WJ-R and the WJ-III batteries, interval scale measures, provide researchers with the ability for use in comparisons across these factors and in later structural equation modeling (SEM) investigating the selection criteria for adults with learning disabilities.

Model Comparison

Structural equation modeling (SEM) creates a structural model that links latent (unobserved) and observed variables. LISREL, a popular computerized application of SEM, is used to generate the two-part model inherent in SEM. "The first part, the structural equation model, describes the theoretical relationships between unobserved or latent variables. The second part, the measurement model, describes the measurement of latent variables by one or more observable indicator variables" (Bollen 1989, p. 102). Therefore, the second part of SEM is a CFA model, which measures the latent variables for the extent to which each of them actually measures the construct it purports to measure. The SEM can play a significant role in the comparison of model to determine the "best fit" model for identifying selection criteria for adults with learning disabilities. Due to the ability of SEM to account for latent unobserved variables, data used in the past for clinical but not statistical decision-making could become part of a model. Certainly, in such fields as physics, the importance of latent variables (partials) that are not visible become central to theory development (Wallace 1972, p. e). As Bollen stated, "Biological species is an abstraction not always measurable" (p. 78). Researchers in the field of learning disabilities have spent a significant amount of time generating theories very dependent upon observed variables but with very little attention on theory. Some initial work using SEM examine phonological and orthographic knowledge (Abbott and Berninger 1995; McBride-Chang 1995; Wagner, Torgesen, and Rashotte 1994) and reading components (Leong 1988; Rupley, Willson, and Nichols 1998; Willson and Rupley 1997) have started to have an impact on issues pertaining to reading.

CLINICAL JUDGMENT

The National Joint Committee on Learning Disabilities (NJCLD), in its May/June 1997 report *Operationalizing the NJCLD Definition of Learning Disabilities for Ongoing Assessment in Schools*, provided a well thought-out critique of the use of clinical judgment in the diagnostic process (see report for in-depth discussion). Learning disabilities, in this document, are considered a multi-dimensional construct, changing in manifestation across age, experiences, and ability. The report addresses the issue of "significant difficulty" that surrounds the operationalization of discrepancy across definitions and selection criteria. The report concludes, "significant difficulty cannot be determined solely by a quantitative test score" (p.6). The NJCLD report encourages use of both quantitative test scores in diagnostic decision-making and affirms that cognitive ability/achievement discrepancies should be used cautiously because a "learning disability can exist when a numerical discrepancy does not" (p. 6).

Among evaluators, faith in the "statistical" reliability and validity of test instruments often takes precedence over professional judgment. As Mather (1993) cautioned, "test results assist with judgment; they are not a substitute" (p. 188). Observed variables (test scores) are often weighed more heavily as predictors of ability/disability than is the relationship between latent variables (intelligence, reading compensation), which should be the actual measurement goal of an examiner. Given the lack of empirically based theoretical constructs underlying selection criteria models used for the diagnostic of learning disabilities among the adult population, the professional judgment of evaluators is integral to decision-making. As Smith (1988) stated, "where there is no need for professional judgment, there is no need for professionals" (p. 62).

Professional judgment will be vital to the development of SEM models to locate the "best fit" variables (both observed and latent) that can be used to support inclusion in models for selection criteria. One of the advantages of CFA or SEM is the use of theory over simple numbers in the construction of models used to investigate complex relationships. Such structural models are particularly important in the examination of latent variables.

SUMMARY

The pioneers in the field of learning disabilities provided the constructs from which the definitions of and selection criteria for learning disabilities have evolved (Gregg and Scott 2000). Over the years, significant discussion has focused on the most accurate predictors to be used in the diagnoses of adults with learning disabilities. With the development of sophisticated statistical models (EFA, CFA, and SEM), the opportunity to combine the knowledge of our early pioneers in learning disabilities with current research and theory (as well as statistical applications) is at hand. At last, sophisticated models for selection criteria can be developed—models that can be tested across factor analyses (EFA, CFA, and SEM) through comparisons of "best fit" criterion. Dependent and integral to the testing of such models will be interval-scaled assessment measures (such as the WJ-R), current theory across the constructs being investigated (intelligence, reading, language) and an openness by researchers to explore the relationships among many different observed and latent variables. It is an extremely exciting time to be a part of the field of learning disabilities. Model development of selection criteria can lead to more accurate diagnoses and access to accommodations for the adult population.

ACKNOWLEDGMENTS

I would like to extend a sincere thank you to three people who contributed significantly to the development of this paper. First, Susan Vogel, Ph.D for providing the opportunity for the ideas in this paper to be expressed. Second, Chris Coleman, M.A., whose technical and theoretical skills redirected my wandering thoughts. Finally, Nancy Mather, Ph. D. for reviewing and adding her expertise to fine tune the theoretical questions raised throughout the paper.

REFERENCES

Abbott, R. D., and Berninger, V. W. 1995. Structural equation modeling and hierarchical linear modeling: Tools for studying the construct validity of orthographic processes in reading and writing development. In *The Variables of Orthographic Knowledge: Vol. 1. Theoretical and Developmental Issues*, ed. V. W. Berninger. Dordrecht, The Netherlands: Kluwer Academic Publishers.

Bartlett v. New York State Board of Law Examiners, 1–131. 1998. United States Court, Southern District of New York.

Berninger, V., Hart, T., Abbott, R., and Karovsky, P. 1992. Diagnosing reading and writing disabilities with and without IQ: A Flexible developmental approach. *Learning Disabilities Quarterly* 15:105–18.

Berninger, V. W. 1994. *Reading and Writing Acquisition: A Developmental Neuropsychological Perspective.* NY: Westview Press.

Berninger, V. W., and Abbott, R. D. 1994. Redefining learning disabilities: Moving beyond aptitude-achievement discrepancies to failure to respond to validated treatment protocals. In *Frames of Reference for the Assessment of Learning Disabilities: New Views on Measurement*, ed. G. Reid Lyon. Baltimore: Paul. H. Brookes Publishing Company.

Bollen, K. A. 1989. *Structural Equations with Latent Variables.* NY: Wiley-Interscience Publication.

Brackett, J., and McPhearson, A. 1996. Learning disabilities diagnostics in postsecondary students: A comparison of discrepancy-based diagnostic models. In *Adults with Learning Disabilities: Theoretical and Practical Perspectives*, eds. N. Gregg, C. Hoy, and A. Gay. NY: Guilford Press.

Carroll, J. B. 1993. *Human Cognitive Abilities: A Survey of Factor-analytic Studies.* NY: Cambridge University Press.

Carroll, J. B. 1997. The Three-stratum Theory of Cognitive Abilities. In *Contemporary Intellectual Assessment: Theories, Tests and Issues*, eds. D. P. Flanagan, J. L. Genshaft, and P. L. Harrison. NY: Guilford Press.

Carver, R. P. 1998. Relating reading achievement to intelligence and memory capacity. In *Advances in Cognition and Educational Practice*, Vol. 5, eds. W. Tomic and Kingma, S.. Greenwich, CT: JAI.

Cattell, R. B. 1941. Some theoretical issues in adult intelligence testing. *Psychological Bulletin* 38:592 [Abstract].

Cattell, R. S. 195). *Personality and Motivation Structure and Measurement.* New York: Worhl Book.

Crowley, S. L., and Fan, X. 1997. Structural equation modeling: Basic concepts and applications is personality assessment research. *Journal of Personality Assessment* 68:508–31.

Ehri, L. C. 1980. The development, in orthographic images. In *Cognitive Processes in Spelling*, ed. U. Frith. London: Academic Press.

Ehri, L. C. 1998. Research on learning to read and spell: A personal-historical perspective. *Scientific Studies of Reading* 2:97–114.

Fassinger, R. E. 1987. Use of structural equation modeling in counseling psychology research. *Journal of Counseling Psychology* 34:425–36.

Flanagan, D. P., Andrews, T. J., and Genshaft, J. L. 1997. The functional utility of intelligence tests with special education populations. In *Contemporary Intellectual Assessment: Theories, Tests, and Issues*, eds. D. P. Flanagan, J. L.Genshaft, and P. L. Harrison. NY: Guilford Press.

Frith, U. 1985. Beneath the surface of developmental dyslexia. In *Surface Dyslexia: Neuropsychological and Cognitive Studies of Phonological Reading*, eds. K. E. Patterson, J. C. Marshall, and M. Coltheat. London: Lawrence Erlbaum Associates.

Greenspan, S., and Drisoll, J. 1997. The role of intelligence in a broad model of personal competence. In *Contemporary Intellectual Assessment: Theories, Tests, and Issues*, eds. D. A. Flanagan, J. L. Genshaft, and D. L. Harrison. NY: Guilford Press.

Gregg, N. 1994. Eligibility for learning disabilities rehabilitation services: Operationalizing the definition. *Journal of Vocational Rehabilitation* 4:86–95.

Gregg, N., Heggoy, S., Stapleton, M., Jackson, R., and Morris, R. 1994. The Georgia model of eligibility for postsecondary students. *Learning Disabilities: A Multidisciplinary Journal* 7:29–36.

Gregg, N. and Scott, S. 2000. Definition and documentation: Theory, measurement, and the courts. *Journal of Learning Disabilities* 33:5–13.

Gregg, N., Scott, S., McPeek, D., and Ferri, B. 1999. Definitions and eligibility criteria applied to the adolescent and adult population with learning disabilities. *Learning Disability Quarterly* 22:213–23.

Horn, J. L. 1991. Theory of fluid and crystallized intelligence. In *Encyclopedia of Human Intelligence*, ed. R. J. Sternberg. NY: MacMillan.

Horn, J. L., and Noll, J. 1997. Human cognitive capabilities: Gf Gc theory. In *Contemporary Intelligence Assessment: Theories, Tests, and Issues*, eds. D. P. Flanagan, J. L. Genshaft, and P. L. Harrison. NY: Guilford Press.

Hoy, C., Gregg, N., Wisenbaker, J., Bonham, S., King, M., and Moreland, C. (1996). Clinical model versus discrepancy model in determining eligibility for learning disabilities services at a rehabilitation setting. In *Adults with Learning Disabilities: Theoretical and Practical Perspective*, eds. N. Gregg, C. Hoy, and A. Gay. NY: Guilford Press.

Hoyle, R. H., and Smith, G. T. 1994. Formulating clinical research hypothesis as structural equation models: A conceptual overview. *Journal of Counseling and Clinical Psychology* 2:429–40.

Kaufman, A. S., and Kaufman, N. L. 1993. *Manual for the Kaufman Adolescent and Adult Intelligence Test (KAIT), Circle Pines, MN: American Guidance Service.*

Keith, T. Z. 1997. Using constructs measured by intelligence tests. In *Contemporary Intellectual Assessment: Theories, Tests, and Issues*, eds. D. P. Flanagan, T. L. Genshaft, and P. L. Harrison. NY: Guilford Press.

Leong, C. K. 1988. A componential approach to understanding reading and its difficulties in preadolescent readers. *Annals of Dyslexia* 38:97–119.

Mather, N. 1993. Criteria issues, in the diagnosis of learning disabilities addressed by the Woodcock-Johnson Psycho-educational Battery-Revised. *Journal of Psychoeducational Assessment* [Monograph Series: WJ-R Monograph] 103–22.

McBride-Chang, C. 1995. What is phonological awareness? *Journal of Educational Psychology* 87:179–92.

McGrew, K. 1994. *Clinical Interpretation of the Woodcock-Johnson-Revised Tests of Cognitive Ability-Revised.* Boston: Allyn &Bacon.

McGrew, K.S. 1994. Analysis of the major intelligence batteries according to a proposed comperhensive Gf-Gc framework. In D. P. Flanagan, J. L. Genshaft, and P. L. Harrison (eds.). *Contemporary Intellectual Assessment: Theories, Tests, and Issues* (pp. 151–180). NY: Guilford Press.

McGrew, K. S., and Kaopik, S. N. 1993. The relationship between the WJ-Rf-Gc cognitive clusters and writing achievement across the life span. *School Psychology Review* 22:687–95.

McGuire, J., Madaus, J. W., Litt, A. V., and Ramirez, M. O. 1996. An investigation of documentation submitted by university students to verify their learning disabilities. *Journal of Learning Disabilities* 29:297–304.

Morris, R. 1996. Relationships and distinctions among the concepts of attention, memory and executive functions: A developmental perspective. In *Attention, Memory, and Executive Function*, eds. G. R. Lyon and N. A. Krasnegor. Baltimore, MD: Paul H. Brookes.

National Joint Committee on Learning Disabilities 1997. *Operationalizing the NJCLD Definition of Learning Disabilities for On-going Assessment.*

Perfetti, C. A. 1997. The psychologuistics of spelling and reading. In *Learning to Spell: Research, Theory, and Practice across Languages*, eds. C. A. Perfetti, L. Rieben, and M. Fayol. NJ: Lawrence Erlbaum Associates.

Rupley, W. H., Willson, V. L., and Nichols, W. D. 1998. Exploration of the development components to elementary school children's reading compensation. *Scientific Studies in Reading*, 2:143–58.

Siegel, L. 1989. IQ is irrelevant to the definition of learning disabilities. *Journal of Learning Disabilities* 22:469–86.

Siegel, L. S., and Himel, N. 1998. Socioeconomic status, age, and the classification of dyslexics and poor readers: The dangers of using IQ scores in the definition of reading disability. *Dyslexia* 4:90–104.

Silvern, L. E. 1984. Emotional-behavioral disorders: A failure of system functions. In *Malformations of Development: Biological and Psychological Sources and Consequences*, ed. E. S. Gollin. NY: Academic Press.

Smith, F. 1988. Professional judgment in the diagnosis of specific learning disabilities. In *SLD Eligibility Conference Handbook*, ed. GLRS. Atlanta, GA: Metro East and West Georgia Learning Resources System.

Stanovich, K. E. 1993. The construct validity of discrepancy definitions of reading disability. In *Better Understanding Learning Disabilities*, eds. G. R. Lyon, D. B. Gray, J. F. Kavanaugh, and N. A. Krasnegor. Baltimore: Paul H. Brookes.

Stanovich, K. E., and Siegel, L. S 1994. Phenotypic performance profile of children with reading disabilities: A regression-based test of the phonological-coe variable-difference model. *Journal of Educational Psychology* 86:24–53.

State University of New York, 4 NDLR Sec 432. (Complaint No. 02-93-2088) (OCR Region II 1993).

Swanson, H. L. 1991. Information processing: An introduction. In *A Cognitive Approach to Learning Disabilities*, eds. K. Reid, W. P. Hresko, and H. L. Swanson. Texas: PRO-ED.

Torgesen, J. K., Wagner, R. K., and Rashotte, C. A. 1994. Longitudinal studies of phonological processing and reading. *Journal of Learning Disabilities* 27:276–86.

Wagner, R. K., and Torgesen, J. K. 1987. The nature of phonological processing and its causal role in the acquisition of reading. *Reading Research Quarterly* 24:402–433.

Wagner, R. K., Torgesen, J. K., and Rachotte, C. A. 1994. Development of reading-related phonological processing abilities: New evidence of bi-directional causality from a latent variable longitudinal study. *Developmental Psychology* 30:73–87.

Wallace, W. A. 1972. *Causality and Scientific Explanation, Vol. 1*, Ann Arbor: University of Michigan Press.

Wechsler, D. 1981. *Manual for the Wechsler Adult Intelligence Scale-Revised*. San Antonio, TX: Psychological Corporation.

Willson, V. L., and Rupley, W. H. 1997. A structural equation model for reading comprehension based on background, phonemic, and strategy knowledge. *Scientific Studies of Reading* 1:45–63.

Woodcock, R. W. 1990. Theoretical foundations in the WJ-R measures of cognitive ability. *Journal of Psychoeducational Assessment* 8:231–58.

Woodcock, R. W. 1993. An information processing view of Gf-Gc theory. *Journal of Psychoeducational Assessment* [Monograph Series: WJ-R Monograph] 80–102.

Woodcock, R.W., and Johnson, M.B. (1989a). *Woodcock-Johnson Tests of Cognitive Abilities-Revised*. Chicago: Riverside.

Woodcock, R. W., and Johnson, M. B. 989b. *Woodcock-Johnson Tests of Achievement Revised*. Chicago: Riverside.

Woodcock, R., McGrew, K., and Mather, N. 2000. *Woodcock-Johnson III*. Itasca, IL: Riverside.

Chapter • 7

Screening and Support for Dyslexia in Adults in the United Kingdom

Angela J. Fawcett

Dyslexia in children is among the most widely researched of developmental disabilities, representative estimates suggesting that probably around 5% of children are dyslexic (Badian 1984; Jorm et al. 1986). There is a consensus that dyslexia is constitutional in origin (Critchley 1964; Smith et al. 1983), and that one cannot "grow out of" dyslexia. Clearly, then, around 5% of the adult population must also be dyslexic, though of course the established incidence is very much lower, owing to the absence of diagnostic tests for dyslexia when many adults were young. It is very likely that many dyslexic adults would benefit if their dyslexia were diagnosed (see the recent book by Vogel and Reder 1998, which discusses the implications of learning difficulties for adult life). Benefits might include improved self esteem and improved self understanding, as well as more specific benefits such as better career information and career support, and also specific allowances for their disability in formal settings such as university courses (see the work of Professor Susan Vogel in the U.S., and the work of other authors in this book; see also Gilroy and Miles 1995, and McLoughlin, Fitzgibbon, and Young 1994, for approaches to support in adults in the U.K.). Unfortunately, however, there is very little agreement on how to diagnose dyslexia in adults, and still less on how diagnosis can be cost-effective.

In this chapter, I present the findings of an eight-year series of studies and surveys aimed at the development of a cost-effective methodology for a screening → assessment → support system for dyslexia in adults. This research was undertaken at the University of Sheffield, in collaboration with Professor Rod Nicolson. Based on the findings of an international survey we conducted on the diagnosis of dyslexia in adults (Nicolson, Fawcett, and Miles 1993), we concluded that a two-stage procedure (an initial screening followed if necessary by a thorough diagnosis) was the only viable method for cost-effective diagnosis. This research is presented in greater detail in Fawcett and Nicolson 1998. The first part of this chapter explains the procedure for a full-scale diagnostic measure, the Adult Dyslexia Index (ADI), and outlines its rationale and validity checks. The second part outlines the procedure for the Dyslexia Adult Screening Test (DAST), which has been designed to provide a quick check of the abilities of adults, and leading to a quantitative assessment of whether they are "at risk" of dyslexia. I argue that initial administration of the DAST (by a support officer), followed, only if necessary, by administration of the ADI (by a chartered psychologist), provides a valid and cost-effective solution to the otherwise intractable problem of large scale testing for dyslexia in adults. It should be emphasized that this assessment phase is seen as only the initial stage in the development of an effective assessment and support system. In the third section, I discuss the need for intervention and support geared to the individual needs of the adult.

Our approach to this topic benefited from our recent international survey (Nicolson, Fawcett, and Miles 1993) which established a clear consensus in the dyslexia community that was particularly impressive, given that the respondents were specialists whose opinions spanned the spectrum of approaches to dyslexia and adult literacy. Researchers and practitioners generally expressed satisfaction with methods of diagnosis in children, but found the present system far less appropriate for adults. There was consensus that it would be feasible to introduce screening procedures that do not require the direction of a trained clinician/diagnostician, and could therefore be carried out cost-effectively in centers such as adult literacy centers, units for young offenders, or job centers. However, endorsement of this suggestion was subject to the provisos that a follow-up second stage testing procedure would be available, and that the screening would be integrated within a support framework.

In addition to this consensus on the need for further work on screening, diagnosis, and research, this survey highlighted the need for further research with adults and indicated a number of unresolved issues awaiting input from the research community. Although the survey was carried out around 1991, I believe that its main conclusions remain valid. In particular, it is vital to derive a cost-effective yet valid method for large scale screening of adults for dyslexia. It is equally important to develop a system to provide the support necessary for a dyslexic adult to obtain the help needed to achieve his or her current objectives. In this chapter, I concentrate on the first requirement, that of a cost-effective screening/diagnostic system, and outline progress toward support.

These issues have recently become more critical in the U.K., following the publication of the Disability Discrimination Act (1995) and its associated Code of Practice. In many ways, this act goes beyond Section 504 of the US Rehabilitation Act of 1973, which applies largely to education, and is similar to the American with Disabilities Act (ADA) of 1990 (see Vogel 1998). The Disability Discrimination Act had the greatest impact on employment, making it unlawful to discriminate against people with disabilities in connection with employment. Disability here is defined as physical or mental impairment that has a substantial and long-term adverse effect on ability to carry out normal day-to-day activities, and includes dyslexia and other learning difficulties. Section 4.2 of the Act makes it unlawful to discriminate against people with disabilities in the following areas: in the terms of employment; in the opportunities for promotion, transfer, or training; or by dismissing, or subjecting to any other detriment.

Although the impact of this act on education has been somewhat less clearly defined, all Higher Education Institutes in the U.K. had to publish a "Disability Statement" by September 1996, explaining how they plan to identify and support students with dyslexia and other disabilities, both physical and mental. The objective here was to produce something like the Code of Practice for schools, with a template for disability statements including: policies and procedures (including admissions and exams); support services (including those specific to dyslexia); staff development; information technology (IT) provision; and monitoring the effectiveness of the service.

Recently (2001–2003), a new Code of Practice, making it unlawful to discriminate against disabled students, among others, was linked to the Special Educational Needs and Disability Act 2001. It may be seen that for the first time it has become a legal requirement to make some provision for adults with dyslexia. Against this background, the need for a cost-effective screening → assessment → support system has escalated, providing the current focus for research on dyslexia in adults in the U.K.

DIAGNOSIS OF DYSLEXIA IN ADULTS

The traditional definition of dyslexia is that provided by the World Federation of Neurology (1968): "a disorder in children who, despite conventional classroom experience, fail to attain the language skills of reading, writing and spelling commensurate with their intellectual abilities." As noted earlier, this definition is of limited value for adult diagnosis because reading is a poor criterion for identifying dyslexia in adults, in that their single word reading might well be normal. Consequently, single word reading alone is not an adequate criterion for dyslexia in adults. More useful indicators are spelling (Thomson 1984) and reading speed (Yap and van der Leij 1993), which are less amenable to remediation. A diagnosis of dyslexia in childhood is also not sufficient, because, although childhood testing is better understood, the testing procedures are variable, and symptoms may change, so childhood diagnoses are therefore not sufficient in themselves. Furthermore, use of an IQ test in testing for dyslexia is also controversial (Siegel 1989; Stanovich and Siegel 1995, though see also Nicolson 1996) in that it is probably more useful to develop a test that identifies positive indicators of dyslexia (Miles 1983) rather than the problematic reliance on discrepancy between IQ and reading performance.

Our objective in developing the Adult Dyslexia Index was to design a thorough test that not only assesses intelligence (necessary to distinguish between dyslexic adults and adults of generally low IQ), but also tests explicitly for positive indicators of dyslexia likely to be present in adults and leading to an objective composite score reflecting the severity of the dyslexia.

Positive Indicators of Dyslexia in Adults

A number of researchers have noted that dyslexic children tend to show a "spiky" profile of abilities on IQ sub-tests, with excellent performance on some tests together with below average performance on others. Typical of these problems is the so-called ACID profile (Thomson 1984) on the Wechsler Intelligence Scale for Children (Wechsler 1976) in which specific difficulties are shown in two or more of the Arithmetic, Coding, Information, and Digit span scales. It is known that problems in working memory persist into adulthood, as do general problems in terms of speeded information processing (see, for example, McLoughlin et al. 1994). Consequently, it seems reasonable to assume that the tests equivalent to the ACID tests in the WAIS-R are namely Arithmetic, Digit Symbol (the adult equivalent of Coding), Information, and Digit Span. A similar approach is used with the WAIS III, which also gives a series of scales, notably processing speed, which are typically impaired in dyslexia.

Deficits in reading and spelling skills for children of average or above average intelligence are the criteria for diagnosis in children. Dyslexic adults, however, may show relatively normal reading skills (especially if speed is not considered). It is therefore more appropriate to take deficits in single word spelling, rather than single word reading as a measure of deficit in adults, because spelling is typically more impaired and more resistant to remediation in both dyslexic adults and children (Thomson 1984).

Research on identification of dyslexia in adults (Felton et al. 1990) has indicated that, even for a high achieving dyslexic adult with a large sight vocabulary, reading of nonsense words is impaired (in that nonsense words can only be read by grapheme-phoneme conversion, an area of continued difficulty for even the more competent adult dyslexics). Nonsense word reading is rather an unnatural task, and Finucci et al. (1976) established that a Jabberwock type passage, in which real words and nonsense words are interspersed (see also Gross-Glenn et al. 1990) provided a sensitive index of dyslexia, especially if performance is scored for speed as well as accuracy.

As noted earlier, the procedures for diagnosis of dyslexia in children (though far from perfect) are considerably better grounded than those for adults. Furthermore, it is believed that dyslexia is constitutional in origin, and hence (even if the major symptoms are alleviated by adulthood) a dyslexic child will necessarily become a dyslexic adult. Consequently, diagnosis of dyslexia as a child provides strong (though not conclusive) evidence of dyslexia in an adult.

The Adult Dyslexia Index

The traditional method for assessing dyslexia in adults is to administer an adult intelligence test (formerly WAIS-R, now typically WAIS III) to check that the adult has an IQ of 90 or more, and then to administer a test of single word reading (a suitable modern test would be the Wechsler Objective Reading Dimension (WORD) reading test). A WORD reading age of 14 or less, together with an IQ of 90 or more, might then be taken as a reasonable indicator of dyslexia. As noted earlier, this procedure lacks theoretical motivation and is of doubtful validity. The WAIS is a restricted test, and its administration is a lengthy procedure requiring skill. It is unfortunate that the above method is costly as well as unsatisfactory. In designing the Adult Dyslexia Index (ADI), we wished to augment this traditional procedure in a principled manner so as to improve its validity without adding substantially to the testing time. We achieved this by first assessing the above four positive indicators for adult dyslexia: namely the WAIS-R "ACID" profile[1]; WORD spelling; nonsense passage reading; and previous diagnosis of dyslexia. It is also valuable to combine these four indicators into a

---

[1]Note that dyslexic females may show superior performance on the Coding subtest of the ACID profile (Vogel 1982). However, females show equally poor performance as males on the Arithmetic, Information, and Digit Span components. This means that they can still generate a score of 1.0 on the ACID profile.

single, objective, composite score which gives an index of severity—the Adult Dyslexia Index—and this can be done simply by adding them. This procedure leads to a score of 0, 0.5, or 1 on each of the four measures, and a composite ADI (Fawcett and Nicolson 1993) ranging from 0 to 4 in steps of 0.5. In a slight modification of earlier work (Brachacki, Fawcett, and Nicolson 1994) we now use a score of 3.0 or more as a strong indicator of dyslexia, a score of 2.5 as clear evidence of dyslexia, scores of 1.5 to 2.0 as borderline evidence, and scores of 1 or less as no evidence of dyslexia. I provide an illustrative example of the procedure at the end of this chapter.

SCREENING FOR ADULT DYSLEXIA

In common with the views of many dyslexia theorists, the bulk of our theoretical work has been on understanding, diagnosing, and remedying dyslexia in childhood, with our driving principle being that the earlier one can detect dyslexia, the easier it is to prevent it from adversely affecting the attainments and morale of the children involved. We believe that the two stage procedure (screening then full assessment) is appropriate for childhood diagnosis. Over the past three years, we have developed, tested, normed, and published screening tests for school use. These are the Dyslexia Early Screening Test [DEST] (Nicolson and Fawcett 1996) for children aged 4:6 to 6:5 years and the Dyslexia Screening Test [DST] (Fawcett and Nicolson 1996) for children aged 6:6–16:5. These tests are designed to be administered by lightly trained school professionals, and to take no more than 30 minutes to produce a profile of performance on a range of tests indicative of dyslexic type difficulties, including phonological skills, memory, speed, motor skill, balance, and knowledge. The tests were designed to check positive indicators of dyslexia, and they use an approach similar to that pioneered by Miles (1983). The DEST and the DST have been based on extensive theoretical work over the past decade that has revealed persistent deficits in a wide range of skills in dyslexia, including many unrelated to reading (Nicolson and Fawcett 1994; 1995, Fawcett and Nicolson 1994a and b; Fawcett, Pickering, and Nicolson 1993). An important contribution for early screening has been the identification of problems in balance in dyslexic children, which is explicable in terms of a cerebellar deficit (Nicolson and Fawcett 1990; Nicolson, Fawcett, and Dean 1995; Fawcett, Nicolson, and Dean 1996). We coupled this work with the established evidence of deficits in phonological skills and naming (e.g. Bradley and Bryant 1983; Denckla and Rudel 1976, Frith et al. 1995) to produce screening tests that provide data on the majority of deficits associated with dyslexia. The DEST and DST involve 10 and 11 sub-tests respectively, have been normed on around 1000 and 800 children, and take about half an hour to administer. They permit the tester to derive a quantitative "at risk" index based on the composite score across the tests, together with a profile of abilities that highlights areas of relative strength and weakness and may form the basis for development of a remediation strategy. This early screening approach fits well within the framework of the 1993 Education Act and the subsequent "Code of Practice on the Identification and Assessment of Special Educational Needs" (Department for Education 1994). The school aged screening tests have been well received, and are now ranked among the best sellers of the Psychological Corporation Europe.

The Dyslexia Adult Screening Test

In parallel with this work on childhood screening, we have modified the DST to support adult screening, leading to the development of the Dyslexia Adult Screening Test (DAST). Tests for adults must be designed with considerable care, so as to be non-threatening to adults with a history of difficulty in literacy tests, while avoiding seeming trivial or patronizing, and nonetheless fulfilling the criterion of successfully identifying disabilities (Fawcett 1995). Following an extensive series of trials with various adult user groups and professionals associated with adult literacy testing (for further details see Fawcett and Nicolson 1998a and b), we have derived the set of sub-tests outlined in table I. Note that the majority of tests are intended to identify specific weaknesses of the test taker, but two (tests 8 and 11) are intended to assess strengths. This is a valuable aspect both to avoid deliberate underachieving by the test taker and to allow a more representative pattern of strengths and weaknesses to be identified.

A prototype non-verbal reasoning test was designed and evaluated, and data collected for dyslexic students and controls. An example of the Non-Verbal reasoning test is given in figure 1 below.

In theory the combination of the DAST and the ADI together implement our proposal for a two stage screening procedure, with the DAST fulfilling the function of a quick, but informative, screening procedure, and the ADI fulfilling the requirements for an objective and valid dyslexia diagnosis. In the next section of this chapter, we present a case study of how we are using this methodology in diagnosing dyslexia in students. Given the incidence of around 5%, this screening process should lead to considerable savings in the overall cost of testing.

Table I.   Components of the Dyslexia Adult Screening Test

	Test	Description	Skills tapped
Test 1	Rapid naming	Time taken to name all the simple pictures on a card	Speed of lexical access and articulation
Test 2	One minute reading test	The number of words on a card read in one minute	Reading fluency
Test 3	Postural stability	The disturbance in balance caused by a calibrated push in the back	Balance
Test 4	Phonemic segmentation	The ability to split a word up into its constituent phonemes	Phonological skill
Test 5	Two minute spelling test	The number of words spelled correctly in two minutes (tester speaks them)	Spelling fluency
Test 6	Backwards digit span	The maximum number of digits that can be correctly repeated in the reverse order	Working memory
Test 7	Nonsense passage reading	The score on a Jabberwock type passage	Grapheme/phoneme translation fluency
Test 8	Non-verbal reasoning	A short nonverbal IQ test	Nonverbal reasoning (OK for dyslexic adults)
Test 9	One minute writing test	The number of words of a sentence that can be correctly copied in one minute	Transcription fluency
Test 10	Verbal fluency	The number of words beginning with S that can be thought of in one minute	Verbal fluency
Test 11	Semantic fluency	The number of animals that can be thought of in one minute	Semantic fluency (should be OK for dyslexic adults)

DIAGNOSIS OF DYSLEXIA IN STUDENTS

Many universities have established a systematic approach to diagnosis and support of dyslexic students, but until recently the approaches adopted have been piecemeal. The Disability Discrimination Act (1994) requires that all Higher Education institutes must publish a disability statement explaining how they will identify and support students with disabilities. Specific Learning Difficulty (Dyslexia) is specifically included. Consequently, each institution is now obliged to identify and provide for the needs of dyslexic students. As outlined

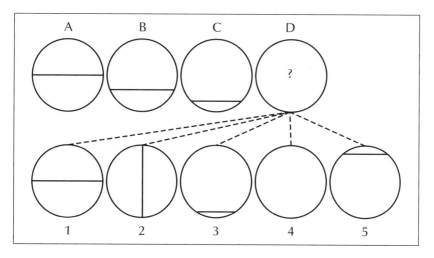

Figure 1.   Example of the Non-verbal reasoning test
(i) Next one in sequence (1 min 30 sec)
The three shapes A, B, and C go in sequence. You have to work out what the
next one in the sequence (D) will be. Look for shape D in the set of 5 possibilities in the next line, and enter the number in the middle of shape D.
(The answer is 3!)

above, all Higher Education institutes were required to publish their
disability statements by September 1996. Singleton (1996) notes that

> . . . in many institutions the situation is now regarded as one of crisis,
> with academic and administrative staff unsure about how this problem
> should be tackled. In particular, there is uncertainty regarding what
> university resources should be allocated to assessing students who sus-
> pect they may be dyslexic, and to supporting those who are diagnosed
> as dyslexic (pp. 10–16).

The underlying basis for this crisis is the number of students affected by dyslexia, which is currently estimated as between 1% and
2% of the student population. Moreover, the increase in mature students, many of whom would be predicted to be dyslexic, means that
this figure may well underestimate the level of demand.

It should also be noted that diagnosis of dyslexia in a student in
the U.K. makes him or her eligible for a support grant from the appropriate local authority which typically involves computer purchase.
Naturally, local authorities are concerned to ensure that diagnoses of
dyslexia are made by appropriately qualified professionals, and that
computer recommendations are likely to meet the real needs of the
student. Recent modifications to the Disabled Student Allowance (au-
tumn 1998) mean that the most impaired students would be eligible

for up to $15,000 per annum for non-medical support. Given the high numbers of those potentially eligible, and the high costs of testing, the need for a systematic and cost-effective system for screening students becomes clear.

In our view there is little alternative to the two stage screening/diagnosis procedure. The majority of those screened would have no difficulties and require no further allocation of resources, but a minority would need extra support to enable them to progress. Our hope would be that most of those identified would make up their lost ground with extra help, leaving a small number needing further full diagnostic assessment and intensive support. This has the advantage of being cost-effective, because it ensures that resources are concentrated on those with the greatest need and on those whose difficulties are the most intractable. At the University of Sheffield, we have for some years provided a full diagnostic service, and we have been evaluating the effectiveness of the two stage DAST screening, followed if appropriate by ADI diagnosis procedures. We start with the results of our evaluation of the ADI using our previously existing database of student testing.

Using the ADI for testing students

We have analyzed the costs involved in providing a full diagnostic service for dyslexic students in Sheffield. The results showed that the major bottleneck in checking our diagnosis and assessment data was the need for an expert judgment. This was because it was necessary to produce a firm diagnosis for subjects who showed a very patchy performance across a range of skills. Many of these subjects were intellectually able, as befitted their student role, but showed very specific problems in restricted areas. In some ways, however, this diagnosis smacked of the "judgment of Solomon," because on the basis of this expert judgment, decisions would be made on the allocation of funding under the disabled students' allowance. It was also clear that the funding system, if it was to remain solvent, could not possibly provide full financial support for every degree of dyslexia. We were left with the situation where the onus fell on the expert to evaluate the relative merits of each dyslexic case against the needs of others, to establish which case was the most deserving of support. The algorithmic system of the ADI (see table II) was developed to meet this need.

In order to determine whether the objective system produced results equivalent to those of the local dyslexia expert, we checked back over our previous records of diagnosis. The diagnostic procedure adopted had involved administration of the WAIS-R, tests of reading and spelling age, history of difficulties, and (in all but 41 cases) admin-

Table II.   Illustrative Use of the four tests to derive the Adult Dyslexia Index

Criterion Measure	Score	ADI Score	Scoring criterion
Previous diagnosis of dyslexia	No	0	1 for psychologist's report, 0 otherwise
WORD spelling scale (age equiv.)	16.3	0.5	0.5 for 16-17 1 for <16
Nonsense word passage Error score	9	0.5	0.5 for >7 errors
Completion time	166 secs	0.5	0.5 for >59 seconds
WAIS-R profile Av. WAIS score (non-ACID) Arithmetic Digit Symbol Digit Span Information	13.9 7 (-6.9) 5 (-8.9) 7 (-6.9) 12	0.5 0.5	0.5 for discrepancy (>3 points) in one of the ACID sub-tests compared with non-ACID mean 1 for two or more discrepancies
WAIS IQ scores Full-scale IQ Performance IQ Verbal IQ	113 104 109		IQ must be 90 or more for diagnosis of dyslexia
Overall Adult Dyslexia Index		**2.5**	2.5 points-dyslexic 1 point -non-dyslexic
Overall Diagnosis	**Evidence of Dyslexia**		

istration of the Finucci nonsense passage. The evidence was then assessed and a clinical judgment made as to whether the student was dyslexic. We subsequently checked the cases using the ADI method, and found very good agreement overall. For the 64 assessments on which data for all four ADI tests were available, concordance of the ADI with the expert judgment was excellent, with a disagreement on only one out of the 64 pairs of judgments. For the 41 assessments for which the nonsense passage data had not been collected, there was agreement on all but one of the cases. In both cases of disagreement the ADI gave a "not dyslexic" judgment whereas the expert gave a "borderline dyslexic" judgment. In both cases the deficits on the ACID profile just failed to reach significance for ADI, but a borderline diagnosis of 2 would have been obtained if the discrepancy between the ACID tests and the WAIS-R non-ACID score had been even 0.10 greater. This analysis therefore provides strong support for the ADI method of objectively combining the scores into a composite dyslexia index.

It should be noted that the ADI algorithm is applied strictly in terms of recommendations for funding for computer provision (an ADI score of at least 2.5 is needed). However, there is also a requirement within the university to make recommendations regarding examination concessions. Here we consider it appropriate to recommend extra time not only for students with ADI of 2.5 or more, but also for students whose performance is low borderline (1.5 or 2) who also show particular difficulties in, for example, speeded performance, spelling, or writing.

Interestingly enough, students are now presenting for assessment with somewhat less clear-cut evidence of deficit. This may reflect greater public awareness of dyslexia, which leads a greater number of students to question their patchy profile of skills. This trend is entirely consistent with expert judgment, which found that the satisfactory classification of students has become increasingly difficult over this time period. This is largely because dyslexic students in the early 1990s had IQ's which fell in the superior range, and a striking discrepancy between potential and achievement. The typical student presenting for assessment since 1994 has a somewhat lower IQ, and consequently their discrepancies are less severe. Similarly, if we compare the two groups, we also find a greater proportion (19%, compared with 1%) who were diagnosed as non-dyslexic. Nevertheless, the majority of students who we have tested have some aspects of peformance that justify presenting for assessment, if only poor study skills.

It should also be noted that the number of students requesting assessment appears to be escalating, with an increase of some 30% per annum in recent years. Moreover, semesterization, with the introduction of a further set of examinations in the winter, has meant that the demand for assessments has become constant throughout the academic year. It is clear that the demand for diagnosis is likely to become somewhat daunting.

Using the prototype DAST for screening students

The above considerations highlight the need for a quick, but effective, screening test that allows students to determine whether or not it is worth going to the expense of a full diagnostic ADI screening. The DAST was developed for just this purpose. Two years ago we administered prototype versions of the DAST as well as the ADI to many students referred for dyslexia assessment. Comparison of the DAST screening with the (definitive) assessment produced by the ADI permits the analysis of DAST "hit" rate (the proportion of those identified as dyslexic by the ADI who were screened as at risk by the DAST) and its "false alarm" rate (the proportion of those identified as not dyslexic by the ADI who were screened as at risk by the DAST). An ideal screening test would have a high hit rate and a low false alarm rate.

In order to estimate the hit rate and false alarm rate for the prototype version of the DAST, we collected control data on approximately 150 non-dyslexic students for the DAST sub-tests. The mean and standard deviation for each sub-test from this database were used to derive a rough "at risk" measure for the DAST assessed students. Each score on each sub-test of the DAST was allocated an index of 0, 1, 2, or 3 (with 0 indicating normal or above normal performance, and the 1, 2, and 3 categories indicating increasingly severe "at risk" danger[2]). The average of the individual sub-test indices was taken as the overall DAST index, and an overall index of 1.0 or more was taken as an at risk indicator for dyslexia (by analogy with the procedures used in the DST). Table III presents the analysis of the scores of the 15 students who were tested on both ADI and DAST and who scored 2.5 or more on the ADI (diagnosis of "dyslexic").

As may be seen from the bottom line of table III, the results of this analysis are encouraging. Fourteen of the 15 students (94%) identified by the ADI as dyslexic were also screened as at risk by the DAST (a hit rate of 94%). Analysis of false alarm rate is limited by the fact that most of the students presenting for assessment in this set were identified as dyslexic. Of the four students identified as "borderline dyslexic" by the ADI, three were screened as at risk by the DAST. Only one student was identified as not dyslexic by the ADI (ADI of 1.0) and he received an "at risk" screening (1.25) from the DAST. The right hand column of table III gives an indication of the false alarm

Table III.   Validation of prototype DAST performance using the ADI database

Scores are standardized relative to the mean and standard deviation of the control data, with positive scores reflecting deficits. A score of 1.0 or more is taken as "at risk" performance on the sub-test in question. See the text for further details of the scoring procedure. Data were available only for eight of the DAST sub-tests.

DAST Sub-test	Dyslexic Students		Control Students	
	Mean	Incidence (%)	Mean	Incidence (%)
Rapid naming	1.00 (0.97)	69	0.22 (0.56)	16
One minute reading	2.00 (0.89)	94	0.17 (0.46)	11
Postural stability	1.44 (1.36)	63	0.19 (0.70)	8
Phonemic segmentation	2.06 (1.18)	81	0.08 (0.34)	5
Two minute spelling	2.25 (0.77)	100	0.16 (0.52)	11
Backwards digit span	1.00 (0.73)	75	0.14 (0.39)	12
Nonsense passage reading	2.63 (1.02)	88	0.24 (0.60)	17
2 minute writing	2.00 (1.41)	75	0.21 (0.57)	14
Overall mean	**1.72 (0.52)**	**94**	**0.18 (0.52)**	**0**

[2]An index of 3 indicates performance at least 3 standard deviations below the mean (a "z-score" of –3 or worse); an index of 2 indicates a z-score of –2.0 to –2.99; an index of 1 indicates a z-score of –1.0 to –1.99; and an index of 0 indicates a z-score better than –1.

rate for the control group of 150 students from whom the norms were derived. It may be seen that none of these (0%) had an at risk DAST score. Therefore, the DAST does an excellent job of discriminating between clearly dyslexic and clearly non-dyslexic students (hit rate of 94%; false alarm rate of 0%). With students for whom the ADI diagnosis is less clear cut, the prototype DAST tends to give an "at risk" assessment, suggesting the need for a full ADI test.

Given that the prototype DAST "missed" one dyslexic student, we checked the reasons for this discrepancy. It turns out that this was a high IQ student with a childhood diagnosis of dyslexia who had improved her literacy skills nearly to the normal range. Consequently the DAST gave a low score (0.71) with positive scores on reading, spelling, backwards span, and postural stability (1, 1, 1, and 2 respectively) and zero scores on rapid naming, the nonsense passage, and on segmentation (only 7 of the DAST tests were administered). By contrast, the ADI total was 2.5, made up of: 1 for a previous diagnosis; 1 for a discrepancy on the WAIS-R on two of the ACID tests; and 0.5 for mild impairment on WORD spelling. The DAST cannot pick up either the previous diagnosis or the WAIS discrepancy, hence the low DAST score. In response to this difficulty, the published version of the DAST has been amended to include a nonverbal ability test (good performance on this is a positive indicator, in that it increases the chances of a discrepancy) together with the requirement that the student bring to the DAST assessment any evidence of previous diagnosis. Moreover, a further classification of "mild risk" has been introduced, based on scores of 0.7 or greater.

It is also possible to undertake an equivalent analysis of hits and false alarms for each individual sub-test. It can be seen from table III that every sub-test yields a fairly high mean index (1.0 to 2.63) and high incidence (63% to 100%) for the dyslexic students compared with the control students (mean index 0.08 to 0.24 and incidence 5% to 17%). Analysis of the hit rates and false alarm rates allows one to see which tests would benefit from "tuning," and the relatively low hit rates of the phonemic segmentation and postural stability sub-tests have led us to redesign these tests somewhat so as to make them more challenging. This was achieved in the first instance by introducing a timed "spoonerism" component into the segmentation task, which is difficult even for competent adults with dyslexia. Similarly, the relatively high false alarm rates for nonsense passage reading have also led to redesign of this test, to include a greater percentage of nonsense words within a more complex passage. This captures all the dyslexic students and correctly classifies their performance.

The 100% incidence of deficit for dyslexics on the two minute spelling test is particularly striking, and leads to the question of whether it alone (or possibly a combination of spelling and one minute reading) would be sufficient for an initial screening. The relatively high false alarm rates (11% for each) are unsatisfactory—most academics are well aware of the high incidence of poor spelling in the student population. A further problem is the obvious opportunity for a student to "cheat" by scoring low deliberately on these literacy tests.

Note that the costs of a false alarm are likely to be high. Whereas the DAST could be undertaken by an appropriately trained support officer, the full ADI test plus report, which must be undertaken by a qualified psychologist, requires around 3 to 4 hours to complete, with commensurate costs. It is likely that an adult would be responsible for at least some part of the ADI costs, and those most disgruntled would be those who pay the money only to find out that they do not have dyslexia. Consequently, in our view the extra discriminative power obtained by applying the full DAST test is well worth the extra time involved (20 minutes or so).

The Published DAST

Having checked that our prototype DAST was effective, the next task was to norm the DAST for the adult population. Norming the test involved collecting data on the performance of two groups; first students and second the general population, aged from 17 to 75. Students were drawn from a range of institutions, including some demanding high academic achievement and others with less stringent entrance requirements. Students were enlisted to represent both science and arts backgrounds, differing socio-economic status and areas of the country. This was relatively straightforward. However, norming an adult screening test such as the DAST on the general population proved to be particularly challenging. Unlike children or even students, who are naturally available within the educational system, groups of adults are not readily available and therefore need to be recruited on an individual basis. Note that the tally for data collection was based closely on that of the WAIS-R (Weschler 1986) and demanded that around 65% of the sample had left school before the age of 17, without further education. The team approached this challenge by contacting a series of groups within the general population, testing adults in the army, the bank, the police force, the library, church groups, support groups for the elderly, supermarket workers, and unemployed adults at the local job center. The norms were derived from nationwide testing in 1997 and 1998, involving over 1,100 adults in Sheffield, Kent, Leeds, London, Middleton-in-Teesdale, and Bristol. As outlined above, separate norms were collected for students and for the general population, with the general population $n = 618$ (with norms for five age groups, from 17–65), and students

$n = 550$ (with norms for two age groups, and performance on some tests superior to general population). Views of user groups on the sub-tests suggested that all were acceptable to adults. The DAST was published in October 1998 by the Psychological Corporation (Europe).

The final stage in completion of a new screening test is based on the validation of the norms against existing data. Twenty-one students who had been diagnosed as dyslexic using the ADI were also given the published version of the DAST, and their data compared with the published norms. Twenty out of the 21 achieved an "at risk" score of 1.0 or greater, confirming that they were all strongly at risk. The student norms also identified the remaining dyslexic student, who scored a risk factor of 0.82, indicating mild risk (based on a risk level of 0.7 or above). The mean "at risk" score for these dyslexic students was 1.46 with a standard deviation of 0.39. Overall at risk scores for the individual dyslexic students ranged from 0.82 (mild risk) to 2.18 (severe risk). The data is presented in table IV below. A full analysis of the data would be necessary to identify whether there were any false alarms. Interpretation of this data is not straightforward, in that one would expect a proportion of the student population to include undiagnosed dyslexics. However, a similar analysis was undertaken with a subgroup selected at random and drawn from Bristol, which consisted of fourteen students aged between 19 and 25. Six out of these 14 students showed an "at risk" score on at least one of the sub-tests. Three showed naming speed deficits, three showed speed deficits in one minute reading, and three others showed problems in nonsense pas-

Table IV.   Validation of DAST performance against final student norms using a second sample of dyslexic students from the 1998 ADI database
Scores here are compared with the student norms for the age group. A score of 1.0 or more is taken as "at risk" performance on the sub-test in question, and a score of 0.7 or greater indicates mild risk. See the test manual (Fawcett and Nicolson 1998b) for further details of the scoring procedure.

| DAST Sub-test | Dyslexic Students (n21) | |
	Mean	Incidence (%)
Rapid naming	1.14 (1.06)	71
One minute reading	1.88 (1.11)	82
Postural stability	1.26 (1.19)	63
Phonemic segmentation	1.14 (1.20)	57
Two minute spelling	2.29 (0.96)	90
Backwards digit span	1.71 (1.15)	81
Nonsense passage reading	2.52 (0.68)	100
Nonverbal reasoning	0.95 (1.08)	55
2 minute writing	2.00 (1.41)	71
Verbal fluency	1.00 (1.22)	52
Semantic fluency	0.38 (0.74)	24
Overall mean	**1.46 (0.39)**	**95%**

sage reading. Only one student showed any impairment in memory span. However, none of these students was identified as even at "mild risk" of dyslexia, with scores ranging from 0 to 0.4. From these figures, the published DAST is successful in identifying students known to be dyslexic, and does not generate any false alarms in the sub-group whose performance was checked for this chapter.

Let us consider here which of the DAST tests are the most successful in identifying dyslexia. It is particularly striking that 100% of the dyslexic students showed deficits on the nonsense passage reading. This prompts one to wonder whether it would be sufficient to rely on this test alone to identify adults with dyslexia. Interestingly enough, however, 21% of the non-dyslexic students also show problems with this test, although none of this group shows problems overall. As discussed above, the fewer tests used for screening, the larger percentage of students identified as "at risk," and the greater number of false positives generated. We therefore recommend the full DAST test be administered where feasible.

In terms of strengths in dyslexia, it is interesting to note here that the semantic fluency test is particularly successful as a measure of strengths in dyslexia, with only 24% of the dyslexic students showing problems on this test, and a risk factor of only 0.38. Somewhat by contrast, the evidence for strengths in non-verbal reasoning is more mixed, with some dyslexic students showing considerable strengths in this test, and others experiencing some difficulty. It is interesting to note, however, that only 10% of this sample shows severe problems on this test based on performance in the lowest 5 percentiles. This is entirely consistent with earlier work in our lab with the Raven's matrices, which indicates that some dyslexic children with higher verbal than performance IQ's do not show strengths on non-verbal reasoning tests. We address this in the DAST by including tests designed to identify verbal or non-verbal strengths, or both. Interestingly enough, following recent changes that allow non-psychologists with expertise in dyslexia to diagnose, the DAST has become the instrument of choice in many institutions in the UK.

SUPPORT FOR ADULTS WITH DYSLEXIA AND OTHER LEARNING DIFFICULTIES

In recent research, the Sheffield team has been working on the development of a computer based system for supporting adults with dyslexia and other learning difficulties, funded by the Leverhulme Trust. This system is known as "RITA," the Reader's Interactive Teaching Assistant, and it was designed to help the teacher or support officer in developing a structured program for support, using the benefits of computer-based record keeping. In order to develop an effective program, we consider that assessment must be geared to development of a support program individually designed for the adult in question. Components of such an assessment should include objective measures of reading, writing, and spelling fluency[3], on tests appropriate for adults, coupled with an in-depth interview to analyze not only the strengths and weaknesses of the adult, but also his or her goals. Over the past few years, we have undertaken a series of case studies, with students, adults in employment, and young offenders, in addition to those described in Fawcett and Nicolson 1998. Our experience suggests that it is not enough to consider the literacy needs of the adult, and that the major problem for dyslexic adults may lie in the wider ramifications of dyslexia in everyday life (see also Vogel and Reder 1998, for a series of chapters on learning disabilities in education and employment).

Informal Assessment for Support

In previous work (Fawcett and Nicloson 1998) we have argued that supporting adults with dyslexia may not be appropriate for the chartered psychologist administering the diagnostic testing. This is an equally demanding role requiring extensive experience along with current knowledge of support tools and interaction methods.

An ideal support assessment session would involve the following components: the adult with dyslexia [the client] who needs to analyze his or her higher-order goals in order to outline his or her requirements for support; a dyslexia specialist who can comment on the formal assessment; a support specialist to advise on methods for the achievement of the goals; and a representative of the client's work environment to advise on the demands of the client's work. The goal of the meeting would be to build on collaborative discussions between these experts, in order to develop an "individual development plan." This plan would identify the key objectives for the client and provide a blueprint of the steps needed to achieve those objectives, together with a means of checking that the client was "on course" at subsequent stages of the development plan. This plan would then form the backbone of the subsequent support program, with reasonably frequent subsequent meetings available to monitor progress and to revise the development plan as appropriate. This framework is exactly

---

[3]This aspect of skilled performance is overlooked in many tests of literacy skills. We currently address this by administering components of our DAST test, including 1 minute reading, 1 minute writing, and 2 minute spelling, in addition to a structured interview.

that prescribed by the 1994 U.K. Code of Practice for children with special educational needs, and seems equally appropriate for adults. However, the two critical differences between supporting children and adults are first that the requirements of children are relatively stereotyped acquisition of literacy skills and appropriate knowledge whereas the needs of adults are diverse; and that there is a well-established school educational system that needs merely to be adapted to fit the special needs of exceptional children, whereas for adults there is typically no system available.

In short, therefore, assessment for support is a difficult process requiring not only excellent interactional skills and insight on the part of the support assessor, but also a knowledge of the methods of support available, and how these might be tailored to the client's particular goals. Furthermore, continual monitoring of progress should be available. Consequently, although there are aspects of support assessment that are generic, the assessment should be seen as an integral part of the support process, rather than as an independent stage. We turn now to a discussion of support methods.

Support

As outlined above, support systems need to address the specific problems for each individual, both in terms of their profile of abilities and aspirations, and their circumstances at work or unemployment. This must, of course, be coupled with attempts to ameliorate the more general problems likely to occur for adults with dyslexia. Strikingly, literacy deficits are often accompanied by poor presentation of work and deteriorating performance under time pressure. Moreover, problems in dynamic working memory make it difficult for adults with dyslexia to hold information in mind while they manipulate it, thus leading to a further range of difficulties. Arguably the strongest general problems lie in organizational skills and in the ability to check work. These are natural consequences of limitations in working memory; by slow speed of processing; and by difficulties in skill automatization (Nicolson and Fawcett 1990). McLoughlin et al. (1994) argue strongly (see also Vogel and Adelman 1992) that an even higher level difficulty —a failure to understand one's own strengths and weaknesses, and in particular to predict the effects that dyslexia will have on one's performance—could be the most basic problem, which should be tackled as soon as possible. Consequently, it is clear that any attempt to address just one source of difficulty is likely to lead to only partial success.

There is, of course, a series of well written self-help books, such as Gilroy and Miles (1995) on dyslexia at college, and these, coupled with talks on study skills, are valuable. However, this theoretical approach is limited unless one adds a strong practical component. Adults with dyslexia are particularly vulnerable here, because they may have good reasons to mistrust academic advice, and may not have the self-confidence to attempt to put it into practice. Ideally, training should be based on one-to-one support from a sympathetic and knowledgeable expert, involving both hands-on involvement and insightful feedback. Unfortunately, this type of support is extremely expensive (Higgins and Zvi 1995), and few experts can have both the knowledge of dyslexia and the subject knowledge across the range of topics to fulfill this role adequately.

The entrenched nature of literacy-related disabilities in adults with dyslexia should be acknowledged, in order that nobody be disheartened by relatively slow progress. Often adults have undergone a series of interventions, and they may well have developed a jaundiced view of their ability to succeed. Although we would not advocate avoiding these tricky areas, it may well be helpful to restore the adults' confidence by building in opportunities for success on a different front. The exciting aspect of this work is that adults can make significant strides, but improvement of this type is normally characterized by exceptional levels of determination to succeed. Generally, improvement is a drawn-out process, demanding high levels of motivation and commitment from the client. Consequently, it is important to prioritize each client's requirements, and tailor support to high-priority but achievable targets. In fact, adults typically need more generalized support than children with disabilities, because the difficulties they experience affect all aspects of their life and work. In terms of a general analysis, one can therefore distinguish between literacy-related skills and life-related skills (especially work-related skills). We shall consider each briefly in turn.

Literacy-related Support

Many adults with dyslexia will have struggled with their literacy-related skills such as reading and spelling since childhood. Consequently, they are likely to benefit most from well-tuned individual support, targeted to their skills. Because many adults have become discouraged by their struggles, many would benefit from a fresh approach as well as more traditional support. The best opportunities include computer-based methods, utilizing multimedia resources. However, current computer programs do not provide the systematic and rich support, targeted to the strengths and weaknesses of the user, that a skilled human tutor can provide. We have been working on the development of a complete system for supporting the acquisition of literacy.

Reasons for failure to develop such a system are manifold. Consider the scenario where an experienced teacher is approached by an adult with literacy problems. Open learning principles (e.g., Lewis 1984; 1987) advise that the tutor should start with a discussion in which the learner's wishes are discussed in general terms, followed by an outline discussion of how these aims might be achieved, followed by more detailed discussions that break down the general aims into a series of fully specified objectives, and then develop a plan for the attaining of each objective (starting with the current profile of skills and knowledge and moving to the desired profile of skills and knowledge). It should be clear that this demands a daunting level of expertise (interviewing expertise, for establishing what the learner would really wish to achieve; planning expertise, for determining an appropriate and achievable development plan to achieve these aims; assessment expertise, for assessing the learner's current skills and knowledge; and teaching expertise for working out a method for achieving each objective). Moreover, the teacher also needs access to a very wide range of teaching resources preferably a fully developed, complete teaching system that prescribes a method for helping the learner progress from his or her current state of knowledge/skill to the required next stage as specified on the development plan.

Computers can help at all stages in this process: in presenting spelling and reading programs; in keeping records and compiling progress reports; in semi-automatic assessment of the learner's current profile of skills and knowledge; and in advising the tutor which resources are appropriate and how to structure objectives. This approach is based on the "Teaching Assistant" (Nicolson 1990; Nicolson and Fawcett 1994) a computer system that helps rather than replaces the teacher. Rather than attempting to replace the teacher, this approach takes the point of view of an experienced teacher, and constructs an integrated package to provide help where appropriate. The system involves an established system for automatically maintaining progress records in a "workbook" for each learner, and providing immediate access to a range of teaching resources in a "Resource Book" that can be accessed directly by the teacher to specify, say, a half hour computer-based session. RITA—the "Readers' Interactive Teaching Assistant"—addresses the needs of those with persistent and severe disabilities in literacy in adolescence and adulthood. However, our experience suggests that support for adults should address a wider context, which I outline below.

Wider Support

Problems in literacy may be the least of the difficulties experienced by adults with dyslexia. They may have significantly greater problems with life skills, organizational skills, and working memory limitations. Consequently, although constructing a development plan is appropriate, it is necessary to consider much wider-ranging support.

Naturally enough, the problems for adults in work are very different from those of students. Problems in literacy skills may be relatively intractable, and adults may not wish to struggle with these, nor are there natural sources of support in literacy. It is particularly important to identify people's priorities. Although the primary deficit in dyslexia is in terms of reading, especially at school, difficulties for adults with dyslexia are much more widespread. They can be characterized as consisting of deficits in a range of skills, including the following: lack of automatization (complete fluency) on a wide range of skills; problems in working memory; weakness in time awareness; problems with modes of interaction; and difficulty in concentration. These difficulties may lead to problems with both interpersonal and organizational skills, and thus to difficulties in holding down a job.

Nevertheless, there may be sources of support within the working environment, and I draw here on an analysis from Callahan and Garner (1997), two of the most influential researchers in this area. A particularly valuable component of their approach is that "we seem to be learning over and over again (or forgetting over and over again) the tremendous natural resource that is available in co-workers and friends from the workplace" (p. 75). They then go on to develop what they call the seven phase sequence for support which goes as follows:

1. Communicate natural ways of working (workplace culture, ways of doing job, specifics of job, assisting relationships [involvement of co-workers and supervisors] and procedures);
2. Promote natural means of training (analyze existing training approaches, motivating strategies [flexibility etc.], rules [especially the subtle unwritten rules of the culture]);
3. Utilize natural people for support (supervisors, co-workers, mentors, etc.);
4. Facilitate successful performance (with support from job trainer [PSO]);

If support is successful, no further action will be needed except for occasional monitoring. Otherwise one needs to move to more specialist support, which might include the following:

5. Support/assist/substitute for natural people (co-workers, employees from another shift, job trainer);
6. Reconsider natural means of training (suggest/adjust training and motivating strategies, negotiate rules);

7. Adapt/modify/change natural ways of support (negotiate natural procedures, redo content steps and methods).

This approach is intended for severely disabled (physically disabled or mentally handicapped) people, and the opportunities for use with dyslexia are more limited. Nonetheless, the stress on natural means of support is an important one. It is far more satisfactory if difficulties and training needs are met by natural means. There are clear opportunities here for dyslexia support, but one crucial difference is that, because the severe disabilities are all too obvious, it is relatively easy to engage the sympathy of workmates so that they naturally support the physically learning disabled (PLD) adult. Furthermore, such adults will have been pre-diagnosed, and so it is obvious that pre-emptive support will be valuable. By contrast, because dyslexia is relatively invisible (and because sensitivities to working culture in dyslexic adults are often reduced) it is all too easy to move rapidly to a situation where the obvious sources of natural support are already against the dyslexic adult. Consequently, one obvious need for a good support strategy is to identify who is dyslexic and therefore more likely to need support (especially when changes such as greater reliance on IT) are being considered.

CONCLUSIONS

There is a pressing need to develop valid and objective methods of diagnosing dyslexia in people of all ages. This has been exacerbated by the demands of the U.K. Disability Discrimination Act, which forces support systems to be created for education and employment. There is a reasonable consensus throughout the dyslexia community that a two stage diagnosis process may be the most cost-effective solution to this need. The first stage of a typical two stage diagnostic process involves an initial low-cost screening undertaken by a support officer. Those screened as being "at risk" should then be given the option of a much more thorough, objective test for dyslexia administered by a fully qualified psychometric tester. This testing procedure should lead in turn to the development of an individual development program tailored to the individual's profile of strengths, weaknesses, and objectives. In this chapter, I have described the Adult Dyslexia Index (ADI), which fulfills the criteria for an objective and valid full test for dyslexia. The ADI diagnoses dyslexia, and quantifies its severity. I have also outlined the Dyslexia Adult Screening Test which fulfills the requirements for a quick but informative screening test. The DAST is a 30 minute screening test that not only provides a quick dyslexia index but also identifies areas of strength and weakness. Specific applications within higher education have been outlined, but it should be emphasized that the approach is of general applicability, and can be used in a variety of populations, from young offenders to adult literacy classes to general personnel selection and employee support. It is argued that there is limited value in assessing for dyslexia unless this leads naturally into a systematic support system designed to be appropriate for the specific needs of that adult. A major component of any support system is therefore the development of an individual development plan, identifying areas the adult seeks to change. The major implications of this concluding section are the need to tackle problems before they become too entrenched, in order to ensure the most successful outcome.

ACKNOWLEDGMENTS

This research was partially supported by a grant from the Leverhulme Trust and the Psychological Corporation (Europe).

REFERENCES

Badian, N. A. 1984. Reading disability in an epidemiological context: Incidence and environmental correlates. *Journal of Learning Disabilities* 17:129–36.

Bradley, L., and Bryant, P. E. 1983. Categorising sounds and learning to read: A causal connection. *Nature* 301:419–21.

Brachacki, G. W. Z., Fawcett, A. J., and Nicolson, R. I. 1995. Impaired recognition of traffic signs in adults with dyslexia. *Journal of Learning Disabilities* 28:297–308.

Callahan, M. J., and Garner, J. B. 1997. *Keys to the Workplace: Skills and Supports for People with Disabilities.* Baltimore, MD: Paul H. Brookes.

Critchley, M. 1964. *Developmental Dyslexia.* London: Heinemann.

Denckla, M. B., and Rudel, R. G. 1976. Rapid 'Automatized' naming (R.A.N.). Dyslexia differentiated from other learning disabilities. *Neuropsychologia* 14:471–79.

Department for Education 1994. *The Code of Practice on the Identification and Assessment of Special Educational Needs.* London: HMSO.

Fawcett, A. J. 1995. Case studies and some recent research. In *Dyslexia and Stress*, eds. T. R. Miles and V. Varma. London, Whurr.

Fawcett, A. J. and Nicolson, R. I. 1993. *Validation of the Adult Dyslexia Index*, Internal report LRG 93/16, University of Sheffield, Dept. of Psychology.

Fawcett, A. J. and Nicolson, R. I. 1995a. Persistent deficits in motor skill for children with dyslexia. *Journal of Motor Behavior* 27:235–40.

Fawcett, A. J. and Nicolson, R. I. 1995b. Persistence of phonological awareness deficits in older children with dyslexia. *Reading and Writing: An Interdisciplinary Journal* 7:361–76.

Fawcett, A. J. and Nicolson, R. I. 1994c. Naming speed in children with dyslexia. *Journal of Learning Disabilities* 27:271–76.

Fawcett, A. J. and Nicolson, R. I. 1996. *The Dyslexia Screening Test.* London: The Psychological Corporation (Europe).

Fawcett, A. J. and Nicolson, R. I. 1998. *The Dyslexia Adult Screening Test.* London: The Psychological Corporation (Europe).

Fawcett, A. J., Nicolson, R. I., and Dean, P. 1996. Impaired performance of children with dyslexia on a range of cerebellar tasks. *Annals of Dyslexia* 46:259–83.

Fawcett, A. J. and Nicolson, R. I. 1998. Learning disabilities in adults: screening and diagnosis in the U.K. In *Learning Disabilities, Literacy and Adult Education.* Baltimore: Paul H. Brookes.

Fawcett, A. J., Pickering, S., and Nicolson, R. I. 1993. Development of the DEST test for the early screening for dyslexia. In *Facets of Dyslexia and its Remediation*, eds. S. F. Wright and R. Groner. Amsterdam: Elsevier Science Publishers B.V.

Felton, R. H., Naylor, C. E., and Wood, F. B. 1990. Neuropsychological profile of adult dyslexics. *Brain and Language* 39:485–97.

Finucci, J. M., Guthrie, J. T., Childs, A. L., Abbey, H., and Childs, B. 1976. The genetics of specific reading disability. *Annals of Human Genetics* 50:1–23.

Frith, U., Landerl, K., and Frith, C. 1995. Dyslexia and verbal fluency: More evidence for a phonological deficit. *Dyslexia* 1:2–11

Gilroy, D. E. and Miles, T. R. 1995. *Dyslexia at College.* 2nd edition. London: Routledge.

Gross-Glenn, K., Jallad, B., Novoa, L, and Helgren-Lempesis V. 1990. Nonsense Passage reading as a diagnostic aid in the study of adult familial dyslexia. *Reading and Writing* 2:161–73

Higgins, E. L. and Zvi, J. C. 1995. Assistive technology for postsecondary students with learning disabilities: From research to practice. *Annals of Dyslexia* 45:123–42.

Jorm, A. F., Share, D. L., McLean, R., and Matthews, D. 1986. Cognitive factors at school entry predictive of specific reading retardation and general reading backwardness: A research note. *Journal of Child Psychology and Psychiatry and Allied Disciplines* 27:45–54.

LaBerge, D. and Samuels, S. J. 1974. Toward a theory of automatic information processing in reading. *Cognitive Psychology* 6:293–323.

Lewis, R. 1984. How to tutor and support learners. *Open Learning Guide 3*, London: CET.

Lewis, R. 1987. How to help learners assess their progress. *Open Learning Guide 2*, London: CET.

McLoughlin, D., Fitzgibbon G. and Young, V. 1994. *Adult Dyslexia: Assessment, Counselling and Training.* London: Whurr.

Miles, T. R. 1983. *Dyslexia: The Pattern of Difficulties.* London: Granada.

Nicolson, R. I. 1990. Design and Evaluation of the SUMIT Intelligent Tutoring Assistant for Arithmetic. *Interactive Learning Environments* 1:265–87.

Nicolson, R. I. 1996. Developmental dyslexia: Past, present and future. *Dyslexia: An International Journal of Research and Practice* 2:190–208.

Nicolson, R. I. and Fawcett, A. J. 1990. Automaticity: A new framework for dyslexia research? *Cognition* 35:159–82.

Nicolson, R. I and Fawcett, A. J. 1994a. Comparison of deficits in cognitive and motor skills among children with dyslexia. *Annals of Dyslexia* 44:147–64.

Nicolson, R. I. and Fawcett, A. J. 1994b. Reaction times and dyslexia. Quarterly Journal of *Experimental Psychology* 47A:29–48.

Nicolson, R. I. and Fawcett, A. J. 1994c. Spelling remediation for dyslexic children: A skills approach. In *Handbook of Spelling: Theory, Process and Intervention*, eds. G. D. A. Brown and N.C. Ellis. Chichester: Wiley.

Nicolson, R. I. and Fawcett, A. J. 1995. Dyslexia is more than a phonological disability. *Dyslexia: An International Journal of Research and Practice* 1:19–37.

Nicolson, R. I. and Fawcett, A. J. 1996. *The Dyslexia Early Screening Test.* London: The Psychological Corporation (Europe).

Nicolson, R. I., Fawcett, A. J., and Dean, P. 1995. Time estimation deficits in developmental dyslexia: Evidence for cerebellar involvement. *Proceedings of the Royal Society* 259:43–47.

Nicolson, R. I., Fawcett, A. J., and Miles, T. R. 1993. Feasibility study for the development of a computerised screening test for dyslexia in adults. Report OL176, Employment Department.

Siegel, L. S. 1989. IQ is irrelevant to the definition of Learning Disabilities. *Journal of Learning Disabilities* 22:469–78.

Singleton, C. 1996. Dyslexia in higher education: Issues for policy and practice. In *Proceedings of 'Skill' Conference "Dyslexic Students in Higher Education: Practical Responses to Student and Institution Needs."* Huddersfield: University of Huddersfield/National Bureau for Students with Disabilities.

Smith, S. D., Kimberling, W. J., Pennington, B. F., and Lubs, H. A. 1983. Specific reading disability: Identification of an inherited form through linkage and analysis. *Science* 219:1345–7.

Stanovich, K. E. and Siegel, L. S. 1994. The phenotypic performance profile of reading-disabled children: A regression-based test of the phonological-core variable-difference model. *Journal of Educational Psychology* 27:91–103.

Thomson, M. E. 1984. *Developmental Dyslexia: Its Nature, Assessment and Remediation.* London: Edward Arnold.

Vogel, S. A. 1998. Adults with learning disabilities: What learning disabilities specialists, adult literacy educatiors and other service providers want and need to know. In *Learning Disabilities, Literacy and Adult Education,* eds. S. A. Vogel and S. Reder. Baltimore: MD: Paul H. Brookes Co.

Vogel, S. A. and Adelman, P. B. 1992. The success of college students with learning disabilities; Factors related to educational attainment. *Journal of Learning Disabilities* 25:430–41.

Wechsler, D. 1976. *The Wechsler Intelligence Scale for Children - Revised* (U.K. edition). Sidcup, Kent: The Psychological Corporation.

Wechsler, D. 1986. *The Wechsler Adult Intelligence Scale - Revised* (U.K. edition). Sidcup, Kent: The Psychological Corporation.

Wechsler, D. 1986. *The Wechsler Objective Reading Dimension.* Sidcup, Kent: The Psychological Corporation.

Wechsler, D. 1998. *The Wechsler Adult Intelligence Scale–III* (UK) London: The Psychological Corporation.

World Federation of Neurology 1968. Report of research group on dyslexia and world illiteracy. Dallas: WFN.

Vogel, S. A, and Reder, S. eds. *Learning Disabilities, Literacy and Adult Education.* Baltimore: Paul. H. Brookes.

Yap, R. L., and van der Leij, A. 1993. Word processing in dyslexics: An automatic decoding deficit? *Reading and Writing: An Interdisciplinary Journal* 5:261–79.

PART • III

Program Models and Support Services Issues in Higher Education

Part three includes four chapters that present support services issues regarding students with learning disabilities in higher education. The first chapter in this section (Chapter 8) addresses the more general question of who shall determine the nature of these models and services. Noel Gregg, Margaret Morrison, and Phillip Cohn encourage us to listen to the voices of the consumers (the students with learning disabilities), service providers, and faculty in constructing the models and providing support services to students with learning disabilities in higher education. The authors stress the importance of hearing the personal narratives of all the participants and recommend employing the strategies of PAR (participant action research) and collaborative research.

The next three chapters in this section deal with issues pertaining to ADHD, assistive technology, and faculty attitude and knowledge regarding students with learning disabilities. Lynda Katz (Chapter 9) focuses on the support services she feels are needed by students with ADHD in higher education. After briefly reviewing issues of identification, requirements for documentation, gender differences, and co-morbidity, she discusses interventions and accommodations. These interventions include mediation as well as education and self-awareness components of support programs. Katz also discusses the use of coaching in the context of higher education.

In Chapter 10, Marshall Raskind and Eleanor Higgins focus on the use of assistive technology as a support service for postsecondary students with learning disabilities. They provide a history of the use of this technology with this population, describe both the range of the technologies currently available as well as the various models used to deliver the services, and discuss the current research on the effectiveness of these technologies.

The final chapter in this section (Chapter 11) looks at a very different aspect of university life that has an impact on students with learning disabilities. It focuses on faculty knowledge, attitudes, and practices towards these students. Yona Leyser, Susan Vogel, Sharon Wyland, Andrew Brulle, Varda Sharoni, and Gila Vogel conducted a cross-cultural study of knowledge and attitudes of faculties at Northern Illinois University in the United States and Beit Berl College in Israel. The researchers examined faculty attitudes as expressed in their willingness to make accommodations in both teaching and examinations, and compared views regarding students with learning disabilities enrolled in teacher education as opposed to other fields. In an effort to understand the identified differences, they examined the impact of several background variables (age, gender, academic degree, and years of college teaching) on faculty attitudes and practices. The results indicated the need for increasing institution-wide awareness and knowledge regarding LD and closer cooperation between support services staff and faculty.

Chapter • 8

Service Provision: Listening to the Dialogue Among and Between Critical Voices

Noel Gregg, Margaret Morrison, and Phillip Cohn

The extremely litigious atmosphere currently observed in the United States, while stimulating important discussion surrounding definition, documentation, and accommodation for disabilities, has unfortunately often been viewed as the stalwart of best practice by many Americans. It is important to remember that the courts in the United States operate from the nondiscrimination mandates of Section 504 of the Rehabilitation Act (1992) and the Americans with Disabilities Act (1990), examining objective evidence to ensure nondiscrimination in individual circumstances (Gregg and Scott, 2000). The framework for best practice, rather than being constructed by court cases, is best based upon theory and empirically based research across disciplines. Action research generated by consumers and professionals involved in post-secondary services and research should be the driving force guiding practice. As Gregg and Scott (2000) stated, "These professionals need to structure college services that address nondiscrimination mandates but are grounded in current research and theory pertaining to LD and ADHD" (p. 10). Future research needs to focus directly on the definition and selection criteria that is most effective in matching accommodation needs across severity and contexts for the college population with learning disabilities. The issues surrounding definition and selection criteria for college students with learning disabilities are addressed in depth by Gregg in this book (see chapter 6).

The purpose of this chapter is to encourage closer attention to the voices of consumers, service providers, and faculty in our attempts to construct effective system supports for college students with learning disabilities. Listening to these voices and connecting them to research-based knowledge is vital to a more meaningful understanding of learning disabilities (Gregg and Ferri 1996). As Gregg and Ferri (1996) stated, careful attention to these voices provides a unique observation of the "passion behind the words testifying to a lived reality that can rarely be voiced or named from a distance" (Hooks 1994, p. 517).

THEORETICAL FRAMEWORK

Mikhail Bakhtin's literary and linguistic theories will be used to inform and critique this discussion of engaging the voices of consumers, service providers, and faculty in directing our vision of current and future access to the needs of college students with learning disabilities. Bakhtin (1981) proposed that language is never unitary, but rather that utterances are always spoken in relationship to another's word (heteroglossia). He argued that all voices must be heard, some often speaking in conflict with the language that attempts to marginalize or silence. Essential to Bakhtin's theories is the idea that meaning is always dialogically associated with voices that are "inherently situated in a sociocultural context" (Wertsch 1991, p. 66). Meaning, according to Bakhtin, requires participation rather than observation (Emerson and Holquist 1986). Therefore, understanding and constructing meaning demands that a person have access to orient herself or himself to a context and engage in dialogue across differences (Morris 1994).

The concept of polyphony, a belief in a "plurality of equally valid consciousnesses" or voices (Morris 1994, p. 93) is also central to Bakhtin's theories. It was his belief that there is never one voice even within a single word uttered by an individual, but rather that there are many voices that interact dialogically. Therefore, one voice should not be engulfed by another (Morris 1994) and it should be recognized that even the self in conversation with the self is peopled with others (Emerson and Holquist 1986).

Silence, in the Bakhtinian view, is the "great enemy" of dialogue since dialogue depends on reciprocity, not sameness (Pearce 1994). Either refusing to speak or not being allowed to speak represents power over others, eliminating shared understanding of meaning across contexts. As Gregg and Ferri (1998) noted, "To truly engage in a dialogue with a narrative, one must listen carefully to gaps, silences, and even contradictions" (Chase 1992) (p. 518). Most importantly, Bakhtin suggested that we always place dialogue within its larger social, cultural, and historical context in order to interpret its meaning to self and others (Clark and Holquist 1986).

The work of Bakhtin has contributed to a better understanding of the importance of the narrative. Bakhtin's theories stress that "the lived experience as told through narratives be used to dialogue with self in exploring the boundaries between centrality and marginality" (Gregg and Willingham 1999, p. 10). Narratives provide a means by which to allow oppressed voice agency. In addition, narratives provide multiple interpreters of the many voices representing the oppressed across different social, cultural, and political contexts (Gregg and Willingham 1999).

PARTICIPATORY ACTION PROCESS

Recent interest in participatory action research (PAR) provides a strategy for integrating the meaning generated by the dialogue among consumers, service providers, and faculty that is true to the theories of Bakhtin. Participatory action research recognizes the need for persons being studied to participate in designing and conducting all phases of the research that affects them. As Whyte, Greenwood, and Lazes (1990) noted, PAR has its roots in social anthropology and sociology. In PAR, " some of the people in the organization or community under study participate actively with the professional researcher throughout the research process from the initial design to the final presentation of results and discussion of their action implications" (Whyte, Greenwood, and Lazes 1990, p. 20). Participatory action research is an approach to or a strategy for research, not a methodology (National Institute on Disability and Rehabilitation Research, November 1994). Therefore, PAR is an independent process, not dependent one. Participatory action research can be used with qualitative and/or quantitative research designs. "Active involvement with practitioners struggling to solve important practical problems is highly likely to open up researchers' minds to new information and new ideas, leading to advances in theory as well as in practice" (Whyte, Greenwood, and Lazes 1990, p. 54). Use of PAR in future research and service projects focusing on the college population with learning disabilities appears to be an effective means of better understanding the meaning behind the voices of consumers, service providers, and faculty engaged in university communities.

CONSUMER VOICES

The voice of students with learning disabilities has been the most predominant narrative voice in the literature, yet the most underrepresented voice if one were to evaluate from a PAR framework.

Very little research, qualitative or quantitative, is conducted in the field of learning disabilities utilizing a PAR framework. Although there is a growing number of personal accounts from consumers (Adelman and Wren 1990; Cohn 1998; Lee and Jackson 1992; Murphy 1992; Reiling n.d.; Stolowitz 1995; Wren and Segal 1991) describing experiences in higher education, the ability of these consumers to participate in the design and conducting of research (PAR) exploring issues that have an impact on the adult population with learning disabilities has been sorely lacking across disciplines. In addition, the voices from a larger sample of college students, representing greater diversity, are needed so that we can better understand the full spectrum of individuals with learning disabilities and the effects of living with learning disabilities across the life span.

The personal narratives of college students with learning disabilities, however, do provide rich and descriptive data by which to interpret service and research agendas. Scott and Gregg (in press) reviewed these personal accounts with respect to their implications for faculty development. They found limited but interesting results showing that college students with learning disabilities reported physical, programmatic, and attitudinal barriers to higher education (West et al. 1993). Cohn (1998) and Lee and Jackson (1992) eloquently testified to the pain and fear of dealing with learning disabilities at a post-secondary institution, a theme frequently encountered across many consumer narratives (Ferri 1998). In particular, Cohn (1998) described issues surrounding feelings of alienation, intense drive to succeed, and a need to wear masks that led to a feeling of loss of self. "Fear of losing face with peers and professors may stimulate students with LD to mask their secret shame and avoid situations in which they have to perform in their weak areas" (Cohn, p. 516). Cohn further explained that in his determination to avoid the anxiety associated with fear of rejection and feelings of shame, he often protected his selfesteem by wearing masks of super-competence and activity. By pretending that he was always involved in some project and could talk his way out of any situation, Cohn attempted to exude an aura of self-confidence and stability that hid his weaknesses.

Ferri (1998) reported the testimony of Hali, a woman with learning disabilities attending college, whose words eloquently encapsulate this threat to the sense of self:

> My shadow self is the person who is defeated by life. I used to be very defeated. [I] never thought that I was worth anything. Sometimes, when I least expected it, those aggravating feelings creep back into my life Anyway, that shadow has been lurking over my shoulder during my graduate school career and I will be glad to be finished with this leg of my journey. Maybe the shadow will disappear for awhile (p.93).

The feeling of loss of identity by the wearing of masks, "faking it," or trying to appear identical to the able in society is a theme that appears throughout the narratives of many college students with learning disabilities. These voices of students with learning disabilities remind us that "anyone who thinks that it is not a big deal to transpose a number or misspell a word" (Ferri 1998, p. 187) should be informed that a single misspelled word can call up past negative memories of being punished or laughed at for being different. The significance of an error to a person with learning disabilities should not be underestimated or discounted, as memories can dominate current performance or perceptions of self/others. The fear that students with learning disabilities will lose the respect of others when their disabilities are discovered can be so intense that it prevents them from achieving their true potential. In fact, "in their determination to achieve equal respect with peers, in what they see as an extremely critical society, individuals with LD often keep stored years of repressed negative thoughts and emotions" (Cohn 1998, p. 516).

Researchers, service providers, and faculty listening to the voices of these students with learning disabilities might choose opportunities that will incorporate consumer voices as well as active participation into future research and service activities. Listening to and validating student voices by co-authorship or co-research opportunities raises the consumer from a position of marginalized powerlessness. In addition, the recent longitudinal follow-up research on adults with learning disabilities discussed throughout this text will contribute to a better understanding of the voices of consumers (Buca et al. 1998; Raskind et al. 1998).

SERVICE PROVIDER VOICES

Service providers represent another voice critical to better understanding the construction of effective services to college students with learning disabilities. Service providers make many of the important decisions regarding the provision of services and the involvement of consumers and faculty at post-secondary institutions. To truly change best practice, the voices of the people doing the practicing need to be heard. The majority of research focusing on service providers has been collected with questionnaires; little qualitative interviewing can be found that features, in the words of service providers, their perceptions and feelings about their multiple roles. Much of this questionnaire-based research has focused on service providers' attitudes and perceptions of services for students and the role of faculty. It is the responsibility of service providers to reinforce the federal mandates being implemented daily on college campuses, as well as to operationalize the broader mandates of campus support services. Yet this central and mediating collective voice is rarely given the stage to present its own narratives. The emphasis in the literature from a service provider perspective has been on what services are provided rather than on listening to the who and the why in service provision. Interestingly, there are currently several list-serves where service providers' voices are heard over e-mail, indeed very active list-serves. Yet very few narratives of service providers, in their own voices, are seen in the learning disabilities literature, particularly in research journals. To create and evaluate a more effective system of service delivery at the post-secondary level, we need to better understand the how and why by listening to the voices of service providers.

FACULTY VOICES

Faculty voices can be read in the literature through anecdotal accounts ranging from extremely negative to positive descriptions of students with learning disabilities. For instance, Lampkin (1995) reported comments from an e-mail survey asking faculty about their experiences working with students with learning disabilities: "Making arrangements for students is a frustrating waste of time"; "Stop telling us how we have to lower standards for learning needs people." Yet other faculty in this same survey reported, "I have often found the students with learning disabilities to be very, very good students who have learned how to cope to the point that many refuse extra consideration" (Lampkin 1995, p. 13). There appears to be a range of viewpoints from individual faculty in response to the roles of providing programmatic access for students with learning disabilities (Scott and Gregg, in press). Such a diversity of responses is likely related to the extent that faculty are able to incorporate access efforts with their faculty roles and what are used as reinforcers (Scott 1992; Scott and Gregg, in press).

    The majority of research investigating faculty participation with college students with learning disabilities, like research on service providers, does not focus on the faculty's own voice in defining their roles and relationships. Predominately, the research has assessed, via questionnaire, faculty attitudes toward students with learning disabilities and their willingness to accommodate such students in instructional settings. Scott and Gregg (in press) discuss a systemic approach, based on the literature, to faculty education at individual, institutional, and disciplinary levels. However, what is missing from their suggestions is the integral role PAR can play in the development of faculty educational needs in providing access for college students with learning disabilities. More opportunity for faculty to talk to each other, service providers, and consumers is what is really missing from the process of evaluating current systems and designing more collaboration between agencies and disciplines on college campuses. This can only add to everyone's ability to handle the complications and difficulties of providing services. The faculty attitude studies being conducted by Ben-Uehunda et al. (1998) discussed in this text are leading the way in better understanding faculty voices.

CONCLUSION

A narrative is the form by which "life events are conjoined into coherent, meaningful, unified themes" (Polkinghorne 1994, p. 126). The narration of an individual represents a self in dialogue with itself and the world, grappling "with the confusion and complexity of the human condition" (Josselson 1995, p. 32). Using the narratives and stories of others is an interpretive exercise requiring listening to (rather than giving) knowledge (Riessman 1993). The stories people tell about themselves are a constantly changing and socially constructed means by which to view perceptions and beliefs individuals have.

Bakhtin's theories were presented as a theoretical framework that has much to offer consumers, service providers, faculty, and researchers searching for ways to develop and evaluate appropriate and effective services for college students with learning disabilities. Yet the use of these theories, operationalized through PAR, require participation—not observation—on the part of the entire social context being studied. Participatory action research laces motives and concepts dialectically, beginning with the unit of activity (Leontiev 1978). Unlike mechanistic or behavioral models, the individual in such a theory is integrally involved in the process of knowing. Paradigms or theories focusing on the verb or action form of knowledge appear to provide a critical perspective necessary in addressing many of the issues related to the college population with learning disabilities (Gregg and Ferri 1996). In addition, as Wertsch (1991) noted, "A Bakhtinian orientation to meaning leads down paths not often traveled in social science analysis, paths that explore voices, social language, speech genres and dialogicality" (p. 6). These paths will lead to the use of different paradigms, theories, and methods.

Valuing by recognizing and listening to the voices of consumers, services providers, and faculty, thereby allotting power to such voices, is the critical first step in developing future research and service agendas for accommodating students with learning disabilities at the post-secondary level. The underlying principle of PAR is that many voices are participants interested in helping to solve the problems facing individuals with disabilities. All voices are needed in identifying possible improvements to programmatic access. Gregg and Ferri (1996) cautioned that use of the plural "voices" is critical to recognizing that many different voices across and within the groups representing consumers, service providers, and faculty must be heard, not just those that are politically in tune with the philosophy of the researcher, service agency, or professional organizations representing different advocacy issues.

The need for collaborative research and service activities between consumers, service providers, faculty, and researchers will "disrupt and transform the relationships, boundaries, and claims of expertise between researchers and the researched" (Gregg and Ferri 1996, p. 47). Narrative accounts of perceptions and experiences representing all of the partners (consumers, service providers, and faculty) need to be presented in allotted space across professional journals. For as Shakespeare, 1995, noted, "having the space to tell them [our stories], and an audience which will listen all starts with having a voice" (p.16). Unfortunately, very few editors of the major research journals in the field of learning disabilities are willing to include narratives. The silencing of the voices of consumers, service providers, and faculty by excluding narratives from research journals allows academics and researchers to control the power and knowledge disseminated about the needs of college students with learning disabilities. Allowing these voices to be represented provides the connection between meaning as perceived by those who speak and the larger bodies of research-based knowledge, with the outcome being further understanding and dialogue.

REFERENCES

Adelman, P., and Wren, C. 1990. Learning disabilities, graduate school, and careers: The student perspective. (Available from Learning Opportunities Program, Barat College, 700 Westleigh, R., Lake Forest, IL, 60045).
Bakhtin, M.M. 1981. *The Dialogic Imagination: Four Essays.* M. Holquist, C. Emerson, and M. Holquist, Trans. Austin. University of Texas Press.
Bakhtin, M. M. 1986. *Speech Genres and Other Late Essays.* C. Emerson and M. Holquist, eds.: V. W. McGee, Trans. Austin: University of Texas Press.
Ben-Uehunda, M., Leyser, Y., Vogel, S., and Vogel, G. 1998. Faculty attitude towards students with learning disabilities. Paper presented at the International Conference on Adults with Learning Disabilities in Higher Education, July 7–9, Beit Berl College, Israel.
Buca, S. L., Satz, P., Seidman, L., and Lipsitt, L. 1998. Defining learning disabilities: The role of longitudinal research. *Thalamus* 16(2):14–29.
Chase, J. 1992. The self and collective action: Dilemmatic identities. In *Social Psychology of Identify and the Self-concept*, ed. G. M. Breakwell. London: Surrey University Press.

Clark, K., and Holquist, M. 1986. A continuing dialoge. *Slavic and East European Journal* 30,1: 96–102.

Cohn, P. 1998. Why does my stomach hurt? How individuals with learning disabilities can use cognitive strategies to reduce anxiety and stress at the college level. *Journal of Learning Disabilities* 31:514–17.

Emerson, C., and Holquist, M. (eds.). Bakhtin, M. M. 1986. *Speech Genres and Other Late Essays* V. W. McGee, Trans. Austin: University of Texas Press.

Ferri, B. 1998. The construction of identity among women with learning disabilities: The many faces of the self. Unpublished dissertation, The University of Georgia.

Gregg, N., and Ferri, F. 1998. Paradigms: A need for radical reform. In *Adults with Learning Disabilities: Theoretical and Practical Perspectives*, eds. N. Gregg, C. Hoy, and A. Gay. New York: Guilford Press.

Gregg, N., and Scott, S. 2000. Definition and documentation: Theory, measurement and the courts. *Journal of Learning Disabilities*. 33:5–13.

Gregg, N., and Willingham, C. 1999. Ambiguity and alienation: Beauvoirs, Bakhtin and Women with disabilities. Paper presented at 50th Anniversary of the Second Sex, IRESCO-CNRS, Paris, France.

Hooks, B. 1990. Postmodern blackness. In *Yearnings*. Boston: South End Press.

Josselson, R. 1995. Imagining the real: Empathy, narrative, and the dialogic self. In *Interpreting Experience: The Narrative Study of Lives*, eds. R. J. Jacobsen and A. Lieblich. Thousand Oaks, CA: Sage.

Lampkin, P. 1995.Faculty survey. Unpublished manuscript. University of Virginia, Charlottesville.

Lee, C., and Jackson, R. 1992. *Faking It: A Look into the Mind of a Creative Learner*. Portsmouth, NH: Boynton/Cook.

Leontiev, K. 1968. The novels of Count L. N. Tolstoy: Analysis, style and atmosphere. In *Essays in Russian Literature: The Conservative View*, Ed. S. Roberts. Athens, Ohio: University Press.

Morris, P. (ed.). 1994. *The Bakhtin Reader: Selected Writings of Bakhtin, Medvedev, Voloshinov*, NY: Edward Arnold.

Murphy, S. 1992. *On Being LD: Perspectives and Strategies of Young Adults*. New York: Teachers' College Press.

Pearce, L. 1994. *Reading Dialogics*. NY: Edward Arnold.

Polkinghorne, D. E. 1994. *Narrative Knowing and the Human Sciences*. Albany, NY: State University of New York Press.

Raskind, M. H., Higgins, E. L., Goldberg, R. J., and Herman, K. 1998. Patterns of change and predictors of success in individuals with learning disabilities: Results from a twenty-year longitudinal study. *Thalamus* 16:40–64.

Reiling, C. undated. How significant is "significant?" A personal glimpse of life with a learning disability. (Available from the Association on Higher Education and Disability, PO Box 21192, Columbus, OH, 43221–0192.)

Reissman, C. K. 1993. *Narrative Analysis*. Newbury Park, CA: Sage.

Scott, S. 1992. National survey of special education faculty involvement with college students with disabilities. *Teacher Education and Special Education* 15(4):284–294.

Scott, S., and Gregg, N. In press. Meeting the evolving education needs of faculty in providing access for college students with learning disabilities. *Journal of Learning Disabilities*.

Shakespeare, T. April 1995. Disability, identity, difference. Paper presented at the "Chronic Illness and Disability: Bridging the Divide" conference, Leeds, UK.

Stolowitz, M. 1995. How to achieve academic and creative success in spite of the inflexible, unresponsive higher education system. *Journal of Learning Disabilities* 28:4–6.

Wertsch, J. V. 1991. *Voices of the Mind: A Sociocultural Approach to Mediated Action.* Cambridge, MA: Harvard University Press.

West, M., Kregel, J., Getzel, E., Zhu, M. Ipsen, S., and Martin, E. 1993. Beyond Section 504: Satisfaction and empowerment of students with disabilities in higher education. *Exceptional Children* 59(5):456–67.

Whyte, W. F., Greenwood, D. J., and Lazes, P. 1990. Participatory action research: Through practice to science in social research. In *Participatory Action Research*, ed. W. F. Whyte. Newbury Park, CA: Sage.

Wren, C., and Segal, L. 1991. College students with learning disabilities: A student's perspective (Available from Project Learning Strategies, DePaul University, SAC 220, 2323 N. Seminary, Chicago, IL, 60614).

Chapter • 9

Students with ADHD in Higher Education

Lynda J. Katz

Although attention-deficit/hyperactivity disorder (ADHD) is commonly diagnosed in childhood with prevalence rates of between 6% and 9% reported among the school-aged population (Anderson et al. 1987; Safer and Krager 1988), systematic epidemiological data on rates of adults with ADHD are lacking (Wilens, Spencer, and Biederman 1995). However, a number of long-term follow-up studies have found that in as many as 50% of adults diagnosed with ADHD in childhood, symptoms of the disorder remain problematic (Gittelman et al. 1985; Weiss and Hechtman 1986). It has been estimated as well that 1% to 3% of the college-aged population has ADHD with symptoms severe enough to warrant treatment and/or accommodations (Barkley 1993). Data likewise indicate that an increasing number of students with learning disabilities are entering post-secondary institutions (Henderson 1995; Dowdy, Carter, and Smith 1990; Mangrum and Strichart 1988). Studies of children diagnosed with learning disabilities have found comorbidity rates of 40% to 60% for ADHD (Cantwell and Baker 1991), so there is reason to suppose that these same rates would hold for the college-age population.

Entrance into college marks a major event in the life of any young adult. When adjustment to post-secondary academic life is complicated by a pre-existing or yet-to-be-diagnosed underlying attention deficit disorder, the potential for failure is high. This chapter focuses on those factors that affect the transition to the college/university setting of students with ADHD as well as their successful matriculation thereafter. Specifically, I look at the issues of identification and diagnosis, current requirements for documentation, gender differences, confounding variables such as comorbidity and substance abuse, the use of medications, guidelines for reasonable accommodations, and appropriate interventions at the post-secondary level.

THE DIAGNOSTIC PROCESS

For a diagnosis of ADHD to be made, diagnostic criteria as set forth in the *Diagnostic and Statistical Manual of Mental Disorders* (DSM-IV) of the American Psychiatric Association (1994) must be met. Six or more symptoms of inattention and/or hyperactivity-impulsivity must be present and must have persisted for at least six months to a degree that is maladaptive (clinically significant impairment) and inconsistent with developmental level. In addition, some of the symptoms must have been present before the age of seven, and some impairment from the symptoms must be present in two or more settings. Finally, the symptoms do not occur exclusively during the course of another disorder or are not better accounted for by another mental disorder. Three subtypes are identified: Attention-Deficit/Hyperactivity Disorder, Combined Type; Attention-Deficit/Hyperactivity Disorder, Predominantly Inattentive Type; and Attention-Deficit/Hyperactivity Disorder, Predominantly Hyperactive-Impulsive Type. A fourth category, Attention-Deficit/Hyperactivity Disorder Not Otherwise Specified (NOS) is provided for disorders with prominent symptoms of inattention or hyperactivity-impulsivity.

Amen and Goldman (1998) have used SPECT studies in their diagnostic work with individuals as an adjunct to the evaluation process. Their work stems from the earlier PET data reported by Zametkin et al. (1990), which found underactivity in the prefrontal cortex in response to a cognitive challenge. In addition, other studies have reported that the basal ganglia are smaller in individuals with ADHD (Castellanos et al. 1994; Castellanos et al. 1996). A significant amount of dopamine is produced in the basal ganglia which then sends nerve tracks through the limbic system and on to the frontal lobes. Studies also support the notion that ADHD has a large genetic component which involves dopamine availability in the brain (Comings et al. 1991; Blum et al. 1996). In fact, most recently in five separate studies a link has been uncovered between ADHD and DRD4, a repeater gene, and that the 7-repeat form of the gene was over-represented among children with ADHD (Lahoste et al. 1996). This gene has been previously associated with high novelty seeking behavior (Benjamin et al. 1996; Ebstein et al. 1996). A variant of this gene affects responsiveness to certain psychiatric drugs (Van Tol et al. 1992); and the gene seems to affect post-synaptic sensitivity, primarily in frontal and prefrontal cortical regions, regions believed to be associated with executive functions and attention (Swanson et al. 1997).

Based upon their SPECT studies, Amen and Goldman (1998) postulated five clinical subtypes of ADHD: (1) ADHD, combined type with symptoms of both inattention and hyperactivity-impulsivity; (2) ADHD, primarily inattentive type (both types show decreased activity in the basal ganglia and prefrontal cortex during a concentration task); (3) Over-focused ADD, with increased activity in the anterior cingulate gyrus and decreased prefrontal cortex activity and associated with obsessive type behaviors; (4) Temporal Lobe ADD, with increased or decreased activity in the temporal lobes and decreased prefrontal cortex activity and associated with aggressive behaviors; and (5) Limbic ADD, with increased central limbic system activity and decreased prefrontal cortex activity with associated low arousal.

Although research into subtypes, such as the work of Amen, continues to occur, currently DSM-IV criteria must still be met before a diagnosis of ADHD can be made. However, the application of these criteria to adults has been somewhat problematic. As Stein et al. (1995) point out, the establishment of these criteria was based primarily on studies of boys. Therefore, issues of gender and maturation, with accompanying levels of social awareness and acculturation, were not necessarily taken into consideration. Further, the symptoms of inattention are much less often found to be as problematic as hyperactivity, by teachers in the classroom or by parents, even though the prevalence of the inattentive subtype may be far greater than the other subtypes (Weiss and Hechtman 1986; Wolraich et al. 1996).

The predominantly hyperactive-impulsive type may well be a precursor to the combined type (Barkley 1997), as indicated by the fact that in the field trial for ADHD in the DSM-IV this type was found primarily among preschool children (Applegate et al. 1995). According to Barkley (1997), symptoms of inattention associated with the Hyperactive-Impulsive Subtype emerge later in the development of the disorder and are primarily manifest as problems with sustained attention (persistence) and distractibility. The types of problems with inattention "seen in the Predominantly Inattentive Type appear to have their onset even later than those eventually associated with hyperactive-impulsive behavior" (p. 67). Barkley, citing the work of Barkley, DuPaul, and McMurray (1990) and Lahey and Carlson (1992), adds that research on the Inattentive Subtype suggests that symptoms of daydreaming, spacing out, being in a fog, being easily confused, staring frequently, and being lethargic, hypoactive, and passive are far more common than with the other two subtypes. In addition, the Inattentive Subtype has a deficit in speed of information processing and in focused or selective attention (Goodyear and Hynd 1992; Lahey and Carlson 1992). Finally, the type of inattention seen in older children and adolescents with ADHD, Combined Type (lack of persistence and distractibility), is still "qualitatively different" from the inattention seen in those classified as the Inattentive Type (Barkley 1997a, p. 67).

IDENTIFICATION CONFOUNDS

Many individuals with ADHD leave high school and arrive at college previously undiagnosed, often with a changing picture of symptoms, or the products of their own coping strategies which have been developed over the years and significantly influenced by the external environment and the "executive functioning" provided by caring parents. Because they are frequently bright and personable with the ability to grasp ideas quickly and to manipulate concepts facilely, the disorder in these young adults often goes unrecognized. In their diagnostic work with adults, Ratey et al. (1992) described a number of positive variables that mask the underlying attentional disorder, including above-average intelligence, previous school performance that was at least adequate, extreme effort to accomplish personal goals, compensatory strategies to deal with symptoms, and protective support systems. Sometimes erratic academic performance or achievement at less than expected levels is regarded as lack of motivation, lack of interest, lack of persistence, or just plain laziness. In other cases, young females are referred to as "space cadets" or young males as "out to lunch."

Highly structured environments, one-to-one interactions, and highly stimulating surroundings or activities have the capacity to mask and/or alter the symptoms of ADHD. The daily attendance requirement of the elementary and secondary school program, mandatory homework assignments, frequent assessment periods, and the opportunity for classroom discussion provide the necessary external structure for these students, whose internal attentional regulatory system is highly stimulus-bound. Parents who regulate study time, monitor task completion, awaken the young person in the morning, set limits on social activities, and prioritize and organize competing interests and activities, among other duties, constitute an external repository for the regulation of executive cognitive functions which otherwise cannot be accessed. The opportunity to engage in physical activities or highly competitive and high risk sports on a regular basis allows for falling asleep at a regular hour. Working with a tutor or private instructor provides the necessary structure for on-task behavior to be maintained.

In addition, many individuals with ADHD have a built-in mechanism that allows them to sustain periods of highly concentrated mental and/or physical energy. Identified as the condition of "hyperfocus," this ability to zoom in on an activity and block out any and all other attentional foci often causes the observer to doubt the existence of an underlying attentional disorder. Parents and teachers have reported over the years that "he can pay attention when he wants to." Many will recall the hours that their son spent playing with Lego toys or a video game, or the super attention demonstrated during a sports competition. While the individual in hyperfocus appears to have super-attentive skills, the super-attention is only selectively functional. The energy required and expended in hyperfocus is exhausting and self-limiting. The individual may be able to successfully compete in a snow board contest over the course of seven or eight hours, but then will find it necessary to sleep for the next 12 to 15 hours. Another individual can work on a jewelry-making project for ten hours on end, but given a book to read will then be asleep inside of one hour. Thus, while college students with diagnosed or undiagnosed ADHD start out strongly, they begin to falter scholastically as in-depth study becomes the requirement for success over general knowledge and problem-solving agility.

GENDER ISSUES

Additionally confounding the process of identification is the issue of gender. Historically, females have been underdiagnosed or misdiagnosed, with sex ratios of 9:1 and 6:1 reported in clinically referred samples (Gittleman et al. 1985; Weiss et al. 1985; American Psychological Association 1994). In a meta-analysis of research literature available between 1979 and 1992, Gaub and Carlson (1997) were able to locate only 18 studies which specifically included samples of females. Although their analysis suggested some gender differences between girls and boys, many of the differences were clearly mediated by source of referral and methodological limitations. In the few studies available involving rating scales and structured interviews (Auchenbach 1991; Bauermeister 1992; Eme 1992; Zoccolillo 1993; McDermott 1996), community-based studies (Berry, Shaywitz, and Shaywitz 1985; Breen 1989; Horn et al. 1989), and brain metabolism (Ernst et al. 1994), findings are divergent with respect to gender differences, some studies suggesting that women have a greater prevalence of comorbid internalizing and learning problems. Beiderman et al. (1994), in a systematic study of the differential expression of ADHD between the sexes, found women to have equal rates of major depression and anxiety disorders with their male counterparts.

In a more recent study by Rucklidge and Kaplan (1997), 102 women aged 26 to 59, half of whom fulfilled criteria for ADHD diagnosed in adulthood, were interviewed and asked to complete structured questionnaires in an effort to look at issues such as coping, locus of control, self-esteem, and the presence of anxiety and/or major depression. Results from this study found that the women who were diagnosed with ADHD were more apt to report depressive symptoms, were more stressed and anxious, had more external locus of control, lower self-esteem, and engaged more in emotion-oriented vs. task-oriented coping strategies. However, the interviewers were not blind to ADHD status, and the women selected for the study were all members of Children and Adults with Attention Deficit/ Hyperactivity Disorder (CHADD) and thus may not have been representative of all ADHD women. However, the study does highlight the possible risks of not being diagnosed with ADHD until adulthood (Rucklidge and Kaplan 1997).

The recent work of Katz, Goldstein, and Geckle (1998) found women in their sample to have a far greater degree of psychological distress than males with ADHD as measured by the Beck Depression Inventory (Beck 1978), the MMPI-II (Hathaway and McKinley 1989), the SCl-90-R (Derogatis 1992), and the MCMI-II (Millon 1987). Included in the study were 75 subjects who met DSM-III-R criteria for ADHD (49 males and 26 females) and for whom extensive neuropsychological and personality data were available. The mean age for both genders was 28 years with a mean educational level of 14 years. Ninety-five percent of the group was Caucasian with a socioeconomic status falling in Hollingshead's Class I or II. There were no significant differences between the genders on account of age, race, IQ, or level of education. In addition, the women did not differ from the men in terms of comorbidity for either learning disabilities or depression. However, the women did demonstrate more efficient working memory and short-term visual memory on several of the cognitive measures administered: California Verbal Learning Test, Short and Long Delay Free Recall (Delis, Kramer, Kaplan, and Ober 1987); Digit Symbol subtest of the WAIS-R (Wechsler 1981); and the Visual Memory Scale (Index) of the Wechsler Memory Scale-Revised (Wechsler 1987). Both findings (more efficient cognitive strategies and greater psychological distress) suggest possible hypotheses regarding the potential for the underdiagnosis and/or misdiagnosis of ADHD in adult women.

COMORBIDITY

Comorbidity is another factor that significantly influences both diagnostic and identification processes in adults. Levine (1992) has written that most commonly in the study of attention deficit disorders, the comorbid patterns comprise overlapping affective disorders, information processing deficits, social cognitive weaknesses, conduct disordered/ oppositional problems, and the classically manifest symptoms complex of attentional dysfunction. Levine explains, "It is the exceptional (perhaps even rare) case that exhibits dysfunction in only one of these domains" (p. 450).

The percentage of adults diagnosed with ADHD who also have a learning disability has been found to reach 40% (Katz, Goldstein, and Geckle 1998) with estimates of concurrent learning disabilities among children with ADHD varying from 10% to 90% (Sandler 1995). Henker and Whalen (1989) suggest that learning disabilities frequently occur with ADHD and may "concur with ADHD, as do much less frequently, internalizing disorders such as dysthymia, depression, or anxiety" (p. 216). And although previous studies have suggested a close resemblance between the cognitive and behavioral profiles of children with ADD without hyperactivity and those with learning disabilities (Ackerman et al. 1986; Epstein et al. 1991), work by Stanford and Hynd (1994) failed to support an overlap in the behavioral domain. Morgan et al. (1996) found a significantly higher prevalence of math learning disabilities in predominantly inattentive children; this finding is congruent with the earlier data of Hynd et al. (1991) that showed a higher prevalence of math disabilities in children with ADD without hyperactivity. In a study examining cormorbidity, cognition, and psychosocial functioning in adults with ADHD, Biederman et al. (1993) found adults with ADHD to have experienced significantly higher rates of repeated grades, tutoring, placement in special classes, and reading disability than adults without the disorder.

With respect to other major psychiatric disorders, in the same study with 84 adults diagnosed with ADHD (two-thirds of whom were male), Biederman reported rates of 31% for major depressive disorder, 25% for substance abuse, 43% for generalized anxiety disorder, and 52% for overanxious disorder. In an earlier study, Biederman et al. (1991) had reported a greater familial risk for anxiety disorders among all members of their sample of boys with ADD than among the normal comparison group, and that there was a tendency for ADD probands' relatives who themselves had ADD to have a higher risk for anxiety disorders than probands' relatives who did not have ADD.

In their examination of comorbidity among children and adolescents with depression, Angold and Costello (1993) reviewed epidemiological studies conducted in New York, Puerto Rico, New Zealand, and Pittsburgh. Their findings concluded that although conduct or oppositional disorder and anxiety disorders are definitely more common in depressed than non-depressed children and adolescents, attention deficit disorder is probably more common as well. Additional work by Jensen et al. (1993) comparing children with attention deficit disorder, children with other psychiatric disorders, and children in the community found that children with ADD and hyperactivity and those with other psychiatric disorders reported significantly more depression and anxiety than did the children in the community. Also, children with ADD and hyperactivity plus a comorbid anxiety or depressive disorder had higher levels of coexisting life stresses than did those with a single diagnosis of ADHD.

In their clinical sample of "unrecognized attention-deficit hyperactivity disorder in adults presenting for outpatient psychotherapy," Ratey et al. (1992) reported that the most frequent Axis I diagnosis among these 60 patients was mood disorders (47%). Fifteen percent presented with anxiety disorders; another 15% were grouped in a category including eating disorders, sleep disorders, and somatization; 13% had a primary diagnosis of drug abuse; and 5% met criteria for an obsessive-compulsive disorder. The authors write: "Distractibility and impulsivity in school, work and relationships were common themes" (p. 270). And while they presented with symptoms such as low self-esteem, generalized anxiety, or depression, they also had a "coexisting disorder of distractibility, inattention, and impulsivity" (p. 270). Their depression, rather than a true unipolar depression, was a chronic disaffection, "a demoralized view of themselves" (p. 270).

The overwhelming evidence regarding comorbidity leads to the conclusion that "with our current diagnostic nomenclature, a heterogeneous group of children receive the diagnosis of ADHD, the majority of whom have at least one other comorbid diagnosis" (Halperin, Newcorn, and Sharma 1991, p.15). The same may be said for adolescents and adults since ADHD is a neurodevelopmental disorder that does not disappear with puberty as was once believed (Biederman et al. 1993); accordingly, the issue of appropriate assessment strategies is of concern.

THE TOOLS OF ASSESSMENT

Although a consistent diagnostic test for ADHD does not exist (NIH Consensus Statement 1998), historically, behavior-rating scales and clinical interviews have been employed with children. Behavior-rating scales have been the mainstay in the clinical assessment of children with ADHD for more than 20 years (Halperin, Newcorn, and Sharma 1991). However, even with children, teacher ratings suffer from halo effects (Schachar, Sandburg, and Rutter 1986), and parent ratings have been found to have poor reliability (Rapoport et al. 1986). In addition, generally these scales have not been particularly helpful in the diagnosis of the inattentive type of ADHD, which may well be comprised of a higher proportion of females (NIH Consensus Statement 1998).

Another approach to identifying symptoms of ADHD in both children and adults is the use of neuropsychological assessment. Neuropsychological assessment is comprised generally of a battery of tests, including, but not limited to: intellectual evaluation; psychoeducational measurement; tests of attention, memory, and perceptual/motor functions; and measures of executive brain functions. And although no single measure has been found to definitely discriminate children with ADHD from those without ADHD (Douglas 1983; Greenblatt, Mattis, and Trad 1991; Halperin, Newcorn, and Sharma 1991; Rudel, Denckla, and Broman 1978; Rugel 1974), the value of psychometric and process-oriented assessments lies in the data which derive from the evaluation in terms of establishing the co-existence of learning disabilities, for example, as well as demonstrating the effects of an underlying attention deficit disorder on various cognitive abilities. In addition, personality evaluation is an integral part of the neuropsychological approach, which further rules out the possibility of other comorbid disorders.

Further, as the diagnosis of ADHD is more difficult to make in the case of older adolescents and adults because of the tendency to imitate other psychological/psychiatric and/or medical disorders, the need for a more comprehensive evaluation approach appears essential. In their clinical study of 30 adult outpatients who met criteria for ADHD, Ratey et al. (1992) administered a battery of neuropsychological tests using Kaplan's Boston Process Approach (1988). The resultant patterns compatible with ADHD in these adults included uneven performance across a range of tests, selective impairment on tests loading on attention, evidence for the coexistence of specific learning deficits, signs of anomalous motoric dominance, and results indicating focal areas of cognitive superiority.

In another study by Klee, Garfinkel, and Beauchesne (1986), two groups of adult males were compared, one with diagnoses of ADHD and the other a normal comparison group. The measures employed included a rating scale as well as a continuous performance test (CPT), the Kagan Matching Familiar Figures Test, and the Coding and Arithmetic sub-tests from the Wechsler Intelligence Scale for Adults (WAIS). Results revealed significant differences between the groups on the WAIS Digit Symbol, omission errors on the CPT, and a summary measure from the CPT. Poor performance on the Digit Symbol sub-test has been found to be related to difficulties in new learning, visual scanning, and distractibility (Kaufman 1979). With respect to the self-rating scale, although the two groups differed in their ratings of childhood behaviors, they did not do so with respect to current behavioral symptoms. The index group rated themselves as having been more restless, active, nervous, and impulsive as well as having more problems with concentration and lower frustration tolerance. The similarity between the two groups on current behavior rating occurred because the index group rated themselves as much improved as compared with their childhood ratings. These findings again demonstrate the limitations of relying on rating scales to identify symptoms in adults, when in fact the nature of symptoms in adults may well be altered.

In a later study, Katz, Goldstein, and Geckle (1998) found several neuropsychological measures to differ significantly between a group of adults with ADHD as compared to a group diagnosed with a mood disorder. An extensive neuropsychological battery including personality measures was administered to both groups. Both the ADHD and depression groups were subdivided with regard to comorbid depression in the ADHD group and developmental learning disorders in both groups. Using discriminant function analysis, variables derived from the California Verbal Learning Test (CVLT) (Delis et al. 1987), the Paced Auditory Serial Addition Test (PASAT) (Gronwall 1977), and the Stroop Color Word Test (STROOP) (Golden 1987) were found to discriminate among the various subgroups at a level significantly exceeding chance. Further, although the neuropsychological tests appeared to be quite sensitive to ADHD, they also were found to be sensitive to depression in some cases. Results would suggest that the differential diagnosis of ADHD and depression in adults may be complicated to some extent because of the shared characteristics of the disorders in adults (Katz, Goldstein, and Geckle 1998).

DOCUMENTATION REQUIREMENTS AT THE POST-SECONDARY LEVEL

In light of the diagnostic confounds present with adolescents and adults, the Educational Testing Service (ETS) has published a policy statement regarding documentation of ADHD in adolescents and adults (1998). The materials used in the policy statement were adapted from a document developed by a group of professionals from various organizations who formed the Consortium on ADHD Documentation. The purpose of both documents was to establish standard criteria that post-secondary personnel, licensing and testing agencies, and consumers requiring documentation would use to determine appropriate accommodations for individuals with ADHD. Documentation requirements include the following: a qualified professional must conduct the evaluation; the documentation must be current (generally within the previous three years); documentation must be comprehensive (evidence of early impairment, evidence of current impairment); alternative diagnoses or explanations should be ruled out; relevant testing must be provided; DSM-IV criteria must be identified; a specific diagnosis must be provided as well as an interpretative summary; each accommodation recommended must include a rationale; and confidentiality must be assured.

With respect to the standard "relevant testing information must be provided" (ETS 1998), the document speaks to the importance of neuropsychological or psycho-educational assessment in determining the impact of the disorder on the "individual's ability to function in academically related settings" (p. 6). It is further recognized that test scores or sub-test scores alone should not be used as a sole measure for the diagnostic decision, and that checklists or surveys do not substitute for clinical observations and sound diagnostic judgment. Finally, the Interpretive Summary must include the elimination of alternative explanations; an indication of how the patterns of inattentiveness, impulsivity, and/or hyperactivity across the life span and across settings are used in the diagnostic process; whether the individual was on medication at the time of the evaluation; the extent of the substantial limitations to learning for which accommodations are being requested; and why specific accommodations are needed and how the ADHD symptomology is mediated by the accommodations.

With the transition from high school, students with ADHD, as well as those with learning disabilities, move from an environment in which school personnel are required to identify their needs and provide appropriate services to one in which the students are expected to provide documentation of their disability and to request specific accommodations. Many students with ADHD may not have had access to special education services under P. L. 94-142 or IDEA, but are eligible for reasonable accommodations under Section 504 of the Rehabilitation Act or the ADA (Americans with Disabilities Act). On the other hand, those who had been previously identified during their elementary or secondary school years may expect proactive services to continue during the post-secondary years. Others may choose to "de-identify" themselves because of the fears of stigma that they have encountered over the years, desiring instead a fresh start in a new environment.

In any case, there is a need for students with ADHD and/or learning disabilities to understand and personally apply the construct "otherwise qualified" as set out in Section 504 of the Rehabilitation Act and as further clarified under case law. To be considered otherwise qualified, the individual must be able to meet the requisite academic and technical standards despite his or her disability when provided reasonable accommodations (Davis v. Southeastern Community College 1979). No student may be denied benefits of a program because of the absence of educational auxiliary aids. However, provision of services is required only if the student informs the institution of the handicapping condition and requests services

(Salvador v. Bell 1985). For those students who have difficulty with self-disclosure or with an underlying denial of the negative impact that their disorder can have on their academic progress, access to reasonable accommodations can be jeopardized.

Unlike the elementary and secondary school years, once a student obtains specific accommodations, that student is responsible to monitor his or her own academic performance. Students with ADHD need to be able to evaluate their progress and recognize when additional or different modes of accommodation are needed. The procedures and safeguards inherent in IDEA that provide for a network of supportive personnel in the academic setting are no longer applicable. Students must now identify and establish their own personal support network. Although it would be most desirable for students with ADHD to enter college prepared to self-advocate based upon a well grounded self-understanding of their disorder, this is the exception rather than the rule. Often it is the parent who reads the necessary evaluation documentation rather than the student, just as they have served as the "executive function" over the years. At other times, it is not until the student is faced with repeated failure during his or her collegiate experience that a willingness to accept and deal with the negative impact of inattention, distractibility, impulsivity, and/or the inability to initiate or follow through on academic performance occurs.

INTERVENTIONS AND ACCOMMODATIONS

Medication

In terms of interventions, there is a considerable amount of clinical research to support the use of medication to treat ADHD symptoms in adults (Wender et al. 1981; Mattes, Boswell and Oliver 1984; Gaultieri et al. 1985; Wender et al. 1985; Wender, Wood and Reimherr 1985; Wender and Reimherr 1990; Zametkin et al. 1990; Ratey, Greenberg, and Lindem 1991; Spencer et al. 1995; Wilens et al. 1995; Wilens, Biederman, and Spencer 1995). However, in contrast to the more than 100 studies evaluating the efficacy of stimulants in children, there are fewer than ten controlled studies on the use of stimulants with adults (Wilens, Spencer, and Biederman 1995). According to Wilens, Spencer, and Biederman (1995), in contrast to the consistent robust responses to stimulants in children and adolescents of approximately 70%, studies with adults have shown more equivocal results ranging from 25% to 73%. In addition, the NIH Consensus Statement (1998), while confining itself primarily to the diagnosis and treatment of ADHD in children, goes on to recommend both studies of long-term treatment (longer than one year) and prospective controlled studies up to adulthood of the risks and benefits associated with childhood treatment with psycho-stimulants. However, although controlled studies with adults are few in number, clinical practice has established the use of medication as a necessary intervention with the college-aged population at times, in conjunction with a number of psycho-social and educational interventions and accommodations.

Psycho-stimulants are the first-line medications for treating both combined and inattentive types of ADHD (Wilens, Spencer, and Biederman 1995; Amen and Goldman 1998). It is hypothesized that these medications increase dopamine output from the basal ganglia which subsequently increases activity in the prefrontal cortex, the area of the brain most closely associated with the executive functions of planning, organization, response inhibition, social judgment, and working memory. Functionally, a broad division is made between the dorsolateral and the medio-orbital prefrontal cortex (Pliszka et al. 1996). Individuals with dorsolateral lesions tend to have impairments such as loss of attention to details, poor generation of response alternative, and perseveration, while those with medio-orbital lesions show greater impulsivity, deficits in social functioning, and emotional lability, but less cognitive deterioration (Stuss and Benson 1986). Barkley (1994) has suggested that this latter profile is more consistent with ADHD, conceptualizing ADHD as a primary deficit in inhibitory control. Further, glucose metabolism studies in both adolescents and adults demonstrate decreased metabolism in the left anterior frontal areas (Zametkin et al. 1990; Ernst et al. 1994).

However, a multistage hypothesis has also been formulated which may have clinical relevance for the varying symptom pictures seen in individuals with ADHD. This hypothesis suggests that the central norepinephrine system may be dysregulated in ADHD and thus does not efficiently prime the cortical posterior attention system to external stimuli, while effective mental processing of information involves an anterior executive attention system that may depend on dopaminergic input. Third, the peripheral epinephrine system may be a critical factor in the response of individuals with ADHD to stimulant medication (Pliszka, McCracken, and Maas1996). These data may give some rationale for the efficacy of tricyclic antidepressants such as imipramine and desipramine as they are strong blockers of the re-uptake of norepinephrine but have very little direct effect on the dopaminergic system (Bolden-Watson and Richelson 1993).

Wilens, Spencer, and Biederman (1995) conclude that "(P)harmacotherapy serves an important role in reducing the core symptoms of ADHD and other concurrent psychiatric disorders in adults" (p. 183). Its administration should be integrated into a multimodal approach to treatment/intervention. Although there is a paucity of data on effectiveness and dosing parameters for adults, "the stimulant medications continue to be the first-line drug of choice for uncomplicated ADHD in adults, with tricyclic antidepressants (TCAs) and bupropion for nonresponders or adults with concurrent psychiatric disorders" (p. 184).

The issue for the college aged student is not necessarily whether medications are an effective intervention strategy to control the effects of inattention and distractibility on academic performance and/or interpersonal interactions, but the individual's "mind-set" with respect to the use of medication in the first place. Non-compliance is a serious issue in medication management with adolescents and young adults for a number of reasons. With individuals diagnosed at an earlier age, medication management often was used as a means to control behavior either in the classroom or at home. When a young adult enters this developmentally appropriate stage of independence from parental control, discontinuance of medication becomes a ready means to herald a kind of "liberation." At the same time peer-endorsed drug and alcohol experimentation adds to the illusion of being able to engage in independent judgment and deal effectively with consequent behaviors. Some of those very students, who argue that prescribed "drugs" are changing their personalities, altering their creativity, and restricting their usual level of high energy, find themselves self-medicating with nicotine, caffeine, marijuana, LSD, and alcohol.

Often, these are the students who have never been given the responsibility by treating clinicians to understand the consequences of the disorder on their lives. Medications are prescribed with little education of the student, and/or dosages are not always titrated with enough attention to target behaviors. As a result, students are left with no real understanding of what prescribed medications are intended to do. In addition, the popular press has at times added to underlying feelings of guilt associated with years of being told by persons in authority that the student is just lazy or unmotivated, and medication is seen as an easy fix to social irresponsibility.

Education and Self-Awareness

The medication issue aside, the single most important intervention in dealing with ADHD for the college-aged student and young adult is self-education which results in self-awareness. Self-education, while including a well-informed decision regarding the use of medication, also includes an understanding of the roles and expectations involved in being a college student. Roles and expectations derive from a knowledge of the environment in which the individual student is expected to function and the various skills needed to achieve successful adjustment there.

TIME MANAGEMENT

Time management is critical to a successful transition to the college environment. Students with ADHD must learn how to adjust to the lack of external structure which they will face now on a daily basis. Because classes will not meet every day and often the day of classes is truncated, the individual student will need to plan not only study time but down time as well. Because there is often no requirement to attend class and no extra credit for completing assignments, exam grades are a major determinant of class performance. Cramming, so long a relatively effective coping mechanism in times past for dealing with procrastination, proves to be less so because papers very often are all due within several days of each other. Use of a daily planner in a way that facilitates time management strategies will most probably need to be taught. Micro-managing a set of operating procedures will begin with how not to misplace the planner or forget to bring it to class, followed by back-tracking from a due date a list of the discrete tasks that need to be performed to meet the established goal within an established time frame.

ORGANIZATION AND PLANNING

Priority-setting and organization of study space, study materials, and class notes are also important skills to be developed. Having the necessary paper, texts, and writing tools in one area in one's room will facilitate portability, should study in the library or laboratory be more appropriate. Using a strategy such as a double-column notebook will facilitate review of class notes and the extraction of main themes from supporting details. Having a file for each class, properly designated and easy to access, will support efforts at organization and counteract problems with forgetfulness, short-term memory deficits, and a tendency to lose things. Students with ADHD are known to be non-linear thinkers and as such can see scores of permutations when dealing with concepts or ideas. With the tendency to get lost in myriad ideas and simultaneous modes of response, students will be required to make a conscious effort to organize either oral or written language in terms of priorities or hierarchies, a task that does not come naturally and must be learned. Also, since highly attention-provoking activities are likely to be more attractive (sports competition, listening to music, playing video games, talking with friends, favorite classes) than out-of-class assignments from less stimulating or required courses, establishing which activities must take priority over others will be essential.

INDIVIDUAL LEARNING SUPPORTS

Often, learning what is the most effective way to study will vary with the individual student. For some students, listening to music through earphones enhances their ability to concentrate when doing assigned readings. Students have explained that the music "occupies one part of their brain," allowing the other part to concentrate on the task at hand. For other students, absolute quiet is essential. When the student shares a room, the distractions from a roommate and/or visiting friends in the dormitory may make it impossible for the student to use his or her dorm room as a major study site. In this case, the student must find a place where the external auditory and/or visual distractions are at a minimum.

For students who have spent their previous school years skim-reading required materials, reading for detail required in a science class, for example, will necessitate a different way to approach written text. Margin noting, the use of colored highlighter pens in a systematic fashion, and using visual maps that associate main ideas with supporting details will need to be taught and consistently used. Approaching math equations with colored markers will do much to control the numerous calculation errors that occur because of number misalignments and/or the misreading/omission of operational signs. Getting lost in a calculus problem when the entire page begins to look the same and working memory fails to hold onto separate, but highly dependent, operations is a common problem that the use of color to aid visual memory can help to remedy.

In addition to study skills, time management, and organization strategies, knowing how and when to access additional support from the classroom faculty and/or a learning support service will be most helpful. Finding out when faculty have office hours, where and when teaching assistants have study labs, and when writing-center staff are available to help proof final manuscripts are necessary if such reasonable accommodations are to be used effectively. Making sure a faculty member knows that exams will be taken separately under extended time conditions in a non-distracting setting is something that both the student and the support service staff will need to ensure. If concomitant problems exist with written language expression, use of a computer and/or oral examinations are reasonable accommodations as long as they are appropriately justified in the student's documentation of disability.

College faculty will be asked to provide reasonable accommodations in their classrooms as students begin the process of self-advocating. Although some faculty will be more eager than others to participate in such accommodations, the obligation remains. In addition, the consequences of indifference are enormous. Accommodations that may prove useful as well as easily administered include such things as providing access to study guides, setting appointments with students for individual discussion of class material, and cooperating with arrangements for proctored exams or alternative approaches to the examination process. It is important also that college faculty recognize that students with ADHD are some of the brightest students they may encounter in a classroom. And for all the disabling aspects of the disorder, students with ADHD are often agile thinkers with an unusual ability both to link ideas across traditional categories and to recognize the unexpected. Weiss (1994) compiled a list of 29 positive attributes of individuals with ADHD including: empathy, feeling deeply, inventiveness, high energy, spontaneity, natural creativity, and looking beyond the surface to the core of people, situations, and issues, among others. It is easy to forget these attributes when confronted with the effects of the dysregulation of attention on academic performance. However, seeing the end result of allowing a student to "learn differently" will reward any teacher worth his or her salt.

IMPORTANCE OF PHYSICAL EXERCISE

Many young adults enter college having previously competed in sports or participating in athletic activities extramurally. According to Pliszka, McCracken, and Maas (1996), a fundamental dysregulation in the central norepinephrine and peripheral epinephine systems might alter the brain's signal-to-noise ratio which plays a role in mobilizing the body's response to stress. As a result the posterior attention system would lose its ability to disengage efficiently from the old stimuli, shift attention to the new data, and read it out to the anterior system. Stimulant response may be a result of the "resetting" of the brain's norepinephrine producing center through a rise in peripheral epinephrine (McCracken 1991) so that the locus ceruleus, which plays a major role in attention, can more robustly respond to external stimuli. Energy-expending physical activities may have been a natural means of stimulating the body's attempts to re-regulate the peripheral sympathetic norepinephrine system. The absence of this means and the presence of increased demands for sustained attention appear to affect the body's own efforts at self-regulation negatively. Anecdotally, students frequently report increased attentional capacity after engaging in vigorous exercise such as running or bicycling on a regular basis.

AVOIDING THE PITFALLS

Finally, students may find themselves reverting to previous dysfunctional coping strategies if the nature of the underlying attention deficit disorder is not taken seriously. Skim-reading, procrastination, socializing with friends, partying until the late hours, staying awake until early morning, missing morning classes, sleeping during the afternoons instead of studying, eating irregular meals, and missing the opportunity to engage in daily physical activity because of poor time management often result in failure and academic probation. Discouraged by the fruitless efforts to affect grades, which are often based upon previous academic experiences and which seem extraordinary, the student gives way to old habits: "If reading the text didn't change my grade, I guess I'll just use someone else's notes," or "All that time I put in was useless; I'll just stay up and cram like I did in high school the night before the exam." Eventually, several nights of cramming result in days of fatigue when nothing else gets done, classes are missed, and rationalizations begin: "Well, I've missed so many classes now, there's no real reason to go for the rest of the semester." Depression sets in and attempts to alleviate the feelings of failure and low self-worth often are made through the use of alcohol and drugs.

Understanding how to avoid these pitfalls is critical to the first year experience. Taking part in ADHD support groups where empathy, constructive confrontation, and suggested strategies are offered can counter the conning game in short order. At other times personal counseling is extremely valuable in helping a young adult understand the ramifications of his or her ADHD on personal relationships. Learning how to communicate honest feelings is not an easy task for young adults. Recognizing for the first time how the unintended consequences of impulsive comments, distractibility, forgetfulness, and problems with time management can affect dating relationships seriously and negatively or unduly burden friendships is not an easy accomplishment. Both developmental learning tasks can be facilitated through a counseling relationship and/or the use of a coach, should one be accessible.

COACHING AND OTHER HIGHLY STRUCTURED COLLEGIATE PROGRAMS

The process of coaching has gotten a fair amount of press most recently. According to Ratey (1997), "coaching is about a partnership, it's about helping the person learn how to manage their brain" (p. 8). Coaching is a process whereby an individual with ADHD is assisted with the development and use of particular structures that are necessary for him or her to function effectively as well as being taught practical approaches to the challenges of daily life. Coaching is also an example of a point of performance intervention (Barkley 1997). Barkley has suggested that the problem concerning individuals with ADHD is not a skill deficit but rather a difficulty with behavioral execution. Because of difficulties in executive functions such as inhibition and strategic behaviors (planfulness or task completion), successful performance is impaired despite the student's existing knowledge of effective coping strategies. The skill is present; its application is highly inconsistent or at times absent. Consistent with Barkley's theoretical perspective, Turnock (1998) reported the results of a survey conducted at Colorado State University involving students with ADHD. His results suggested that among the 151 undergraduates surveyed, students in the high symptom group used significantly less coping behavior than their low-symptom peers. In addition, coping strategy, not intelligence, was significantly related to academic success among the low symptom group. High symptom students approached studying in a less organized, less methodical way, procrastinated more, and employed fewer self-control/self-disciplinary behaviors. Academic success among this group was related primarily to their level of intelligence, but significantly lower grades and higher drop-out rates were greater among this group than among their low symptom peers.

Although neither tutoring nor coaching are required accommodations under the ADA, there are colleges that are beginning to provide coaching services for their students (Disability Compliance for Higher Education 1997). West Chester University, for example, received a TRIO grant to cover the cost of hiring graduate students to serve as coaches for students with ADHD. At Kenyon College, a great deal of coaching was conducted through e-mail with a former dean of academic advising who credited, at least partly, her informal coaching practice with a low attrition rate and improved grades among her students with ADHD (Disability Compliance for Higher Education 1997).

In an unpublished manuscript, Coleman and Sussman, who are both professional coaches in the San Francisco area, suggest that a comprehensive approach toward coaching people with ADHD can be summarized in four words: structure, support, skills, and strategies. They define structure operationally as (1) clearly defined vision, goals, and values, clarified in the early phases of coaching; (2) systems for managing daily life (shopping, bill paying, handling mail); (3) a time management system that enables the individual to identify priorities, break them into manageable steps, and schedule them into a calendar; (4) daily or weekly appointments that are scheduled, reliable, and consistent; (5) a single daily action taken every day to reinforce a sense of accomplishment; and (6) daily habits that are small constructive actions done on a daily or routine basis.

Support is provided through a variety of means. The coach serves the role of witness and empathizer, a provider of feedback, someone who acknowledges wins, and someone who helps to sustain the client's vision when that vision gets forgotten during the hard times. A coach also champions his or her clients, standing by the individual when he or she doubts or questions his or her own abilities. Celebrating, creating trust, and providing an opportunity for active listening as the individual clears away preoccupations and situations or mental states are also part of the supportive role undertaken by a coach.

Skill building focuses on skills becoming more consistent and reliable. The need for consistency is generally most apparent in the area of time management, goal setting, setting boundaries, and dealing with transition. Another important area is teaching the individual with ADHD how to deal with the inner critic. Years of external criticism result in a personal tendency to self-doubt and to assume responsibility for all problems or mishaps in the course of relationships or activities. As two individuals have recently commented, "It's no wonder people with ADD have anxiety attacks; we're always messing up and waiting for the axe to fall."

Strategies, according to Coleman and Sussman (unpublished manuscript), are the creative tools used by coaches to help individual students with ADHD deal with everyday life and achieve their personal goals. Strategies include such factors as: identifying high energy times for engaging in tasks that require concentration and stamina; coupling activities or times for events so that one triggers the memory of the other; setting realistic study times by blocking off periods for intense concentration followed by a pre-set break time; identifying issues that may block work completion such as old patterns of resistance so that the individual can learn how to bypass them in the future; establishing concrete methods of demarcating the end of steps in a multi-step operation, and finally, setting up contingency awards on a consistent basis (Peterson, unpublished manuscript).

Other strategies that may prove helpful for students with ADHD are techniques such as mind mapping, visualization, verbalization, keeping personal notebooks, and creating a "home" for thoughts. Mind mapping is particularly useful for students who tend to get overwhelmed because they see the whole picture and cannot pick out the details. The technique can be used also with detail-intensive texts where the student is trying to put a complex of ideas into order or into perspective. Visualization is a means to help students deal with time, for example, so that their mental image is one involving size and shape.

Verbalization is a means to enable students to "download" extraneous thoughts so that they can focus on the task at hand. Specifically, the coach sets a specified amount of time for individuals to verbalize myriad thoughts and ideas that at times are racing in their heads. After this initial "downloading," students can be redirected to a topic of concern or a class assignment. Another technique (Peterson's unpublished manuscript) is getting students to write their creative ideas or distracting thoughts at the point at which they occur rather than allowing these intrusive thoughts to divert them from the task at hand. Peterson calls this creating a home for thoughts, a parking lot of sorts. Use of this strategy can enable students to gain more control over their creative ideas while at the same time modifying the dysfunctional nature of impulsivity.

Finally, as McCormick (1998) has written, accommodations alone are not enough to enable students with ADHD to succeed academically and personally in college. Comprehensive programming, addressing personal, social, and academic needs, is seen as essential. McCormick goes on to suggest a number of strategies that traditional colleges can employ to foster retention among students with ADHD. Among these is collaborative programming. A collaborative program approach among and within various student service providers on campus will ensure that proactive strategies are undertaken at the time of orientation to reach first year students before they begin to fail, for example. The use of peer mentors, who can be trained to provide coaching for students with ADHD, is a second viable recommendation. This strategy takes into account the fiscal restraints that college service providers may face, while at the same time providing a point of performance intervention. For example, a study buddy is there to help get the student with ADHD to begin his or her work at hours when typical student services are not provided. In addition, advising and continuity of advising are viewed as key institutional factors in supporting students with ADHD: "Though many institutions are moving toward a one-stop, one shop model for advising, one-on-one advising should still be an option for selected populations of students, i.e., students with disabilities" (McCormick 1998, p. 89).

Landmark College in Putney, Vermont, is an example of a nontraditional college whose entire program is geared toward students with learning disabilities and/or ADHD. All faculty use a multisensory, multi-modality teaching approach and all classrooms, regardless of content, adhere to this systematic method of instruction. Techniques such as using double-column note taking, visual mapping, and the use of manipulatives are reinforced in the classroom. In addition, each student is provided with a tutor who is also a faculty member. This individual works with the student two to four hours weekly in order to identify individual strengths and weaknesses that bear on the learning process, provide opportunities for remediation, develop strategies for new learning and study skills, reinforce time management and organization skills, and generally support the student throughout the learning experience. For students with ADHD, the tutor is their "coach" as well. In addition, each student has an academic advisor who acts as a "case manager" of sorts across the student's academic and residential life on campus.

The bottom line, regardless of whether the collegiate program is non-traditional as in the case of Landmark or one that incorporates some or all of the elements of successful programming for students with ADHD as discussed by McCormick (1998), is clear. Post-secondary education can play a major role in affecting the ultimate success or failure of the college student with ADHD. Without their co-operation and ownership of the need for specific interventions, accommodations, and coping strategies, these students may well fail. However, without the appropriate supports and structures that a post-secondary academic setting can and should proactively provide, they run even a greater risk of failure. Tinto (1993) in his work on student attrition factors in the college setting writes, "Colleges and universities are like other human communities; student departure, like human communities generally, reflects both the attributes and actions of the individual and those of the other members of the community in which that person resides" (p. 5).

REFERENCES

Ackerman, P. T., Anhalt, J. M., Dykman, R. A., and Holcomb, P. J. 1986. Effortful processing deficits in children with reading and/or attention disorders. *Brain and Cognition* 5:22–40.

Amen, D. G., and Goldman, B. 1998. Attention-Deficit Disorder: A guide for primary care physicians. *Primary Psychiatry* July, 76–85.

American Psychiatric Association. 1994. *Diagnostic and Statistical Manual of Mental Disorders.* Washington DC: American Psychiatric Association.

Americans with Disabilities Act (ADA), P. L. 101–336, 42 U.S.C. 1201 et seq.

Anderson, J. C., Williams, S., McGee, R., and Silva, P. A. 1987. DSM-III disorders in preadolescent children. *Archives of General Psychiatry* 44:69–76.

Angold, A., and Costello, E. J. 1993. Depressive comorbidity in children and adolescents: Empirical, theoretical, and methodological issues. *American Journal of Psychiatry* 150 (12):1779–91.

Applegate, B., Lahey, B. B., Hart, E. L., Waldman, I., Biederman, J., Hynd, G. W., Barkley, R. A., Ollendick, T., Frick, P. J., Greenhill, L., McBurnett, K., Newcorn, J., Kerdyk, L., Garfinkel, B., and Shaffer, D. 1995. The age of onset for DSM-IV attention-deficit hyperactivity disorder: A report of the DSM-IV field trials. Manuscript submitted for publication.

Auchenbach, T. M. 1991. *The Child Behavior Checklist—1991.* Burlington: University of Vermont, Department of Psychiatry.

Barkley, R. A., DuPaul, G. J., and McMurray, M. B. 1990. Comprehensive evaluation of Attention Deficit Disorder with and without hyperactivity as defined by research criteria. *Journal of Consulting and Clinical Psychology* 58:775–89.

Barkley, R. A. 1993. *Attention Deficit Hyperactivity Disorder: Workshop Manual.* Worcester, MA: Author.

Barkley, R. A. 1994. Impaired delayed responding: A unified theory of Attention Deficit Hyperactivity Disorder. In *Disruptive Behavior Disorders: Essays in Honor of Herbert Quay,* ed. D. K. Routh. New York: Plenum.

Barkley, R. A. 1997a. Behavioral inhibition, sustained attention, and executive functions: Constructing a unifying theory of ADHD. *Psychological Bulletin* 121 (1):65–94.

Barkley, R. A. 1997b. *ADHD and the Nature of Self-control.* New York: Guilford Press.

Bauermeister, J. 1992. Factor analyses of teacher ratings of attention-deficit hyperactivity and oppositional defiant symptoms in children aged four through thirteen years. *Journal of Clinical Child Psychology* 21:27–34.

Beck, A. T. 1978. Beck Depression Inventory. San Antonio, TX: *The Psychological Corporation.*

Benjamin, J., Li, L., Patterson, C., Greenberg, B. D., Murphy, D. L., and Hamer, D. H. 1996. Population and familial association between the D4 dopamine receptor gene and measures of novelty seeking. *Nature Genetics* 12:81–4.

Berry, C. A., Shaywitz, S. E., and Shaywitz, B. A. 1985. Girls with Attention Deficit Disorder: A silent majority? A report on behavioral and cognitive characteristics. *Pediatrics* 76:801–809.

Biederman, J., Faraone, S. V., Keenan, K., Steingard, R., and Tsuang, M. T. 1991. Familial association between Attention Deficit Disorder and anxiety disorders. *American Journal of Psychiatry* 148 (2):251–56.

Biederman, J., Faraone, S. V., Spencer, T., Wilens, T., Norman, D., Lapey, K. S., Mick, E., Krifcher Lehman, B., and Doyle, A. 1993. Patterns of psychiatric co-morbidity, cognition, and psychosocial functioning in adults with attention deficit hyperactivity disorder. *American Journal of Psychiatry,* 150 (12):1792–98.

Blum, K., Cull, J. G., Braverman, E. R., and Comings, D. E. 1996. Reward deficiency syndrome. *American Scientist* 84:132–45.

Bolden-Watson, C., and Richelson, E. 1993. Blockade by newly developed antidepressants of biogenic amine uptake into rat brain synaptosomes. *Life Science* 52:1023–9.

Breen, M. J. 1989. Cognitive and behavioral differences in ADHD in boys and girls. *Journal of Child Psychology and Psychiatry* 30:711–16.

Cantwell, D. P., and Baker, L. 1991. Association between Attention Deficit-Hyperactivity Disorder and learning disorders. *Journal of Learning Disabilities* 24 (2):88–95.

Castellanos, F. X., Giedd, J. N., Eckburg, P., et al. 1994. Quantative morphology of the caudate nucleus in attention-deficit hyperactivity disorder. *American Journal of Psychiatry* 151(12).

Castellanos, F. X., Giedd, J. N., Eckburg, P., et al. 1996. Quantitative brain magnetic resonance imaging in attention-deficit hyperactivity disorder. *Archives of General Psychiatry* 53 (7):607–16.

Coleman, S., and Sussman, S. 1996. The four S's: A comprehensive program for coaching people with ADD. Unpublished manuscript.

Comings, D. E., Comings, B. G., Muhleman, D., Dietz, G., Shahbahrami, B., et al. 1991. The dopamine D2 receptor locus as a modifying gene in neuropsychiatric disorders. *Journal of the American Medical Association* 266:1793–800.

Davis v. Southeastern Community College, 442 U.S. 397. 1979.

Delis, D. C., Kramer, J. H., Kaplan, E., and Ober, B. A. 1987. *California Verbal Learning Test: Adult Version.* San Antonio, TX: The Psychological Corporation.

Derogatis, L. R. 1992. SCL-90-R. Towson, MD: Clinical Psychometric Research, Inc.

Disability Compliance for Higher Education. 1997. Volume 3, Issue 5.

Douglas, V. I. 1983. Attentional and cognitive problems. In *Developmental Neuropsychiatry,* ed. M. Rutter. New York: Guilford Press.

Dowdy, C. A., Carter, J. K., and Smith, T. E. C. 1990. Differences in transitional needs of high school students with and without learning disabilities. *Journal of Learning Disabilities* 23:343–354.

Ebstein, R. P., Novick, O., Umansky, R., Priel, B., Osher, Y., Blaine, D., Bennett, E. R., Nemanov, L., Katz, M., and Belmaker, R. H. 1996. Dopamine D4 receptor (D4DR) exon III polymorphism associated with the human personality trait of novelty seeking. *Nature Genetics* 12:78–80.

Educational Testing Service (ETS) 1998. Policy Statement for Documentation of Attention-Deficit/Hyperactivity Disorder in Adolescents and Adults. Office of Disability Policy Educational Testing Service, Princeton, NJ.

Eme, R. F. 1992. Selective female affliction in development of disorders of childhood: A literature review. *Journal of Clinical Child Psychology* 21:354–64.

Epstein, M. A., Shaywitz, S. E., Shaywitz, B. A. and Woolston, J. L. 1991. The boundaries of Attention Deficit Disorder. *Journal of Learning Disabilities* 24:78–86.

Ernst, M., Liebenauer, L. L., Jons, P. H., King, A. C., Cohen, M. D., and Zametkin, A. J. 1994. Sexual maturation and brain metabolism in ADHD and brain metabolism in ADHD and normal girls. Presentation at 41st Annual Meeting American Academy of Child and Adolescent Psychiatry, New York.

Gaub, M., and Carlson, C. 1997. Gender differences in ADHD: A meta-analysis and critical review. *Journal of the American Academy of Child and Adolescent Psychiatry* 36 (8):1036–44.

Gaultieri, C. T., Ondrusek, M. G., and Finley, C. 1985. Attention Deficit Disorder in adults. *Clinical Neuropharmacology* 8:343–56.

Gittleman, R., Mannuzza, S., Shenker, R., and Bonagura, N. 1985. Hyperactive boys almost grown up: I. Psychiatric status. *Archives of General Psychiatry* 42:937–47.

Golden, C. J. 1987. *Stroop Color and Word Test.* Chicago, IL: Stoelting Company.

Goodyear, P., and Hynd, G. W. 1992. Attention deficit disorder with (ADD/H) and without (ADD/WO) hyperactivity: Behavioral and neuropsychological differentiation. *Journal of Clinical Child Psychology* 21:273–305.

Greenblatt, E., Mattis, S., and Trad, P. V. 1991. The ACID pattern and the freedom from distractibility factor in child psychiatric population. *Developmental Neuropsychology* 7 (2):121–30.

Gronwall, D. M. A. 1977. Paced auditory serial-addition task: A measure of recovery from concussion. *Perceptual and Motor Skills* 44:367–73.

Halperin, J. M., Newcorn, J. H., and Sharma, V. 1991. Ritalin: Diagnostic comorbidity and attentional measures. In *Ritalin Theory and Patient Management*, eds. L. L. Greenhill, and B. Osman. Larchmont, NY: Mary Ann Liebert.

Hathaway, S. R., and McKinley, J. C. 1989. *Minnesota Multiphasic Personality Inventory-II.* Minneapolis, MN: University of Minnesota Press.

Henderson, C. 1995. College freshmen with disabilities. A triennial statistical profile. American Council on Education, HEATH Resource Center.

Henker, B., and Whalen, C. 1989. Hyperactivity and attention deficits. *American Psychologist* 44:216–23.

Horn, W. F., Wagner, A. E., and Ialongo, N. 1989. Sex differences in school-aged children with pervasive Attention Deficit Hyperactivity Disorder. *Journal of Abnormal Child Psychology* 17:109–25.

Hynd, G. W., Lorys, A. R., Semrud-Clikeman, M., Nieves, N., Huettner, M. I. S., and Lahey, B. B. 1991. Attention deficit disorder without hyperactivity (ADD/WO): A distinct behavioral and neurocognitive syndrome. *Journal of Child Neurology* 6:37–43.

Individuals with Disabilities Education Act (IDEA), P. L. 101-476, 20 U.S.C. 1400 et seq.

Jensen, P. S., Shervette, R. E., Xenakis, S. N., and Richters, J. 1993. Anxiety and depressive disorders in attention deficit disorder with hyperactivity: New findings. *American Journal of Psychiatry* 150 (8):1203–9.

Kaplan, E. 1988. A process approach for neuropsychological assessment. In *Clinical Neuropsychology and Brain Function Research, Measurements, and Practice*, eds. T. Boll and B. Bryant. Washington, DC: American Psychological Association Press.

Katz, L. J., Goldstein, G., and Geckle, M. 1998. Neuropsychological and personality differences between men and women with ADHD. *Journal of Attention Disorders* 2 (4): 239–48.

Kaufman, A. S. 1979. *Intelligence Testing with the Wisc-R.* New York: Wiley.

Klee, S. H., Garfinkel, B. D., and Beauchesne, H. 1986. Attention deficits in adults. *Psychiatric Annals* 16 (1):52–56.

Lahey, B. B., and Carlson, C. L. 1992. Validity of the diagnostic category of Attention Deficit Disorder without Hyperactivity: A review of the literature. In *Attention Deficit Disorder Comes of Age: Toward the Twenty-first Century*, eds. S. E. Shaywitz and B. Shaywitz. Austin, TX: PRO-ED.

Lahoste, G. J., Swanson, J. M., Wigal, S. B., Glabe, C., Wigal, T., King, N., and Kennedy, J. L. 1996. Dopamine D4 receptor gene polymorphism is associated with Attentional Deficit Hyperactivity Disorder. *Molecular Psychiatry* 1:121–24.

Levine, M. 1992. Commentary: Attentional disorders: Elusive entities and their mistaken identities. *Journal of Child Neurology* 7:449–53.

Mangrum, C. T., and Strichart, S. S. 1988. *College and the Learning Disabled Student: Program Development, Implementation, and Selection.* Philadelphia, PA: Grune & Stratton.

Mattes, J. A., Boswell, L., and Oliver, H. 1984. Methylphenidate effects on symptoms of Attention Deficit Disorder in adults. *Archives of General Psychiatry* 41:1059–63.

McCormick, A. 1998. Retention interventions for college students with AD/HD. In *Re-thinking AD/HD*, eds. P. Quinn and A. McCormick. Bethesda: Advantage Books.

McCracken, J. T. 1991. A two-part model of stimulant action on Attention-Deficit Hyperactivity Disorder in children. *Journal of Neuropsychiatry and Clinical Neurosciences.* 3:201–209.

McDermott, P. 1996. A nationwide study of developmental and gender prevalence for psychopathology in childhood and adolescence. *Journal of Abnormal Child Psychology* 24 (1):53–66.

Millon, T. 1987. *Millon Clinical Multiaxial Inventory II.* Minneapolis, MN: National Computer Systems, Inc.

Morgan, A. E., Hynd, G. W., Riccio, C. A., and Hall, J. 1996. Validity of DSM-IV ADHD predominantly inattentive and combined types: Relationship to previous DSM diagnoses/subtype differences. *Journal of the American Academy of Child and Adolescent Psychiatry.* 35 (3):325–33.

NIH Consensus Statement. 1998. Diagnosis and Treatment of Attention Deficit Hyperactivity Disorder, Nov. 16–18.

Peterson, K. Coaching Interventions and Strategies for Adults with Attention Deficit Disorder. Unpublished manuscript.

P. L. 94-142. The Education for All Handicapped Children Act of 1975, 20 U.S.C. SS1401 eq seq., 45 C.F.R. 121 (a).

Pliszka, S. R., McCracken, J. T., and Maas, J.W. 1996. Catecholamines in Attention-Deficit Hyperactivity Disorder: Current perspectives. *Journal of American Academy of Child and Adolescent Psychiatry* 35 (3):264–72.

Rapoport, J. L., Donnelly, M., Zametkin, A., and Carrougher, J. 1986. Situational hyperactivity in a U.S. clinical setting. *Journal of Child Psychology and Psychiatry* 27:639–46.

Ratey, J., Greenberg, M., and Lindem, K. 1991. Combination of treatments for Attention Deficit disorders in adults. *Journal of Nervous Mental Disorders* 176:699–701.

Ratey, J. J., Greenberg, M. S., Bemporad, J. R., and Lindem, K. J. 1992. Unrecognized attention-deficit hyperactivity disorder in adults presenting for outpatient therapy. *Journal of Child and Adolescent Psychopharmacology* 2 (4):267–75.

Ratey, N. 1997. Supporters give ADD coaching credit for low attrition rates, improved grades. *Disability Compliance for Higher Education* 3:5.

Rucklidge, J. J., and Kaplan, B. J. 1997. Psychological functioning of women identified in adulthood with attention-deficit/hyperactivity disorder. *Journal of Attention Disorders* 2 (3):167–76.

Rudel, R. G., Denckla, M. B., and Broman, M. 1978. Rapid silent response to repeated target symbols by dyslexic and nondyslexic children. *Brain and Language* 6:52–62.

Rugel, R. P. 1974. WISC subtest scores of disabled readers: A review with respect to Bannatyne's recategorization. *Journal of Learning Disablities* 7:48–55.

Safer, D. J., and Krager, J. M. 1988. A survey of medication treatment for hyperactive/inattentive students. *Journal of the American Medical Association* 260: 2256–8.

Salvador v. Bell, 622 F. Supp. 438 (N.D. III. 1985), affd, 800 F. 2d 97 (7th Cir. 1986).

Sandler, A. D. 1995. Attention deficits and neurodevelopmental variation in older adolescents and adults. In *A Comprehensive Guide to Attention Deficit Disorder in Adult*, ed. K.G. Nadeau. New York: Brunner/Mazel.

Schachar, R., Sandberg, S., and Rutter, M. 1986. Agreement between teacher ratings and observations of hyperactivity, inattentiveness, and defiance. *Journal of Abnormal Child Psychology* 14:331–35.

Section 504 of the Rehabilitation Act of 1973, 29 U.S.C. 794, 45 C.F.R. 81, 84.

Spencer, T., Wilens, T. E., Biederman, J., Faraone, S. V., Ablon, S., and Ras, J. F. 1995. A double blind comparison of methylphenidate and placebo in adults with Attention Deficit Hyperactivity Disorder. *Archives of General Psychiatry* 52.

Stanford, L. J., and Hynd, G. W. 1994. Congruence of behavioral symptomatology in children with Add/H, ADD/WO, and learning disabilities. *Journal of Learning Disabilities* 27 (4):243–53.

Stein, M. A., Sandoval, R., Szumowski, E., Roizen, N., Reinecke, M., Blondis, T., and Klein, Z. 1995. Psychometric characteristics of the Wender Utah Rating Scale (WURS): Reliability and factor structure for men and women. *Psychopharmacology Bulletin* 31:423–31.

Stuss, D. T., and Benson, D. F. 1986. *The Frontal Lobes*. New York: Raven Press.

Swanson, J. M., Sunohara, G. A., Kennedy, J. L., Regino, R., Fineberg, E., Wigal, E., Lahoste, G. J., and Wigal, S. 1997. Association of the dopamine receptor D4 (DRD4) gene with a refined phenotype of attention deficit hyperactivity disorder (ADHD): a family-based approach. Submitted for publication, University of California at Irvine.

Tinto, V. 1993. *Leaving College: Rethinking the Causes and Cures of Student Attrition*. (2nd edition). Chicago: The University of Chicago Press.

Turnock, P. 1998. Academic coping strategies in college students with symptoms of AD/HD. In *Re-thinking AD/HD* Bethesda MD: Advantage Books.

Van Tol, H. H. M., Wu, C. M., Guan, H., Ohara, K., Bunzow, J. R., Civelli, O., Kennedy, J., Seeman, P., Niznik, H. B., and Jovanovic, V. 1992. Multiple Dopamine D4 variants in the human population. *Nature* 358:149–52.

Wechsler, D. 1981. Wechsler Adult Intelligence—Revised. San Antonio, TX: The Psychological Corporation.

Wechsler, D. 1987. *Wechsler Memory Scale—Revised.* San Antonio, TX: The Psychological Corporation.

Weiss, G., and Hechtman, L. 1986. *Hyperactive Children Grow Up.* New York: Guilford Press.

Weiss, G., Hechtman, L., Milroy, T., and Perlman, T. 1985. Psychiatric status of hyperactives as adults: A controlled prospective 15-year follow-up of 63 hyperactive children. *Journal of the American Academy of Child Psychiatry* 24:211–20.

Weiss, L. 1994. *The Attention Deficit Disorder in Adults Workbook.* Dallas, TX: Taylor Publishing Company.

Wender, P. H., Reimherr, F. W., Wood, D., and Ward, M. 1985. A controlled study of methylphenidate in the treatment of attention deficit disorder, residual type, in adults. *American Journal of Psychiatry* 142:547–52.

Wender, P. H., Reimherr, F. W., Wood, D., et al. 1981. A controlled study of methylphenidate in the treatment of attention deficit disorder residual type in adults. *American Journal of Psychiatry* 142:547–52.

Wender, P. H., and Reimherr, F. W. 1990. Bupropion treatment of attention-deficit hyperactivity disorder in adults. *American Journal of Psychiatry* 147 (8):1018–20.

Wilens, T. E., Spencer, T. J., and Biederman, J. 1995. In *A Comprehensive Guide to Attention Deficit Disorder in Adults,* ed. K. G. Nadeau. New York: Brunner/Mazel, Inc.

Wilens, T. E., Biederman, J., Mick, E., and Spencer, T. 1995. A systematic assessment of tricyclic antidepressants in the treatment of adults with attention deficit disorders. *Journal of Nervous and Mental Disease.* 183: 48–50.

Wilens, T. E., Biederman, J., and Spencer, T. 1995. Venlafaxine for adult ADHD (letter). *American Journal of Psychiatry.* 152: 1099–100.

Wolraich, M. L., Hannah, J. N., Pinnock, T. Y., Baugaertel, A., and Brown, J. 1996. Comparison of diagnostic criteria for attention-deficit hyperactivity disorder in a county-wide sample. *Journal of the American Academy of Child and Adolescent Psychiatry* 35:319–24.

Zametkin, A. J., Nordahl, T. E., Gross, M., King, A. C., Semple, W. E., Rumsey, J., Hamburger, S., and Cohen, R. M. 1990. Cerebral glucose metabolism in adults with hyperactivity of childhood onset. *New England Journal of Medicine* 323:1361–6.

Zoccolillo, M. 1993. Gender and the development of conduct disorder. *Development and Psychopathology* 5:65–78.

Chapter • 10

Assistive Technology for Post-secondary Students with Learning Disabilities: *An Overview*[1]

Marshall H. Raskind and Eleanor L. Higgins

Over the last decade, the number of students with learning disabilities (LD) entering post-secondary programs in the United States has grown faster than any other disability classification (American Council on Education 1992, 1995). According to the National Center for Education Statistics (1999), as of 1998, there were approximately 195,870 post-secondary students who identified themselves as LD. This number represents almost 50% of all students with disabilities in post-secondary settings. Students with LD now make up the single largest disability group on United States campuses.

This increase in the population of students with LD, coupled with federal legislation (Section 504 of the Rehabilitation Act of 1973, Subpart E) mandating "academic adjustments" for students with disabilities, prompted post-secondary institutions to develop LD support service programs aimed at promoting academic retention and success (Beirne-Smith and Deck 1989; Vogel 1987; Vogel and Adelman 1993). Although the specific services offered by individual programs vary (Shaw, McGuire, and Brinkerhoff 1994; Vogel 1993), programs often

---

[1]This section draws heavily from previous publications—Raskind and Scott (1993) and Raskind and Higgins (1998)—but is updated to reflect the most current technological developments.

provide readers, note takers, tutors, counselors, academic advisors, advocates, compensatory strategy instruction, diagnostic assessment, and test-taking modifications. In addition to the above services, post-secondary LD support programs are offering increasing levels of assistive technology (sometimes referred to as "auxiliary aids" or "adaptive technology"; Adelman and Vogel 1993; Bryant, Rivera, and Warde 1993; Mellard 1994; Raskind and Scott 1993; Rothstein 1993; Shaw, McGuire, and Brinkerhoff 1994).

According to the Technology-Related Assistance for Individuals with Disabilities Act of 1988 (P.L. 100-407), an assistive technology device refers to "any item, piece of equipment, or product system, whether acquired commercially off-the-shelf, modified, or customized, that is used to increase, maintain, or improve the functional capabilities of individuals with disabilities." For the purposes of this chapter, assistive technology is further delineated as any technology that enables an individual with LD to compensate for specific deficits. In some instances the technology may assist or augment task performance in a given area of disability, while in others it is used to circumvent or "bypass" (not remediate) specific deficits entirely.

A review of the approximately 1,000 listings in Peterson's Colleges with Programs for Students with Learning Disabilities (Mangrum and Strichart 1997) indicates that virtually all LD support service programs provide some form of assistive technology (listed under "auxiliary aids") to their students. These assistive technologies are most likely to include basic devices such as tape recorders, word processors, spell checkers, and calculators. To a much lesser extent, many programs also offer speech synthesizers, optical character recognition (OCR) systems, listening aids, and speech recognition systems.

The purpose of this chapter is to provide an overview of assistive technology as it relates to post-secondary students with LD. Specifically, we will (a) briefly trace the development of assistive technology service for post-secondary students with LD; (b) identify basic models of assistive technology service delivery and specific services; (c) provide a description of specific assistive technologies; (d) review research on the effectiveness of assistive technology with post-secondary students with LD, with a focus on the authors' three-year federally funded study; and (e) conclude with a summary and recommendations.

THE DEVELOPMENT OF ASSISTIVE TECHNOLOGY SERVICE DELIVERY

It is difficult to determine the precise factors that lead to assistive technology use with post-secondary students with LD. The entry of assistive technology into post-secondary LD programs was undoubtedly the result of multiple forces and influences both within and outside of post-secondary institutions, and reflects the growing interest in and use of technology in society as a whole. Such forces likely include the growth of technology (e.g., academic computing, electronic information systems) on post-secondary campuses, the tremendous influx of persons with LD into post-secondary settings, combined with federal legislation that mandates "academic adjustments" (including the availability of auxiliary aids) and increases the financial and personnel demands of providing support services to the ever-growing population of individuals with LD (Vogel 1987). The provision of assistive technology (e.g., tape recorders, OCR) to students with other disabilities may also have acted as a catalyst. Additional factors included an early awareness on the part of several technology developers/manufacturers (e.g., Xerox, Humanware, Arkenstone) of the need for LD products, and the vast LD market; the passage of the Americans with Disabilities Act of 1990; Section 508 of the Rehabilitation Act of 1973 (the Act was amended in 1986); the Individuals with Disabilities Education Act of 1990 (which now includes specific mention of assistive technology); and the Technology-Related Assistance for Individuals with Disabilities Act of 1988.

There are a number of other traceable forces that made a major contribution to promoting the use of assistive technology, although it is impossible to determine the exact manner in which they influenced post-secondary LD programs or their degree of impact. These forces include the establishment of the High-Tech Center for the Disabled of the California Community Colleges Chancellor's Office in 1986, which led to a network of more than 100 High-Tech Centers for the Disabled. These centers were designed to provide students with disabilities, including LD, "training in, and access to, supportive technologies that [would] allow them to compete effectively in both academic and workplace environments" (Brown, Norris, and Rivers 1989, p. 389) and also establish a research, evaluation, and training facility for directors of disabled student service programs at all of the 107 California community colleges. Project EASI (Equal Access to Software and Information), founded in 1988 as a special interest group of EDUCOM (a consortium of more than 600 colleges and universities and approximately 100 corporate associates), also played a prominent role in promoting the use of assistive technology for post-secondary students with LD. This group acted as a leading resource for the higher education community on developing computer support service for persons with disabilities, via seminars, online workshops, and numerous publications on "adaptive computing technology," including technology for persons with LD.

The California State University, Northridge (CSUN), Center on Disability also had an impact on the area of assistive technology and post-secondary students with LD when it initiated (in 1985) one of the first conferences on technology and disability, and created a specific topical strand on assistive technology and post-secondary students with disabilities. This provided a forum for some of the first presentations in the area. The CSUN program also established a comprehensive LD support service program and computer access lab in 1985, which provided a vast array of assistive technology to students from a number of disability categories, and the opportunity to intensively explore the potential benefits of numerous assistive technologies for post-secondary students with LD. These initial informal investigations set the stage for a series of formal research studies on the effectiveness of several assistive technologies with post-secondary students with LD, which will be discussed later in this article.

In addition to the aforementioned organizations and programs, Murphy (1991), in a report from the National Council on Disability, identified 17 exemplary technology support programs for post-secondary students with disabilities, nine of which include services for students with LD. These programs have acted as models in the area of assistive technology and post-secondary students with LD and include Disabled Student Services, University of Wyoming; the Assistive Technology Center, University of Minnesota; the Disabled Computing Program, University of California, Los Angeles; the Office of Services for Students with Disabilities, University of Nebraska; the Adaptive Computing Technology Center, University of Missouri; the Adaptive Technology Laboratory, Southern Connecticut State University; and the Center for the Vocationally Challenged, Grossmont Community College in El Cajon, California. The two remaining programs include those already discussed, the California Community College High-Tech Center and the CSUN program.

DELIVERY OF ASSISTIVE TECHNOLOGY TO POST-SECONDARY STUDENTS WITH LD

Assistive technology service delivery models and services vary considerably among institutions. Although at the time this paper was written, no nationally representative random sample of assistive technology service delivery for students with LD is available, basic models and practices can be discerned from a review of the limited literature (Brown 1987; Burgstahler 1992; Cutler 1990; EASI 1991; Horn and Shell 1990; Murphy 1991; Raskind and Scott 1993). First, the institutional office or department charged with managing assistive technology services varies from campus to campus. In most instances, the provision of assistive technology is managed by either student service offices for the disabled, academic/departmental computing services, or the institution's central computing department. Murphy indicated that of the nine exemplary technology support programs reporting LD services, four were coordinated by the office of disabled student services, four by the central computing department, and one program was "self-managed." Similarly, Burgstahler, in a survey of technology services for students with disabilities at 1,200 post-secondary institutions, found that the departments most likely to manage computing services were, in descending order, student service offices for the disabled, central computing services, and departmental computing services.

The location of the assistive technology also differs from one institution to the next, with some programs distributing assistive technology throughout the campus (distributive model) at existing computer sites, and others providing assistive technology at a central location. Proponents of the distributive approach assert that it is more in line with federal regulations mandating integration of students with disabilities, and that it helps ensure greater access to the full range of campus-computing resources, while advocates of the centralized model argue that housing assistive technology services in a central location results in greater levels of student satisfaction and success, as well as more efficient delivery of services (Burgstahler 1992). According to Burgstahler, the majority of post-secondary service providers for disabled students endorse the distributive model.

In addition to the management and location of assistive technology, programs also vary considerably in regard to the specific services provided. These variations can involve (a) a range of assistive technologies available (e.g., OCR, spell checkers, word prediction, abbreviation expansion, speech recognition, outlining, speech synthesis); (b) the specific brands or models of assistive technology provided (e.g., DragonDictateTM vs. Kurzweil VoiceTM speech recognition); (c) the extent and model of training or support provided; (d) the background/expertise of the personnel providing training or support; (e) the degree of technical support offered to students; (f) the presence or absence of "user groups"; (g) whether an equipment loan program exists; and (h) provisions for funding. Again, to date, there are no published data to help determine the exact assistive technology services provided to post-secondary students with LD across the nation.

OVERVIEW OF ASSISTIVE TECHNOLOGIES

This section will present an overview of assistive technologies currently available for assisting adults with LD (space limitations will not permit a discussion of all technologies; see note 1). The technologies discussed in this section have been suggested for use with post-secondary LD students by a number of authors (e.g., Brown 1987; Bryant, Rivera, and Warde 1993; Raskind and Scott 1993; Shaw, McGuire, and Brinkerhoff 1994; Raskind and Higgins 1995; Higgins and Raskind 1995; Higgins and Raskind 1997). Recommendations are based primarily on case studies and clinical observations and are not necessarily supported by formal research (research on assistive technologies will be discussed in the next section). The authors of this article have used these technologies with approximately 400 students over an 8-year period in the Learning Disability Program and Computer Access Lab at CSUN (part of the Office of Disabled Student Services).

Technologies will be discussed relative to the difficulties experienced by post-secondary students with LD and grouped according to the area of disability the technology is intended to circumvent. Several of the technologies have more than one application and thus will be listed under more than one heading. It is important to stress that not all the technologies discussed are appropriate for all students with LD, and that a technology that might be extremely valuable to one person might be ineffective, or even detrimental, for another. Therefore, it is imperative that technologies be chosen relative to the particular individual's strengths, weaknesses, interests, and experiences; the function to be performed; and the context of interaction.

Written Language

Word Processing.   The written language difficulties of adults with LD have been well documented (e.g., Gregg and Hoy 1989; Hughes and Smith 1990; Johnson 1987; Vogel 1985). In fact, Blalock (1981) asserted that between 80% and 90% of adults with LD exhibit written language disorders. Several researchers (e.g., Collins 1990; Primus 1990) have found word processors valuable in helping persons with LD compensate for written language difficulties. Unlike the conventional methods of writing with pencil and paper or typewriter, word processors enable users with LD to write without having to be overly concerned with making errors, as text can be easily corrected on-screen prior to printing.

When not preoccupied with the mechanical aspects of writing, persons with LD have a greater opportunity to focus on meaning. This is of particular importance for those individuals who have developed a fear of translating their thoughts into written language as the result of a history of writing problems and the criticism that often follows. Knowing that they can simply generate language and correct errors later may reduce their anxiety, liberate their writing abilities, and ultimately facilitate written expression at a level commensurate with their intelligence. Furthermore, word processing may lead to neater and cleaner documents, which may in turn help foster in students a sense of pride in their written work and enhance their image of themselves as writers.

Spell Checking. Many adults with LD have written language disorders that include difficulty with spelling (Johnson 1987; Vogel and Moran 1982). The use of spell checkers (generally included in word processing programs) can help compensate for such problems, because they permit the user to check for misspelled words within a document before a final copy is made. Spell checkers match the words in a document against words in the spell checker's dictionary, and if a match is not found, the user is alerted by a visual or auditory cue and is presented with a list of words from which to choose the correctly spelled word. The user selects the correct word and the computer automatically corrects the misspelled word in the text. Some spell checkers alert the user to spelling errors while typing (which may be disruptive to some students), whereas others check for mistakes after the document has been completed.

Selecting the correct word from a list of options can be a difficult task for many LD students. Cross-checking the words for synonyms in the word processor's thesaurus or dictionary (if available) can assist in the selection process. The use of a speech synthesizer/screen reader (see the following section) may also help the user identify the correct word.

In addition to spell checkers that are part of word processing programs, there are also battery-operated stand-alone spell checkers that are available in desktop and pocket sizes. Basic units will simply verify and correct spelling on a liquid crystal display (LCD), whereas more sophisticated devices also provide dictionaries and thesauri. Some of these units are now equipped with speech synthesizers, which enable the user to hear, as well as to see, the word in question, along with definitions, synonyms, and help messages.

It is important to note that spell checkers often do not recognize the misspellings of individuals with LD. In some instances, this is because the misspelled forms are the correct spelling of other words (MacArthur 1996). In other instances, the spellings are too far removed from the "rules" used by the spell checker to identify misspelled words. Several products have been introduced that claim to identify more accurately the misspellings (and suggest the correct spelling) of persons with LD, however, research to support the claims have not been published to date.

Proofreading Programs. Adults with LD who experience written language problems may also benefit from the use of proofreading programs. These software programs (now included in many word processors) scan word processing documents and alert users to probable errors in punctuation, grammar, word usage, structure, spelling, style, or capitalization. Most of these programs can be used either to mark probable errors or to mark the error and attach a commentary (e.g., "Be sure you are using 'is' with a singular subject"). Many programs include online tutorials that allow the user to study the language rules checked by the program.

It is important to stress that proofreading programs are not completely accurate and will not pick up all grammatical errors or objectionable phrases in a document. They may also make incorrect suggestions, sometimes prompting the user to correct elements of writing that are not really incorrect. In addition, some individuals with LD may find these programs demeaning, with the technology playing the role of an intolerant "electronic teacher," criticizing them and possibly intensifying feelings of incompetence and low self-esteem.

Outlining / Brainstorming.   Although some individuals with LD may have great ideas in their heads, getting them down on paper may be another story. Writing that first word or sentence can be an insurmountable task, and even if the person can get started, he or she may have difficulty determining how to proceed. Many persons with LD have difficulty organizing a paper with regard to topic, categories, and sequence (Johnson 1987). Outlining programs (now included in most standard word processing programs) can help with such difficulties because they enable the user to "dump," in an unstructured manner, information that can subsequently be placed in appropriate categories and order.

Although each program has it own features, generally, the user types in any idea or thought on a specified topic, without regard to overall organization. By using a few simple keystrokes (or, with a mouse, pointing and clicking), the outlining program will automatically create the Roman numerals for major headings, and letters and numbers for subordinate headings. The user need not be concerned with order, levels of importance, or categories, as text can be easily moved at a later time. Once basic ideas have been written down, those ideas that are related, or that seem to "go together," provide the basis for major headings or categories. Ideas that fall under any major heading can be easily reduced to any level of subordinate heading. Even if the user determines at a later time that an idea does not belong under a certain heading, this does not pose a problem because any piece of text can easily be moved within the outline as many times as necessary. The program automatically reorganizes the Roman numerals, letters, and numbers designated for specific headings. Outlining programs also enable users to limit what is viewed on the computer screen to only the major headings, to facilitate an overview of the document, as well as to select single subordinate headings and view all information under it for a detailed analysis. This may be a useful option for persons who become so focused on details that they cannot see the big picture, or, inversely, for those whose writing is excessively "skeletal" and lacking in detail.

Programs (e.g., Inspiration®) also exist that have graphic capabilities that can facilitate brainstorming by enabling the users to create a diagram of their ideas (semantic webs, "mind maps," cluster diagrams) prior to formulating an outline. The user types in a main idea that is displayed on the screen. Related ideas are then added and appear in specified geometric shapes (e.g., circles, ovals, rectangles) surrounding the central idea. Ideas may be linked with the main idea (and each other) by lines. Ideas can easily be moved, rearranged, and categorized. Detailed notes can also be attached to specific ideas and hidden from view. Ultimately, the graphic representation can automatically be converted to an outline. This nonlinear, "free-form" graphic approach may be even more helpful than simple text-based outlining to some students.

Abbreviation Expanders. Abbreviation expansion is used in conjunction with word processing and allows users to create their own abbreviations for frequently used words, phrases, or standard pieces of text, thus saving keystrokes and, ultimately, the amount of time it takes to prepare written documents. This is an important consideration in light of the fact that some students with LD take longer than their peers without LD to complete tasks (Blalock and Johnson 1987). For example, a student with LD in a history class who has to type out "industrial revolution" frequently in completing written assignments might create the abbreviation "ir." To expand an abbreviation, the user simply types in the abbreviation and presses the space bar on the keyboard (or depending on the particular program, points and clicks), and the abbreviation is expanded into its original form. Abbreviations are easily recorded by executing a few simple commands and can be saved from one writing session to another. Abbreviation expansion is an integral part of some word processing programs and is also available as "memory resident add-on" programs (operating simultaneously with the word processing program).

Speech Recognition. Speech recognition systems appropriate for use by post-secondary students with LD operate in conjunction with personal computers (and specific laptops) and consist of speech recognition software (internal board), software, headphones, and a microphone. Speech recognition systems enable the user to operate the computer by speaking to it. This may be particularly helpful to those individuals with LD whose oral language exceeds their written language abilities (King and Rental 1981; Myklebust 1973). Used in conjunction with word processors, speech recognition systems enable the user to dictate (via microphone) to the computer—converting oral language to written text. These systems automatically learn the phonetic characteristics of a person's voice while that person dictates to the system. The more the system is used, the better it is able to understand what the user is saying.

There are two basic types of systems: discrete and continuous speech. Discrete speech systems (e.g., Dragon Dictate™) require a calculated pause of approximately 1/10 second between words. The word the system "thinks" the person has spoken is placed on the screen. If the word is incorrect, the user can choose the correct word from a menu/list of similar-sounding words that appear on the screen (this feature is not present in all systems). It should be noted that all keyboard editing and control commands (e.g., "delete word") can be done with the voice alone. In contrast to discrete speech, continuous speech systems (e.g., Dragon Naturally Speaking™, IBM Via Voice®) allow the user to dictate without pausing between words. Incorrect words can be corrected by either voice or keyboard commands.

Speech Synthesis/Screen Reading.   Several authors have suggested that speech synthesis be used as an assistive technology for post-secondary students with LD (e.g., Brown 1987; Norris and Graef 1990). Speech synthesis refers to a synthetic or computerized voice-output system usually consisting of an internal board or external hardware device. In conjunction with "screen reading" software, a speech synthesizer will read back text displayed on a computer screen so that the user can hear as well as see what is displayed. Text can be read back a letter, word, line, sentence, paragraph, or screen at a time. Screen-reading programs (e.g., eReader, Read&Write) that are specifically designed for individuals with LD and that simultaneously visually highlight words as they are spoken are now available. In most cases the speed, pitch, and tone of voice can be set to accommodate individual preferences. The voice quality of speech synthesizers varies considerably, from more "human" to more "mechanical" sounding voices. In some instances, the more mechanical-sounding voices are actually more intelligible. There are also synthesizers available that provide the user with the opportunity to select a number of different voices (e.g., male, female, young, old).

Speech synthesis/screen review technology, when combined with a word processing program, may be helpful to students with written language deficits. (The systems discussed here should be differentiated from speech synthesis systems that are tied to specific word processing programs.) This is especially true for individuals who possess oral language skills that are superior to their written language abilities. For these persons, the ability to hear what they have written may enable them to catch errors in grammar, spelling, and punctuation that would otherwise go unrecognized. Having the auditory feedback also helps alert the user with LD to problems regarding the coherence and semantic integrity of his or her document.

Word Prediction.   Word prediction software supports word processing programs by "predicting" the word a user is entering into the computer. Predictions are based on syntax and spelling, as well as frequency, redundancy, and recency factors. Some programs also "learn" the user's word preferences. Typically, word prediction programs operate in the following manner. As the first letter of a word is typed, the program offers a list of words beginning with that letter. If the desired word appears in the list, the user can then choose the word (by pressing a corresponding number, or pointing and clicking) and the desired word will automatically be inserted into the sentence. If the desired word is not displayed, the user enters the second letter of the word and a new list appears with words beginning with those two letters. The user continues this process until the desired word is offered in the list. If the word is not included in the program's database, it can be added for future use. After a word is chosen, the next word in the sentence is predicted, even before the first letter is typed. Again, if the desired word is not present, then the user continues to enter the letters until the word appears.

Word prediction can be helpful to post-secondary students with LD for several reasons. First, because the program minimizes the number of keystrokes it takes to enter a word, students with poor keyboarding skills may find these programs easier and faster to use than standard word processors. Second, the program acts as a compensatory spelling aid, as it automatically spells the word out, and the user need only recognize the word within the list. Additionally, because these programs use grammatical rules to predict words, students with syntactical deficits may find the programs helpful. Finally, students who have word-finding difficulties may discover that the word list acts as a prompt, cuing them to the appropriate word. It is important to realize that, in some instances, word prediction programs may actually interfere with the writing process (Cutler 1991). The word list may be distracting, and having to stop and choose words may slow some students down, especially students who have significant difficulty in word recognition or who are proficient typists.

Word prediction programs are available as add-on programs that work in conjunction with standard word processors, and also as integrated word prediction/word processing software packages.

Reading

Speech Synthesis/Screen Reading.   The benefits of speech synthesis systems are not limited to use with word processors. They may also be used to review materials written by others, including software tutorials, help systems, letters, and reports. These systems will read essentially any text on a computer screen. Some systems will read electronic text on the Internet.

Some organizations, including Recordings for the Blind and Dyslexic and the American Printing House for the Blind, are now producing "books on disk," which make it possible for persons with LD to listen to text by means of a speech synthesis system. Persons with LD are eligible to receive services from these organizations. There are also several online electronic-text library collections available through the Internet, that house large collections of classic works that have the potential to be read aloud by means of a speech synthesis/screen review system.

Optical Character Recognition/Speech Synthesis Systems.   An OCR system might be thought of as a "reading machine." Optical character recognition systems provide a means of putting in text/printed material (e.g., a page in a book, a letter) directly into a computer. Text is put in by using a full-page flatbed scanner in which a page of text is placed face down on the device (much like a copy machine), or a hand-held scanner which the user moves across a page of text (or down, depending on the particular system), or a full-page scanner. "Book-edge" (designed for bound text) scanners and automatic document feeders are also available for several systems. Once the text has been scanned into the computer, it can then be read back to the user by means of a speech synthesis/screen reading system. This technology may be particularly helpful to those LD individuals who exhibit no difficulty comprehending spoken language (Gough and Tunmer 1986), yet have problems understanding language in the written form (Hughes and Smith 1990).

Optical Character Reader systems are of two basic types—"stand alone" or PC-based. Stand alone (or "self-contained") systems have all components built into one device, including the scanner, OCR software/hardware, and the speech synthesizer. Some stand-alone systems are portable (about the size of a briefcase), others are desktop units. The PC-based systems consist of a number of components that are hooked up to a PC. These components consist of a full-page (desktop) or hand-held scanner, an OCR board and/or software, and a speech synthesizer. Several companies have designed systems with the LD individual in mind (i.e., Kurzweil 3000, Arkenstone's WYNN) that simultaneously highlight words as they are spoken back by the system.

In addition to OCR/speech synthesis systems described above, a fully portable, pocket-sized (smaller than a TV remote control) "reading pen" has been introduced into the marketplace (i.e., Quicktionary™ Reading Pen). Using a "miniaturized" optical scanning system, this battery-operated device enables the user to scan single words on a page (e.g., textbook, magazine) and have the word read aloud by means of a built-in speech synthesizer. The product also provides definitions for the scanned words.

Variable Speech Control Tape Recorders.   Portable audiocassette recorders have been recommended by a number of authorities as a compensatory aid for post-secondary students with LD (Mangrum and Strichart 1988; Scheiber and Talpers 1985). Among the possibilities is the use of tape recorders for listening to books on audiotape, which may help students with reading difficulties circumvent their disability by listening to prerecorded text (books, journals, newspapers). Prerecorded text is available from a number of sources, including The Library of Congress, Recordings for the Blind, and several private companies. Although tape recorders may be helpful to some students, they may present problems for individuals with LD who have difficulty processing auditory information at standard playback rates (McCroskey and Thompson 1973). This problem can be alleviated by the use of variable speech-control (VSC) tape recorders, which, unlike conventional tape recorders (or units that simply have different record/playback speeds), enable the user to play back audio taped material slower or faster than the rate at which it was initially recorded, without the loss of intelligibility, which is maintained by adjusting speed and pitch control levers. These devices enable the user to slow down prerecorded text by 25% without loss of intelligibility.

Organization/Memory

Personal Data Managers.   Post-secondary students with LD often have difficulty remembering, organizing, and managing personal information (Mangrum and Strichart 1988; Vogel 1987). It may be a question of scheduling appointments, prioritizing activities, remembering important dates/deadlines, or recording/accessing names, addresses, and phone numbers. The use of personal data managers can compensate for difficulties in this area. Personal data managers are available as software programs as well as self-contained hand-held units and allow the user to easily store and retrieve vast amounts of personal information. Data is input and retrieved via keyboard/keypad or stylus and is displayed on a computer monitor or LCD display. Some pocket-size data managers (e.g., Parrot) allow the user to enter and retrieve data by speaking into the device. Stored data are spoken back in the user's own voice. Additionally, selected hand-held units permit the exchange of information between device and a computer. Data managers have numerous capabilities and a diverse combination of functions. Typical features include monthly calendars, daily schedules/planners/appointments, clocks/alarms, memo files, "to do lists," name/address books, telephone directories (some with electronic dialers), and bankbooks/check registers/money managers.

Free-Form Databases.   Like personal data managers, free-form databases can also be valuable to individuals with organizational and/or memory problems. These software programs work with computers and might be thought of as "computerized Post-It™ note" systems. They are memory resident and can be activated while in a word processor or other program by simply pressing a "hot key." Users can create their own notes, of any length, on any subject, in much the same way people use sticky notes, a notepad, or scraps of paper to jot down important information. Unlike a manual system, free-form databases enable the user to store the notes in the computer's memory electronically, rather than on tiny pieces of paper that are easily misplaced. Perhaps more important than how the information is stored is how it is retrieved. A note can be retrieved by typing in any piece or fragment of information contained in the note. For example, the note *Carl Stevens, Advanced Electronics, Inc., 835 West Arden, Northridge, CA 91330, (818) 306-1954* could be brought up on the computer's screen by inputting any of the following information, including (but not limited to) "Carl," "Advanced," "West," "North," and "818."

Listening Aids

Personal FM Listening Systems.   Research has indicated that some adults with LD have difficulty focusing auditorily on a speaker (Hasbrouck 1980). Such difficulties may lead to misunderstanding or missing information presented during a classroom lecture or meeting. One device that may help students with LD focus on a speaker is a personal FM listening system. These technological aids consist of two basic components: a wireless transmitter with a microphone and a receiver with a headset or earphone. For situations in which there is only one speaker (e.g., a professor in a classroom), the speaker wears the transmitter unit (about 2 to 3 inches in size.), while the user wears the receiver unit (also about 2 to 3 inches in size). The transmitter and receiver are easily clipped to a belt or shirt pocket. The microphone is only about $1^1/2$ inches long and is easily clipped to clothing (e.g., a tie). When there are multiple speakers (e.g., during a meeting), an omni-directional microphone enclosed in a small, stand-alone unit is placed in an area that is the center of the conversation. Essentially, these systems carry the speaker's voice directly from the speaker's mouth to the listener's ear. Volume is easily controlled by a dial on the receiver. These devices run on AA size rechargeable or disposable batteries.

Tape Recorders.   In addition to helping compensate for reading disabilities, tape recorders may also be useful to the student with listening difficulties (as well as those with memory problems). Tape recorders can be utilized to record classroom lectures, as either an alternative or a supplement to taking notes. This may be beneficial for students with LD who have listening difficulties (because of either difficulty processing oral language or attentional disorders), because they can review lectures at a later date, listening to tapes as many times as necessary to comprehend the material. The ability to commit a lecture to permanent record may also aid students with other types of difficulties, including those who find it difficult to take notes and listen simultaneously, students with fine-motor dysfunction, and those with auditory memory problems. Variable speech control tape recorders may be particularly helpful in reviewing taped material, as they enable the user to increase the speech rate (generally up to 100%) in order to reduce the amount of time it takes to "re-listen," or, as previously discussed, reduce speech rates to more comprehensible levels.

Math

Talking Calculators.   A talking calculator is simply a calculator with a speech synthesizer. When number, symbol, or operation keys are pressed, they are vocalized/spoken by a built-in speech synthesizer. In this way, the user receives simultaneous auditory feedback for checking the accuracy of visual-motor operations. Once a calculation has been made, the number can be read back via the synthesizer. This feature enables the user to double-check the answers being transferred from calculator to paper. Bryant, Rivera, and Warde (1993) stressed that post-secondary students with LD are likely to need scientific programmable calculators.

It is important to note that the speed at which calculations are performed may be problematic, because it takes longer to have operations spoken than displayed. Second, some students may experience "stimulus overload" when having to contend with both visual and auditory feedback. As with all technologies, individual profiles and preferences will have to be considered.

RESEARCH ON THE EFFECTIVENESS OF ASSISTIVE TECHNOLOGY

Although increasing, there is still a paucity of formal research regarding the effectiveness of assistive technology for post-secondary students with LD. Indications of effectiveness have been derived primarily from anecdotal reports and case studies (e.g., Brown 1987; Bryant, Rivera, and Warde 1993; Collins 1990; Collins and Price 1986; Cutler 1990, 1991; Norris and Graef 1990; Primus 1990; Raskind and Scott 1993). The limited research that has been conducted in this area is briefly reviewed below. Particular attention will be given to the authors' federally funded research at CSUN.

Collins (1990) conducted a three-year study on the impact of word processing on the writing performance of college students with LD in a required first-year writing course. Results suggested that the use of word processors helped the students complete the course at a rate similar to that of their peers without a disability, achieve grades at least comparable to their peers', and improve their writing fluency. According to the researcher, the use of word processors also led to a significant reduction in writing anxiety among students with LD. Similarly, Primus (1990) studied the impact of word processing on the grades and grade-point averages (GPAs) of university students with LD. Results of the study indicated that first year students' English grades and semester and cumulative grade-point averages were higher for students with LD who used word processors than for non-computer users with LD while they were taking first year English. However, the researcher emphasized that the trend toward higher academic performance was not sustained throughout the participants' academic careers.

McNaughton, Hughes, and Clark (1997) investigated the effect of five writing conditions on the spelling performance of college students with LD: handwriting, handwriting with a conventional print dictionary, handwriting with a handheld spell checker, word processing, and word processing with an integrated spell checker. Results indicated that the word processor with an integrated spell checker provided a statistically significant advantage over the other four conditions in the detection of spelling errors. The word processor with an integrated spell checker also showed a statistically significant advantage over handwriting and word processing (but not over the other conditions) in "correction activities." The authors also reported that the word processor with spell checker demonstrated a significant advantage over handwriting and word processing, but not over handwriting in combination with a spell checker or conventional dictionary.

Elkind, Black, and Murray (1996) studied the use of optical character recognition with speech synthesis, as a compensatory tool for college students with dyslexia. The researchers report that the technology enhanced the reading rate and comprehension of most of the subjects. Furthermore, the technology enabled subjects to increase the length of time they were able to sustain attention to reading.

A comprehensive three-year study on assistive technology for post-secondary students with LD was conducted by the Center on Disability at CSUN. In the first year of the project, the compensatory effectiveness of the following three technologies was investigated: (a) OCR/speech synthesis as a compensatory reading strategy, (b) speech synthesis/screen review as a compensatory proofreading strategy, and (c) speech recognition as a compensatory writing strategy. In years two and three of the project, changes in academic outcomes, behaviors, and attitudes as a result of assistive technology use were studied. The cost effectiveness of these technologies was also investigated in the final year of the project. A brief description and the results of each phase of the project appear below.[2]

During the first year of the study the immediate compensatory effectiveness of the technologies was investigated. Optical character readers in conjunction with speech synthesis were evaluated as to their effectiveness in compensating for difficulties with reading comprehension. Thirty-seven post-secondary students with LD in the area of reading[3] were trained on the technologies and given the Formal Reading Inventory (Wiederholt 1986) under three conditions: (a) reading the test silently without assistance; (b) having the test read aloud by a human reader; and (c) converting (scanning) the test into a computer document using an OCR system, then having it read aloud via a speech synthesis/screen review system. No differences were found in the means of standard scores across the three conditions. This was due to the fact that the technologies helped some readers while interfering with the performance of others. There was, however, a significant correlation ($p = .001$) between silent reading scores and scores obtained via the assistive technology; that is, the greater the disability in silent reading, the more the technology assisted the student to compensate

---

[2]For a complete report on the speech synthesis and speech recognition compensatory effectiveness studies, see Higgins and Raskind (1997), Raskind and Higgins (1995), and Higgins and Raskind (1995), respectively.

[3]Students were selected from the CSUN Learning Disability Program and identified as LD in accord with the criteria of the California State University Chancellor's Office.

for the difficulty. A similar but weaker correlation was found when the test was read aloud by a human reader ($p > .01$). These findings, taken together, suggest that the auditory presentation of text (whether by human voice or by computer) assisted less proficient readers with the decoding process (thus elevating their scores), but interfered with the more efficient silent reading processes for the proficient readers.

Speech synthesis/screen review was also assessed as to its effectiveness in increasing students' efficiency at proofreading written compositions. Thirty-four students with LD in the area of written language composed the first draft of an essay of approximately 500 words in length. The essay was divided into three equal parts, each of which was proofread under the following conditions: (a) without assistance; (b) having the essay section read aloud by a human reader; and (c) having the essay section read by the speech synthesis/screen review system. Students found significantly more errors overall using speech synthesis/screen review than when proofreading without assistance or proofreading while a human reader read the essay section aloud. Additionally, speech synthesis/screen review proved superior at assisting students in finding particular types of errors in comparison to proofreading without assistance.[4] Typographical errors as well as errors in capitalization, spelling, and usage were found at a significantly higher rate using the technology. Having the essay section read aloud by a human reader proved significantly superior to proofreading without assistance for two types of errors, spelling and mechanical grammar errors. Finally, when comparing human readers to speech synthesis/screen review, human readers were superior to the technology at a significant level for one category mechanical grammar errors (Raskind and Higgins 1995).

Finally, speech recognition technology was evaluated for its compensatory effectiveness at improving written composition skills. Twenty-nine post-secondary students with LD in the area of written language were trained on the speech recognition system and asked to write three essays under the following conditions: (a) without assistance (students could either handwrite or use a word processor to generate the "no assistance" essay); (b) dictating the essay to a human transcriber; and (c) using a speech recognition system. The essays were designed to emulate the Upper Division Written Proficiency Examination (WPE), a timed, holistically scored essay required by the university for a student to graduate. Significantly more students received a higher holistic score on the essay written using speech recognition than on the one written without assistance ($p > .05$). A post hoc

---

[4]Error categories included capitalization, punctuation, spelling, usage, grammar-mechanical, grammar-global, typographical, content/organization, and literary style.

analysis of the essays indicated that students used significantly more long words (words of seven or more letters) when using the equipment and, further, that the use of words with seven or more letters was positively correlated with better holistic scores at a significant level ($p > .0001$).

In years two and three of the project, changes in academic outcomes, behaviors, and attitudes as a result of assistive technology use were studied. These results are reported briefly below. It is important to emphasize that this portion of the study was more descriptive than experimental. Data were derived from interviews, questionnaires, and self-reports, supplemented where possible by computer log-on records, official reports, and databases that documented the use of services. It is acknowledged that many of the reported changes may have been due to factors other than those under investigation. It is also possible that the sample self-selected, with participants of particular "psychological constitutions" or having particular personality characteristics being drawn to participate in the study.

The 140 students who received training on the technology over the 3-year period showed several positive academic outcomes: (a) participants significantly ($p > .05$) increased their GPAs for courses with heavy reading and/or composition requirements, whereas a matched control group did not (although these gains were not sufficient to increase overall GPAs so that they reached significance); (b) the university attrition rate for the 140 participants was only 1.4% over the three-year period, compared to 34% for a matched group of students with LD who did not participate in training (and 48% for students without a disability over four years; Office of the Chancellor 1994); (c) although participants in the study showed numbers of withdrawals and incompletes similar to the matched group's, they showed significantly higher rates of repeating the courses until a satisfactory grade was obtained; and (d) participants' WPE first-time passage rate was 95%, compared to 50% passage rates for both the matched group and the population of LD students prior to the study, and a 75% overall passage rate for the general CSUN population.

Examination of log-on programs and responses to pre- and post-training questionnaires revealed several changes in academic behaviors among the participants in the study. These changes included: (a) a 78% increase in hours of use of assistive technology in general, which was accounted for primarily by greater use of word processing; (b) an increase among 75% of the participants in extending the use of word processors for academic purposes other than composition, such as note taking, organizing course content, outlining reading material, and managing time; (c) an increase among 90% of the participants in expanding the use of computers into nonacademic settings (e.g., employment, recreational/social); (d) increases in the use of assistive technologies not utilized in the study (e.g., VSC tape recorders, books on tape); and (e) an eightfold increase in the use of the three technologies under study by persons trained in the study.

An examination of databases documenting use of services through the computer access lab and of questionnaire responses also indicated that participation in the study and/or use of assistive technology was accompanied by changes in the use of compensatory strategies other than technological strategies, including: (a) an initial tendency by newly identified students to increase their use of services offered by the CSUN Learning Disability Program and other campus services, followed by a decrease in the use of services by previously identified students, over the three-year period; (b) an overall increase in independence, suggested by students' less frequent reliance on family members, friends, classmates, and fellow employees to help them compensate for their disabilities; and (c) changed roles in study groups or informal study relationships with classmates from being helped to being a helper.

Previous research on adults with LD (Adelman and Vogel 1990; Gerber, Ginsberg, and Reiff 1992; Raskind et al. 1999) has indicated that successful adults understand the nature of their disability and tend to accept rather than deny the disability, to be users of technology, to use a variety of compensatory strategies in response to situational variables, to be self-advocates in terms of their disabilities, and to be active members of groups that advocate for persons with LD. Questionnaire responses indicated that attitudinal and affective changes had taken place as a result of training and/or participation in the study in the direction of the above cluster of attributes associated with successful adults: (a) two-thirds of the respondents reported having learned more about their strengths and weaknesses, and about LD in general, as a result of participation and training; (b) 80% of the students related that they felt better about themselves academically since discovering more about their disabilities through participation; (c) nearly half the respondents reported that computers had changed their lives for the better, allowing them to accomplish tasks they had previously been unable to do; (d) nearly a third reported that they "couldn't have made it through" without the help of training on assistive technology; and (e) one-third of the students reported alteration of their career goals to include working with other students with LD or related difficulties as a result of participation in the study.

Cost-effectiveness was evaluated for the technologies in year three of the study. The analysis was prepared with regard to the costs that would be incurred by the service delivery point for assistive technology at CSUN, which is a well-established office of services for disabled students with a well-trained technical support staff, a history of attracting many student volunteers, and adequate funding for several student assistants, to provide a variety of services for students with disabilities, including LD. Elements included in the analysis were the initial cost of equipment, equipment repair/maintenance, consumable supplies, and initial training and supervisory/monitoring costs once students were trained (given current staffing and salary schedules). The estimate was then adjusted for projected increases in use of assistive technology services and other support services, on the basis of data gathered from the questionnaire given to students from the study and of log-on times taken from the computer access lab. The estimate was then compared to the cost of providing equivalent non-technological services, such as transcribers, readers, tutors, counselors, and note-takers, given current staffing and salary schedules. Two estimates were computed: (a) a minimal bottom-line cost estimate that covered initial equipment purchases, initial training costs, and post-training monitoring needs for the projected number of students likely to request services, given current turnover rates; and (b) a maximal estimate that, in addition to the costs listed under (a), included some student outreach efforts to previously identified students with LD, needs-assessment of the current population of students with LD, and the provision of specialized training based on that needs assessment.[5] It was determined that the net savings for the Office of Disabled Student Services (ODSS) for the minimal services was $320 (U.S.) per student per semester and $260 (U.S.) for the maximal services. The amount was then adjusted for projected increases in use of other services within ODSS and to other campus service providers, for a net benefit of approximately $310 for the minimal service provision and $234 for the maximal service provision, per student per semester.

It is important to stress that the evaluation of cost-effectiveness of any assistive technology is highly dependent on the context in which the analysis is conducted. Therefore, readers are cautioned not to generalize the results reported herein to other settings (e.g., employment, rehabilitation, etc.)—even to other university/college settings, as even "comparable contexts" may vary markedly as to goals, purposes, and policy regarding the delivery of assistive technology, other support services, the location within the post-secondary

[5]The maximal amount was based on the actual outreach, needs assessment, and service provision costs that were incurred during years two and three of the study. The needs assessment conducted in year two revealed that two areas of need were salient to participants in the study—passage of the WPE and instruction/guidance on how to write a term paper. Two "mini-courses" entitled "Writing a Term Paper Using Technology" and "Passing the WPE Using Technology" were developed. Flyers were sent out to all students with learning disabilities each semester. Sixty students responded and subsequently participated in the mini-courses.

institution of the assistive technology delivery point (e.g., office of disabled student services vs. centralized computing center), and budgetary policy (e.g., soft vs. hard funding for technological training and/or equipment purchases).

SUMMARY AND RECOMMENDATIONS

The practice of providing assistive technology to post-secondary students with LD has had a very short history. Although assistive technology LD support services are growing, considerable investigation, exploration, and experience is still needed to determine which service delivery models, specific services, and technologies are the most appropriate for meeting the needs of individual institutions, LD support service programs, and students with LD. Additionally, although numerous technologies are now available to help post-secondary students with LD compensate for a variety of difficulties, there is a paucity of research to support their efficacy. Only a limited number of studies have been conducted on a narrow range of technologies.

Although research in the area of assistive technology for post-secondary students with LD is quite limited, collective results suggest a number of general conclusions: (a) Select assistive technologies have been found effective for some students in compensating for specific deficits in such areas as writing and reading; (b) a technology that is beneficial for one individual with LD could be counterproductive for another; (c) it is unclear whether the use of assistive technology leads to improved academic outcomes (e.g., improved overall GPA); (d) low-tech or even "no-tech" solutions may be more effective than high-tech assistive technology; (e) specific types of technology (e.g., speech synthesis) may be helpful in compensating for one area of difficulty (e.g., proofreading) but not necessarily for another (e.g., reading); (f) the fact that an assistive technology has compensatory value does not guarantee that it will be cost- or time-effective; (g) a technology may be more effective than alternative strategies in helping one specific area of skill deficit (e.g., speech synthesis in catching usage errors) but not others (e.g., locating grammar-mechanical errors); and (h) some assistive technologies seem to have a positive behavioral and/or psychological/attitudinal effect on specific students.

The use of assistive technology as a means to help post-secondary students with LD compensate for their difficulties and to enhance their academic success looks promising. However, to ensure that the full benefits of assistive technology are achieved, concerted effort will have to be made to conduct research regarding (a) the compensatory effectiveness of select technologies for specific difficulties (and how these technological interventions compare to non-technological strategies); (b) the extent to which specific contexts influence the compensatory effectiveness of select technologies; (c) the possible relationship between assistive technology use and academic outcomes, including grades/performance in specific courses, course withdrawals and incompletes, grade-point averages, and retention/graduation rates; (d) the potential behavioral and/or psychological benefits of assistive technology including changes in levels of independence, perseverance, attitudes toward academic tasks, self-esteem, and self-understanding; (e) the possible social consequences of assistive technology use, including changes in establishing and sustaining friendships and levels and types of social participation; (f) the long-term effects of assistive technology use; (g) valid and reliable assessment practices for determining which students will benefit from assistive technology, and ensuring the best possible match between the student, technology, task, and context; (h) the cost-effectiveness of assistive technology as compared to alternative compensatory strategies in light of the costs associated with specific products, maintenance, consumable supplies, technical support, training, and personnel; and (i) the effectiveness of different service delivery models/practices relative to such factors as the coordinating department, the types and location of technology, personnel, training, technical support, and funding.

To ensure that research will ultimately benefit post-secondary students with LD, mechanisms are needed to close the gap between research and practice, ensuring that what is validated in research is effectively implemented in the post-secondary setting. Translating research into practice is not simply a matter of disseminating research results to post-secondary institutions, but, rather, necessitates that the institutions themselves (to the extent possible) play an active role in the research process. Such participation requires ongoing collaboration and communication between researchers, service providers, administrators, faculty, and students with LD.

Effective implementation also demands that post-secondary institutions have a well-defined, comprehensive, and systematic plan for assistive technology service delivery. This plan needs to clearly delineate (a) goals and objectives; (b) the office/department responsible for coordinating service delivery; (c) the personnel responsible for implementing the plan; (d) service eligibility criteria; (e) timelines for completion; (f) the specific technologies needed, including modpification of existing technologies and systems (e.g., library information systems, e-mail, the Internet); (g) the location(s) of the technology; (h) the hours when the technology is available for student use; (i) the times when training/support is available; (j) training procedures and content; (k) a technical support and maintenance plan; (l) funding mechanisms for initial and continued financial support; (m) procedures for interdepartmental coordination; and (n) a plan for evaluating the efficacy of the service delivery system over time.

Consideration should also be given to (a) initial and ongoing training/information dissemination to faculty, support personnel, administrators, and persons with LD to promote awareness of assistive technology (and related federal regulations); (b) the strategies necessary to ensure that support service providers and students with LD are kept abreast of current technologies, assessment practices, service delivery strategies, legislation, funding opportunities, and research (which would necessitate ongoing contact with manufacturers, conference participation, training, and literature review); (c) the procedures required to foster collaboration with technology manufacturers in order to identify and develop/modify appropriate technologies for individuals with LD; and (d) the safeguards required for ensuring that service delivery is in accord with federal regulations regarding postsecondary institutions and assistive technology.

In conclusion, assistive technology holds great promise for helping post-secondary students with LD reach their full potential. However, only through continued research and carefully planned and executed service delivery systems will this promise be realized. This is our challenge; this is our responsibility.

ACKNOWLEDGMENTS

The authors would like to acknowledge Carl Brown, Dr. Sheryl Burgstahler, Carmela Castorina, Ellen Cutler, Dr. Danny Hilton-Chalfen, Dr. Harry Murphy, Chris Primus, and Tobey Shaw for sharing their expertise in assistive technology.

REFERENCES

Adelman, P. B., and Vogel, S. A. 1990. College graduates with learning disabilities. *Learning Disability Quarterly* 13:154–56.

Adelman, P. B., and Vogel, S. A. 1993. Issues in program evaluation. In *Success for College Students with Learning Disabilities*, eds. S. A. Vogel and P. B. Adelman. New York: Springer-Verlag.

American Council on Education. 1992. College freshmen with disabilities: A statistical profile (Cooperative Agreement No. H030C00001-91). Washington, DC: American Council on Education, Heath Resource Center.

American Council on Education. 1995. College freshmen with disabilities: A statistical profile (Cooperative Agreement No. H030C00002-94). Washington, DC: American Council on Education, HEATH Resource Center.

Americans with Disabilities Act of 1990, P.L. 101-336, 42 U.S.C.A. 12, 101-12, 213 (West Supp. 1991).

Beirne-Smith, M., and Deck, M. D. 1989. A survey of post-secondary programs for students with learning disabilities. *Journal of Learning Disabilities* 22:456–57.

Blalock, J. 1981. Persistent problems and concerns of young adults with learning disabilities. In *Bridges to Tomorrow*, eds. W. Cruickshank and A. Silvers, Vol. 2: The best of ACLD. Syracuse, NY: Syracuse University Press.

Blalock, J., and Johnson, D. 1987. Primary concerns and group characteristics. In *Adults with Learning Disabilities: Clinical Studies*, eds. D. J. Johnson and J. W. Blalock. Orlando, FL: Grune and Stratton.

Brown, C. 1987. Computer access in higher education for students with disabilities. Washington, DC: Fund for the Improvement of Post-secondary Education, U.S. Department of Education.

Brown, C., Norris, M., and Rivers, J. 1989. High tech centers for the disabled: The future of computer access in the California community colleges. In *Transforming Teaching with Technology: Perspectives from Two-year Colleges*, ed. K. Anandam. McKinney, TX: Academic Computing Publications.

Bryant, B., Rivera, D., and Warde, B. 1993. Technology as a means to an end: Facilitating success at the college level. *LD Forum* 19:13–18.

Burgstahler, S. 1992. Computing services for disabled students in institutions of higher education. Unpublished doctoral dissertation, University of Washington, Seattle.

Collins, T. 1990. The impact of microcomputer word processing on the performance of learning disabled students in a required first year writing course. *Computers and Composition* 8:49–68.

Collins, T., and Price, L. 1986. Testimony from learning disabled college writers on the efficacy of word processing in their writing process. Unpublished manuscript. (ERIC Document Reproduction Service No. ED 267 411)

Cutler, E. 1990. Evaluating spell checkers, thesauruses, dictionaries and grammar editors for the community college student with learning disabilities. In *Proceedings of the Fifth Annual Conference on Technology and Persons with Disabilities*, ed. H. J. Murphy 5:163–75.

Cutler, E. 1991, March. Evaluating spell checking, abbreviation expansion and word prediction software. Paper presented at the Sixth Annual Conference on Technology and Persons with Disabilities, Los Angeles.

EASI. 1991. *Computers and Students with Disabilities: New Challenges for Higher Education.* Washington, DC: EDUCOM.

Elkind, J., Black, M.S., and Murray, C. 1996. Computer-based compensation of adult reading disabilities. *Annals of Dyslexia* 46:159–86.

Gerber, P., Ginsberg, R., and Reiff, H. B. 1992. Identifying alterable patterns of vocational success in highly successful adults with learning disabilities. *Journal of Learning Disabilities* 25:475–85.

Gough, P. B., and Tunmer, W. E. 1986. Decoding reading and reading disability. *Remedial and Special Education* 7 (1):6–10.

Gregg, N., and Hoy, C. 1989) Coherence: The comprehension and production abilities of college writers who are normally achieving, learning disabled and underprepared. *Journal of Learning Disabilities* 22:370–72.

Hasbrouck, J. M. 1980. Performance of students with auditory figure-ground disorders under conditions of unilateral and bilateral ear occlusion. *Journal of Learning Disabilities* 13:548–51.

Higgins, E. L., and Raskind, M. H. 1995. An investigation of the compensatory effectiveness of speech recognition on the written composition performance of post-secondary students with learning disabilities. *Learning Disability Quarterly* 18:159–74.

Higgins, E. L., and Raskind, M. H. 1997. The compensatory effectiveness of optical character recognition/speech synthesis on reading comprehension of post-secondary students with learning disabilities. *Learning Disabilities: A Multidisciplinary Journal* 8:75–87.

Horn, C. A., and Shell, D. F. 1990. Availability of computer services in post-secondary institutions: Results of a survey of AHSSPPE members. *Journal of Post-secondary Education and Disability* 8:115–24.

Hughes, C. A., and Smith, J. O. 1990. Cognitive and academic performance of college students with learning disabilities: A synthesis of the literature. *Learning Disability Quarterly* 13:66–79.

Individuals with Disabilities Education Act of 1990, P.L. 101–476. 1993.

Johnson, D. J. 1987. Disorders of written language. In *Adults with Learning Disabilities: Clinical Studies*, eds. D. J. Johnson and J. W. Blalock. Orlando, FL: Grune and Stratton.

King, M. L., and Rental, V. M. 1981. Research update: Conveying meaning in written texts. *Language Arts* 58:721–28.

MacArthur, C. A. 1996. Using technology to enhance the writing processes of students with learning disabilities. *Journal of Learning Disabilities* 29:344–54.

Mangrum, D. T., II, and Strichart, S. S. 1988. *College and the Learning Disabled Student*. Philadelphia: Grune and Stratton.

Mangrum, D. T., II, and Strichart, S. S. 1997. *Peterson's Colleges with Programs for Students with Learning Disabilities*. Princeton, NJ: Peterson's Guides.

McCroskey, R., and Thompson, N. 1973. Comprehension of rate controlled speech by children with specific learning disabilities. *Journal of Learning Disabilities* 6:29–35.

McNaughton, D., Hughes, C., and Clark, K. 1997. The effect of five proofreading conditions on the spelling performance of college students with learning disabilities. *Journal of Learning Disabilities* 30:643–51.

Mellard, D. 1994. Services for students with learning disabilities in the community colleges. In *Learning Disabilities in Adulthood: Persisting Problems and Evolving Issues*, eds. P.J. Gerber and H. B. Reiff. Stoneham, MA: Andover Medical.

Murphy, H. 1991. *The Impact of Exemplary Technology-support Programs on Students with Disabilities*. Washington, DC: National Council on Disability.

Myklebust, H. R. 1973. *Development and Disorders of Written Language: Studies of Normal and Exceptional Children* (Vol. 2). Orlando, FL: Grune and Stratton.

National Center for Education Statistics. 1999. *Profile of Handicapped Students in Post-secondary Education, 1998*. Washington, DC: U.S. Government Printing Office.

Norris, M., and Graef, J. 1990. Screen reading programs for students with learning disabilities. In *Proceedings of the Fifth Annual Conference on Technology and Persons with Disabilities*, ed. H. J. Murphy (ed.) 5:491–99.

Office of the Chancellor, Division of Analytic Studies, California State University. 1994, April. CSU Stateline, pp. 1–2.

Primus, C. 1990. *Computer Assistance Model for Learning Disabled*. Washington, DC: Office of Special Education and Rehabilitation Services, U.S. Department of Education.

Raskind, M. H., Goldberg, R. J., Higgins, E. L., and Herman, K. L. 1999. Patterns of change and predictors of success in individuals with learning disabilities: Results from a twenty-year longitudinal study. *Learning Disabilities Research and Practice* 14 (1):35–49.

Raskind, M. H., and Higgins, E. L. 1995) The effects of speech synthesis on the proofreading efficiency of post-secondary students with learning disabilities. *Learning Disability Quarterly* 18: 141–158.

Raskind, M. H., and Higgins, E. L. 1998. Assistive technology for post-secondary students with learning disabilities: An overview. *Journal of Learning Disabilities* 31:27–40.

Raskind, M. H., and Scott, N. 1993. Technology for post-secondary students with learning disabilities. In *Success for College Students with Learning Disabilities*, eds. S. A. Vogel and P. B. Adelman. New York: Springer-Verlag.

Rehabilitation Act of 1973, P.L. 92-112, 29 U.S.C. 794 1980.

Rothstein, L. F. 1993. Legal issues. In *Success for College Students with Learning Disabilities*, eds. S. A. Vogel and P. B. Adelman. New York: Springer-Verlag.

Scheiber, B., and Talpers, J. 1985. *Campus Access for Learning Disabled Students.* Washington, DC: Closer Look.

Shaw, S. F., McGuire, J. M., and Brinkerhoff, L. C. 1994. College and university programming. In *Learning Disabilities in Adulthood: Persisting Problems and Evolving Issues*, eds. P. J. Gerber and H. B. Reiff. Stoneham, MA: Andover Medical.

Technology-Related Assistance for Individuals with Disabilities Act of 1988, P.L. 100-47, 29 U.S.C. 2201, 2202. 1988.

Vogel, S. A. 1985. Syntactic complexity in written expression of LD college writers. *Annals of Dyslexia* 35:137–57.

Vogel, S. A. 1987. Issues and concerns in LD college programming. In *Adults with Learning Disabilities: Clinical Studies*, eds. D. J. Johnson and J. W. Blalock. Orlando, FL: Grune and Stratton.

Vogel, S. A. 1993. The continuum of university responses to Section 504 for students with learning disabilities. In *Success for College Students with Learning Disabilities*, eds. S. A. Vogel and P. B. Adelman. New York: Springer-Verlag.

Vogel, S. A., and Adelman, P. B. 1993. *Success for College Students with Learning Disabilities.* New York: Springer-Verlag.

Vogel, S. A., and Moran, M. R. 1982. Written language disorders in learning disabled students: A preliminary report. In *Coming of Age*, Vol. 3: The Best of ACLD, eds. W. M. Cruickshank and J. W. Lerner. Syracuse, NY: Syracuse University.

Wiederholt, J. L. 1986. *Formal Reading Inventory.* Austin, TX: PRO-ED.

Chapter • 11

American and Israeli Faculty Attitudes and Practices Regarding Students with Learning Diabilities: *A Cross-Cutural Study*[1]

Yona Leyser, Susan A. Vogel, Sharon Wyland, Andrew Brulle, Varda Sharoni, and Gila Vogel

Educational systems and educational institutions around the world are facing new challenges and difficulties as they enter the new millennium. One of these main challenges is related to changes in student population. Examples of such changes include growth in the number of students with disabilities in schools, particularly in developing countries (Csapo 1993); changing demographics (i.e., an increase in the cultural and linguistic diversity of students, especially in nations where immigration is on the rise); and a reported increase in the number of learners that are at risk for school failure (see, e.g., Friend and Bursuck 1999). The student school population is also changing as a result of civil rights movement legislation, special education laws, and policy guidelines regarding provision of special education and related services in the least restrictive environment, passed in many nations around the world in the last quarter of the 20th century.

For example, the Salamanca Statement and Framework for Action on Special Needs Education (UNESCO 1994) reaffirmed the right to education of every individual and endorsed the principle of inclusive

---

[1]This chapter is an overview and extension of recent work by Leyser, Vogel, Brulle et al. (1998), Leyser, Vogel, Wyland et al. (2000), Brulle et al. (1998), and Vogel et al. (1999).

education where all children, regardless of their physical, intellectual, social, emotional, linguistic, or other conditions, should be enrolled and accommodated in regular schools "unless there are compelling reasons for doing otherwise." Indeed, as reported by many authors, the endorsed or mandated mainstreaming or inclusion principles are implemented in many industrialized western nations as well as in many developing countries (Booth and Ainscow 1998; Cavanagh 1994; Leyser, Kapperman, and Keller 1994; UNESCO 1998). In the USA, landmark legislation PL 94-142, the Education for All Handicapped Children Act of 1975, and subsequent legislation, PL 101-476, The Individuals with Disabilities Act (IDEA 1990) and its amendment PL 105-17 (IDEA 1997) resulted in the placement of almost 75 percent of all students with disabilities receiving their education either in general education classrooms on a full-time basis or in a combination of general education and resource room placements (US Department of Education 1998).

In regard to students with disabilities in higher education, PL 101-476 (IDEA 1990) mandated that an Individual Transition Plan (ITP) be included in the Individual Education Plan (IEP) to prepare all students with disabilities for transition to postsecondary education or employment. As a result, individuals with disabilities, their parents, counselors, and teachers became aware of a variety of college and university options for students with disabilities. Students who had not previously aspired to higher education also found that postsecondary institutions were more responsive to their needs because of passage of Section 504 of the Rehabilitation Act of 1973, which mandated that higher education institutions receiving federal assistance must make campus and program modifications and accommodations to qualified students with disabilities that would allow them to participate fully in educational programs.

As a result of the removal of barriers, a dramatic increase in the number of students with disabilities in higher education in the 1980s was noted (Brinckerhoff, Shaw, and McGuire 1993; Vogel and Adelman 1993). According to the HEATH Resource Center, the national clearinghouse on postsecondary education for individuals with disabilities of the American Council on Education (ACE), the proportion of first-time, full-time freshmen with disabilities attending college increased more than threefold between 1978 and 1994, from 2.6% to 9.2% (Henderson 1995). An analysis of these data by disability indicates that the overall increase is due to the significant increase in the number of students with learning disabilities, from 15% of the total number of students with self-reported disabilities in 1988 to 32% of first-time, full-time freshmen with disabilities in 1994, representing slightly more than a twofold increase in students with LD.

In Israel, special education law, modeled after the American law, PL 94-142 of 1975, was passed in 1988 (Israel Knesset 1988). This law and subsequent regulations by the Ministry of Education, Culture, and Sport required (among other key provisions) that members of the placement committee give priority to the placement of students with a disability in general education settings wherever appropriate. The regulations clearly state that the goals of the mainstreaming placement recommendation were to assure that students with disabilities are integrated in general education classrooms and to reduce the number of referrals of students to placement committees. Another provision established flexible organizational and professional structures at the local and regional level (MATIA) in order to better serve students with disabilities in general education settings (Brandes and Nesher 1996). Statistical data reported since the passage of the law reveal a decrease in the percent of students with disabilities served in segregated special education settings (Sprinzak et al. 1997).

Regulations by the Ministry of Education, Culture, and Sport (1996) provided guidelines for needed adaptations for students with disabilities, particularly students with learning disabilities, during matriculation examinations which are required for entry into postsecondary institutions. Indeed, a major trend has been reported by many universities and colleges to provide accommodations and support systems for students with disabilities (Kosminsky 1995; Vogel 1998). To date, no enrollment figures for students with disabilities in postsecondary schools are available. Margalit, Breznitz, and Ahroni (1997), however, reported that 3% of students in higher education in Israel have learning disabilities.

Among the key factors contributing to the achievement and successful degree completion of students with disabilities in higher education is a positive faculty attitude and a willingness to provide accommodations for these students (Baggett 1994; Fonosch and Schwab 1981; Moore, Newlon, and Nye 1986). Several studies on faculty attitudes and awareness of the needs of students with disabilities have been reported in the literature. Although one study reported negative views of college faculty toward students with disabilities (Minner and Prater 1984), most studies reported that faculty expressed positive attitudes toward the students' integration into college classroom environments (Aksamit, Morris, and Leuenberger 1987; Fonosch and Schwab 1981; Leyser 1989; Satcher 1992). Moore, Newlon, and Nye (1986) reported contradictory findings in a survey of students with visual, hearing, and orthopedic impairments. They found that respondents in all groups, particularly students with visual and hearing impairments, noted some lack of faculty awareness of their needs.

Researchers who explored faculty attitudes and willingness to make accommodations found that the attitudes of faculty were related to a number of selected demographic variables. Such variables included (a) gender (female faculty expressed more positive attitudes toward individuals with disabilities than male faculty members [Aksamit et al. 1987; Baggett 1994; Fonosch and Schwab 1981]); (b) information (faculty with more information about disabilities had more positive attitudes than those with less information [Aksamit et al. 1987]); and (c) academic field (faculty in education were found to have more positive attitudes toward individuals with disabilities than faculty in business and in social sciences [Fonosch and Schwab 1981]). Nelson et al. (1990) reported that College of Education faculty responded more favorably to making accommodations for students with learning disabilities than did faculty in the Colleges of Business and Arts and Sciences. Finally, experience had an impact on attitude and accommodations (faculty with more contact and teaching experience with students with disabilities had more positive attitudes and were more comfortable allowing accommodations than those with less experience [Fichten et al. 1988; Fonosch and Schwab 1981; Satcher 1992]).

When faculty familiarity with special education disability legislation, experience with students with disabilities, and knowledge of support services on campus were examined, the reported results indicated mixed responses. For example, Baggett (1994) found that many faculty in a large state university reported lack of familiarity with disability laws and university support services. Limited experience in teaching students with disabilities was also indicated. Aksamit et al. (1987) reported that faculty members had limited knowledge about students with learning disabilities. Leyser (1989), on the other hand, reported that a large majority of faculty members (85%) were familiar with special education legislation pertaining to the rights of individuals with disabilities. Findings regarding experience in teaching students with disabilities are mixed. Some researchers found limited experience (Baggett 1994) while others found that faculty had teaching experiences, particularly with students with learning disabilities (Satcher 1992) and with physical and sensory disabilities (Leyser 1989; McCarthy and Campbell 1993).

Overall, investigations regarding faculty attitudes toward making accommodations revealed that faculty members expressed a willingness to provide various teaching accommodations in their classrooms (Baggett 1994; Houck et al. 1992; Leyser 1989; Matthews, Anderson, and Skolnick 1987; Nelson, Dodd, and Smith 1990; Satcher 1992). However, evidence from these investigations has also shown that faculty were generally less willing to allow exclusive extra credit; overlook misspelling, incorrect punctuation, and poor grammar; permit substitutions for required courses; or allow students to turn in tape recorded assignments (Matthews et al. 1987; Nelson et al. 1990; Satcher 1992). As these researchers observed, faculty were willing to accommodate, but not to the extent of what faculty perceived as lowering certain course standards.

One of the issues that has received some recognition in the literature (Brulle 1996; McGee and Kauffman 1989; Yanok 1987) awaiting further discussions and answers, is related to the question of students with documented learning disabilities who opt for teaching as a career choice. As noted by McGee and Kauffman (1989), it is necessary for colleges and universities to balance the right of students with disabilities to choose their own direction, with the general public expectations and the call from the National Commission on Teaching and America's Future (1996), that all teachers be well prepared and capable of performing their duties in an exemplary manner.

Although empirical findings on faculty perceptions and practices regarding students with disabilities have been reported in the literature, further research is needed to replicate the reported results in a variety of colleges and universities, especially because of the reported increases in the numbers of students with disabilities entering institutions of higher education, including students with learning disabilities in teacher education programs. Furthermore, because of the increase in the worldwide commitment to educating students with disabilities in inclusive educational environments and the growing interest in supporting these students in postsecondary institutions, it is important to initiate research into faculty attitudes and practices in different countries. Such data will be useful in providing guidance for the development of policies and the provision of accommodations and support services on campuses throughout the world.

In this chapter we report results from a cross-cultural study which (a) examined faculty attitudes, experiences, and willingness to make accommodations for students with disabilities in general and for students with learning disabilities in particular in two institutions, one in the USA and the other in Israel; and (b) compared faculty views and practices in these two teacher preparation colleges regarding students with learning disabilities enrolled in teacher education; and (c) examined the impact of selected background variables on faculty attitudes and practices. A related goal of this research was to serve as an impetus for future collaborative cross-cultural studies between universities and colleges and encourage networking in different regions and nations.

METHODOLOGY

Participants

Participants in the US sample consisted of 1,050 faculty at a large doctoral degree-granting midwestern university, Northern Illinois

University (NIU), with an enrollment of 23,000 undergraduate and graduate students. The university is composed of seven major colleges (humanities, business, social sciences, law, natural sciences, education, and engineering). Survey forms were sent to all full-time faculty and temporary instructors teaching half-time or more. Forty percent responded to the survey ($n = 420$). In this chapter, we report on the responses of 142 faculty teaching in the college of education and in other colleges on campus (e.g., humanities, social sciences) who indicated that they were involved or had been involved in teacher preparation (e.g., methods courses, clinical supervision). Findings from studies on the total sample of faculty at NIU are available in several recent publications (Leyser et al. 1998; Vogel et al. 1999). The College of Education has 130 full-time faculty and another 60 part-time faculty in seven departments. Approximately 2,000 undergraduate and 2,000 graduate students are enrolled in the college.

According to the Center of Access-Ability Resources, 260 undergraduate and graduate full-time and part-time students at NIU with documented disabilities disclosed that they had a disability in the year the survey was distributed to faculty, representing approximately 1.1% of the total student body of 23,000. Interestingly, this represents almost an identical prevalence rate to that reported for similar doctoral degree-granting, research-oriented universities in the National Learning Disabilities Postsecondary Data Bank (Vogel et al. 1998). Moreover, 40.1% of the 260 students had documented learning disabilities. This prevalence rate may be somewhat higher than the one-third rate reported by the American Council on Education (ACE) (Henderson 1995) because the ACE data refer only to full-time first-time freshmen, which were collected two years earlier (in the 1994–1995 academic year), whereas the above NIU data included all part-time and full-time undergraduate and graduate students.

Among the students with documented LD, 25% were in a teacher preparation program within the College of Education (CoE). This proportion dropped off dramatically in the other colleges with 13% majoring in business, 9% in visual and performing arts, and 5% in engineering and engineering sciences. However, this distribution confirmed that students with LD enroll in programs of studies across all disciplines in the university. Currently (1999–2000) the number of students with documented disabilities at NIU is 300, including 188 students with learning disabilities.

Beit Berl College (BBC) is the largest teacher education program in Israel. It is composed of a school of education, a school of art education, an institute for training teachers for the Arab sector of Israel, an in-service teacher program, and several other programs. The total enrollment is approximately 7,000 students, with approximately 3,500 students enrolled in the school of education in both pre- and in-service training. In addition to teaching certification programs, the school of education offers a program in informal education. Students in the school of education are awarded a B.Ed. degree after four years of study, and are admitted directly to the specific departments of the college. The departments include: early childhood, elementary education, junior and senior high school, and special education. Students in the elementary, and junior and senior high school departments select majors in the various disciplines of study as well (math, sciences, literature, history, geography, etc.). Admission requirements include a high school matriculation certificate and a sufficiently high score on a psychometric examination given to all those who apply to teacher colleges or universities in Israel (this exam is similar to the SAT exam in the U. S.). The minimum cut-off score for admission to teacher training colleges is determined by the Ministry of Education. The various departments, however, have the autonomy to set higher cut-off scores or to consider other criteria as well.

At Beit Berl, students who have learning disabilities may apply to a Professional Committee under the auspices of the Office of the Dean of Students and need to provide a recent evaluation. The committee then determines the accommodations that the student is entitled to receive. Students receive a letter listing these accommodations and may show it to faculty members if they so desire. The committee may also recommend that the student receive services at the college's Support Center. The types of services offered at the center include: peer tutoring, an audio center (providing tapes of required reading assignments), individualized support by professional staff, and a series of workshops on topics including note-taking, test-taking and study skills, and techniques for improving memory. Staff of the Support Center also meet with and advise faculty members when necessary. Beit Berl also has an assessment center and students who have not been identified earlier in their academic careers may be evaluated at this center. The fee for the evaluation is subsidized by the college.

The number of students with recognized learning disabilities in the college has grown dramatically over the past three years. There are currently 150 students with documented learning disabilities at Beit Berl. The Support Center was established during the 1996–1997 academic year. During that year it served 15 students. The number of students served grew to 38 during the 1997–1998 academic year, and to 50 during the 1998–1999 academic year. Currently (1999–2000), the Support Center is providing services to 70 students.

Surveys were sent to 400 full- and part-time faculty teaching in the school of education, including faculty who teach courses in the various disciplines such as literature, science, and math as well as to those who teach courses in education, psychology, and sociology. Response rate of the survey was 30% (116 questionnaires). (Findings from the Beit Berl study can be found in Sharoni and Vogel 1998.)

Survey Instrument

The English version of the survey instrument was composed of 35 items and titled "A Faculty Survey on Students with Disabilities." It was designed to measure faculty attitude, knowledge, and practices regarding students with disabilities. The instrument was a modified and expanded version of a scale used in a prior study on faculty attitudes and practices (Leyser 1989). In the revised survey, new items specifically regarding students with LD were added from several other instruments (i.e., Houck et al. 1992; Nelson et al. 1990; Rose 1993; Satcher 1992).

The instrument was divided into five parts: (1) background information, (2) faculty contact with individuals with disabilities, (3) willingness to provide teaching and examination accommodations for students with learning disabilities and judgment of fairness of accommodations, (4) accommodations for teacher certification candidates with learning disabilities, and (5) faculty suggestions and comments.

The survey contained structured 4-point Likert-type items (1 = low degree of support or willingness to accommodate, and 4 = a high level of support, willingness to accommodate, or strong agreement with statement). Also included were multiple-choice items (for background information), several open-ended questions regarding other accommodations faculty had made, and a section for faculty suggestions.

Prior to its use, the English version was reviewed by several faculty from other universities who were experts in learning disabilities and in statistics within and outside the university, for their input and suggestions regarding the survey design, wording, and clarity of items. A Cronbach alpha coefficient of reliability for the revised survey used in this study yielded a coefficient of .87.

For the faculty sample at BBC in Israel, the survey was translated into Hebrew and adapted to the educational experiences of faculty in an Israeli postsecondary institution. Following the first translation of the form, it was translated back from Hebrew into English by an independent translator to ensure the similarity of items. The final Hebrew form was composed of the 35 original items in the English survey and 13 additional items that were of interest to Beit Berl College. Prior to its use, the Hebrew version was administered and reviewed by six faculty members at BBC to obtain their suggestions and wording recommendations. The Cronbach alpha coefficient of reliability for the Hebrew version of the items in the original scale was .84.

Procedures

In the study at NIU, a list and mailing labels for all full-time teaching faculty and temporary faculty (instructors) were obtained. Each participant was sent, via campus mail, the faculty survey, a cover letter, and a campus addressed return envelope. The letter explained the purpose of the questionnaire and the importance of faculty input for the development of programs and services for students with disabilities. The cover letter assured anonymity and indicated that participation was voluntary. Respondents were allowed two weeks to complete and return the survey. A follow-up reminder postcard was sent to all faculty shortly after the deadline.

At Beit Berl, the questionnaires were distributed to faculty members through campus mail. A cover letter was included that explained the purpose of the study and indicated that it was part of a large study conducted in collaboration with NIU. Faculty were asked to return the completed form to the department of special education or leave it in a mail box in the teachers' lounge. Faculty were given three weeks to return the questionnaire. A reminder letter was sent to all faculty as well.

Method of Analysis

Descriptive item analysis was conducted regarding the frequency of the responses to all items on the questionnaire for faculty at BBC and for faculty in the College of Education (CoE) at NIU. The frequency of responses for faculty who responded to the survey at the other colleges at NIU was also calculated. Chi square tests were applied to examine differences in responses by faculty at BBC and faculty in education at NIU to the survey items.

In addition, five subscales were constructed from the survey form. The first subscale was titled "General Attitudes" (AT) and was composed of the average of three items exploring the overall faculty disposition toward making accommodations for students with disabilities in general and the judgment of fairness to other students of accommodations made specifically for students with LD. The Cronbach alpha reliability coefficient was .52. The second subscale titled "Experience, Knowledge, and Information" (EK) was composed of seven items from Part 1 of the scale. Higher scores on these variables have been found in the literature to be related to more acceptability and willingness to make accommodations for individuals with disabilities (Cronbach alpha .75). The third subscale was titled "Teaching Accommodations" (TA) and included six items from Part III of the survey that related to specific teaching accommodations for students with LD (Cronbach alpha .64). The fourth subscale was titled "Examination Accommodations" (EA). It was composed of 10 items also from Part III related to testing accommodations (Cronbach alpha .84). The fifth subscale was titled "Students with LD in Teacher Education" (LDT). It was composed of five items from Part IV of the scale asking for faculty perceptions of students with learning disabilities seeking teacher certification (Cronbach alpha .74). Differences between BBC faculty and education faculty at NIU on these five subscales were examined using t-tests.

Finally t-tests and one-way ANOVAs were calculated to determine how background variables such as gender, age, highest degree earned, and teaching experience were related to faculty responses to the five subscales. When one way ANOVAs were significant, post hoc tests were used to determine where the differences were. An alpha level of .05 was used to determine significance.

RESULTS

A. Demographic Background

Background information on participating faculty in the college of education at NIU and BBC is depicted in table I. As can be seen for both samples, there was a representation of faculty with advanced degrees (masters and doctorates) and a range of age groups and years of teaching experience. The sample at NIU also represented all academic ranks. Some differences, however, between groups should be noted. Many more faculty members at NIU, a graduate degree-granting school, hold a doctorate degree (73.0%) as compared to faculty at BBC (31%). Interestingly, the faculty at BBC was composed of a large majority of female members (72.4%), while at NIU the percent of male and female faculty in the College of Education was about the same (50%). As can be seen, the age distribution of the two faculties was quite similar. Somewhat more faculty members at BBC (51.7%) than at NIU (43.2%) had ten or fewer years of teaching experience, while more faculty at NIU (35.5%) had 16 and more years of teaching experience in higher education than had faculty at BBC (25%).

B. Comparisons of Responses by Faculty at NIU and BBC

Table II depicts the comparison between CoE faculty members at NIU and BBC faculty on the five subscales of the survey. The first subscale score was composed of items exploring general attitude and disposition toward providing accommodations for students with disabilities and judgment of fairness of accommodations for students with LD

Table I. Demographic Information for Faculty in Education for NIU (*n* = 141) and BBC (*n* = 116)

	NIU		BBC	
	Frequency	Percent	Frequency	Percent
Degree:				
Bachelor's	1	.7	2	1.7
Master's	35	24.8	75	64.7
Doctorate	103	73.0	36	3l.0
Other	2	1.4	3	2.6
Gender:				
Female	70	49.6	84	72.4
Male	70	49.6	29	25.0
Not reported	1	.7	3	2.6
Years College Teaching:				
1-5	36	25.5	36	31.0
6-10	25	17.7	24	20.7
11-15	25	17.7	21	18.1
16+	50	35.5	29	25.0
Missing	5	3.5	6	5.2
Age Group:				
24-35	13	9.2	6	5.1
36-45	44	31.2	38	32.7
46-55	53	37.6	48	41.3
56+	28	19.9	19	16.4
Missing	3	2.1	5	4.3
*Rank:				
Instructor	36	25.5	——	
Assistant Professor	36	25.5	——	
Associate Professor	27	19.1	——	
Professor	40	28.4	——	
Missing	2	1.4	——	

*Presently no academic ranks are used at BBC.

Table II. Comparison between Education Faculty at NIU and BBC on Five Composite Scores

	NIU		BBC		t	P
Composite Score	Mean	SD	Mean	SD		
General attitudes (AT)	3.71	.45	3.54	.50	2.35	.020
Experience, knowledge, and information (EK)	2.16	.66	1.99	.64	1.84	.067
Willingness to make teaching accommodations (TA)	3.49	.55	3.53	.43	-.457	.646
Willingness to make examination accommodations (EA)	3.36	.61	3.73	.30	-5.52	.001
Students with LD in Teacher Education (LDT)	3.07	.61	3.38	.55	-3.56	.001

(AT). As can be seen, faculty at NIU expressed a significantly more supportive attitude toward students with disabilities in higher education than did faculty of BBC (t190 = 2.35, p = .020). Comparison of responses to items composing this subscale using a standard complex chi square procedure (Bruning and Kintz 1977) revealed that faculty at NIU expressed overall significantly more willingness to provide accommodations for students with disabilities in general (chi = 43.38, p = .001) than did faculty at BBC. On another question on the survey (not included in this subscale) faculty at NIU also reported spending significantly more time making accommodations for students with disabilities than did their counterparts (chi = 22.43, p = .001). However, no significant differences were noted between groups regarding whether or not making instructional and examination accommodations specifically for students with learning disabilities would be unfair to non-disabled students. Despite the reported difference on the total AT subscale score, a majority of faculty in the two groups expressed a very supportive attitude toward students with disabilities. For example, on the "willingness to accommodate" item, 98.5% of faculty at NIU and 83.9% at BBC were supportive or very supportive (ratings of 3 and 4 on a 4-point scale). Also on the fairness questions, 93.4% of faculty at NIU and 97.2% at BBC agreed or strongly agreed that providing TA accommodations for students with LD was fair to non-disabled students; while 89.3% and 94.7% respectively agreed that providing EA accommodations was fair.

However, on the question about the amount of time spent making accommodations, only 33.8% of faculty at NIU and 24.4% at BBC reported spending much or very much time, and for those who made accommodations, the majority (about 70%) indicated that the average amount of time spent per week was less than 30 minutes.

The second subscale was composed of items that explored faculty experience, knowledge, and information about resources and disability legislation (EK). The overall score for faculty at NIU on this variable was higher than for their counterparts at BBC, yet only approached statistical significance (t219 = 1.84, p = .067). Analyses of individual items included in this variable revealed the following. Faculty at BBC reported more overall personal contact with individuals with disabilities (chi = 15.18, p = .002), but more faculty at NIU reported contact with colleagues (chi = 20.83, p = .001) and friends with disabilities (chi = 39.02, p = .001). Faculty at NIU, in contrast to BBC, also reported having more exposure to students with disabilities in their college teaching experience although the difference only approached statistical significance (chi = 6.60, p = .086). Regarding specific disabilities, faculty at NIU reported significantly more experience with students who are identified as blind (chi = 51.64, p = .001), deaf (chi = 48.97, p = .001), and with a physical disability (chi = 18.75, p = .001). However, no significant differences were found in reported teaching experience with students with learning disabilities. Faculty at NIU reported having significantly more knowledge and skills regarding making accommodations (chi = 18.56, p = .001)) and were more aware of resources and services on campus for students with disabilities (chi = 34.92, p = .001) than BBC faculty. No differences between groups were found on the question regarding training in the area of disabilities.

Faculty responses to specific items on the second subscale also showed the following. (a) A large number of respondents in both groups (43% at NIU, and 55.5% at BBC) indicated having no experience in teaching students with disabilities in higher education. (b) Two thirds of faculty at NIU (66.1%) compared with less than half at BBC (47.3%) indicated they had a lot or a great deal (rankings 3 and 4) of knowledge and skills in making accommodations. (c) Quite a low percentage of faculty, 28.7% at NIU and 36.9% at BBC, reported a lot or a great deal of training in disabilities, and only 49.0% and 23.9% respectively reported being aware of services and resources on campus. (d) In both groups, only about one third indicated they had a lot or a great deal of familiarity with various disability laws.

On the third subscale, regarding willingness to provide teaching accommodations (TA) specifically for students with learning disabilities, no significant differences were found between groups (t199 = –.457, p = .646). However, on several specific accommodations significant differences were noted. For example, faculty at NIU were more willing to provide students a copy of their lecture notes (chi = 17.33, p = .001) while significantly more faculty at BBC reported willingness to make comments on drafts of papers (chi = 12.00, p = .007), and to allow students to complete assignments in a different format (e.g., oral presentation instead of written projects) (chi = 16.35, p = .001). No significant differences were found on willingness to make accommodations such as providing a copy of an overhead transparency, clarifying lecture assignments, or allowing students to tape record classroom lectures. Overall responses obtained to the items of this subscale revealed that 80% to 95% of faculty in each group expressed a high degree of willingness to provide students with learning disabilities with most of these teaching accommodations. Willingness to provide students with a lecture outline was, however, only 73.8% for NIU and 47.6% for BBC.

Findings for the fourth subscale exploring willingness to provide examination accommodations (EA) specifically for students with learning disabilities indicated that significantly more faculty at BBC than NIU expressed a strong willingness to provide such accommodations (t187 = –5.52, p = .001). Chi square tests for items comprising this variable revealed that significantly more faculty at BBC than at NIU were willing to allow additional time on tests (chi = 14.39, p = .002), allow the use of calculators (chi = 9.03, p = .029), provide paraphrased test questions (chi = 54.94, p = .001), allow oral or tape recorded responses to questions rather than written responses (chi = 22.08, p = .001), allow for an alternative format of exams, (e.g., multiple choice instead of essay) (chi = 14.95, p = .002), and consider the process as well as the final solution in grading (chi = 10.01, p = .018). No group differences were found on faculty willingness to allow exams to be monitored in a supervised location other than the classroom and to allow students to use a word processor or electronic spell-checker. Responses to items in this domain showed that 80% to 98% of faculty at BBC expressed a strong willingness to offer these accommodations; in contrast to faculty at NIU where 55% to 75% were willing to provide these same accommodations. The lowest support by NIU faculty was given to accommodations providing an alternative format for exams, paraphrasing questions, and giving partial credit for the correct process.

Responses on the subscale regarding faculty views about students with learning disabilities in teacher training programs (LDT) revealed that faculty at BBC expressed overall a significantly more supportive attitude than did their counterparts at NIU (t191 = –3.56, p = .001). Faculty at BBC expressed significantly stronger agreement with the statement that the minimum grade point average required for entry into teacher education may be modified for students with LD (chi = 52.74, p = .001). However, no significant differences between groups were noted in their positive support for the statements that skills needed for entry into teacher education could be demonstrated in ways other than standardized tests, and that during clinical experiences students may be given their assignments early to allow extra time to complete them, and that they be allowed to use assistive technology. Both groups (more than 80%) strongly supported the statement that students with learning disabilities may be as effective as teachers without learning disabilities. Overall, both groups indicated a strong supportive attitude toward students with learning disabilities in teacher training, except in regard to the modification of the GPA. Seventy percent of faculty at BBC versus only 20 percent at NIU were in support of this modification.

Demographic Variables and Faculty Responses

T-tests and one-way ANOVA tests were computed to examine the impact of faculty background variables on their responses to the five subscales.

The demographic variables included: (1) gender, (2) age (divided into four levels: 25–35, 36–45, 46–55, 56+), (3) academic degree (doctorate vs. non-doctorate), and (4) years of college teaching (divided into four groupings: 1–5, 6–10, 11–15, 16+).

BEIT BERL COLLEGE

Several background variables were found to have an impact on faculty responses.

Gender. Significant differences were found between females and males in their responses to the following subscales: Experience, Knowledge, and Information (t84 = −3.07, p = .001), Teaching Accommodations (t92 = −4.24, p = .006) and Examination Accommodations (t76 = −3.24, p = .002). In all of the three subscales, females obtained significantly higher scores than males.

Academic degree. Significant differences were found between faculty without a doctorate and faculty with a doctorate for the following two subscales: General Attitudes (t66 = 2.38, p = .020) and Teaching Accommodations (t93 = 2.59, p = .011). On these subscales, faculty without a doctorate obtained significantly higher scores than their colleagues with a doctorate.

Age. No statistically significant differences were found for this variable.

Teaching experience. Years of college teaching were found to be related to the following subscales: Experience, Knowledge, and Information (EK) (F3,81 = 3.35, p = .023), Examination Accommodations (EA) (F3,73 = 4.43, p = .006), and views about Students with LD in Teacher Education (LTD) (F3,74 = 4.28, p = .008). The post hoc comparisons indicated that for the EK subscale, faculty with 1 to 5 years of teaching experience obtained significantly higher scores (p < .05) than faculty with 6 to 10 years of experience on the modified LSD post hoc test (SPSS 1994). For the EA subscale, faculty with 1 to 5 years of teaching experience had again significantly higher scores (p < .05) than faculty with 6 to 10 years on the Scheffé post hoc test. For the LDT subscale, faculty with 1 to 5 years of teaching experience had significantly higher scores (p < .05) than faculty with 6 to 10 years, on the Scheffé test. Their scores were also higher than of faculty with 16+ years of experience, but this difference only approached significance (p = .058).

NORTHERN ILLINOIS UNIVERSITY

No statistically significant differences were found between demographic variables of gender, academic degree, and years of college teaching and responses to the five subscales. For the variable of age, a significant difference was found on the subscale Examination Accommodations ($F_{3,101}$ = 3.67, p = .015). Scheffé tests, however, revealed that only faculty in the 46 to 55 age group obtained significantly higher scores ($p < .05$), namely expressed more willingness to provide EA, than faculty in the 36–45 age group.

DISCUSSION

The purpose of this study was to explore faculty attitude and practices toward students with disabilities in postsecondary institutions with the focus on a cross-national/cross-cultural comparison. Participants were faculty members in a College of Education at a large state university in the USA and faculty at BBC, the largest teacher training college in Israel. Given the substantial increase in the proportion of students with disabilities (and particularly students with LD) in higher education, we considered it important to start an international initiative to research faculty attitude and practices in order to guide the further development of support services on college and university campuses in different cultures and to plan professional development activities based on faculty needs and interests.

A number of factors need to be considered in seeking to understand the results of the present study and similar future cross-cultural studies. Such factors include cultural similarities and differences between the USA and Israel's legislative histories regarding individuals with disabilities, and the size and mission of the two participating institutions.

Although Americans and Israelis share many similar norms and values, and have frequent contacts, some of the reported findings may have resulted from different interpretations of the wording or the language used in the survey form, as well as to a different pattern of responding to questions influenced by cultural expectations, beliefs, values, and norms.

Regarding the legislative histories, it should be stressed that the US has a much longer history and commitment to disability rights legislation compared to Israel. Findings showed that faculty at NIU had more experience in teaching students with disabilities than their counterparts at BBC, particularly students with sensory and physical disabilities. Note also that the American law PL 94-142, mandating free appropriate public education for all students with disabilities and their integration into inclusive environments, was passed in 1975, while a similar law in Israel was passed in 1988, 13 years later. In the US the law resulted in the full- or part-time placement of more than almost 75% of all students with disabilities in regular education classrooms (US Department of Education 1998). In Israel too, a decrease in the numbers of students in segregated special education placements has been recently documented (Sprinzak, Bar, and Piterman et al. 1997). As members of a College of Education, faculty were aware of this educational trend. Furthermore, an increased enrollment of students with disabilities in postsecondary schools in the US has resulted from disability legislation such as Section 504 and ADA. In Israel, similar legislation has not yet been passed, though it is in a draft stage. (See chapter on legislation in this volume.) Not surprisingly, then, more faculty at NIU reported contact with students with disabilities and more awareness of support services on campus. Furthermore, the Student Support Center at BBC described above was only opened during the 1996–1997 academic year, and this survey was conducted in 1997. Faculty at NIU also felt they had more knowledge regarding accommodating students with disabilities. Overall, however, about half of the faculty in both institutions indicated they had no teaching contacts with these students, suggesting that over the years relatively few students with disabilities enrolled in their university courses. Although both groups reported a strong willingness to make accommodations, the significantly higher composite score on the Attitude subscale by NIU faculty than BBC faculty may be a result of the former's having more years of experience and knowledge in working with students with different disabilities. However, with the reported increase in the US and in Israel in the number of students with documented LD in post-secondary institutions, many faculty members in both samples reported that the largest group with which they had teaching experience were students with LD. Such experiences probably had an impact on the positions of the majority of faculty in both institutions that providing accommodations to students with LD was fair to students without disabilities.

Although many faculty members in both groups (about two thirds) reported limited training in the area of disabilities and many (about 50%) had limited personal contact or teaching experience with individuals with disabilities, it was interesting that a very large majority expressed positive attitudes, or a positive disposition, toward students with disabilities in general in higher education. Similar positive attitudes in general by faculty have been reported by other investigators (Aksamit et al. 1987; Leyser 1989; Satcher, 1992). Note that data reported here were obtained only from Education Faculty. Previous comparisons between faculty from CoE and faculty in other disci-plines at NIU (Leyser et al. 1998; Vogel et al. 1999) revealed that the CoE faculty reported more contact with and more training in disabili-ties, a greater familiarity with the law as well as more willingness to provide some TA and EA accommodations. This finding was also sup-ported by several other investigators who reported more positive atti-tudes by faculty in the College of Education than in all other colleges within the university (Fonosch and Schwab 1981; Nelson et al. 1990).

Findings here are similar to those reported by a number of other researchers (Houck et al. 1992; Matthews et al. 1987; Nelson et al. 1990; Satcher 1992) indicating faculty willingness in both groups to provide various instructional and examination accommodations while expressing less willingness to offer some other accommoda-tions. For example, a large majority of faculty in both institutions ex-pressed willingness to provide instructional accommodations such as to allow students to tape record lectures; to clarify assignments on a one-to-one basis; or to comment on drafts of papers. They were less willing, however, to provide students with a copy of a lecture outline or with a copy of an overhead transparency, possibly because many faculty do not lecture from an outline or from formal notes. In regard to examination accommodations, a large majority of faculty in both groups expressed willingness to modify the setting (i.e., to allow exams to be proctored in a supervised location), to change the timing (to allow students additional time to complete exams), and allow the use of assistive technology (e.g., a calculator or word processor) which in today's society has a high level of acceptance and is widely available. Faculty in both institutions, however, were less willing to change the presentation format (e.g., multiple choice instead of essay) and less willing to adjust the grading (e.g., give partial credit for a correct process).

Significant differences, however, were found between the two groups on a few instructional accommodations, especially in the area of student evaluation. In the area of instructional accommodations, significantly more faculty at NIU than at BBC expressed willingness to provide students with a copy of their lecture notes, while significantly more faculty at BBC were ready to make comments on drafts, and allow for changes in the format of presentation (i.e., oral presentation instead of written projects). Regarding examination accommodations, significantly more faculty at BBC than at NIU were ready to adjust the timing (allow additional time), and modify the grading procedures (i.e., give partial credit). However, faculty in both groups were not strongly supportive of giving partial credit.

Faculty at BBC expressed a significantly higher willingness to modify the format of an exam (e.g., multiple choice instead of essay) to paraphrase questions upon student request, and to change the response format (e.g., allow oral or tape recorded rather than written responses).

These differences between faculty members can possibly be explained by the fact that NIU is a large graduate degree granting institution that fosters a strong research orientation, in contrast to BBC, which primarily focuses on teaching—not research and writing—and where faculty may view themselves as more student-oriented, hence their greater willingness to make examination accommodations. Faculty at NIU, on the other hand, may be concerned more about the academic integrity of their program as compared with other programs on campus, and seek reassurance that in their teaching and evaluation procedures students achieve mastery of the material, while at the same time they maintain fairness for all students. Similar findings regarding faculty perceptions were also reported by other researchers in studies in the US (e.g., Nelson et al., 1990; Satcher, 1992). Results from studies of faculty in doctoral degree granting institutions in Israel may be more similar to those reported here for NIU.

Making classroom accommodations may often demand a great deal of time. Indeed, faculty were asked to indicate if they had spent extra time, and if so, what was the average amount of time they spent per student per week. A majority (about 70%) at both institutions reported that they spent less than 30 minutes per week making accommodations. It can be argued that this is the amount of time that faculty actually felt was needed to make accommodations, or that it was all the time faculty were willing to give. Considering the types of accommodations faculty reported that they were willing to make, it seems that most were quite straightforward (yet necessary) and that they did not demand a great expenditure of time. It would be of interest to examine whether students with disabilities view the amount of time spent by faculty as sufficient.

An important question explored in this study was how faculty in colleges of education view students with learning disabilities who wish to enter and study in programs leading to teacher certification. The issue of the commitment of education faculty to the rights of students with disabilities on the one hand, while at the same time having a major responsibility of ensuring that only qualified competent teachers obtain certification, has been raised by several authors (i.e., Brulle 1996; Brulle et al. 1998; McGee and Kauffman 1989; Wertheim, Vogel, and Brulle 1998; Yanok 1987). Findings revealed that regarding admissions regulations for entry into teacher education, namely modifying the required grade point average (GPA) for students with LD, a majority of faculty at NIU expressed opposition to lowering the academic standards in order to accommodate these students, in contrast to their counterparts at BBC. In the US, the national accreditation standards

(NCATE 1997) specify a minimum GPA of at least 2.50 for entry into and continuation in a teacher education program (NIU has adopted a similar standard of 2.5). As noted, faculty did not support modification of this requirement (BBC seems to allow for more flexible entrance requirements). Furthermore, that stand by faculty at NIU was also supported by their unwillingness to provide accommodations that, based on their perception, might compromise the quality of the program or of their instruction. However, the majority of faculty at NIU, as at BBC, supported the idea that reasonable accommodations could be made in the assessment of students' basic skills (i.e., allowing students to demonstrate these competencies in ways other than standardized tests). Both groups felt that such an alteration for students with LD assures an equal opportunity for participation in teacher education.

Overall, faculty expressed a positive disposition toward students with learning disabilities in preservice teacher preparation programs. A large majority supported the idea that during clinical experiences, providing these students with assignments early to allow extra time to complete them, and allowing the use of assistive technology are examples of reasonable accommodations. Perhaps this support is due to the easy access to most technologies. For example, these days just about everyone has access to a calculator or a word processing program.

These technologies are now such a part of everyday life that perhaps most faculty were not concerned with their use. Another very supportive and encouraging finding was that the majority of faculty members believed that students with LD may be as effective as teachers who are non-disabled, taking the position that with reasonable accommodations students with LD are capable of pursuing careers in teaching.

In our exploration of demographic variables that have an impact on faculty attitudes and practices, several were found to have a significant role. Findings regarding faculty at BBC revealed that the variables of gender, academic degree, and college teaching experience were related to responses on the subscales. For example:

(1) Female faculty reported significantly more experience and knowledge than male faculty about disabilities and more willingness to provide teaching and examination accommodations. More supportive attitudes of female faculty members toward students with disabilities were also reported in other studies (Aksamit et al. 1987; Baggett 1994; Fonosch and Schwab 1981).

(2) Faculty members with less than a doctorate degree obtained significantly higher scores than those with a doctorate on the attitude measure and on willingness to provide teaching accommodations. This finding may be related to the fact that faculty with a doctorate, many of whom also hold a teaching position at a doctoral degree-

granting university, may spend more of their time in research and writing, thus may find less time for making accommodations.

(3) Faculty members with fewer years of college teaching experience, compared with faculty with more teaching experience, reported having more knowledge, experience, and information about disabilities; more willingness to provide examination accommodations; and more positive attitudes toward students with LD in teacher education (see also Brulle et al. 1998). Perhaps these beginning instructors, many of whom previously worked in public schools and/or were recently trained at universities, had more exposure to students with disabilities in general education classes and to recent information on laws and practices than did faculty with more years of college teaching. In an earlier study, Center and Ward (1987) reported that teaching experience was negatively related to attitudes toward integration of students with disabilities in general education classrooms.

For faculty members at NIU, the demographic variables were not found to be related to attitudes and practices. In a previous study of faculty at the same College of Education at NIU, Leyser (1989) also found that gender or years of teaching experience were not related to attitudes and accommodations. Faculty at NIU and BBC differed on several demographic variables, which may have had an impact on these results. For example, at NIU almost 75% of faculty, as compared to only 30% at BBC, had a doctorate. Also, while half of the faculty at NIU were female, their percentage at BBC was close to 75%.

The findings reported in this cross-cultural study have several implications for practice and future research. Many faculty at both institutions reported limited training in disabilities, limited knowledge of resources, limited skills for making accommodations, and limited familiarity with disability laws. These results suggest that there is a need for faculty development activities. Faculty should be provided with information about disabilities, recent disability legislation, and support services on campus. Also, faculty could benefit from examples of reasonable instructional and course-related accommodations. Such lists are available in the literature in English (Vogel and Adelman 1993) and in Hebrew (Vogel 1998). Faculty, however, need reassurance that these modifications do not lower academic standards. A dialogue among faculty members should continue regarding the critical question of how to find a balance between the public demand for competency in the teaching profession and the moral obligation to provide an equal opportunity for students with disabilities (Brulle 1996; Brulle et al. 1998; Wertheim, Vogel, and Brulle 1998; Yanok 1987).

The recommendations made by Brulle (1996) may still be well advised. He recommended that faculty in teacher preparation programs have, for each student with a learning disability, clear written documentation regarding the expectations, the accommodations, and the feedback provided to each student with a learning disability to ensure that the student has clearly demonstrated that he or she can meet the demands of teaching and that the institution has provided all necessary accommodations.

It is well known that faculty members have a very busy schedule teaching, conducting research, writing, and serving on university committees. Therefore, they may not have time to participate in presentations, workshops, and seminars. Suggestions made by faculty at NIU indicate that they would prefer to receive information through printed materials such as newsletters, pamphlets, and handbooks. Information could also be disseminated through campus e-mail, the internet, and the university newspaper. Preparing a showcase and displays in the education building or in the faculty lounge with updated information could be an effective way to disseminate information.

Several limitations of this study need to be addressed. First, because the survey included faculty in only one institution in the US and one in Israel, caution is required in generalizing these findings to other institutions and nations. Additional studies are needed in other universities and colleges in different countries and regions of the world to support or refute our findings. Information gathered from international studies may be important for the development of a large database that will be useful for policy makers and for faculty development activities.

Second, the response rate by faculty in both institutions was acceptable, yet lower than desirable. Attempts should be made to secure higher response rates in studies in other institutions (e.g., sending out multiple reminders after the deadline and soliciting the support of department chairs and deans). Third, responses obtained to a self-report questionnaire may not represent the true feelings and, in particular, the actual teaching behavior in the classroom. Other methodologies of data collection such as interviews, observations of faculty classroom teaching, use of focus groups, and obtaining input from students with disabilities should be employed to confirm findings on faculty attitudes and accommodations that are being used.

EPILOGUE

Since the time this study was completed, several activities and initiatives have been undertaken. Although the survey instrument was found to be reliable and useful, information received from participating faculty was used to revise the survey form. Major changes included the addition of three new items and the use of 6-point Likert-type scales instead of 4-point scales. Furthermore, the revised survey requests faculty to respond not only to items by stating their willingness to make teaching and examination accommodations, but also by indicating whether they have actually made these accommodations.

Northern Illinois University has decided to serve as a future national and international bank for data on faculty attitudes and practices regarding students with disabilities. Letters in this regard have been sent to many institutions of higher education that indicate an interest in participating and information has been published in newsletters. The revised survey form is currently being administered in several colleges and universities in the USA. The revised edition has also been translated into Hebrew and will be used both at Beit Berl College and other teacher training colleges and universities in Israel. It is hoped that the aggregated data will provide additional insight into faculty views and practices toward students with disabilities, and provide recommendations to increase faculty knowledge, ability, and enhance more supportive attitudes.

REFERENCES

Aksamit, D., Morris, M., and Leuenberger, J. 1987. Preparation of student services professionals and faculty for serving learning-disabled college students. *Journal of College Student Personnel* 28:53–59.

Baggett, D. 1994. A study of faculty awareness of students with disabilities. Paper presented at the annual meeting of the National Association for Developmental Education, Kansas City, MO. (ED 369 208)

Booth, T., and Ainscow, M. 1998). Introduction. In *From Them to Us: An International Study of Inclusion in Education*, eds. T. Booth and M. Ainscow. London, New York: Routledge.

Brandes, O., and Nesher, P. 1996. Equal but not separate - Students with special needs. In *The Third Leap: Changes and Reform in the Educational System in the 1990s*, ed. O. Brandes. Jerusalem, Israel: Ministry of Education, Culture, and Sports. (Hebrew)

Brinckerhoff, L. C., Shaw, S. F., and McGuire, J. M. 1993. *Promoting Postsecondary Education for Students with Learning Disabilities: A Handbook for Practitioners*. Austin, TX: PRO-ED.

Brulle, A. R. 1996. Students with learning disabilities and teacher preparation. *Critical Issues in Teacher Preparation* 6:13–20.

Brulle, A. R., Leyser, Y., Vogel, S., and Wyland, S. 1998. Competencies and accommodations: Faculty attitudes toward students with learning disabilities in teacher preparation. *Critical Issues in Teacher Education* 7:24–32.

Bruning, J. L., and Kintz, B. L. 1977. *Computational Handbook of Statistics* (2nd ed.). Glenview, IL: Scott Foresman.

Cavanagh, I. N. M. 1994. Disability and special education provisions for children with disabilities in low income countries. *European Journal of Special Needs Education* 9 (1):67–79.

Center, Y., and Ward, J. 1987. Teachers' attitudes toward the integration of disabled children into regular classrooms. *The Exceptional Child* 34:41–56.

Csapo, M. 1993. Special education in crisis. *International Journal of Special Education* 8:201–208.

Fichten, C. S., Amsel, R., Bourdon, C. V., and Creti, L. 1988. Interaction between college students with a physical disability and their professors. *Journal of Applied Rehabilitation Counseling* 19:13–21.

Fonosch, G. G., and Schwab, L. O. 1981. Attitudes of selected university faculty members toward disabled students. *Journal of College Student Personnel* 22:229–35.

Friend, M., and Bursuck, W. 1999. *Including Students with Special Needs: A Practical Guide for Classroom Teachers* (2nd ed.). Boston: Allyn and Bacon.

Henderson, K. 1995. *College Freshmen with Disabilities: A Triennial Statistical Profile*. Washington, DC: American Council on Education and HEATH Resource Center.

Houck, C. K., Asselin, S. B., Troutman, G. C., and Arrington, J. M. 1992. Students with learning disabilities in the university environment: A study of faculty and student perceptions. *Journal of Learning Disabilities* 25 (10):678–84.

Israel Knesset. 1988. Special Education Law of 1988. Rules Book 1256. Jerusalem, Israel: Author.

Kosminsky, L. 1995. Needs of students with learning disabilities in institutions of higher education. *To Be Like All* (NITZAN Magazine) 12:4–9. (Hebrew)

Leyser, Y. 1989. A survey of faculty attitudes and accommodations for students with disabilities. *Journal of Postsecondary Education and Disability* 7 (3 and 4):97–108.

Leyser, Y., Kapperman, G., and Keller, R. 1994. Teacher attitudes toward mainstreaming: A cross-cultural study in six nations. *European Journal of Special Needs Education* 9:1–15.

Leyser, Y., Vogel, S., Brulle, A., and Wyland, S. 1998. Faculty attitudes and practices regarding students with disabilities: Two decades after implementation of Section 504. *Journal of Postsecondary Education and Disability* 13:5–19.

Leyser, Y., Vogel, S., Wyland, S., Brulle, A., Sharoni, V., and Vogel, G. 2000. Students with learning disabilities in higher education: Perspectives of American and Israeli faculty. *International Education Journal* 29:47–67.

Margalit, M., Breznitz, Z., and Ahroni, M. 1997. Task Force Study of Students with Learning Disabilities in Institutions of Higher Education: Final Report. Jerusalem, Israel: Ministry of Education, Council for Higher Education.

Matthews, P. R., Anderson, D. W., and Skolnick, B. D. 1987. Faculty attitude toward accommodations for college students with learning disabilities. *Learning Disabilities Focus* 3 (1):46–52.

McCarthy, M., and Campbell, N. J. 1993. Serving disabled students: Faculty needs and attitudes. *NASPA (National Association of Student Personnel Administration) Journal* 30 (2):120–25.

McGee, K. A., and Kauffman, J. M. 1989. Educating teachers with emotional disabilities: A balance of private and public interests. *Teacher Education and Special Education* 12 (3):110–16.

Ministry of Education, Culture and Sport 1992, April. Procedures for the placement of students in special education (Special regulations). Jerusalem, Israel: Author.

Ministry of Education, Culture and Sport 1996, September. Learning disabilities (Special regulations). Jerusalem, Israel: Author.

Minner, S., and Prater, G. 1984. College teachers' expectations of LD students. *Academic Therapy* 20:225–29.

Moore, C. J., Newlon, B. J., and Nye, N. 1986. Faculty awareness of the needs of physically disabled students in the college classroom. *AHSSPPE* 4:137–45.

National Commission on Teaching and America's Future. 1996. What matters most: Teaching for America's future. New York: Author.

National Council for Accreditation of Teacher Education (NCATE). 1997. Standards, procedures, and policies for the accreditation of professional education units. Washington, DC: Author.

Nelson, R. J., Dodd, J. M., and Smith, D. J. 1990. Faculty willingness to accommodate students with learning disabilities: A comparison among academic divisions. *Journal of Learning Disabilities* 23 (3):185–89.

Rose, E. 1993. Faculty development: Changing attitudes and enhancing knowledge about learning disabilities. In *Success for College Students with Disabilities*, eds. S. A. Vogel and P. B. Adelman. New York: Springer-Verlag.

Satcher, J. 1992. Community college faculty comfort with providing accommodations for students with learning disabilities. *College Student Journal* 26 (4):518–24.

Sharoni, V., and Vogel, G. 1998. Attitudes of college faculty toward students with disabilities in general and students with learning disabilities in particular. *Dapim* 27:59–77.

Sprinzak, D., Bar, E., and Piterman, D. 1997. The Educational System in Numbers. Ministry of Education, Culture and Sport. Jerusalem, Israel (Hebrew).

SPSS 6.1. 1994. *Syntax Reference Guide.* Chicago, IL: SPSS, Inc.

The Rehabilitation Act of 1973 (PL 93-112), Section 504, Rules and Regulations—Nondiscrimination on the basis of handicaps in federally-assisted programs 1977. Federal Register 42:22675–94.

US Congress 1975. Public Law 94-142. The Education of All Handicapped Children Act. Washington, DC: Author.

US Congress 1990. Public Law 101-476. Individuals with Disabilities Education Act amendments (IDEA). Washington, DC: Author.

US Department of Education 1998. Twentieth annual report to Congress on the implementation of the individuals with disabilities education act. Washington, DC: Author.

UNESCO 1988. Review of the present situation of special education. Paris, France: Author. (ERIC Document Reproduction Service No. ED 312 820)

UNESCO 1994. The Salamanca statement and framework for action on special need education. Paris, France: Author.

Vogel, S. 1998. *Students with Learning Disabilities in Institutions of Higher Education: A Guidance Manual.* Jerusalem, Israel: LESHEM. (Hebrew)

Vogel, S. A., and Adelman, P. B. 1993. *Success for College Students with Learning Disabilities.* New York: Springer-Verlag.

Vogel, S. A., Leonard, F., Scales, W., Hayeslip, E., Hermanson, J., and Donnell, L. 1998. The National Learning Disabilities Postsecondary Data Bank: An overview. *Journal of Learning Disabilities* 31 (3):234–47.

Vogel, S., Leyser, Y., Wyland, S., and Brulle, A. 1999. Students with learning disabilities in higher education: Faculty attitudes and practices. *Learning Disabilities Research & Practice* 14 173–86.

Wertheim, C., Vogel, S. A., and Brulle, A. 1998. Students with learning disabilities in teacher education programs. *Annals of Dyslexia* 49:293–309.

Yanok, J. 1987. Equal opportunity in teacher education programs for the learning disabled. *Journal of Teacher Education* 38 (1):48–52.

PART • IV

Social-emotional Impact of Learning Disabilities

In Part IV, Social-emotional Impact of Learning Disabilities, there are two chapters. In Chapter 12, Michael Baron-Jeffrey, Susan Vogel, and Angela Baron-Jeffrey propose a model for a support group for adults with learning disabilities based on the research of Paul Gerber and his colleagues. The focus of this support group is to enable the participants to understand and develop strategies pertaining to social and emotional adjustment that researchers have found to be characteristic of adults with learning disabilities who lead highly successful lives. The chapter depicts the strategies, outlines each session as well as the objectives for the participants and the group leader, and discusses a number of practical considerations that can contribute to the successful establishment and continued functioning of such a support group.

Lea Kozminsky (Chapter 13) also focuses on successful adults with learning disabilities. Kozminsky interviewed 33 successful Israeli adults with learning disabilities and described their cognitive and emotional approach to their disability. She describes their sources of support and their own personal strategies for dealing with their problems. In addition, she describes three different intervention and support programs that were designed on the basis of her results and implemented in Beer Sheva, a city in southern Israel.

Chapter • 12

Support Groups for Adults with Learning Disabilities

Michael C. Baron-Jeffrey, Susan Vogel,
Angela C. Baron-Jeffrey

This chapter provides a practical approach for developing and conducting a support group for adults with learning disabilities who wish to build and enhance skills for employment success. The group affords participants the opportunity to identify their strengths, interests, and abilities and to develop skills and techniques to build upon while addressing or learning to cope with deficits that hinder their progress.

The chapter is intended for use by group leaders in community settings, on college campuses, including those with limited resources for this population, and in any other context where adults with learning disabilities may benefit from participation in the support group. It provides guidelines for selecting participants, instructions for conducting exercises that facilitate the growth and development of the desired skills and abilities, and insights on group process. An appendix of resource materials is also provided. The psycho-educational approach offers adults with learning disabilities the opportunity to change the way they conceptualize, understand, and relate to their environment. The model is based on one that emerged from the work of Gerber, Ginsberg, and Reiff (1992).

GERBER'S MODEL OF EMPLOYMENT SUCCESS

Gerber, Ginsberg, and Reiff (1992) conducted research to determine factors that contribute to success in employment among adults with learning disabilities. They identified two themes that distinguished highly from moderately successful adults with learning disabilities: internal decisions and external manifestations. Internal decisions consist of desire, goal orientation, and reframing. External manifestations involve persistence, goodness of fit, learned creativity, and social ecology. Gerber and his colleagues found that the degree to which adults with learning disabilities control these themes correlates positively with the level of success they achieve.

To identify successful adults with LD, professionals in the field of learning disabilities were asked to nominate successful adults (Gerber, Ginsberg, and Reiff 1992). Potential participants were rated on five indicators of employment success: income level, education level, job classification, prominence in one's field, and job satisfaction. Five experts in the field of learning disabilities then rated the candidates on each variable. Panel members discussed discrepancies in ratings for each candidate until a consensus was reached on each criterion. Participants were placed in the high success group if they received high ratings on four of the five variables, and no low ratings. They were placed in the moderately successful group if they received a majority of moderate ratings and no more than one low rating among the five criteria.

To control confounding variables, participants were matched on several variables. In addition to the demographic variables, participants in the two groups were matched on severity of disability and specific learning disability. To maximize the identification of key variables associated with high levels of success, whenever possible two high success participants were matched with one member of the moderately successful group. This selection process yielded 71 participants, including 46 highly and 25 moderately successful adults with learning disabilities.

The support group for college students with learning disabilities that we describe later in this chapter integrates materials and exercises designed to help participants understand and develop the themes that Gerber and his colleagues indicated as characteristic of the highly successful adults with LD.

Themes

Desire.   According to Gerber, Ginsberg, and Reiff (1992), the strength of an individual's desire to succeed is critical for success. They found highly successful adults express desire through conspicuous and powerful statements about personal motivation. These adults are determined not to fail and frequently are anxious about the prospect of failure. Gerber, Ginsberg, and Reiff found that moderately successful adults also express desire. However, their expressions are less intense and less resolute.

Goal Orientation. Highly successful adults are goal-oriented (Gerber, Ginsberg, and Reiff 1992). They know what they want, figure out what it takes to get it, and persistently pursue it. They consciously set concise and explicit long-term and short-term goals. By contrast, Gerber, Ginsberg, and Reiff found that moderately successful adults with learning disabilities have ambivalent and less lofty goals. When they do identify goals, they set short-term goals but few long-term ones. They also frequently report distraction as the cause of failure.

Reframing. According to Gerber, Reiff, and Ginsberg (1996), reframing is a process through which individuals change the way they think about themselves. This change results in altering a person's perspective. Instead of focusing on weaknesses, this change builds upon strengths. The process results in recognition, acceptance, and understanding of one's learning disability leading to action. Success requires accurate assessment and action, so it is not surprising that Gerber, Ginsberg, and Reiff (1992) included an action-oriented process of self-assessment in their model.

Recognition. Highly successful adults with learning disabilities see themselves for who they are. Recognition of their disability and its disadvantages was evident among the highly successful adults. They realize that they see and do things differently, and that this difference hinders them in some ways. Gerber, Ginsberg, and Reiff (1992) found this awareness occurs at various stages in life, some early, some late.

Acceptance. Successful self-awareness goes beyond recognition. Highly successful adults with learning disabilities accept themselves and their disability. These adults express acceptance of the fact they will always have to confront the disability. Gerber, Ginsberg, and Reiff (1992) found evidence of acceptance in their willingness to share information about their disability. Although highly successful adults vary in the amount of information about their disability that they disclose to others, they do not try to hide the fact they have a learning disability. Conversely, moderately successful adults expressed a need to hide their disability.

Understanding. In the reframing process, Gerber, Ginsberg, and Reiff (1992) found that highly successful adults with learning disabilities go beyond recognition and acceptance of weaknesses. These adults acknowledge the limits of their weaknesses and understand how to use personal strengths to compensate for them. They reframe the typical deficit perspective associated with disability into a perspective that accentuates strengths and fortifies vulnerabilities. Thus their focus goes beyond limitations and a need to cover up, to one that uses personal strengths to compensate for the consequences of their learning disability.

Action.   As may be expected, insightful self-awareness and acceptance is not sufficient for success. Highly successful adults act upon this awareness to reach their goals. Gerber, Ginsberg, and Reiff (1992) found that highly successful adults with learning disabilities distinguished themselves from moderately successful adults by choosing to make decisions built on accomplishments. These decisions included taking action that increased desire, that focused on goals, and that changed perceptions of self.

Gerber, Ginsberg, and Reiff (1992) found the degree of progress through each of these four stages differed among highly successful and moderately successful adults with learning disabilities. Moderately successful adults expressed more difficulty than highly successful peers regarding acceptance, and they understood less about their disability and their strengths. They were also less active in the pursuit of goals and desires. They exhibited more blaming of self, others, and circumstances, as well as more avoidance, and other forms of "holding back" than highly successful adults with learning disabilities. Gerber, Ginsberg, and Reiff concluded that movement through the four stages of reframing was limited among moderately successful adults with learning disabilities, but not among their more successful peers.

External Manifestations

External manifestations are adaptive behaviors that increase the probability of success. Gerber, Ginsberg, and Reiff (1992) identified four characteristics of this theme: persistence, goodness of fit, learned creativity, and social ecology.

Persistence.   Gerber, Ginsberg, and Reiff (1992) found that highly successful adults describe themselves as exceptionally persistent. Obstacles, including their disability, are unacceptable causes of failure. They see themselves working much harder than their peers and accept this type of persistence as a way of life. By contrast, moderately successful adults express less determination, report taking fewer risks, and recall being more easily distracted from goals and desires.

Goodness of Fit.   Goodness of fit is a state of being that results from the process of seeking environments that are compatible with personal interests, abilities, skills, and strengths (Gerber, Ginsberg, and Reiff 1992). All participants in Gerber, Ginsberg, and Reiff's sample described themselves as finding compatible work environments.

At the same time, adults in the high success group expressed greater enthusiasm about their work and reported greater control over their working environment than their moderately successful peers.

Learned Creativity. According to Gerber, Ginsberg, and Reiff (1992), learned creativity is a skill characterized by divergent problem-solving methods that builds upon strengths, and results in a collection of compensatory strategies and mechanisms that enhance performance. Most successful adults with learning disabilities use compensatory strategies and techniques, such as modern technology, to adapt to their environment. Gerber, Ginsberg, and Reiff found that highly successful adults use more sophisticated and creative compensatory strategies. For example, some use anticipatory skills, a process that involves predicting various possible outcomes and preparing responses for the most probable ones. In general, highly successful adults devise ways to address their disability instead of hiding, avoiding, or neglecting it.

Social Ecology. Social ecology is an environment that is characterized by social support and a commitment to self-improvement (Gerber, Ginsberg, and Reiff 1992). Highly successful adults develop relationships that provide emotional support and vocational guidance. They receive and accept encouragement from individuals with whom they have key personal relationships like spouses, friends, and colleagues. They also seek guidance from consciously selected mentors, and participate in self-improvement programs. Gerber, Ginsberg, and Reiff found moderately successful adults with learning disabilities were more frequently apt to reject support, depend on others to compensate for their disabilities, and seek less guidance and support than their highly successful peers.

OVERVIEW OF A SUPPORT GROUP FOR COLLEGE STUDENTS

The following section contains information on the purpose and scope of the support group. A section follows on goals and objectives of the support group. It contains lists of specific objectives for participants and group leaders. Required skills and characteristics of group leaders are discussed, followed by a section on methodology and content that provides general information on content and methods to be used when conducting a support group and specific topics for each session. The practical considerations section that follows gives guidelines for screening group members and scheduling meetings, dealing with attrition, and managing group development. Evaluation, an important, but sometimes overlooked component, is also included. Suggested activities, materials, and resources are provided for each session.

Purpose

The primary purpose of a support group is to engage its members in a process of exploring and applying principles and skills that facilitate success, personally, academically, and vocationally, with special emphasis on vocational success. This group experience also provides a safe and structured environment in which to explore new ways of behaving and to discuss and share current life experiences. Members have the opportunity to see others who struggle with similar problems, discover new ways to deal with them, and experience care and support. These experiences tend to reduce the level of stress experienced by members of the group.

Scope

Rather than providing an open, unstructured forum for discussion and support, this support group focused on the development of the themes that differentiate highly successful adults with learning disabilities from moderately successful adults. Gerber, Ginsberg, and Reiff (1992) found that the amount of control individuals have over two themes distinguishes these populations. Participation in the support group improved the general functioning of its members by increasing member awareness of these themes in their lives and by facilitating the development of skills needed to achieve vocational success. This is accomplished through brief teaching segments, guided discussions of current life events, and homework assignments.

Goals and Objectives

The primary goal of this support group was to improve the functioning of its members by increasing self-awareness and personal knowledge of behaviors that promote success. In addition to learning to identify these behaviors, participants learned to increase their personal use of them.

Participant Objectives

Participants:

1. Learned to identify two themes that differentiate between highly successful and moderately successful adults with learning disabilities as outlined by Gerber, Ginsberg, and Reiff (1992).
2. Gained a greater understanding of the qualities and principles that embody each theme.

3. Assessed the presence of each theme in their lives. They determined how and under what conditions they exhibited particular behaviors and the functions they served, as well as what prevented them from exhibiting others.
4. Understood the techniques for developing themes of highly successful adults with learning disabilities to improve self-concept, personal performance, and satisfaction.
5. Identified at least one characteristic they wished to improve.
6. Applied the principles and techniques to develop the characteristic(s) they selected to attain or improve their lives.

Group Leader Objectives

1. Group leaders convened and maintained the group and helped the group develop and respect its culture (expectations and norms).
2. Group leaders helped members discover:
   strongly held desires,
   individual interpersonal style,
   life events that reflect personal persistence,
   personal strengths and weaknesses, particularly those
      influenced by learning disabilities,
   environmental resources, and
   individual creativity.
3. Group leaders helped members learn:
   to convert desires into goals and objectives,
   to develop strategies for reaching goals and objectives,
   to reframe personal life experiences, shaped by their
      learning disabilities, in ways that reduce
      discouragement and increase motivation, and effort,
   to identify persistence in other group members,
   to assess the adequacy of accessible resources to
      complement their strengths and weaknesses in ways
      that facilitate goal attainment,
   to enhance their creativity in problem solving,
      the importance of social support, and
      ways to increase the support they receive.

Group Leader Skills and Characteristics

Group leaders should have group leadership skills and experience working with adults with learning disabilities. As in most groups, group leaders must communicate attitudes and beliefs that inspire group participation. Group leaders exhibit genuine concern and caring, along with the courage to confront challenges openly, and an unwavering belief in the group process. This is particularly important because adults with learning disabilities are vulnerable to experiences of frustration and alienation. Unattended, these experiences can lead to agitation, despair, depression, and reduced motivation.

In addition to basic listening and group leadership skills (Corey 1995), group leaders should ideally be competent with both cognitive-behavioral and process-oriented leadership techniques. Cognitive-behavioral techniques are emphasized during the teaching segments of the program, and can promote growth during the sharing segments. Modeling, shaping, and reinforcing behaviors will help members learn and use group expectations and encourage them to provide each other with much needed interpersonal feedback.

METHODOLOGY AND CONTENT

Methodology

In each group meeting, the group leader:
1. Provided graphic representation and verbal definitions of each theme.
2. Led discussions and defined, illustrated, and provided examples that helped participants understand the principles and techniques associated with developing each theme in their lives.
     Used "I statements" to describe both moderately and
        highly successful adults with learning disabilities.
     Discussed current events or case studies.
3. Encouraged participants to explore what to do and why it works.
     In each group meeting, participants had to complete the
        following assignments:
     Find self among (I) statements.
     Reflect on situation and re-examine personal behavior,
        response, feelings, etc.
     Write brief journals.
4. Share personal growth experiences with group members.

Content

Corey (1995) emphasizes the need for group leaders to possess skills that facilitate both individual and interpersonal growth. This is particularly important in this group, because its purpose is to increase personal knowledge, understanding, and skills, as well as to increase self-awareness of one's interpersonal style. Group leaders who find it difficult to switch readily between these roles may pay closer attention to the individual learning needs of members during the teaching segment of sessions, and attend more closely to relationship issues during the sharing or processing segments of the sessions.

Topics. The support group is designed to discuss the following topics over 12 sessions.

Session 1: *Introduction.* Acquaint members with each other and with the group process. Discuss group expectations of confidentiality, respect, attendance, and participation. Describe the rationale for the group. Share and discuss members' hopes and expectations for the group.

Session 2: *Success.* Note its personal quality. Identify and describe successful people.

Session 3: *The role of desire.* Discuss differences between intrinsic and extrinsic motivation. Facilitate discussion of personal desires and motivations. Begin to classify personal desires as intrinsically or extrinsically motivating.

Session 4: *Goal orientation.* Introduce concept. Discuss difference between desires and goals. Begin to identify measurable short- and long-term goals.

Session 5: *Reframing:* Define, then discuss the value of reframing one's learning disabilities experience into a productive, growth-oriented experience.

Session 6: *Persistence.* Understand the centrality of persistence and its manifestations. Identify strategies to enhance persistence.

Session 7: *Learned creativity.* Understand problem-solving techniques and creative strategies for success.

Session 8: *Goodness of fit.* Understand strategies to create a comfortable and productive match between self and environment. Facilitate exploration of ways to select or tailor personal environments to fit specific needs, to utilize strengths, and to compensate for learning disabilities.

Session 9: *Social ecology.* Facilitate discussion that identifies people who are supportive, and that explores ways to develop and refine one's personal social support network and improve one's skills.

Session 10: *Discuss and clarify* any concept and strategies introduced earlier. Share examples of particular applications of these concepts from the participant's own lives.

Session 11: *Review.* Briefly review topics. Facilitate discussion of additional participant skill and coping strategies.

Session 12: *Reflection.* Discuss what each person has received from the support group. Share strengths seen in other members of the group. Complete evaluations.

PRACTICAL CONSIDERATIONS

Meeting Logistics

This support group program is designed to meet for twelve weeks. Optimally, the group should meet for an hour and a half, once a week. The ninety-minute session allows a fifteen- to twenty-minute teaching segment, a forty-five minute processing segment, and time to check in and check out. A time that is convenient for most interested participants should be selected. Consider the context of the group when scheduling meeting times. For example, groups on college campuses may begin the second week of the semester, end the week before finals, and meet during late afternoons to avoid conflicts with class schedules. Groups meeting in community agencies may need to be scheduled in the evenings and around public school holidays to avoid conflicts with work schedules and the demands of parenting. If desired, continuity beyond the 12-week program may be provided through informal meetings.

Participant Selection

Screening interviews should be conducted to assure selection of appropriate members. The primary criterion is the presence of a learning disability, including attention deficit disorders, and a desire to enhance future employment success. Most members should have sufficient social skills to interact in the group and all should be free of substance abuse, personality disorders, and psychotic behaviors that impair group development. To determine other criteria for selection, group leaders may wish to consult with programs and organizations that serve adults with learning disabilities within the context in which they intend to conduct the support group. The purpose, format, and expectations should be described to prospective members during the screening interview. Their motivation and ability to comply with group expectations should be assessed. Prospective group members should be encouraged to determine whether the group will meet their current needs. Their degree of willingness to participate should be taken into consideration in the selection process.

Minimizing Attrition Rate

Group therapy research indicates that clients drop out of groups prematurely regardless of what the therapist does (Yalom 1995). Applying proper method of selection as outlined earlier and establishing meeting times based on the convenience of most interested participants will help minimize the attrition rate. In addition, group leaders should communicate their confidence in the group process and their expectation that the participants will use the process for effective work. They should also explain that periods of discouragement are normal, which will minimize negative surprises for group members (Yalom 1995).

When group leaders model the behaviors of punctuality and regular attendance, they convey personal conviction of their importance to the group process and participants are apt to follow their lead and hold each other accountable to do so. Leaders should encourage clients to call in advance when they know they will be late or absent because an individual's absence or lateness affects the group. In the case of repeated absences or tardiness, Yalom (1995) suggests attending to group maintenance and norm-setting tasks first by attempting to correct the behavior, and later, when the timing is right, attempting to help the member explore the meaning of his or her behavior.

Group Development

The initial stage of group development is characterized by attempts to "fit in" and understand group expectations and personal purpose. Members frequently seek acceptance and approval, clarify their purpose for participation, and establish their level of commitment to the group. Group leaders can facilitate member participation by modeling appropriate behaviors, reviewing and clarifying expectations, helping members identify goals, and by acknowledging and reinforcing appropriate group behavior. Because some form of language processing deficit underlies most learning disabilities, the group leader must be concerned to help each member understand the purpose of the group. Soliciting support from group members in clarifying issues will facilitate relationships and begin to build cohesion among group members.

According to Yalom (1995), hostility characterizes the next phase of group development. Members may hog "air time," become uncharacteristically silent, or express hostility toward the group leader or other members of the group. Difficulty in clarifying personal purpose, processing group expectations, and/or handling a stressful life event may cause some members to bring high levels of anxiety to group meetings. Leaders can help members deal with frustration and anxiety by identifying it, labeling it, and reminding members of group expectations. They can also encourage other members to share similar experiences, reinforce attempts by group members to reach out and respond to one another, and encourage members to provide each other immediate feedback. Reinforcing and facilitating personal interaction among group members will provide relevant individual feedback and practice in developing much needed social skills. This interaction will also help members apply the content of the teaching segments to their personal lives.

After members feel safe in confronting personal anxiety in the group, a sense of mutual trust and an increase in morale can develop. This will encourage members to disclose information about themselves more freely, confront one another constructively, and more readily apply what they learn in the group outside the group. Encouraging and reinforcing relationship building among group members will facilitate greater self-exploration and discovery among group members.

Termination, the final stage of group development can be particularly meaningful for group members. Group leaders should prepare members for termination one or two weeks before the final session. Members should be encouraged to reflect on what they learned and come prepared to share this with others. During the final session, group leaders should encourage members to identify growth they saw in each other as well as individual plans to secure the support they need.

EVALUATION

Feedback should be solicited from group members on a regular basis during the twelve weeks. Group leaders might use this information to tailor sessions to meet the current needs of the participants. In addition, a formal written evaluation should be collected from each participant during the last session of the group. Evaluation forms should solicit information on the program content, the group process, the logistics (meeting location and times), as well as the value of the support group to participants. A number of group evaluation forms are available in the literature. Group leaders might pay particular attention to feedback about the topics and teaching style. Although the selected content areas appear valid, specific teaching methods should be responsive to individual learning styles.

CONCLUSION

Although some authors provide guidelines for self-help groups for adults with learning disabilities, few describe those groups designed to promote employment success. In this chapter, we attempted to fill that void on the basis of the research and model of vocational success of Gerber, Ginsberg, and Reiff (1992). This self-help group integrates a psycho-educational model with cognitive-behavioral and interpersonal techniques to facilitate development of themes, behaviors, and attitudes that promote success among adults with learning disabilities.

REFERENCES

Corey, G. 1995. *Theory and Practice of Group Counseling* (4th ed.). Pacific Grove: Brooks/Cole.

Gerber, P. J., Ginsberg, R., and Reiff, H. B. 1992. Identifying alterable patterns of employment success in highly successful adults with learning disabilities. *Journal of Learning Disabilities* 25:475-87.

Gerber, P. J., Reiff, H. B., and Ginsberg, R 1996. Reframing the learning disabilities experience. *Journal of Learning Disabilities* 29 (1):97-101.

Yalom, I. D. 1995. *The Theory and Practice of Group Psychotherapy* (4th ed.). New York: Harper Collins.

APPENDIX

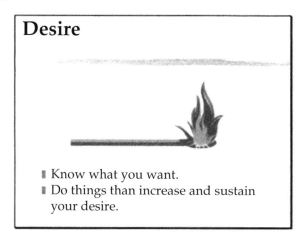

Desire

❚ Know what you want.
❚ Do things than increase and sustain
your desire.

Definition: A strong feeling that is motivating.

As you read through the following examples of statements about desire made by adults with learning disabilities, ask yourself:

Where do I fit?

Which statements sound most like me?

Highly successful adults with LD say:
❑ I am driven. Tell me it can't be done, and I will do it.
❑ I believe in determination. It is three-fourths of the battle. I absolutely have to stick with it.
❑ I have a burning feeling to be successful.
❑ I fight until I can't fight anymore, then I fight some more.
❑ I use negative messages to motivate me instead of to discourage me.

Moderately successful adults with LD say:
❑ I'm just really someone who's been plodding along.
❑ I don't know what I want most in life.
❑ I am uncomfortable with competition, so I change what I want to avoid it.
❑ I often settle for less, taking what I can get.

Desire that leads to success.

Everyone has desires. Some successful people display desires that are stronger than others.

Highly successful adults with learning have desires that are:
- Obvious and very powerful
- Unquenchable

Developing skills for greater success.
Take action:
What am I willing to do regardless of the cost?

Which of my hopes, dreams, or aspirations come to mind over and over again?

Which of these am I willing to pursue until I fulfill them?

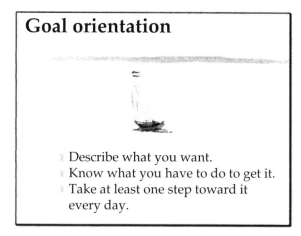

Goal orientation

- Describe what you want.
- Know what you have to do to get it.
- Take at least one step toward it every day.

Definition: Goals are specific desires accompanied by a decision to pursue them. Goal orientation is a state of being that consistently focuses and acts upon one or more goals.

As you read through the following examples of statements about *goal orientation* made by adults with learning disabilities, ask yourself:

Where do I fit?

Which statements sound most like me?

Highly successful adults with LD say:
- ❑ I must have a plan, goals, and strategies, otherwise I will fly through the clouds and hit mountains.
- ❑ I identify goals, set out to accomplish them, and don't care when I take longer than others to reach them.

Moderately successful adults with LD say:
- ❑ Much of what happened to me just happened.
- ❑ Although I know what I want, I don't know what it takes to get it.
- ❑ Making plans just makes life complicated. I'd rather live for today.
- ❑ I have lots of goals; I just don't follow through on them.
- ❑ Goals are great; however, I frequently find myself distracted.
- ❑ I have so many goals it's difficult to choose which to work on.
- ❑ I don't take myself seriously. I hate disappointment.

Goal orientation that leads to success.
Most people have some goals. Successful adults with learning disabilities consciously set goals based upon their desires.

Highly successful adults with learning disabilities:
- Describe in detail their strongest desires and prioritize them.
- Know and describe steps that must be taken to make their desires a reality.
- Focus on and act upon important goals daily.
- Develop and use specific problem-solving strategies to attain their goals.

Developing skills for greater success.
Take action:

What are my strongest desires (describe in specific detail)?

What steps must I take to make these desires a reality?

What will I do today, tomorrow, and next week to make my desires a reality?

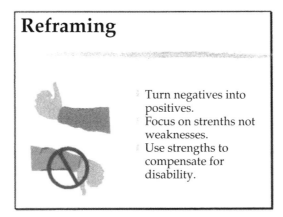

Reframing

- Turn negatives into positives.
- Focus on strenths not weaknesses.
- Use strengths to compensate for disability.

Definition: The process of changing negative and counterproductive thoughts into positive ones.

As you read through the following examples of statements about reframing made by adults with learning disabilities, ask yourself:

Where do I fit?

Which statements sound most like me?

Highly successful adults with LD say:
- ❏ I know I can succeed in spite of the fact that I do not read well. I have other abilities.
- ❏ In junior high school I began to realize that I was good in math. I could handle more complicated stuff. I no longer thought I was stupid.
- ❏ I accept who I am, what I can do, what I cannot do, who I should try to be, and who I should not try to be.

Moderately successful adults with LD say:
- ❏ I approach life as if I am a second-rate human being. Dyslexics don't feel as good about themselves as other people do.
- ❏ I feel like a prisoner locked in myself.
- ❏ I wish I'd wake up one day without my disability.
- ❏ I've never told anyone I have a learning disability. I am too ashamed.

Reframing that leads to success.

Many successful adults with learning disabilities recognize and accept their limitations and their strengths.

Highly successful adults with learning disabilities:
- See themselves for who they really are.
- Recognize that they see and do some things differently and that these differences have both disadvantages and advantages.
- Accept themselves with their disabilities.
- Are willing to share information about their disabilities.
- Understand and use personal strengths to compensate for their weaknesses.

Developing skills for greater success.
Take action:

What strengths do I have that make me feel good about myself?

How do I use personal strengths to compensate for my disability?

How might I use other strengths to compensate for my disability?

What will I do this week to build upon my strengths?

Persistence

Willing to do whatever it takes to achieve my goals.

Work harder than anyone else.

Definition: Sustained effort towards a specific goal, even in the presence of defeat, failure, adversity, or some other challenge.

As you read through the following examples of statements about persistence made by adults with learning disabilities, ask yourself:

Where do I fit?

Which statements sound most like me?

Highly successful adults with LD say:
❑ I overcame my problem with sheer grit and determination.
❑ I would adapt by doing extra work.
❑ I reached my goals by working harder and longer than others.
❑ I never stop trying . . . I have an incredible amount of persistence.

Moderately successful adults with LD say:
❑ I dislike conflict and would rather "give in" than fight for what I want.
❑ People will think I'm pushy if I stand up for my rights, or if I insist upon having my needs met.
❑ It just isn't worth it . . . it's too much to ask of myself.
❑ I can't bear the pain, the ridicule, the isolation it takes to reach my goals.

Persistence that leads to success.

Persistence toward some desires are common. Most people remember seeing a young child begging or even screaming for candy or a toy in a store.

Highly successful adults with learning disabilities:
- Persist toward major goals, even when they face great difficulty.
- Put forth effort after failure.
- Believe desired goals are worthy of sustained effort.
- Practice persistence as a way of life.
- Do whatever it takes to accomplish their goals.
- Work harder than anyone else does.

Developing skills for greater success.
Take action:

When I am persistent, what desires and goals are involved?

What goal or goals have I abandoned where persistence might have made the difference?

What goal am I willing to work harder to achieve?

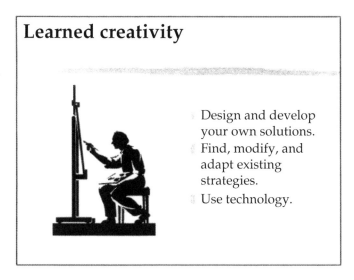

Learned creativity

- Design and develop your own solutions.
- Find, modify, and adapt existing strategies.
- Use technology.

Definition: The act of searching, finding, modifying, adapting, and creating unique solutions that enhance ability to perform well.

As you read through the following examples of statements about learned creativity made by adults with learning disabilities, ask yourself:

Where do I fit?

Which statements sound most like me?

Highly successful adults with LD say:
- ❑ I create scenarios about what I will have to do under certain circumstances in order to succeed.
- ❑ I developed my own way of doing things. For example, I use photographs, pictures, and drawings to improve my retention.
- ❑ I taught myself lip-reading which helped me perceive sounds correctly and comprehend conversation.

Moderately successful adults with LD say:
- ❑ I minimize my mistakes by taking few risks.
- ❑ I fear others will find out that I'm faking it, and call me a fraud.
- ❑ My learning disability makes me very defensive.
- ❑ Yes, I have weaknesses, but I find ways to cover them up or avoid doing things that reveal them.
- ❑ I manipulate myself into such a position that I can't make a mistake.

Learned creativity that leads to success.

Successful adults with learning disabilities use a variety of strategies and techniques to cope with their disability. Highly successful adults with learning disabilities excel through the regular use of creativity strategies. They:

- Use sophisticated and creative schemes to cope.
- Build on inborn and learned strengths.
- Excel through the use of creativity.
- Use modern technology.
- Develop anticipatory skills.
- Use a variety of strategies, techniques, and mechanisms to enhance their ability to perform.

Developing skills for greater success.

Take action:

What unique solutions do I use to address common problems (e.g., keeping appointments, keeping track of things)?

What creative schemes would make my life easier, but I hesitate to try them?

What techniques or strategies will I try, over the next three days, in an effort to enhance my performance?

Goodness of fit

- Choose environments that work for you.
- Adapt to your environment.

Definition: A measure of compatibility between a person and his or her environment.

As you read through the following examples of statements about goodness of fit made by adults with learning disabilities, ask yourself:

Where do I fit?

Which statements sound most like me?

Highly successful adults with LD say:
❑ I took advantage of my strong personality in selecting a career in sales.
❑ I chose my job because I enjoy it, and do it well.
❑ I chose to specialize in dermatology because there was little writing and the medical textbooks had lots of pictures.

Moderately successful adults with LD say:
❑ I took the first job I could get.
❑ I can handle a more challenging job and would find it more enjoyable; however, my current job is quite secure.
❑ It's a job . . . it pays the bills . . . I don't have to like it.

Goodness of fit that leads to success.

Highly successful adults with learning disabilities:
- Choose environments (majors, jobs, friends, gadgets, etc.) that complement their strengths and interests.

- Change their environment to meet their needs and desires.
- Seek or create environments that are conducive to achievement, and that are comfortable.

Developing skills for greater success.

Take action:

How have I changed my environment to make my life more pleasant?

What three things can I change that will make me more productive in my work environment?

What academic choices are most compatible with my strengths and interests?

What occupational choices are most compatible with my strengths and interests?

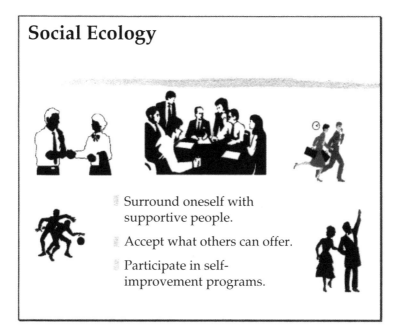

Social Ecology

- Surround oneself with supportive people.
- Accept what others can offer.
- Participate in self-improvement programs.

Definition: A state of being that includes encouragement, help from others, and self-improvement.

As you read through the following examples of statements about social ecology made by adults with learning disabilities, ask yourself:

Where do I fit?

Which statements sound most like me?

Highly successful adults with LD say:
- ❏ I value the support and guidance I get from friends.
- ❏ I find and use a mentor for guidance when I take a promotion or other position involving new and complex responsibilities.
- ❏ I know exactly what types of support I need and call upon others when my responsibilities require them.

Moderately successful adults with LD say:
- ❏ If I could do it all over again, I'd ask for more help.
- ❏ It's foolish to let people know your weaknesses, so I just try on my own, and don't ask others for help.
- ❏ I often find it difficult to accept help from others.

Social ecology that leads to success.

No one can survive alone; however, many act as if they can.

Many people hide their weaknesses.

Highly successful adults with learning disabilities

- Surround themselves with supportive and helpful people.
- Find and develop significant personal relationships (e.g., spouse and close friends).
- Willingly seek, appreciate, and accept help from others.
- Seek out and use guidance from others who have experience.
- Improve themselves by learning and using self-help skills and strategies.

Developing skills for greater success.

Take action:

Who encourages me to accomplish my desires and goals?

Whom will I ask for help over the next three days and what will I ask them to do?

What can I do to improve myself?

Who might be a good mentor for me?

ASSESSMENT OF SUPPORT GROUP EXPERIENCE

Please respond to the following statements regarding the group in which you participated this semester.

1	2	3	4	5
Do Not Agree		Neutral		Agree

_____ 1. I gained hope that I could resolve the challenges of my disability.

_____ 2. I understand better that other people have problems similar to mine.

_____ 3. I received helpful guidance and/or information about how to approach my challenges.

_____ 4. I helped other group members by offering support, re-assurance, and suggestions.

_____ 5. I learned to act differently in response to my challenges.

_____ 6. By observing others, I learned new ways of thinking about my life and new ways to act.

_____ 7. I discovered something important about myself by being in this group.

_____ 8. I felt close to other group members.

_____ 9. There is at least one meeting I remember as being very important to me in helping me with my challenges.

_____ 10. Overall, this group helped me accomplish the goals that brought me to the group.

_____ 11. I learned something new about success as an adult with a learning disability.

_____ 12. The organization of presentations by the co-leaders was clear.

_____ 13. The clarity of presentations by the co-leaders was clear.

Adapted from Counseling and Student Development Group Evaluation Form at Northern Illinois University.

What will you take away from this experience? What did you learn? How did it change the way you think? How did it change the way you feel?

What didn't you get that you hoped you would?

What might we consider doing differently in the next group?

What did you learn from other group members?

Would you participate in a group like this again?   Yes   No

Chapter • 13

Successful Adjustment of Individuals with Learning Disabilities

Lea Kozminsky

A learning disability represents a persistent developmental impairment that can interfere with an individual's ability to function as an adult (Gerber 1986; Zeltin and Hosseini 1989). Success as an adult is measured by employment outcomes (Gerber, Ginsburg, and Reiff 1992) and social and emotional adjustment, but persistent learning difficulties may cause an individual to find professional and social adjustment especially challenging (White et al. 1982; Gerber et al. 1990). We often hear statements such as "Einstein the scientist, Churchill the statesman, and Degas the artist all had a learning disability." New names are constantly added to this list, such as Thomas Edison, Woodrow Wilson, Hans Christian Andersen, and Leonardo da Vinci. Although parents and the individuals with learning disabilities themselves may find consolation in the knowledge that such eminent individuals are "suspected" of having learning disabilities, two researchers (Adelman and Adelman 1987) have published a cautionary statement concerning the retroactive diagnosis of celebrated historical figures based on unreliable information. They claim that such statements create myths that, while heartwarming, can act as boomerangs, actually causing harm to the population with learning disabilities. Comparisons between these successful figures and a specific student may lead to unrealistic expectations or to the student being blamed for his or her poor scholastic achievement, with the claim that "even Edison had a learning disablity and see what wonderful inventions he came up with despite his disability."

When names of famous individuals with learning disabilities are cited, it is particularly important to try to understand what contributed to their success. How did these people succeed in compensating for and rising above their difficulties to the extent that their disabilities did not present an obstacle to their success? Because in most cases we do not have first-hand testimonies concerning famous historical figures, living examples of successful people can be used to understand effective ways of grappling with disabilities. This type of knowledge can serve as a basis for the development of intervention and support programs.

In order to examine the characteristics of successful Israeli adults with learning disabilities, we interviewed 33 adults. We heard, from the perspective of the adults themselves, the cognitive and emotional approach to their disabilities, the sources of support they had for good adjustment despite their disabilities, their own personal ways to deal effectively with their problems, and their recommendations of how to succeed.

STUDY POPULATION

Thirty three adults (17 women and 16 men, aged 18 to 56) were individually interviewed by means of a structured interview (see interview form: appendix 1).

Type of Disability

From their own testimonies concerning difficulties they experienced or were still experiencing, a varied picture of problems came to light, including difficulties in reading (21), writing (19), math (5), attention (4), social life (4), and motor responses (3). (The figures add up to more than the number of individuals we interviewed because many said they suffer or suffered from more than one problem.)

Diagnosis of Disabilities

From the testimonies of the individuals participating in the study, it emerged that very few had been diagnosed as learning disabled during their early school years. In most cases, the disabilities were diagnosed in the middle or towards the end of their elementary school years. The time of diagnosis is divided as follows: primary grades (first to third grade), five interviewees; middle to end of elementary school (fourth to sixth grade), nine interviewees; high school, four interviewees; post-high school, 13 interviewees.

Occupation

The interviewees are currently adults involved in a variety of occupations. Some said that they were still studying a profession (12); five had academic professions, such as teacher, nurse, or attorney; and 16 were blue-collar workers, such as warehouseman, driver, mechanic, contractor, hairdresser, and children's nursemaid.

Extent of Success

Each interviewee was asked about his or her personal feeling: "Do you consider yourself a successful person today?" The question was worded in this way in order to rate the extent of the interviewee's success according to his or her own personal criteria. This scale was later used in determining the elements conducive to these adults' sense of success. By their own testimony, ten of the interviewees considered themselves successful to a high degree; five attested to a moderate level of success, and eight to a low level.

Based on the research of Gerber and his colleagues (Gerber et al. 1992), and on the testimony of the study participants, we constructed a model to describe the elements conducive to the success of these adult Israelis with learning disabilities (see figure 1).

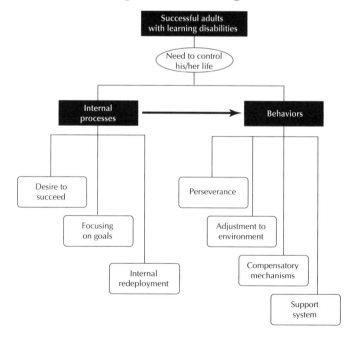

Figure 1. Elements of the model of the successful adult with learning disability.

The leading principle of this model is that successful adults with learning disabilities acknowledge that they need to have control over their own lives, and, as one put it, "Not to allow circumstances to dominate me, but rather to dominate circumstances. To create a circle in which things work according to my own tempo and direction—I am the one who decides, who controls; not aggressively, but by taking control of the situation." Adults who control the circumstances of their lives manifest internal processes for attaining control, as well as the ability to translate these processes into behaviors directed at attaining control. The internal processes include the desire to succeed, the ability to focus on a goal, and the ability to interpret the experience of failure. Successful adults translate these internal processes for attaining control into a collection of behaviors directed at the attainment of control. These behaviors are characterized by perseverance, adjustment to one's environment, the creative use of compensatory mechanisms adapted to individual needs, as well as the identification, creation, and use of a supportive environment. Below, each of the elements in the model is illustrated by means of quotes from the interviews.

The internal processes for the attainment of control include the desire to succeed and the ability to focus on goals and to redeploy internally.

A Desire to Succeed

The desire to succeed is reflected in an aspiration to excel, which may manifest itself early in life, or develop later on. The following quotes from various successful interviewees reflect this desire:

- "I hope to succeed in graphics and advertising. What does it mean to succeed? To be among the best in the field, to make a name for myself in this profession."
- "Everyone wants to succeed in life, but I want to succeed as much as possible."
- "I was very highly motivated. If I hadn't wanted it, and if I hadn't put in more effort than everyone else, I wouldn't have succeeded. My success didn't come on its own. It was always because that was what I wanted."
- "I think that I succeeded partly because I didn't want to disappoint my cousin, and secondly because I put a great deal of effort into succeeding. And also because I had to bring my report card to my husband. But these are all excuses. I did it because I wanted to succeed. I told them that it was for them, but it was really for me."

Focusing on the Goal

The second component in the internal process contributing to the attainment of control over one's life is the ability to focus on a goal and succeed. This is a conscious setting of clear goals and the expression of realistic and attainable aspirations. Examples of focusing on goals can be found in the following quotes.

- "I divide my life into stages, and each time, I grapple with a stage in the present, complete it, and move on to the next one."
- "The best and most important suggestion: to sit down and figure out what I want from life—to make a list of things."
- "The first thing I do is to work on myself. I think that a person can change himself if he knows exactly where he wants to go. For example, once I used to answer immediately. Today I am more prudent, and ask for time to think.

Internal Redeployment

The third internal component likely to contribute to success is called internal redeployment. This refers to a change in one's attitude toward the disability and to a new personal interpretation of the experience of disability. From this point on, the individual no longer treats the disability as a destructive and restrictive experience but as a constructive one. This time of change is reflected in comments by one interviewee, who said, "I am dyslectic, but I am not an idiot. I found that there is an association that treats dyslexia, so I have just recently decided to see what can be done, how to move ahead... There must be ways in which I can help myself that I don't know about."

There are four interrelated stages in the changing attitude toward the disability and the internal redeployment: recognizing the disability, deciding whom to inform, understanding the problem, and planning what action to take.

RECOGNITION OF THE DISABILITY

This refers to the willingness of individuals to accept their weaknesses and strengths. They realize that they are special and that they do not have to be identical to others in order to feel equal. They accept themselves with their advantages and disadvantages. The following statements illustrate this recognition of strengths and weaknesses:

- "I see something once and I remember it well, and that is an advantage I have over other people. I usually distinguish small details that others don't notice. I had a meeting with an engineer about an agricultural machine that separates stones from earth that we saw during a trip abroad, and we tried to copy the idea. The engineer couldn't remember how it worked. I remembered the details and that helped us figure out how it worked."

Statements Illustrating Recognition of Strengths

- "The advantage I have is that I know how to understand people, how to empathize with their feelings and understand their situations. I know how to compromise, and I am easy to live with."
- "I am very aware of my surroundings. I have an understanding of those around me that in my view is extraordinary. When I hear a word, I immediately make the connection and put two and two together with everything else."

Statements Illustrating Recognition of Weaknesses

- "I have a problem expressing myself in writing. There are a lot of things I know on a test but I don't write them because I can't phrase what I know well, and I have spelling mistakes."
- "In foreign languages, I always make spelling mistakes."
- "When reading, I have problems concentrating. I often find myself reading and then I realize that I haven't been paying attention to what I read and I have to go back and read it all over again."
- "I find it difficult to make friends."

DECIDING WHOM TO INFORM

Following the decision to recognize strengths and weaknesses, individuals decide with whom to share the information about their difficulties. The decision itself is more important that the content of the decision. Individuals can decide whether they are interested in sharing their problems with others, or whether they wish to share that information only in certain cases. The component that is conducive to success is the sense of personal control over the decision concerning whether to share the information. The following examples of statements made by interviewees focus on the decision to share the information, to share it randomly or not at all.

- "I think that when you don't hide things and talk about them openly, people accept things at face value. They simply ask and you explain."

- "I cannot hide it. It is like asthma, which you also have to let people know about, but the thing is how you say it. You can discuss it as if it is a major issue, or you can mention it incidentally, which is what I do today. I don't direct the conversation in the direction of my disability."
- "I would not suggest being completely open or candid with new people who don't know your history. You don't have to tell anyone about your disability because people don't understand and they may think you are weird."

UNDERSTANDING THE PROBLEM

This involves the need to understand the essence of the disability—how it can influence one's life and have an impact on the development of methods to deal with the problem. This includes the insight that certain ways of responding, such as blaming oneself or various educational institutions, withdrawal, or isolation, may be counterproductive to encouraging success. The following are quotes from interviewees' statements:

- "I explain that I have a problem with reading and writing and that I read on the level of a fourth grader. Sometimes people ask more specific questions and I go into the details. I explain that I get confused, forget letters, and that I don't know how to spell. I also explain that I have a problem with the camera between my eyes and my brain and that it is the result of a problem that occurred during birth."
- "I decided to go for a diagnosis, and they discovered that I have a problem with math and that I am LD. I was so happy to learn that I have a problem and to tell everyone that it's not that I'm lazy, that I'm not someone who just wastes other people's time and doesn't make an effort and fails in the end, but that I have a real problem and that it doesn't depend only on me."
- "When I call someone on the telephone and it turns out to be wrong number, I apologize and I know that I must have switched digits, that I jotted down the number wrong".

PLANNING ACTIONS

The successful person with learning disabilities is an individual who consciously plans his or her actions and acts in accordance with that plan in order to succeed. This planning is reflected in the following statements by interviewees.

(Woman, 56, who immigrated to Israel as an older adult) "Everyone with a disability finds it difficult to start new things. Some of that is my credo. I can't reach a good level of writing in Hebrew— it's easier for me to continue in English. My priority is to improve my reading level in Hebrew, which is easier for me. After that, it is to express myself out loud. I cannot see that writing in Hebrew will be particularly practical for me in four years' time when I plan to take early retirement. All my writing will be in English rather than in Hebrew."

- "In the area of computers, which I find very difficult but which I cannot escape, I plan to take courses and study."

Successful adults with learning disabilities translate these internal components into a series of behaviors that propel them on the way to success. The contributing behaviors include perseverance, adjustment to one's environment, learned creativity, and the development and use of a support system. The following are examples from personal testimonies from Israeli adults with learning disabilities concerning these contributing behaviors.

Perseverance refers to resolve and the willingness to put in effort and hard work in order to succeed. The following are quotes from interviewees in whom the component of perseverance is prominent.

- "I would suggest to people like myself not to give up, to keep trying again and again even if things don't come easily. There are all kinds of people in the world and I am the type that has to work very hard to accomplish a little."
- "There is no one precise remedy or recipe. You just have to sweat that much more."
- "I would keep notes in a notebook, get home, decipher what I wrote and write it again. I would sit at it until two o'clock in the morning."
- "Even while I was still in high school and until I completed my army service, I studied English on my own. I took books from my brothers and sisters and started to write words. I tried to learn to read on my own. I would ask everyone around me the meanings of any word I didn't understand. I looked up words in the dictionary. I would go over every word a thousand times, reading and writing. I took books out of the library, and I read and translated and wrote... I wasn't ashamed to ask, to open books, dictionaries. I didn't give up even if I had to write each word a thousand times. I think that I succeeded only thanks to my willpower and the effort I put in... Today I know that I can carry on a conversation in

English if I need to and can read many words without mistakes and even understand what they mean."

- "On the day Nitzan had its special campaign, they showed how they work with dyslectic children in the United States. One of the parts that moved me and with which I identify was when they showed a group of dyslectic children with a counselor actually climbing up a mountain, while at the same time explaining to the kids what they will have to do. I found myself telling my father that that is how I feel, that I am constantly climbing up to the top of the mountain. And the climb is long and hard."

The second component in the behaviors that are conducive to success is that of *adjustment to one's environment*. This refers to the ability to identify or actually create environments in which it is possible to exploit one's strengths and succeed. There is, of course, a mutual dependence among the various components of the model. Thus, in order to identify the environment conducive to their success, individuals must also be aware of the nature of their individual disability as well as of their individual strengths. The environmental adjustment component includes choosing an occupation and place of occupation that they enjoy, where they feel they are their own master and can control their progress and future.

Here are a number of quotes from interviewees that relate to adjustment to their environments.

- "I am an aerobics teacher. Aerobics is in no way related to my dyslexia. It has improved my self-confidence. It helps with my right-left direction. Because of the aerobics, I find things easier. It also helps emotionally... Someone looking at me cannot tell that I have dyslexia."
- "I run a metal shop and my work is my hobby. At work, other people do all the paperwork. I am the manager and I decide who does what."
- "If I worked for someone else rather than being self-employed, I might not have succeeded to the same extent and probably would have encountered more difficulties."
- "When I learned that I was learning disabled, I decided to quit college. I decided to study something else that I really enjoy and that I am good at. I studied hairdressing. I always noticed people's hair and I was picked on for it. Now, I notice things that other people don't see and I really enjoy that."
- "At present I am in charge of food supplies. I work independently. I don't like it when others tell me what to do. I manage well when I have only one boss and no more."

- "At a certain stage, I felt that I was not a good sergeant and I asked to be transferred to another post where I wouldn't have to give orders, but only to organize things and come up with solutions to different types of problems."

Studies in the field of learning disabilities have shown that a learning disability is a chronic condition. It is a persistent ongoing situation that extends throughout the life of the individual and is reflected in different ways at life's different stages. Successful individuals are those who recognize their difficulties and develop individual ways to grapple with them appropriate to them and their environment. They are creative, finding and inventing varied ways to compensate, and succeed in maneuvering the environment so that their strengths find greater expression. They are sophisticated in the use of such strategies, many of which demonstrate an extensive use of technology to compensate for individual difficulties, such as word processors or dictaphones. The following statements illustrate the many variations in the use of *compensatory mechanisms*.

- "I try not to do tests and prefer papers. When I write a paper, I am under less time pressure. Also, I let someone else check my papers for spelling mistakes before I hand them in."
- "I am constantly looking for tricks and ways to overcome my difficulties. Technology is the most helpful tool. I use a spell checker and a pocket calculator. I collect different words that I know are difficult for me but that are useful and I take lists of such words with me when necessary."
- "I found it very difficult to learn the names of drugs. I learned to write the words in Hebrew and in English, to hear the word and say it. Today, in order to avoid spelling mistakes, I write very slowly and when I have to use a word that I am unfamiliar with, I replace it with one I know. I also had trouble with anatomy. I just couldn't remember the names. I made a sketch of the human body and wrote the names of all the organs on a transparency. I learned how to write the names and gradually removed the transparency and remembered the words."
- "I am currently completing my matriculation exams at Kaye College. I am allowed to take the tests orally. Today, I record the lectures on tape, and then I listen at home and take notes slowly, at my own pace. I have a subscription to the library for the blind in Jerusalem, where I can take out books recorded on tape, and you get a special tape recorder."
- "I use the telephone a great deal as an alternative to writing letters."

- "I have developed other ways to learn, such as using logic and working with my hands."

The fourth component in the set of behaviors of the successful Israeli adult with learning disabilities involves a *support system*. This is a support network surrounding the individuals, their parents, and family members, but it also includes the construction of such a support system, the kind of network that individuals consciously surround themselves with. Successful individuals surround themselves with supporters and know how to use their talents to compensate for their own shortcomings, to back themselves up and emphasize their strengths. Dyslexic students study for tests together with friends who are good at organizing information. Lawyers and business people hire employees skilled in those areas in which they have difficulty, for example, a secretary skilled at reading and writing, who will read various memos for them and highlight the most important items. Afterward, they will study the memo and decide if it requires additional attention from themselves. The following statements from interviewees illustrate the social ecology developed by these successful adults with learning disabilities:

- "It is very important to have someone supportive because it would be very difficult to handle all the things on my own. When you have someone that believes in you and supports and helps, it is easier to overcome the difficulties."
- "I am aware of my disability and deal with it in various ways. I involve friends and superiors so that they will help and support me."
- "My father believed that I could succeed at anything. He helped me organize things in my life so that I could study."
- "Other people help me when I have to write. I sit with them and tell them what I want and they write it for me."

SUMMARY AND CONCLUSIONS

From these testimonies from Israeli adults with learning disabilities, we learn that although the learning disability persists throughout adulthood, it should not necessarily be considered a limiting situation throughout life. The theme in all the components of the "successful model" is the successful individuals' need to take control over their lives. This control is reflected in the setting of goals and in the planning of action. It is also reflected in the behaviors themselves, in which the individuals are aware of and recognize their disability and decide what to do so that it does not overshadow their lives. One of the interviewees put it this way: "In life there are things that can be changed and things that cannot be changed and you have to know how to distinguish between them. I think this is the way I always wanted to act to see what in life I can change and what I cannot change, and I have to look carefully to see the differences between them, because there are things that you cannot change in life like the learning disability. But in the learning disability itself there are things that I can control. Then I can do it and there is a sense of completeness. I am not frustrated because I don't want to control anyone else, only myself, and I do that only through my own actions."

An examination of the interviews with adults with learning disabilities shows that the various components that contribute to success are mutually dependent. Recognition that an objective difficulty exists and awareness of its nature and its characteristics contribute to the individual's success because these factors serve as a basis for future action. In addition, it reflects the faith that the components of success can be cultivated and learned. Successful Israeli adults with learning disabilities describe themselves as responsible for their lives, as people who have decided to succeed, and who set clear goals for themselves. They have the ability to redeploy internally, which includes the recognition and understanding of the disability, an awareness of their weaknesses and strengths, and the knowledge that they do not have to be the same as everyone else. This is the source of the successful adults' decision to share or not to share information about themselves with others, and they consciously plan the steps they must take to overcome their difficulties and succeed. Successful adults with learning disabilities have found occupations that they are enthusiastic about and in which they feel comfortable and can be their own master. They succeed in using strategies to bypass difficulties, and surround themselves with support networks, which may include a spouse, family members, parents, and friends. When adults accept their disabilities and succeed in building the necessary internal systems needed to deal with them, they are also willing to use effectively the support of their surroundings without becoming unnecessarily dependent on them.

EDUCATIONAL IMPLICATIONS

The first-hand testimonies from Israeli adults with learning disabilities who have found their way in life provides us with information that may serve as the basis for the development of early intervention and support programs. In Be'er Sheva, Israel, we have employed three different programs to foster the components of success among students with learning disabilities of different ages. A description of each of the programs follows.

A CAUSAL ATTRIBUTIONAL RETRAINING PROGRAM

This is a program geared to ninth graders with learning disabilities. These students study in separate classes in large comprehensive high schools. They participated in the program throughout their entire first year in high school, and the purpose of the program was to retrain their causal attributions ascribed to events such as academic success and failure. Weiner's causal attributional theory (Weiner 1979, 1986) maintains that in situations of success and failure, people tend to analyze for themselves what led to the outcome of success or failure. This analysis reflects the perceived self-efficacy and beliefs of the individual rather than the objective reality concerning the source of the success or failure. These causal attributions, or to what people attribute responsibility for successes and failures, will influence their self-perception, expectations concerning the outcome of future events, feelings about the ability to influence these events, as well as learning motivation. The students in this intervention program learned to attribute their achievements to the learning effort they put in and the right use of learning strategies, which they practiced. Instead of claiming that they succeeded at a learning task because they were lucky, or that they failed because it was too difficult (external attribution out of their control), we taught them to attribute their successes and failures to internal controllable factors, such as diligent preparation for a test or the use of effective learning strategies.

The attributional dialogue takes place on a "dialogue page," developed by Dr. Eli Kozminsky of Ben-Gurion University and myself; it was tested in the context of the Shalem program (a Hebrew acronym for learning and motivational improvement). Once in three weeks each student is asked to fill in the dialogue page, which serves as the basis for the attributional dialogue between the student and teacher, the purpose of which is to advance attributions that focus on the personal responsibility of the students for their own achievements. In the dialogue page, the students are asked to describe two real events that they experienced in the last week: (1) a successful event (What did I succeed at this week?) and (2) a failure (What did I not succeed at this week?). After describing each event, the students are asked to explain to what they attribute the success (Why did I succeed?) and to what they attribute the failure (Why didn't I succeed?). Additionally, (3) the students write how, in their view, they could have made the week even more successful. The purpose of the third item on the dialogue page is to examine the potential strategies the students are aware of and which in their view may advance them, but which they did not actually use in the events they described.

After the students have completed the third item on the page, all the students' dialogue pages are collected and each student's comments receive a personal written comment from the teacher. (4) After the teacher has finished writing the comments, the papers are returned to the students. Each student reads the teacher's comments and responds to them. (5) A week later they receive the dialogue page again. This time the students respond to an additional item (6) in which they are asked to report on "How I used the suggestions from the dialogue page." This report clarifies to the student the importance of applying the comments, and for the teacher it serves to assess the actions the students did in fact take in order to promote their achievements. As stated, the entire process takes about three weeks. After a week's break new dialogue pages are used, and the process is repeated throughout the academic year.

In the context of an in-service training program held once a week throughout the academic year, the teachers participating in the Shalem program were instructed concerning the principles of the program and how they would be applied. The teachers' responses to the students' comments in these training sessions were discussed in detail, and the teachers were taught to include three elements in their responses:

1. Reinforcement of internal controlled attribution, that is, reinforcement of a response by the students that attributes their outcomes to their efforts and the use of effective strategies.
2. A verbal reflection of the students' attributions that focus on taking personal responsibility for their own learning.
3. Asking the students a leading question intended to guide them to consider specific actions that could enhance their learning, such as how to do homework, how to listen during the lesson, how to prepare for tests, or how to manage their time outside school effectively. The group of students with learning disabilities demonstrated significant changes in their personal attributions. In the course of the year they gradually abandoned their uncontrolled internal or external attributions that characterized the responses to their successes and failures at the beginning of the school year. They shifted to attributing these outcomes to controlled internal factors, while broadening their repertoire of learning strategies, adapting them to varied learning circumstances.

TRAINING IN SELF-ADVOCACY

Because of the unseen nature of the learning disability, it is very important that individuals with learning disabilities learn the skills of self-advocacy. They must understand their unique needs as well as their rights, and they must know how to communicate them to others in order to ensure that their rights are safeguarded. Until now, most of the legislation and the ways learning disabilities were viewed underscored the role of the parents and teachers, minimizing the role of the students themselves in making decisions concerning the manner of their own learning progress. Parents have a considerable role in participating in the planning and in the act of signing of the students' "Individualized Educational Program," and in their willingness to turn to school officials to inform them about their child's learning disability and to make sure his or her rights are upheld. The students themselves were on the sidelines of the process, allowing others "with greater authority" to fight their wars and represent their interests before the establishment.

We developed a self-advocacy program that transfers the responsibility to the learners, increases their overall self-awareness, and increases their understanding of their own strengths and weaknesses. It helps them develop their ability to explain to others what their learning styles are and what their unique organizational and learning adaptation needs are. For students who have taken part in this program to become their own advocates, they needed to acquire a number of skills:

1. Self-awareness: recognition of personal needs, difficulties, and strengths, and awareness of the students' own personal ways of compensating that they have developed for themselves over the years in order to realize their ability and the conditions that the education system places at their disposal in order to do so.

2. The ability to decide: the students' inner faith that they are sovereign over their own life and that they will be the ones to decide whom to inform as to their learning disability and what adjustments to request.

3. The knowledge: how to explain effectively what their personal needs are, using relevant language and the appropriate tone and vocabulary when making the request.

4. Recognition of one's rights in society: An enlightened society enables its members to realize their basic rights to a proper education and satisfying work. Unfortunately, in various education and social contexts, students with learning disabilities are prevented from realizing their right to

succeed. They are liable to refrain from participating in lessons, for example, in order to avoid revealing their reading difficulties, or a young adult may hesitate to reveal his learning disability to his new girlfriend, for fear of rejection. At work too, people with learning disabilities refrain from telling others about their disability, for fear of social alienation, or of being dismissed.

In order to cultivate their self-advocacy skills, we ran a self-advocacy program in Be'er Sheva for students with learning disabilities at the end of elementary school before the transition into junior high school. Using the three-step program offered by Yuan (1994), the students learned how to express their desire to improve with the help of sentences containing positive messages. They learned how to be aware of their personal difficulties and were trained to describe their problem and its current impact on their behavior. They also practiced making specific requests and suggesting concrete methods of action in order to ensure their success.

This program, which was set into action before the beginning of the school year, was highly applauded by the junior high school teachers to whom these students later turned. The junior high school teachers were deeply impressed by the students' awareness of their disabilities, and their ability to insist on their rights and to suggest adjustments to the teacher to make it easier for them to express their knowledge.

WORKSHOP TO CULTIVATE PERSONAL LEARNING STRATEGIES

In the large comprehensive high school in Beer Sheva, seven eleventh-grade students with learning disabilities were found in regular classes. These students were to take their matriculation examinations in civics and history at the end of the school year, and their teachers had doubts about whether to let them take the tests because of their poor chances of passing. It was suggested that this group serve as a learning and self-help group under the guidance of the school's civics and history coordinator and a special education teacher on the school staff. During the school year, the students met with their counselors once a week in the early evening hours. At these meetings they talked among themselves, and became aware of their learning disabilities and of their strong and weak learning points. They acquired and practiced learning strategies specifically adjusted to their individual learning disability (Alley and Deshler 1979; McGuire and O'Donnell 1989;

Pressley and Associates 1990) and bolstered their self-advocacy skills. All the skills and learning strategies were practiced directly in their study of civics and history, with the help of the study coordinator. At the end of the school year, all these students sat for the matriculation examinations in civics and history and passed. The teachers who taught them other subjects said that their participation in the workshop both contributed to their social confidence and improved their academic achievements in subjects other than the subjects focused on in the workshop.

In sum, the three intervention programs presented here—the causal attributional retraining program, the training in self-advocacy, and the workshop to cultivate personal learning strategies—were constructed on the basis of insights drawn from the testimony of successful Israeli adults with learning disabilities. These programs showed the students the importance of persistence and effort and the ways to use personal learning strategies, with emphasis on building confidence in their ability to succeed. The students learned to become aware of their weaknesses as well as their strong points, and the compensatory mechanisms that can be developed in order to succeed. They used this knowledge to safeguard their rights within the educational system. The testimony of the successful adults helped forge the path for the younger students.

REFERENCES

Adelman, K. A., and Adelman, H. S. 1987. Rodin, Patton, Wilson, Einstein: Were they really learning disabled? *Journal of Learning Disabilities* 20:270–79.

Alley, G. R., and Deshler, D. D. 1979. *Teaching the Learning Disabled Adolescent: Strategies and Methods.* Denver, CO: Love Publishing Company.

Gerber, P. J. 1986. The learning disabled adult nexus: European perspectives and emerging American trends. *Journal of Learning Disabilities* 19 (1):2–4.

Gerber, P. J., Ginsberg, R., and Reiff, H. B. 1992. Identifying alterable patterns in employment success for highly successful adults with learning disabilities. *Journal of Learning Disabilities* 25 (8):475–87.

Gerber, P. J., Schnieders, C. A., Paradise, L. V., Reiff, H. B., Ginsberg, R., and Popp, P. A. 1990. Persisting problems of adults with learning disabilities: Self reported comparisons from school-age and adult years. *Journal of Learning Disabilities,* 23 (9):570–73.

McGuire, J. M., and O'Donnell, J. M. 1989. Helping learning disabled students to achieve. *College Teaching* 37 (1):29–32.

Pressley, M., and Associates 1990. *Cognitive Strategy Instruction that Really Improves Children's Academic Performance.* MA: Brookline Books.

Weiner, B. 1979. A theory of motivation and attribution for some classroom experiences. *Journal of Educational Psychology* 75:530–43.

Weiner, B. 1986. *An Attributional Theory of Achievement, Motivation and Emotion.* New York: Springer-Verlag.

White, W. J., Alley, G. R., Deshler, D. D., Schumaker, J. B., Warner, M. M., and Clark, F. L. 1982. Are there learning disabilities after school? *Exceptional Children* 49:273–74.

Yuan, F. 1994. Moving toward self-acceptance: A course for students with learning disabilities. *Intervention in School and Clinic* 29 (5):301–09.

Zeltin, A. G., and Hosseini, A. 1989. Six post-school case studies of mildly learning handicapped young adults. *Exceptional Children* 55:405–11.

APPENDIX 1: INTERVIEW WITH ADULT

Gender _____ Age _____ Family Status _____
Occupation and place of work _____
Date of diagnosis _____ Type of disability _____

Questions

1. Tell me something about yourself so that I can get to know you better.
2. Do you feel good about yourself? Are you satisfied with what is happening in your life?
3. Can you recall a specific occasion where you had real difficulty? Tell me about it. (Bring an example of a difficulty you had. Tell me about your memories of what was difficult for you. How did you resolve the problem in the end?)
4. How and under what circumstances did you discover that you had a disability?
5. What do you find difficult now? What is so difficult about it? (Needs to be clarified: To what does s/he attribute the failures?) Explain to me what your problem is.
6. What have you done and what do you do to overcome your difficulties? What tricks do you have to succeed well? Thanks to what have you succeeded? (Are you successful now?) Who (what) helped you?
7. Do you recall a specific case at which you really succeeded? Tell me about it. Why did you succeed? (Needs to be clarified: To what does s/he attribute his/her success?)
8. What are your strong points? At what are you especially good?
9. Was there a turning point in your development? What was it?
10. What suggestions do you have for people suffering from the same difficulty that you suffer or suffered from?
11. How do you feel about your disability?
12. Do you consider yourself a successful person today? Would you describe yourself as: very successful, fairly successful, or not so successful? Why?
13. What is your personal success index? (How do you define success for yourself?)

PART • V

Meeting the Challenges of LD Across a Lifespan

Part V, Meeting the Challenge of LD across a Life Span, consists of three chapters that deal with outcomes for adults with learning disabilities across the life span. Two chapters (14 and 5) were contributed by Susan Vogel and Pamela Adelman who reported on one of the longest follow-up studies on college-able adults with learning disabilities. Two important aspects of this longitudinal research are that the participants with LD were enrolled in a comprehensive college program designed specifically for students with LD and, in addition, at the time of initial enrollment, Vogel and Adelman identified a comparison group from the general population of students without learning disabilities enrolled in the same setting.

In the first chapter (14), Vogel and Adelman describe the findings from the follow-up study regarding educational attainment, employment, occupational status, job satisfaction and annual salary for both groups. Unlike other follow-up studies of high school graduates who had received LD services while in high school where there were significant differences in educational attainment, income, occupation, etc., they found minimal differences, if any, between those with and without LD. However, some of the adults with LD reported that their learning disability had a negative impact on the job, usually in some aspect of language functioning. In order to overcome the impact of their LD, they developed compensatory strategies including working longer hours, using assistive technology, and relying on their strengths in, for example, oral communication rather than written communication.

In Chapter 15, Adelman and Vogel reported that although there were no significant differences in independence, responsibilities, mobility, and the number and scope of leisure activities, some reported feelings of low self-esteem and lack of self-confidence. In order to avoid situations in which their LD would be apparent, the adults with LD avoided some social situations which may have contributed to their social isolation. Emotional problems were cited as the main way in which their LD affected them including problems with intimate relationships, loneliness, depression, and phobias. Many reported employing appropriate coping strategies such as counseling and support groups intermittently throughout their lives, especially during periods of transitions and when under extreme stress. Lastly, they spelled out the implications of this study including the need for career counseling in high school continuing into the college years, and the need for job experience and acquisition of job search strategies, and the need for information about The Americans with Disabilities Act and issues surrounding disclosure.

In Chapter 16, Rosalie Fink describes the lives of 60 highly successful adults with dyslexia in the U.S. who achieved high levels of success in diverse professions that require reading. Forty-six had achieved advanced degrees and twelve had bachelor degrees from four year colleges or universities. She focused on investigating how these persons developed literacy as well as on their current profiles of literacy strengths and weaknesses. Fink concludes that all the adults she studied had mastered the ultimate goal of reading—the ability to make meaning from a complex text—despite the fact that some still showed ongoing weaknesses in phonological abilities and processing speed. She relates her results to teaching methods for both children and adults with reading disabilities stressing the role of interest-driven instruction. Whether it be these instructional strategies or those described by Vogel and Adelman, there is no doubt that adults with learning disabilities can and do achieve high levels of success in spite of their vulnerability.

Chapter • 14

Adults with Learning Disabilities
8 to15 Years after College

Susan A. Vogel and Pamela B. Adelman

Since the early 1990's, national attention has been focused on improving outcomes for all learners including individuals with disabilities. The impetus for this focus can be attributed at least in part to The National Education Goals 2000 (1991) which focused attention on increasing the college degree completion rate in the nation. In order to determine how those with disabilities fare and improve outcomes, Congress directed the Secretary of Education to determine educational attainment and employment and occupational status of individuals with disabilities. The Stanford Research Institute (SRI) was selected to conduct what has become known as the National Longitudinal Transition Study (NLTS) (Blackorby and Wagner 1996; Marder and D'Amico 1992). This study initially identified a nationwide representative sample of 8,000 young adults from the 13 disability categories as defined by The Education for All Handicapped Children Act of 1975 (PL 94-142). Three to five years after the students initially interviewed had exited from high school, Wagner, D'Amico, Marder, Newman, and Blackorby (1992) contacted a subsample of 327 adults with learning disabilities, ages 26 or younger, and found that 63.6% had graduated from high school, 4.4% attended a 4-year

Vogel, S. A. and Adelman, P. B. 2000. Adults with learning disabilities 8 to 15 years after college. *Learning Disabilities: A Multidisciplinary Journal* 10(3):165–82, a publication of the Learning Disabilities Association of America, reprinted here with permission.

college, and 0.4% had completed a 4-year degree. With regard to employment, 56.7% were employed full-time, however, the mean hourly wage was $6.45 bringing their annual income to only $12,000. With regard to occupational status, 70% of the adults with learning disabilities were employed in low-prestige jobs that required a low level of literacy skills and as many as 39% were employed as laborers. Similarly discouraging findings have been reported by a series of studies funded by Congressional discretionary dollars in the states of Washington (Affleck, Edgar, Levine, and Kortering 1990; Levine 1993; Levine and Edgar 1995), in New Hampshire (Nesbit and Lichtenstein 1992), and in Iowa (Sitlington and Frank 1990).

The NLTS followed these young adults for a maximum of five years, but what happens across the life span? In order to address this question, we turn now to another database, namely, The National Adult Literacy Survey (NALS), which was administered in the early 1990's in the homes of 26,000 adults ages 16–65, a sample that was representative of the adult population in the U.S. (see Kirsch, Jungeblut, Jenkins, and Kilstad 1993, for a full description of the NALS). Within this population, 3% self-reported that they had a learning disability (Reder 1995). Similarly bleak findings emerged regarding educational outcomes (Vogel and Reder 1998) and employment, occupational status, and income levels of adults with learning disabilities across the life span (Reder and Vogel 1997). In regard to educational attainment, slightly fewer than half of the adults with learning disabilities graduated from high school. In contrast to the NLTS, the college or graduate school graduation rate in this sample was 8.7%. In terms of employment status, the percent employed full-time among those with learning disabilities was significantly lower (39%) than the percent employed full time in the total population (51%) and more of the adults with learning disabilities were in lower status occupations (13% vs. 26% held professional, managerial, or technical jobs; 14% vs. 28% were in sales; 45% vs. 28% worked in service jobs; and 28% vs. 18% were laborers). The average annual income of adults with learning disabilities was $14,958 as compared to $23,131 among the general population. These findings translated into greatly reduced earnings and substantially higher risk of poverty for adults with learning disabilities.

As discouraging as these findings are, it is important to keep in mind that some researchers conducted follow-up studies on small samples of adults with learning disabilities and reported that some of the adults with learning disabilities in their studies were highly successful (for a complete review of this literature see Adelman and Vogel 1998). One such study was our first follow-up study (Adelman and Vogel 1990; 1993) on a subgroup of the adults who participated in the present study. In this follow-up study, the participants had exited the college 3 to 7 years earlier, had average or above cognitive abilities, moderate to mild learning disabilities, English as their native language, and no other disability. (For a complete description of cognitive and academic achievement abilities, see Vogel and Adelman 1990).

A total of 56 (63%) out of 89 potential participants responded either verbally or by mail to the follow-up questionnaire. Thirty-six (40%) of the participants had completed their Bachelor's degree and an additional seven (19%) were attending or had completed graduate school. With respect to occupations, the largest proportion of the college graduates (42%) went into some area of business. Six (17%) were employed as teachers: four certified and two non-certified teachers. Other occupations reported were chemist, computer programmer, librarian, and health service provider.

A second college-student follow-up study has since been conducted (Greenbaum 1993). The participants in this study consisted of 49 adults with learning disabilities (there was no comparison group without learning disabilities) who had attended a highly competitive university between 1980 and 1992. Greenbaum reported that 67% of the total group of 81 had completed their undergraduate degree as compared to a graduation rate in the general student population of 63%. Moreover, out of the 44 participants who were not in school at the time of data collection, 83% were employed. Almost three-fourths were employed in professional, technical, or managerial positions, slightly less than one-fourth in sales occupations, and 6% in service occupations. Average annual salary was approximately $20,000 in spite of the fact that many were employed in high status occupations and had completed their Bachelor's degree.

A third very relevant follow-up study of former college students with learning disabilities and their comparison group without learning disabilities was conducted 2 to 8 years after they had graduated from a very highly competitive university (Witte, Philips, and Kakela 1998). Among the 37 former students with learning disabilities who participated in this follow-up study, 87% were employed full-time; 29% were in the highest occupational category, and 20% were in sales. When asked if they had disclosed their learning disability on the job, similar to the Greenbaum (1993) follow-up study, a very small fraction (only 5%) disclosed their learning disability in their employment setting.

Vogel (1996) attributed these often contradictory findings to methodological differences and/or problems including:

1. The lack of a comparison group without learning disabilities;

2. The lack of a sufficient number of years elapsing since exit from high school or college (e.g., in the NLTS study only 3–5 years had elapsed);

3. Some of the individuals who participated in the study were still in school making it invalid to report their educational attainment while it was still in flux;

4. Selection criteria differed, resulting sometimes in over generalization of the findings, e.g. only college graduates were included in the study, but the results were applied to all college students with learning disabilities;

5. Sometimes the participants were self-referred (as in studies of college-able students with learning disabilities); at other times they were school-identified (as in the NLTS sample); and at other times they were representative of the general population (as in the NALS sample).

6. The follow-up studies sometimes looked at different outcomes.

Given these methodological problems, given that there have been so few follow-up studies of college-able adults with learning disabilities and those that did exist often lacked a comparison group without learning disabilities, given that a robust number of years (8–15) had passed since the adults in our first follow-up study had either graduated or exited from the college setting, and given that The Americans with Disabilities Act had been enacted since our first follow-up study was conducted, we felt it was timely to conduct our second longitudinal study and to address the following questions:

1. What was the educational attainment of adults with learning disabilities as compared to their peers without learning disabilities?

2. What was the employment and occupational status, congruity of academic studies and career, employment history (full time vs. part time, number of jobs held, longevity in present employment, job seeking strategies), job satisfaction, and financial status of adults with learning disabilities as compared to their peers without learning disabilities?

3. If there was a negative impact of learning disabilities on the job, did those with learning disabilities disclose that they had a learning disability, if so, why, at what stage, to whom, and what was the reaction of the person to whom they disclosed?

4. How knowledgeable were the adults with learning disabilities as compared to the adults without learning disabilities regarding The Americans with Disabilities Act?

METHODS

Design

Telephone interview was the method used (Bruininks, Wolman, and Thurlow 1990) for several reasons. (1) Telephone interviews have the potential of getting the largest participation rate because participants can speak to the interviewer rather than write their responses; (2) The interviewers could ask for clarification and/or elaboration if a response were unclear; (3) Participants were more likely to provide more detailed responses to open-ended questions if they could speak to a sympathetic and interested listener; (4) Telephone interviews could be very cost effective if done in the evening or on weekends when telephone rates were at their lowest; and (5) Participants may be more willing to give up half an hour or an hour for a telephone interview, but not be willing to respond in writing, to travel, or to have someone come to their home.

The Groups with and without Learning Disabilities

The total number of possible participants consisted of 107 adults with learning disabilities and 153 adults without learning disabilities who entered Barat College between 1980 and 1988 and met the selection criteria for participation. Though more than 107 students were enrolled in the learning disability support program during those years, participants in the longitudinal study had to meet the following criteria: average or above IQ, at least a two-year discrepancy between their cognitive abilities and one or more aspects of academic achievement, English as their native language, and no concomitant disability. The 107 adults with learning disabilities were matched with students without learning disabilities on gender and year of entry to the College. None of the adults without learning disabilities had a history of receiving special education services. (For a more detailed description of the College, the support services, the application process, entrance requirements for students with learning disabilities, and cognitive abilities and academic achievement, see Adelman 1988, Vogel 1982, and Vogel and Adelman 1990.)

Search strategies

Through the use of a variety of search strategies, 57 (53%) of the adults with learning disabilities and 59 (39%) of the adults without learning disabilities were located. Initially, we identified the last known telephone numbers and addresses from the office of the support program, the College Alumni and Development Offices, the registrar's office, telephone books and directories on CD-ROM, and the telephone information service. If the parents of those with learning disabilities had maintained contact with the director of the support services, these parents were contacted and permission requested (and in all cases granted) for the interviewer to contact their son or daughter by phone. If these strategies were unsuccessful, the last step was for a private investigator to search databases in the public domain such as the registries of motor vehicles, marriage licenses, and voter's registration (M. Raskind and E. Higgins, Personal Communication, February 4, 1994; Raskind, Goldberg, Higgins, and Herman 1999).

Participants

Out of those who were located, 50 (88%) of those with learning disabilities and 41 (70%) of those without learning disabilities agreed to participate in the longitudinal study. Cognitive abilities of the participants with learning disabilities were in the normal range (Verbal IQ $M = 104.54$, $SD = 10.72$; Performance IQ $M = 103.98$, $SD = 11.43$; Full Scale IQ $M = 104.57$, $SD = 10.11$) and the adults with learning disabilities performed significantly poorer than those without learning disabilities on timed reading comprehension as measured by the Stanford Diagnostic Reading Test—Blue Level (Karlsen, Madden, and Gardner 1974) ($t = 6.12$ [$df = 69$], $p < .001$), on knowledge of sentence structure (Descriptive Tests of Language Skills, ETS (The College Board 1978) ($t = 4.55$, $df = 71$, $p < .001$), and on the ability to write an essay on an assigned topic ($t = 4.87$, $df = 65$, $p < .001$).

In order to determine if those who had agreed to participate as compared with those who were unwilling to participate comprised a representative sample or one with perhaps more favorable outcomes (Bruininks et al. 1990), the interviewers asked those unwilling to participate two questions, namely, what was their highest level of education and whether or not they were employed. We selected these two questions because we felt that this information could have an impact on a wide variety of other findings, e.g., educational level has an impact on employment status and salary. All of those who refused to be interviewed agreed to respond to these two questions. Upon comparing the participants and non-participants within group, no significant differences were found on either of these two questions confirming that the participants in this study were in fact representative of the total group who had been located.

Instrumentation

The questionnaire consisted of four parts. Part I included basic demographic information such as age, gender, race, marital status, parenting, and educational attainment. In Part II the interviewer asked whether they were presently employed full-time, part-time, or unemployed, their present occupation, salary, job satisfaction, job maintenance, if they were presently looking for another job, congruity of present job and college studies, the timing of the identification of their present career, employment history, and knowledge about The Americans with Disabilities Act of 1990. Questions in Part III pertained to the impact of their learning disability on the job, job satisfaction, job maintenance, compensatory strategies, disclosure, and accommodations, and Part IV addressed quality of life issues. In this article, we will report on most of the questions addressed in Parts I–III of the survey. In addition to the development of the instrumentation, several scripts and a checklist were developed for use during the preliminary phone call, the interview itself, and the end of the interview.

A pilot study was conducted in order to determine (a) clarity of items, (b) the need for additional items, (c) the need for response alternatives rather than open-ended questions, and (d) the length of time to complete the interview. Ten adults with learning disabilities, who had attended other colleges and universities and were not known to the researchers, volunteered to be interviewed. In this pilot study we were able to further refine the interview items, scripts, response checklists, and interview procedures. The last step was to review the response alternatives and revise, as needed, for ease of data entry.

Procedures

Qualifications of Interviewers. Interviewers were selected who were native English speakers and had a pleasant phone manner, clear articulation, and moderate speaking rate. None of the interviewers had any previous contact with the office of the learning disability support program or the participants. Whenever possible, the interviewers were enrolled in or had completed a Master's degree in learning disabilities and had telemarketing experience.

Interviewer Training. Each interviewer received 10 to 15 hours of training and practice. The first 1 to 2 hours of training focused on the purpose of the study, characteristics of adults with learning disabilities, principles of sound interviewing, the survey itself, and the importance of accuracy and consistency of questioning strategies and recording responses. Some of the characteristics of adults with learning disabilities that were discussed included rate of oral language comprehension, memory deficits, and word-finding problems. Interview strategies to minimize the impact of learning disabilities were described and modeled including rate of speech, pauses, the use of advance organizers, and question repetition.

Time was devoted during training to discussion of the various roles of the interviewer and the potential conflict between the role of the interviewer as researcher, helping professional, confidante, counselor, and friend. The interviewers were trained to listen for signs of loneliness and/or depression. If these were suspected, the interviewers offered to provide referrals to helping professionals in the participants' geographic locale. If the interviewers observed that the participant demonstrated suicidal tendencies, they followed a series of steps designed to secure immediate help for the participant. Whereas several of the participants were severely depressed and wanted the names of professionals in their area, none were suicidal.

The second stage in training was memorizing the scripts and items in the questionnaire. We encouraged memorizing the scripts in order to preserve uniformity across interviewers and worked with the interviewers until they sounded natural and spontaneous. In the initial phone contact, the interviewers used a checklist consisting of the points to be covered that served as memory prompts for the interviewer. Based on the participants' responses, some items could be skipped. These instructions were incorporated into the survey. Practice was necessary to enable the interviewers to become very familiar with the guidelines for order of presentation.

In the third stage of training, the interviewers conducted mock interviews with the researchers as subjects. Extensive feedback was provided regarding voice quality and volume, rate of speech, use of *filler* comments while listening to and/or transcribing responses to fill the long silences, style of communication, and when and how to encourage elaboration. During actual interviews, the interviewers' communication (not the participants) was tape recorded to assure that the protocols continued to be followed consistently. The primary co-principal investigator listened to all tapes and provided feedback to interviewers as needed.

Interview Strategies

First Telephone Contact.   During the initial telephone contact, the interviewer's first task was to persuade the listener to participate by describing the purpose of the longitudinal study, the importance of the information that they can provide, and the gift certificate they would receive as a token of appreciation. Once the participants agreed to be interviewed, the interviewer provided an overview of the topics to be covered and assurance that any questions that they did not want to answer could be skipped. The interviewers also explained that the participants would receive two copies of the consent form, a self-addressed stamped return envelope, and outline of the topics to be covered in the interview so they could think about the topics in advance and more easily follow along during the actual interview. Two alternative outlines were developed; one for those with learning disabilities and one for the participants without learning disabilities since those without learning disabilities were not asked questions pertaining to learning disabilities. Lastly, a mutually convenient day and time were determined about 10 days later, which allowed time for the consent letter to be received, signed, and returned.

Reminder Telephone Call. Initially, we found that on occasion participants with learning disabilities were not at home or in their office to receive the phone call at the appointed time and later apologized for forgetting the appointment. Other times they did not send the consent letter back prior to the scheduled interview. We, therefore, instituted a plan whereby four days prior to the interview, the interviewer telephoned the participant to confirm day, time, and phone number for the scheduled interview. Most participants preferred that the interview take place at home in the evening or on the weekend. A few preferred that they be called at their place of work. If the consent letter had not yet been returned, another script was written, to verify the address. Usually faxing the letter to a confidential fax number resolved the problem.

The Interview. At the beginning of the telephone call, the interviewer followed a script thanking participants for agreeing to participate, for returning the consent letter, and then asked if they had the outline in front of them. When they were about to begin, the interviewer indicated that they would begin with questions about basic background information found on page one of the outline of interview topics. Periodically, the interviewer would inform the participant of the page and item number to be discussed next. During and following the participants' responses to questions, the interviewer would indicate with neutral comments, e.g., mmm, I see, or uhuh, that they were listening and recording their responses.

At the close of the interview, along with thanking them for the valuable information they provided, the interviewer ascertained which gift certificate they would like to receive, if they would like information about the ADA, and if they would like to receive a copy of the results. The interviewers also asked permission to get back in touch with them if there were something unclear in their notes, or something they forgot to ask. The interviewer then shared with the participants that we want to maintain contact with them over the years and asked that if they should move, to please fill out the enclosed self-addressed change of address postcard.

Data Analysis

Frequencies were computed for each item in the survey by group and by gender within each group. The group with learning disabilities and the group without learning disabilities were compared on Part I (Background Information) and Part II (Employment Information) of the survey. Categorical data and items that used a five- point scale (e. g., from *not at all*, to *a lot*) were tested between groups using chi-square (x^2) analyses. Examples of categorical data include race, marital status, employment situation, educational level, etc. Dichotomous data arising from *yes-no* responses were compared via tests of proportions. Quantitative data such as salary, number of jobs held since exit or graduation from college, were compared using *t* tests and ANOVA. A separate variance (rather than pooled variance) estimate of the standard error was used when the variances of the groups were significantly different ($p < .05$). Comments made in response to the open-ended questions were categorized and are summarized below.

RESULTS

Background Information

Age.   The adults with learning disabilities were significantly younger ($M = 33.79$, $SD = 5.47$) ($t = -2.78$, $df = 66.10$, $p < .01$) than the adults without learning disabilities ($M = 38.02$, $SD = 8.41$). When we grouped the participants by decade, we found that there was a higher proportion of individuals in the group with learning disabilities in their 30's (62% vs. 53%) and fewer (6%) in the group with learning disabilities in their 40's than in the group without learning disabilities (17%). Thus, the participants with learning disabilities were more often of traditional age (18–24) eight to fifteen years ago when they entered the college. Another factor influencing the age difference was that this college attracted a large proportion of non-traditional age students (defined as 25 years or older at entrance) who chose to return to college studies after their children were of school age (see table I).

Years Since Exit from College or Highest Degree.   Because responses to questions such as the number of jobs held since exit or graduation, annual salary, and present occupation are heavily influenced by the number of years in the work force and/or profession, (rather than age per se), we compared the groups on the number of years that had elapsed since exiting from college (if they had not completed their Bachelor's degree) or the number of years since completing their highest degree. The mean number of years for both groups was almost identical (8 years). We, therefore, concluded that there

Table I.   Age of Participants

Age Range	Adults with Learning Disabilities[a]		Adults without Learning Disabilities[b]	
	N	%	N	%
20–30	16	32	8	20
31–35	23	46	12	29
36–40	8	16	10	24
41–45	1	2	2	5
46–50	2	4	5	12
51–55	0	0	3	7
56–60	0	0	1	2

[a]$N = 50$, $M = 33.79$, $SD = 5.47$
[b]$N = 41$, $M = 38.02$, $SD = 8.41$
$p < .01$

were no significant differences between the groups on years since exit from college or completion of highest degree and we therefore have confidence that years since exit or highest degree completion was not going to have a differential impact on the findings.

Gender.   The gender ratio in both groups was 4:1 females to males, the reverse of the expected ratio for those with LD because this college had been a college for women until 1982 and still attracted more females than males with LD.

Ethnicity.   Forty-three (86%) were Caucasian among the learning disability group (1 was African American, 3 were Hispanic American, and 2 were multi-racial) as compared to 37 (90%) Caucasian in the non-learning disability group (3 African American and 1 Asian American).

Marital Status and Parenting.   Given the tendency for women born around 1970 to marry later in life and to delay marriage and child bearing until after they had established themselves in their careers, it was not unexpected to find that 21 (42%) in the learning disability group were single, which is slightly more than twice the proportion who were single in the group without learning disabilities (8 [20%]). Because more of those in the group without learning disabilities were married (27 [66%] vs. 25 [50%]), the divorce rate was also higher in the group without learning disabilities (10% as compared to 4%). Lastly, it follows logically that many more among the group without learning disabilities were parents (61%) as compared to those in the group with learning disabilities (39%) because the group without learning disabilities was significantly older and more were married. (For an overview of the demographic variables, see table II.)

Table II.   Demographic Variables

Variable	Adults with Learning Disabilities[a]		Adults without Learning Disabilities[b]	
	N	%	N	%
Gender Distribution				
Male	13	26	10	24
Female	37	74	31	76
Ethnicity				
Caucasian	43	86	37	90
African American	1	2	3	7
Asian	0	0	1	2
Hispanic American	3	6	0	0
Multi-racial	2	6	0	0
Preferred not to answer	1	2	0	0
Marital Status				
Single	21	42	8	20
Married	25	50	27	66
Separated	1	2	1	2
Divorced	2	4	4	10
Widowed	1	2	1	2
Parenting				
Yes	20	40	25	61
No	30	60	16	39

[a]N = 50
[b]N = 41

Educational Attainment

There were no significant differences between the groups on educational attainment ($x^2 = 1,000$, $df = 2$, $p > .05$). Twelve (24%) in the group with learning disabilities and 7 (17%) in the group without learning disabilities attended college, but did not complete a degree. In the group with learning disabilities, 2 (4%) earned the Associates of Arts (AA) degree as compared to 3 (7%) in the group without learning disabilities. For thirty (60%) in the group with learning disabilities and 23 (56%) in the group without learning disabilities, the highest degree earned was the bachelor's degree. Moreover, 6 (12%) in the group with learning disabilities completed a graduate or professional degree, 5 completed a master's degree in education, and one completed a degree in law. Among those in the group without learning disabilities, 8 (20%) completed their master's or doctorate. There was more variability in the master's and doctoral degrees earned among the group without learning disabilities, which included social work, Latin American Studies, education, and psychology (see table III).

Table III.   Educational Attainment

Variable	Adults with Learning Disabilities[a]		Adults without Learning Disabilities[b]	
	N	%	N	%
Some College	12	24	7	17
Associate's Degree	2	4	3	7
Bachelor's Degree	30	60	23	56
Graduate/Professional Degree	6	12	8	20

[a]$N = 50$
[b]$N = 41$

Employment

There were no significant differences in the overall employment attainment of the two groups. Thirty-nine (78%) of those in the group with learning disabilities compared to 35 (85%) in the group without learning disabilities were employed outside the home. About three-fourths (72%) of those employed in the group with learning disabilities were employed full-time in contrast to 86% in the group without learning disabilities and the remainder were employed part time (28% of the group with learning disabilities vs. 14% in the group without learning disabilities). Eleven (22%) in the group with learning disabilities and 6 (15%) in the group without learning disabilities were unemployed. Among those unemployed, three in each group chose to be full-time parents/home makers. When the remaining eight with learning disabilities were asked why they were not employed, six responded. One did not work because of health reasons, two stated that they lacked the necessary skills, two indicated that their learning disability affected job performance, and one was unable to work because of an accident. When those without a learning disability who were unemployed were questioned about why they were unemployed, three responded; two indicated lack of specific skills and one indicated having some mild health problems. (See table IV for an overview of employment status.)

Using a scale of 1 to 5 with 1 being *not at all* and 5 being *extremely satisfied*, the participants were asked how satisfied they were with their current employment. There were no significant differences between the groups on job satisfaction for those who were employed full time. About one-third in each group indicated that they were *highly satisfied* (5) and the remaining two-thirds were *somewhat* to *very satisfied* (2–3) with their present jobs. None of those in the group with learning disabilities were dissatisfied with their present job and only one was dissatisfied in the group without learning disabilities.

Table IV.   Employment Status

Variable	Adults with Learning Disabilities[a]		Adults without Learning Disabilities[b]	
	N	%	N	%
Full- and Part-Time	39	78	35	85
Full-Time	28	72	30	86
Part-Time	11	28	5	14
Unemployed	11	22	6	15

[a]$N = 50$
[b]$N = 41$

We were interested to know how the participants found their present jobs. By far, the most common strategy used by about half of the participants in both groups was to have found their present job through family and friends. Of the remainder, the next most frequently used strategy for those with learning disabilities was taking the initiative to start their own business (8 [21%]), a strategy less commonly used by those without learning disabilities. The next most common method of finding a job for those with learning disabilities was using a placement office, a published listing of job openings, or the classified advertisements (10%) (see table V).

We were also interested to know the degree of congruity between their current employment and their college studies. Underlying this question was the concern as to whether individuals with learning disabilities have a more difficult time than those without learning disabilities to find jobs in their chosen field. Using a scale of 1 to 5, we found that there was significantly more congruity between employment and academic major for the adults without learning disabilities as compared to those with learning disabilities ($x^2 = 13.85$, $df = 4$, $p < .01$) (See table VI). However, when we examined this question for those who were employed full time, the difference was only minimally significant ($x^2 = 5.99$, $df = 2$, $p < .05$). Apparently, those who

Table V.   Job Search Strategies

	Adults with Learning Disabilities	(39)	Adults without Learning Disabilities	(35)
Family-Friend	19	(49%)	15	(43%)
Placement Office/ Employment Counselor	4	(10%)	3	(9%)
Newspaper Ad/ Job Listing	4	(10%)	6	(17%)
Headhunter	2	(5%)	3	(9%)
Own Initiative/ Self-Employed	8	(21%)	5	0.14

were employed part time were either unable to find a full time job in their area of expertise and therefore compromised on the congruity of their employment and their preparation in college or graduate school at that time in order to be employed at least part time, or they could only work part time at this point in time and took the job temporarily regardless of the lack of complete congruity with college preparation and career goals (see table VI).

Another approach to determine congruity was to ask those who were employed full time if they considered their current job their career. On a scale of 1 to 5, with 1 being *not at all* and 5 being *most definitely*, 57% in each group answered *most definitely* with 43% of the group with learning disabilities and 37% in the group without learning disabilities indicating a response of either 2, 3, or 4. The follow-up question to this one was when did they identify this profession as their career choice. Not surprising, for the group without learning disabilities, 17% of the respondents had identified this career direction before entering college, 30% identified their career path while in college, and 43% after they completed their undergraduate degree. For those with learning disabilities, a different picture emerged. Only one had identified his or her career direction before college, 20% did so while in college, and 78%, after completing their undergraduate degree.

Given that some of the previously described researchers reported that some individuals with learning disabilities have difficulty not only finding a job, but also keeping a job, we asked the participants how long they had been employed in their present job. Though there was no significant difference between the groups on job maintenance ($t = -.53$, $df = 53$, $p > .05$), the mean number of months for those in the group without learning disabilities was 51.03 months ($SD = 53$) compared to a mean of 45.12 months ($SD = 29.88$) for those with learning disabilities.

It stands to reason that if individuals have not determined their career choice before or during college, they may experiment with different jobs once they exit or graduate from college, namely, they may have a history of a significantly larger number of job changes after college. Our findings confirmed this pattern especially for those with learning disabilities. When asked how many different jobs they had held since leaving college, 10 (20%) individuals with learning disabilities indicated they had held more than five jobs in contrast to 3 (7%) who had held more than five jobs among those without learning disabilities. The mean number of jobs for those with learning disabilities was 4.26 ($SD = 3.73$) and 3.02 ($SD = 1.68$) for those without learning disabilities ($t = 2.10$, $df = 70.94$, $p < .05$). When we examined the individual responses case by case, it became clear that a few individuals in the group with learning disabilities had held a very large number of

Table VI.   Congruity between Employment and College Studies

	Congruity									
	None 1		2		3		4		A lot 5	
	LD[a]	NLD[b]	LD[a]	NLD[b]	LD[a]	NLD[b]	LD[a]	NLD[b]	LD[a]	NLD[b]
	N %	N %	N %	N %	N %	N %	N %	N %	N %	N %
Full and Part Time Employed	6 15	8 23	10 26	0 0	9 23	7 20	8 21	6 17	6 15	14 40
Full Time Employed	3 11	5 17	7 25	0 0	6 21	6 20	7 25	6 20	5 18	13 43

[a]Full and Part Time, N = 39; Full Time, N = 28
[b]Full and Part Time, N = 35; Full Time, N = 30

jobs. Nine individuals with learning disabilities had held more than five jobs since leaving college. Among those, several had held 6 and 7 jobs, and the others had held 8, 9, 12, and 24 jobs. In contrast, in the group without learning disabilities, 4 had held 5 jobs, 2 had held 6, and 1 had held 8 jobs.

In order to refine our understanding further, we divided those employed into two groups, that is, those employed full time and those employed part time. The data revealed that there were no significant differences in the number of jobs held by those who were employed full time, rather it was the number of jobs held by those employed part time that had contributed to the significant difference found in the total number of jobs held since leaving college. For those employed full time, the mean number of jobs was almost identical in the two subgroups: $M = 3.36$, $SD = 2.13$ for the group with learning disabilities compared to $M = 3.23$, $SD = 1.83$ for the group without learning disabilities ($t = 0.24$, $df = 56$, $p < .05$). However, the mean number of jobs held by those employed part time in the group with learning disabilities was 4.45 ($SD = 1.44$) with a range of 1 to 24 jobs as compared to the mean among those without learning disabilities who were employed part time of 2.60 ($SD = 1.14$) with a range of 1 to 8 jobs ($t = 2.53$, $df = 14$, $p < .05$).

Occupations

The occupations/job titles of the participants were grouped into four categories (US Government Occupational Index 1996–1997) for ease in comparing our data to the national longitudinal and cross sectional studies reviewed earlier. The categories were: (1) professional, technical, and managerial jobs; (2) jobs in sales; (3) service/clerical jobs; and (4) laborers. There were no significant differences overall in the categories of jobs for those with learning disabilities employed full time and those without learning disabilities, with slightly more than two-thirds of those in the group with learning disabilities and almost three-fourths of those without learning disabilities holding jobs in category one. A greater discrepancy was seen in the category of sales with twice as many (14%) in the group with learning disabilities in sales as compared to 7% in the group without learning disabilities. (Table VII provides a full overview of the number in each group holding full time jobs in each category.)

Salaries

An overview of the financial status of the two groups appears in table VIII. Because salary and educational attainment are so highly correlated (Reder 1995), only those who had earned at least a four-year

Table VII.   Occupations—Full time Employed

Occupational Category	Adults with Learning Disabilities[a]		Adults without Learning Disabilities[b]	
	N	%	N	%
Professional, Technical, and Managerial	19	68	22	73
Sales	4	14	2	7
Service/Clerical	4	14	6	20
Laborer	1	.5	0	0

[a]$N = 28$
[b]$N = 30$

Table VIII.   Annual Salaries—Full time Employed

Variable	LD[a]		NLD[b]	
	N	%	N	%
< $20,000	1	4	2	7
20.001–30,000	10	36	8	28
30,001–40,000	6	21	5	17
40,001–50,000	6	21	2	7
50,001–60,000	1	4	4	14
60,001–70,000	2	7	3	10
70,001–80,000	1	4	0	0
> 80,001	0	0	1	3
No Response	1	4	4	14

[a]$N = 28$, $M = \$38,500$, $SD = \$16,524$
[b]$N = 29$, $M = \$39,018$, $SD = \$15,676$, Outlier eliminated

degree and were employed full time were considered in this analysis. When the salaries were arranged from highest to lowest, the discrepancy between any two salaries was $8,000 or less with one exception. The exception to this observation was the discrepancy of $81,000 (tenfold larger than the discrepancy between any other two salaries in either group). This discrepancy occurred between the two highest salaries in the group without learning disabilities, which were $69,000 and $150,000. In this way, it was determined that the highest salary in the group without learning disabilities skewed the descriptive data so significantly as to be misleading. Therefore, the highest salary ($150,000) was considered an outlier and was not included in the present analysis. The median salaries for the two groups were $35,000 for the group with learning disabilities and $32,000 for the group without learning disabilities. There was no significant difference between the mean salary for those employed full time for the group with learning disabilities ($38,500, $SD = \$16,524$) and the Group without learning disabilities ($39,018, $SD = \$15,676$) ($t = -0.11$, $df = 47$, $p > .05$) and it is, therefore, possible to conclude that there were no significant differences in the financial status of the two groups. (See table VIII.)

Impact of Learning Disabilities on the Job

Twenty-one (76%) of those employed full time reported that their learning disability had a negative impact on the job. Of those 21, when asked how much their learning disability affected them on the job using a 1 to 5 scale, it was almost a three-way split. Forty percent reported it affected them minimally, 25% reported it affected them at a moderate level, and 35% reported that it affected them a lot. However, 63% of those employed part time reported that their learning disability affected them minimally on the job.

If their learning disability affected them on the job, we asked how it affected them. Out of 63 comments describing the way their learning disability affected them on the job, 27 described a language-related impact including from high to low, written expressive language (43%), spelling (25%), rate of oral comprehension (14%), and reading comprehension and reading rate (both 8%). Twenty-two percent of the comments related to math problems, while 14% described information-processing difficulties such as memory deficits, misperception of oral language, or reversals. Five of the comments (8%) indicated that their learning disability affected their emotional well being. Only two comments related to the positive impact of the learning disability when they stated that it made them creative, it made them unique, and they would never want to give it up.

Compensatory Strategies

If their learning disability had a negative impact on the job, we asked the respondents how they compensated for their learning disability. Out of a total of 89 comments, one type of comment occurred 21 times (24%), namely, using self-knowledge and understanding of their learning disability to find the right job and work environment where they could capitalize on their strengths, compensate for deficits, and avoid situations where they may fail. The second and third most frequently mentioned compensatory strategy with each one mentioned 18 times (19%) involved spending additional time and using technology. The next two most frequent strategies, each mentioned 10 times (11%), involved using written expressive language and asking for help. A few reported using organizational or memory strategies.

Disclosure

If they reported that their learning disability affected them on the job, we wanted to know if they disclosed that they had a learning disability, the reason that they disclosed or did not disclose, at what stage in their employment they disclosed, to whom they disclosed, and the reaction of that individual. Sixteen out of 27 (59%) of those employed who had reported that their learning disability affected them on the job, had disclosed that they had a learning disability and 11 (41%) said they did not disclose. Three out of the 16 disclosed during the job application process. Two out of these three disclosed during the job interview, and one, during pre-employment testing. Among the 13 who disclosed after being hired, 6 out of the 13 disclosed to a co-worker and four to a supervisor. Some disclosed to their secretary whose help they needed to get the job done, others disclosed to a corporate trainer, a customer, an examination board, or the head of the company. From their comments it is apparent that some disclosed to more than one individual.

The 16 who had disclosed gave 30 different reasons that they disclosed. One disclosed to his customers because he wanted them to understand why he charged for fewer hours than he actually worked. He explained to them that his work pace was slow and deliberate because of his learning disability and he did not want them to be concerned that they would be charged for all of the hours he spent on the job. Others disclosed to a corporate trainer who may have noticed that they performed tasks using unique strategies compared to other people or because they sometimes did not understand how to get the job done because of the nature of their learning disability. They needed to learn how to perform a specific aspect of the job differently (e.g., seeing a demonstration instead of reading the manual of instructions), or someone may have observed that the individual with a learning disability had very poor handwriting, were puzzled by it, and may have misinterpreted the reason for the poor handwriting. Some persons with learning disabilities expressed a desire to make others aware of the nature of learning disabilities so co-workers would be more empathetic and understanding regarding their frustrations. Many expressed the feeling that they disclosed because having a learning disability was no big deal, and they did not perceive it as a weakness as long as they could use technology. Others thought learning disabilities was a topic of general interest. A couple stated that they disclosed because having a learning disability was not something they had to hide since they were very successful on the job. Only one person disclosed in order to receive accommodations on a professional accreditation examination. However, this disclosure and request for an accommodation were made only as a last resort after the individual had failed the examination three times and only four tries were allowed.

The 11 out of the 27 who reported that their learning disability affected them on the job and who did not disclose their learning disability reported 16 reasons for not disclosing. Several of them did not disclose because of their fear of being judged as less worthy, less intelligent, or less capable than they had been judged by those same individuals prior to becoming aware that they had a learning disability. Others reported fear of negative consequences if they disclosed, e.g., not being promoted as a result of having disclosed. Several decided not to disclose because they believed this information should remain confidential and was of no importance to others. Lack of awareness and misunderstandings about learning disabilities were expressed by other participants as well. One stated that people would not understand what to do with this information if they had been told they had a learning disability. Lastly, in one instance, the individual reported that he or she did not have to disclose because anyone who needed an accommodation could receive it whether or not they had a disability.

We asked the 16 participants who had disclosed at what stage in their employment history they had disclosed and to whom they disclosed. Three out of the 16 had disclosed during the application process. In response to the questions regarding when and to whom they disclosed, two had disclosed during the interview process to the person conducting the job interview, and one disclosed to the person administering the pre-employment tests. Among the 13 who disclosed after being hired, 7 told a co-worker about the learning disability, 4 told their supervisor, 2 told their secretary, one told a corporate trainer, and one told a customer.

We asked those who had disclosed to describe the reaction of the individual (1 very negative to 5 very positive) upon learning that they had a learning disability. Their assessment indicated the reaction was either moderately or very positive, However, one person commented that the person he or she told did not believe that he or she could possibly have a learning disability. (Table IX provides the distribution of their reactions.)

ACCOMMODATIONS

We wanted to determine if the motivation for disclosing was related to requests for accommodations. We therefore asked those who disclosed if they had requested accommodations, what accommodations they requested, if the accommodations were provided, and, if they

Table IX.   Assessment of Reaction to Disclosure ($N = 11^*$)

Negative 1		2		3		4		Reaction Positive 5	
N	%	N	%	N	%	N	%	N	%
–	–	1	9	3	27	3	27	4	64

*No response from 5.

were not provided, why not. Only 2 out of the 16 individuals who disclosed requested accommodations. In both instances, they requested extra time and received the accommodation.

Familiarity with the Americans with Disabilities Act of 1990

One of the changes that had occurred since the 1990 longitudinal study was passage and implementation of ADA. Therefore, we wanted to know how familiar the respondents were with this law as it pertained to accommodations for employees with learning disabilities on the job. We assigned a value to each of the ratings on a scale of 1 to 5 with 1 *not at all familiar*, and 5 *very familiar* and found that those with learning disabilities were significantly less familiar with ADA ($M = 1.77$, $SD = 1.16$) than the respondents without learning disabilities ($M = 2.50$, $SD = 1.42$) ($t = -2.58$, $df = 81$, $p < .01$). The most surprising finding was that 62% of the group with learning disabilities as compared to 33% of the group without learning disabilities indicated that they were not at all familiar with ADA (see table X).

Discussion

We were only able to locate 53% of the original cohort with learning disabilities and 39% of those in the group without learning disabilities. However, this was a considerably more robust number compared to the location rate of 24% in another institution conducting a 10-year follow-up study (Spekman, Goldberg, and Herman 1992). The proportion who agreed to participate in the group with learning disabilities (88%) was somewhat higher than the participation of 62% and 70% for the group with learning disabilities in the two university follow-up studies described earlier (Greenbaum 1993; Greenbaum, Graham, and Scales 1995; Witte, et al. 1998). Perhaps the fact that the participants were enrolled in an institutional setting with a very individualized approach and that this was the second follow-up study to be conducted had a positive impact on their willingness to participate.

We have a reasonable degree of confidence that the participants and non-participants did not differ in ways that would have biased the outcomes, that is, those who agreed to participate did not have more favorable outcomes. When the non-participants and participants were compared on the two most salient outcomes, i.e., educational attainment and employment status, there were no significant differences. We therefore concluded that participants in this study did not agree to participate because they judged their accomplishments to be more favorable and, therefore, they were more willing to share information.

We used several strategies to locate possible participants, Most recently, telephone number computerized database searches have be-

Table X.   Familiarity with the Americans with Disabilities Act

	Degree								
Not at all 1		2		3		4		Very 5	
LDa	NLDb	LDa	NLDb	LDa	NLDb	LDa	NLDb	LDa	NLDb
N %	N %	N %	N %	N %	N %	N %	N %	N %	N %
29 62	12 33	7 15	8 22	6 13	7 19	3 6	4 11	2 4	5 14

[a]N = 39 (no response from 3)
[b]N = 35 (no response from 5)

come available that will make locating a cohort over time a lot easier. In our highly mobile society and one in which name changes as a result of changes in marital status are not uncommon (because of marriage and divorce for women), tracking a cohort after 15 years or more is extremely difficult. We recommend that the researchers send a first class mailing periodically such as holiday greeting cards to participants. In the event that the mailing is returned, it is important to have a fall back, such as asking participants at the close of the interview to give us permission to contact two non-family members who are likely to know their new address and telephone number (M. Raskind and E. Higgins, personal communication, February 4, 1994). Another strategy based on the premise that the participants are willing participants and want to continue to participate in future follow-up studies is to have them provide their social security numbers, the key to accessing computerized databases in the public domain (M. Raskind and E. Higgins, personal communication, February 4, 1994).

One of the most important findings of this longitudinal study is that 60% of those with learning disabilities completed their Bachelor's degree (their highest degree) at the time of the follow-up study compared to 56% for those without learning disabilities. When those who graduated with a bachelor's, a graduate, or professional school degree were combined, that figure increased to 72% for those with learning disabilities and 76% for those without learning disabilities.

In order to be better able to interpret the findings regarding educational attainment, it is important to have a national perspective. According to The Higher Education Research Institute (Astin, Tsui, and Avalos 1996) which has been conducting national longitudinal research on degree completion rates since 1966, the percent of students in the general population completing their bachelor's degree after 4, 6, and 9 years of study was 39.9%, 44.9%, and 45.7%, respectively. When they divided the population by type of institution, four-year degree completion rates varied substantially; 38.4% had graduated from public colleges, 50.8% from nonsectarian colleges, 55.5%, from Catholic colleges, and 72.0% from private colleges. The bachelor's degree completion rate for the participants in this study for those who had attended Barat College, a previously Catholic college, most closely resembled the national bachelor's degree completion rate for Catholic colleges. We, therefore, concluded that the bachelor's degree completion rates for those with and without learning disabilities were indeed very similar to the national statistics regarding graduation rate for this type of college.

In regard to graduate studies, more of the participants without learning disabilities completed a graduate or professional degree than among those with learning disabilities (20% vs. 12%). It is possible that attitudinal barriers and less awareness of learning disabilities among graduate and professional school faculty may have resulted in fewer students with learning disabilities graduating from graduate or professional school (Vogel, et al. 1998). Such barriers could have created a hostile environment in some graduate and professional schools, thus discouraging students with learning disabilities either from applying, or once enrolled, to persevere. Alternatively, since earlier studies reported that on average it took between one semester (Witte, et al. 1998) and one year longer (Greenbaum, et al. 1995; Vogel and Adelman 1992) for students with learning disabilities to complete their undergraduate degree, we expect that more of the adults with learning disabilities may enroll in a graduate program in the future. Perhaps when the next longitudinal study is conducted, the gap in graduate degrees earned will have been closed.

For those who did complete their master's degree, it is interesting to note that five out of the six participants in the group with learning disabilities completed their master's degree in education. This finding extends those of the earlier longitudinal study in which Adelman and Vogel (1990) reported that 30% of the undergraduates majored in education, (the largest proportion who majored in any one field). Among the participants without learning disabilities, there was more variability in their graduate studies, i.e., social work, psychology, Latin American Studies, and education. The choice of education for those with learning disabilities may also be related to students' perception that the faculty members in the College of Education are more willing to provide accommodations than faculty in other academic disciplines. This finding was partially confirmed by Vogel, et al. (1999) in their study regarding faculty attitude toward students with learning disabilities. They reported that although there was no significant difference between faculty in the College of Education compared to the rest of the faculty regarding willingness to provide instructional/teaching accommodations, faculty in the College of Education were significantly more willing to provide examination accommodations than were faculty in other academic disciplines. However, Vogel and co-workers (1999) pointed out that, in general, there is a high degree of willingness to accommodate which leads us to conclude that there may be additional factors in the decision-making process as to whether to pursue the master's degree in Education.

Another positive outcome in the present research with regard to employment was that there were no significant differences between the groups employed full or part time. These findings are very similar to Greenbaum's findings regarding the employment rate of adults with learning disabilities. However, it is important to keep in mind that employment, even full time employment, is not necessarily in and of itself a measure of success since salary could be at minimum or close to minimum wage. In our findings, the adults with learning disabilities held significantly more part time jobs than the adults without learning disabilities. Certainly, holding a variety of part-time jobs may be indicative of having had difficulty finding and/or keeping full time employment. On the other hand, frequent job changes could indicate that the adults with learning disabilities were searching for an environment in which they could find supportive colleagues, supervisors, and management, referred to as the right *social ecology* (Gerber, Ginsberg, and Reiff 1992). Alternatively, it may indicate that these individuals were searching for the right environment in which they could rely on their strengths and in which their weaknesses played a limited or no role in their performance on the job, a principal referred to by Gerber and co-workers (1992) as *goodness of fit*. The underlying assumption is that these individuals had to have an in-depth understanding of their learning disability and their strengths and weaknesses (as reported above). Self-understanding was also identified as one of the prerequisites to success in employment by Adelman and Vogel (1990), Gerber and co-workers (1992), Rogan and Hartman (1990), Silver and Hagin (1985), and Vogel, Hruby, and Adelman (1993), and enabled adults with learning disabilities to use their insight and understanding of their own learning disability to guide their career choices and employment settings.

Given that part-time employment may often be viewed as temporary and not necessarily in the area of preparation or congruent with one's career goals, we were interested to know if the participants with learning disabilities had more difficulty than their peers without learning disabilities in finding employment in a job related to their undergraduate major. If this were the case, our assumption was that they would report less congruity between these two. Our findings confirmed this assumption, but mainly for those employed part time. Specifically, those with leaning disabilities employed part time reported significantly less congruity between their undergraduate major and their present employment than those in the group without learning disabilities. This finding is not surprising since only 22% of those with learning disabilities had identified a career direction while in college. On the other hand, the finding that 78% of those with learning disabilities had identified their career choice only after they graduated from college lead Halpern (1992) to refer to the years following college graduation as the floundering years in which individuals with disabilities who experienced difficulty in career decision making experimented with a variety of jobs.

A more sensitive measure of employment success than full time employment that has been used nationally is occupational status based on the *Occupational Outlook Handbook*. Compared to other studies of occupational status for adults with learning disabilities, the finding that slightly more than two-thirds of the adults with learning disabilities compared to almost three-fourths of those without learning disabilities held jobs in the most prestigious occupational category, namely, professional/technical/managerial category is an encouraging finding. Our findings are even more surprising in light of the findings of Witte and co-workers (1998) who reported only 29% of the graduates in their sample were in jobs in the highest occupational category. On the other hand, Greenbaum, Graham, and Scales (1996) reported that 71% held jobs in the highest category. Upon close examination of the Witte and Greenbaum samples, it appears that the samples differed on one of the important parameters identified by Vogel (1996) in her analysis of differences in research design and methodology that seem to explain the contradictory findings in follow-up studies. In this case, the three studies varied in the number of years since exit or graduation from college. The Greenbaum sample, similar to the present sample, had been out of school much longer than the Witte sample perhaps allowing the participants to decide on a career choice, find the right job, perhaps complete graduate degrees, and advance in their employment setting.

We asked participants to identify how they found their present job and the largest proportion in both groups reported that they used the family-friends network about half the time. This finding confirms that of others regarding the use of the family-friends network. In a study conducted by Schwarz and Taymans (1991), 84% of the respondents found jobs through this network as did the participants in the Roessler (1990) follow-up study in which 79% reported finding jobs through personal contacts. However, it is interesting to note that about 20% of those with learning disabilities were entrepreneurial in spirit, i.e., were self-employed, perhaps because they had difficulty finding and maintaining a job. Although previous studies reported the frequent use of the family-friends network, our study confirms that this is not unique to those with learning disabilities. The adults with learning disabilities were very much like those without learning disabilities in the use of this specific job finding strategy.

The mean annual salaries for those employed full time was $38,500 for the group with learning disabilities and $39,018 for those without learning disabilities, while the median was $35,000 versus $32,000. Reported annual median income according to the US Bureau of Labor Statistics (1996–1997) for those with a bachelor's degree is $34,666. It is apparent that the median salary of those with learning disabilities is almost identical to the national income for those without learning disabilities who have similar levels of education. Considering how successful the group with learning disabilities was (i.e., there were no significant differences between the groups on educational attainment, proportion employed full time, occupational status, percent in full time jobs, longevity on the job, and annual salary), we asked ourselves what made this group so successful given the significant reading, written expression, spelling, and math deficits they had at entrance to college as compared to their peers without learning disabilities.

Some of the factors contributing to the success of these adults with learning disabilities relate to the screening and admissions criteria for entrance to the college and the support program. Applicants who were accepted to the program had average or above intelligence, mild to moderate learning disabilities, high school academic preparation and performance commensurate with applicants without learning disabilities to the college, a positive attitude toward the teaching/learning environment, a high level of motivation to achieve in college based on letters of recommendation and self-report, and the persistence and stamina to sustain their efforts and delay gratification for a long period of time (Adelman 1988; Adelman and Vogel 1993; Vogel 2000; Vogel and Adelman 1992; Vogel, et al. 1993).

Although all of the applicants were screened and thought to meet these criteria, not all were equally successful. Therefore, we scrutinized their comments in regard to compensatory strategies they used to overcome the negative impact of their learning disability, their reasons for disclosing or not disclosing their learning disability, and advice they would give to other adults with learning disabilities preparing to enter the same profession.

Their comments confirmed some of the key factors that Gerber and co-workers (1992) identified that contributed to employment success. The first was *internal reframing* which refers to . . . *reinterpreting the learning disability experience in a more positive or productive manner.* (p. 481). For example, several of the adults attributed their strengths to their learning disability, that is they believed that they would not have had these strengths if it were not for their learning disability. One specific comment provided evidence of having reached a very high level of acceptance of a learning disability as can be seen in the comment, *I wouldn't give it up even if I could.*

However, the reframing process, according to Gerber and his colleagues, is not sufficient to achieve success unless there are external manifestations of the process. These manifestations became apparent when we asked the participants what advice they would give to other adults with learning disabilities preparing for jobs in their profession. Many of the comments referred to the stamina they had to have, their willingness to work hard and to be persistent as exemplified best by the comment *Never give up.* This finding regarding the perseverance and high level of motivation present in these adults confirms the finding of Gerber and co-workers (1992), Greenbaum and co-workers (1996), Rogan and Hartman (1990), Spekman and co-workers (1992), and Vogel and co-workers (1993).

Another external manifestation of the reframing process is *Learned Creativity* defined as the ability to develop compensatory strategies in order to overcome the effect of the learning disability on performance. The adults with learning disabilities listed 89 strategies that they used to accomplish job responsibilities. Some of the specific strategies were the use of technology, and organizational, memory, and self-awareness strategies. Lastly, is the principle of finding the right *Social Ecology*, that is the environment in which there are supportive and empathetic coworkers, staff, secretaries, supervisors, mentors, and friends. Recognizing the need to find a supportive environment perhaps lead participants with learning disabilities to change jobs more frequently than those in the group without learning disabilities, especially those in part-time jobs.

We were surprised to learn that as many as 59% of those employed and whose learning disability affected them negatively had disclosed their learning disability. Moreover, it was also interesting to learn that about 20% had disclosed during the job application process when the stakes were the highest. When asked why they had disclosed, we were surprised to learn that only one person out of the 16 who reported that their learning disability affected them negatively had disclosed in order to receive an accommodation. The others reported that they disclosed because they wanted their coworkers to understand them better, to be more empathetic, or to understand learning disabilities in general. None disclosed that they had a learning disability to someone in the Human Resources Office. The reasons they had disclosed indicated that many were very comfortable with the fact that they had a learning disability; they did not see it as *a big deal*. They also stated that they felt comfortable in explaining their learning disability to others precisely because they were successful and able to compensate. However, as was reported by Witte and co-workers (1998) and Greenbaum et al. (1996), the 11 participants who did not disclose expressed fear of negative consequences and/or fear of discrimination, e.g., being bypassed for promotion or being looked down upon.

More research is needed regarding the consequences of disclosure and constructive ways of dealing with disclosure issues. The limited familiarity with The Americans with Disabilities Act among those with learning disabilities revealed the need for providing information and workshops about ADA for adolescents and adults with learning disabilities while they are in high school or college. Such discussions could include reasons for disclosure, the pros and cons of disclosure, the timing, setting, wording, and person to whom to disclose, procedures to follow if accommodations are needed, and possible benefits and debits. Such information also needs to be provided to employers at all levels in the work force in order to broaden understanding of learning disabilities, ADA, and alternative accommodations, to dispel myths, and to change attitudes regarding learning disabilities.

Limitations

It is important to keep in mind that this sample was drawn from an institution of higher education with explicit admissions criteria and in which applicants disclosed that they had a learning disability and requested support services in the admissions process. Moreover, the respondents to this telephone interview had participated in a support program in which an extensive battery of tests was administered in order to monitor students' progress, develop an individual plan, and assist in academic advisement and the development of compensatory strategies. The test battery results were explained to the participants thoroughly using non-technical terminology in order to enhance self-understanding regarding the nature of their learning disability, identify goals and undergraduate major, and career directions.

Future Research

This study has provided guidelines for search strategies for location of graduates, for interview and script development, and interviewer training that all institutions could follow. The foundation for follow-up research should be laid while the adults with learning disabilities are still on campus by explaining to them the importance of the longitudinal research program. Offering incentives for their participation such as availability of specific services (e.g., electronic access to career-focused support groups, job coaching, job placement information, notification regarding job fairs and interviewers on campus and/or monetary compensation, gift certificates, tickets to campus activities, and others in exchange for notification of changes of address and telephone numbers will help to increase their willingness to participate in future follow-up studies.

There are several topics that need to be explored in depth in future research. For example, more research is needed regarding the complex issue of disclosure including the decision-making process (to disclose or not to disclose), the benefits and costs of disclosing as opposed to not disclosing, the timing of disclosure, the purpose of disclosure, to whom to disclose, the scripting of disclosure, etc. Increasing awareness and understanding of the complex process involved in disclosure of one's learning disability, whether in higher education, in employment settings, or in one's personal life, has many practical implications. Follow-up studies could also become not only a method of determining outcomes and monitoring changes, but also a meaningful way of providing continuing support, information, and referral, as the needs arise.

ACKNOWLEDGEMENT

This research was supported by a grant from the Thorn River Foundation.

The authors wish to express appreciation to the participants and interviewers who assisted in conducting this study. Special thanks to Ms. Alexa Darby who assisted in the development of the interview strategies, and to Dr. Peter Abrams for his able assistance in data analysis.

REFERENCES

Adelman, P. B. 1988. An approach to meeting the needs of the learning disabled student in a four-year college. In *College and the Learning Disabled College Student: Program Development, Implementation, and Selection,* eds. C. T. Mangrum II and S. S. Strichart, (2nd ed.), (pp. 237–49). Philadelphia: Grune & Stratton.

Adelman, P. B., and Vogel, S. A. 1990. College graduates with learning disabilities: Employment attainment and career patterns. *Learning Disability Quarterly* 13(3), 154–66.

Adelman, P. B., and Vogel, S. A. 1993. Issues in the employment of adults with learning disabilities. *Learning Disability Quarterly* 16(3), 219–32.

Adelman, P. B., and Vogel, S.A. 1998. Adults with learning disabilities. In *Learning about Learning Disabilities,* ed. B. Wong, (2nd ed.), (pp. 657–701). New York: Academic Press.

Affleck, J. Q., Edgar, E., Levine, P., and Kortering, L. 1990, Postschool status of students classified as mildly mentally retarded, learning disabled, non-handicapped: Does it get better with time? *Education and Training in Mental Retardation* 25(4), 315–24.

Americans with Disabilities Act of 1990, PL 101-336, 42 U.S.C. § 12101 et seq.

Astin, A. W., Tsui, L., and Avalos, J. 1996. *Degree Attainment Rates at American Colleges and Universities: Effects of Race, Gender; and Institutional Type.* Los Angeles: Higher Education Research Institute, UCLA.

Blackorby, J., and Wagner, M. 1996. Longitudinal postschool outcomes of youth with disabilities: Findings from the National Longitudinal Transition Study. *Exceptional Children* 62(5), 399–413.

Bruininks, R. H., Wolman, C., and Thurlow, M. L. 1990. Considerations in designing survey studies and follow-up systems for special education service programs. *Remedial and Special Education* 11, 7–17.

The College Board 1978. *Descriptive Tests of Language Skills*. Princeton, NJ: Educational Testing Service.

Education for All Handicapped Children Act of 1975, PL94-142,20 U.S.C. § 1400 et seq.

Gerber, P. J., Ginsberg, R., and Reiff, H. B. 1992. Identifying alterable patterns in employment success for highly successful adults with learning disabilities. *Journal of Learning Disabilities* 25, 475–87.

Greenbaum, B. 1993. A follow-up survey of students with learning disabilities after exiting a postsecondary institution. (Doctoral dissertation. University of Maryland, 1993). *Dissertation Abstracts International* 54–08, Section A, 2981.

Greenbaum, B., Graham, S., and Scales, W. 1995. Adults with learning disabilities: Educational and social experiences during college. *Exceptional Children* 61, 460–71.

Greenbaum, B. L., Graham, S., and Scales, W. 1996. Adults with learning disabilities: Occupational and social status after college. *Journal of Learning Disabilities* 29, 167–73.

Halpern, A. 1992. Transition: Old wine in new bottles. *Exceptional Children* 8: 202–11.

Karlsen, B., Madden, R., and Gardner, E. 1974. *Stanford Diagnostic Reading Test*. New York: Harcourt Brace Jovanovich, Inc.

Kirsch, I. S.. Jungeblut, A., Jenkins. L., and Kilstad, A. 1993, September. *Adult Literacy in America: A First Look at the Results of the National Adult Literacy Survey*. Prepared by Educational Testing Service under contract with the National Center for Education Statistics, Office of Educational Research and Improvement. US Department of Education.

Levine, P. 1993. Gender Differences in Long-term Postschool Outcomes for Youth and Mild Mental Retardation, Learning Disabilities and No Disabilities: Myth or Reality? Unpublished doctoral dissertation, University of Washington, Seattle.

Levine, P., and Edgar, E. 1995. An analysis by gender of long-term postschool outcomes for youth with and without disabilities. *Exceptional Children* 61, 282–301.

Marder, C., and D'Amico, R. 1992. *How Well are Youth with Disabilities Really Doing? A Comparison of Youth with Disabilities and Youth in General*. Menlo Park, CA: National Longitudinal Transition Study, SRI International.

Nesbit, J., and Lichtenstein, S. 1992. Following the lives of young adults with disabilities in New Hampshire. Durham, NH: Institute on Disability/UAP., University of New Hampshire.

Raskind, M., Goldberg, R. Higgins. E., and Herman, K. 1999. Patterns of change and predictors of success in individuals with learning disabilities: Results from a twenty-year longitudinal study. *Learning Disabilities Research and Practice* 14(1), 35–49.

Reder, S. 1995. *Literacy, Education, and Learning Disabilities*. Portland, OR: Northwest Regional Educational Laboratory.

Reder, S., and Vogel, S. A. 1997. Life-span employment and economic outcomes for adults with self-reported leaning disabilities. In *Learning Disabilities and Employment*, eds. P. Gerber and D. Brown, (pp. 371–94). Austin, TX: PRO-ED.

Roessler, R. T. 1990. A quality of life perspective on rehabilitation counseling. *Rehabilitation Counseling Bulletin* 34(3), 82–90.

Rogan. L. L., and Hartman, L. D. 1990. Adult outcome of learning disabled students 10 years after initial follow-up. *Learning Disabilities Focus* 5(2), 91–102.

Schwarz, S. L., and Taymans, J. M. 1991. Urban vocational/technical program completers with learning disabilities. *Journal for Vocational Special Needs Education* 13, 15–20.

Silver, A. A., and Hagin, R. A. 1985. Outcomes of learning disabilities in adolescence. *Annals of the American Society for Adolescent Psychiatry* 12(14), 197–213.

Sitlington, P. L., and Frank, A. R. 1990. Are adolescents with learning disabilities successfully crossing the bridge into adult life? *Learning Disabilities Research and Practice* 8(4), 244–52.

Spekman, N. J., Goldberg, R. J., and Herman, K. L. 1992. Learning disabled children grow up: A search for factors related to success in the young adult years. *Learning Disabilities Research and Practice* 7(3), 161–70.

US Department of Labor. (1996–1997). *Occupational Outlook Handbook.* Bureau of Labor Statistics. Bulletin 2470.

Vogel, S. A. 1982. On developing LD college programs. *Journal of Learning Disabilities* 15, 518–28.

Vogel. S. A. 1996. Adults with learning disabilities: Research questions and methodological issues in planning a research agenda for 2000 and beyond. *The Canadian Journal of Special Education* 11(2), 33–54.

Vogel, S. A. (2000). *College Students with Learning Disabilities: A Handbook for Students with Learning Disabilities, Faculty, Administrators, and Admissions Counselors* (7th ed.). Pittsburgh: Learning Disabilities Association of America.

Vogel, S. A., and Adelman, P. B. 1990. Extrinsic and intrinsic factors in graduation and academic failure among LD college students. *Annals of Dyslexia* (Orton Dyslexia Society) 40, 119–37.

Vogel, S. A., and Adelman, P. B. 1992. The success of college students with learning disabilities: Factors related to educational attainment. *Journal of Learning Disabilities* 25, 430–41.

Vogel, S. A., Leyser, Y., Wyland, S., and Brulle, A. 1999. Students with Learning Disabilities in Higher Education: Faculty Attitude and Practice. *Learning Disabilities Research and Practice* 14(3): 173–86.

Witte, R., Philips, L., and Kakela, M. 1998. Job Satisfaction of College Graduates with Learning Disabilities. *Journal of Learning Disabilities* 31(3): 259–65.

Chapter • 15

Life-Style Issues of Adults with Learning Disabilities
8 to 15 Years after College

Pamela B. Adelman and Susan A. Vogel

Recognition that learning disabilities affect individuals across their life span has resulted in considerable research, within the past 20 years, on college-age students and adults with learning disabilities. Most of this research has focused on educational programming and attainment and on employment (Adelman 1988; Adelman and Vogel 1990; Gerber 1992; Reder and Vogel 1997; Vogel 1982, 1997; Vogel and Adelman 1990; Vogel, Hruby, and Adelman 1993). In contrast to the extensive research in employment and educational attainment, only a few studies have focused on social and emotional well being. Findings from these studies indicated that adults with learning disabilities are often dependent on their families for financial and social support. Many continue to live with their parents well past the traditional age of independence and their social lives tend to revolve around family functions well beyond the norm. Problems with making and keeping friends (Blalock 1981; Bruck 1985; Fafard and Haubrich 1981) and participating in social activities with peers continue into adulthood (Fafard and Haubrich 1981; Haring, Lovett, and Smith 1990; Menkes, Rowe, and Menkes 1967; Scuccimarra and Speece 1990; Spekman et al. 1989).

The Learning Disabilities Association of America (They Speak for Themselves 1996) conducted an in-depth study on attainment of independence in living arrangements, financial management, and social interpersonal relationships in adults with LD. Their survey revealed that 32% of the adults with LD were living with their parents, whereas 25% were living with a spouse and 22% were living alone. Finances were managed independently by 49% of the adults who participated in LDA's survey, while 20% reported that their parents managed finances. Fourteen percent said that spouses managed their finances. Twenty-five percent reported that they had no close friends, while 74% had friends of the same sex and 64% had friends of both sexes. Forty-nine percent rated their social lives as fair or poor.

The National Longitudinal Transition Study (NLTS) initially identified a nationally representative sample of 8,000 young adults from the 13 disability categories as defined by federal law at the time of the study. Blackorby and Wagner (1996) identified a subsample of 1,990 students who participated in data collection in 1985–1986 and again in 1990 when they had been out of secondary school between three and five years. One of the outcomes examined was residential independence. Although the percentage of individuals with LD who were living independently increased from when they were out of secondary school less than two years to when they were out three to five years (14.7% versus 44.1%), they still lagged far behind the general population of youth living independently (60%).

In addition to studies identifying an impact of LD on residential independence, financial management, and social life, there is evidence that learning disabilities have interfered with the psychological well being of adults with LD and have placed their emotional health and physical health at risk (Cohen 1985; Spekman et al. 1989; Werner and Smith 1992). Werner and Smith (1992) conducted an important longitudinal study that investigated the psychological and emotional status of 22 adults with LD (32 years old at last data collection) as compared to their non-LD peers matched on gender, socio-economic status, and ethnic background. This study, sometimes called the Kauai Longitudinal Study, periodically assessed this multiracial cohort of 698 infants born on the island of Kauai in 1955. The 22 individuals from the total cohort who were identified at age 10 as having LD and their matched controls have been studied closely to identify the risk and resiliency factors that have contributed to the reported outcomes. One of the surprising findings of this study is that the outcomes have changed over time from a very discouraging prognosis in their late teens to very positive outcomes in their 30s. In their teens, 27% of LD versus 5% of non-LD individuals had some contact with police. By age 32, the LD and non-LD young adults appeared very similar in that there was no significant difference in the percent who had police records, were divorced, or who had significant mental health problems.

To date, several studies have been conducted on successful adults with learning disabilities where success was based on work related issues, i.e., status of their job, eminence within their occupation,

income, and job satisfaction (Adelman and Vogel 1990; Gerber, Ginsberg, and Reiff 1992; Rogan and Hartman 1990). Using these standards for success, they found that persons with some college
experience fell into the moderately to highly successful group. Because a college education was related to more positive outcomes regarding employment, we are interested in whether having a
postsecondary education resulted in more positive life style outcomes.

Greenbaum (1993) assessed social status of 49 individuals with
LD after graduation from college. She reported that 21 (43%) lived
with their parents, which she attributed to the high cost of living independently. Sixty-one percent received monetary contributions from
their parents. Participants were involved in a number of social activities, and 82% indicated that they were satisfied with their social lives.

Another follow-up study that included a subgroup of 30 college
graduates was conducted by Rogan and Hartman (1990). A major difference of this study's population was age at follow-up. Whereas the
mean age of participants in the Greenbaum study was 26 years old,
the individuals in the Rogan and Hartman study were between the
ages of 30 and 40 years old. Seventy-nine percent of the 28 who responded lived independently with their spouses or alone. Only 18%
were living with parents or another relative. However, only 29% were
married, and only 18% reported having children. Sixty-eight percent
judged their life satisfaction as highly positive.

Vogel and Adelman (see chapter 14) attribute these often contradictory findings to methodological differences and/or problems, such
as: the lack of a non-LD comparison group; the lack of a sufficient
number of years elapsing since exit from high school or college; or differences in selection criteria and/or outcomes. (See Adelman and
Vogel [1993] and Vogel [1996] for a complete review of these methodological differences and/or problems.) In view of: (a) these methodological problems; (b) the paucity of follow-up studies of college-able
adults with LD and, in those that do exist, often a lack of non-LD comparison groups; (c) the number of years (8–15) that had elapsed since
the adults in our first follow-up study had either graduated or exited
from college; and (d) the limited number of studies on adults with LD
who attended or graduated from college that focused on employment
and life style issues, we felt it important to include in our second longitudinal study questions regarding the impact of LD on:

1. achieving independence as an adult
2. one's social life
3. physical and emotional health and
4. factors that caused problems and changes needed to improve the quality of one's life.

METHODOLOGY

The LD and NLD Groups

The total number of possible participants consisted of 107 adults with LD and 153 non-LD (NLD) adults who entered Barat College between 1980 and 1988 and met the selection criteria for participation. Though more than 107 students were enrolled in the LD support program during those years, participants in the longitudinal study had to meet the following criteria: average or above IQ; at least a two-year discrepancy between their cognitive abilities and one or more aspects of academic achievement; English as their native language; and no concomitant disability. The 107 adults with LD were matched with NLD students on gender and year of entry to college. None of the NLD adults had a history of receiving special education services. (For a more detailed description of the college, the support services, the application process, entrance requirements for students with LD, and cognitive abilities and academic achievement, see Adelman 1988; Vogel 1982; Vogel and Adelman 1990.)

Through the use of a variety of search strategies, 57 (53%) of the adults with LD and 59 (39%) of the NLD adults were located. (See chapter 14 for a detailed description of search strategies.) Of those who were located, 50 (88%) of those with LD and 41 (70%) of the NLD agreed to participate in a telephone interview lasting 30 to 60 minutes.

The interview consisted of four parts. The first three parts included basic demographic information, educational attainment, and extensive information regarding employment history, present employment status, and the impact of LD on the job. Results of the first three parts are reported in Chapter 14. Part IV addressed quality of life issues, which included living arrangements, personal responsibilities, mobility, financial status, leisure activities, vacations, presence of other disabilities, counseling and health issues, and specific factors affecting the quality of life (for an in-depth description of the development of the questionnaire and the qualification and training of interviewers, see chapter 14 and Darby, Vogel, and Adelman 2001).

Data Analysis

Frequencies were computed for each item in the survey by group and by gender within each group. The LD and NLD groups were compared on Part IV of the survey. Categorical data and items that used a five-point scale (e.g., from "not at all" to "a lot") were tested between groups using chi-square analyses. Examples of categorical data include race, marital status, living arrangements, etc. Dichotomous data arising from yes-no responses were compared via tests of proportions. Quantitative data, such as number of years receiving counseling or number of years living in the same residence, were compared using t-tests and ANOVA. A separate variance estimate of the standard error was used when the variances of the groups were significantly different (p < .05). Comments made in response to the open-ended questions were categorized. First, categories were identified based on content analysis and qualitative data analysis strategies. Then, comments were assigned to categories independently by the co-authors and the lead interviewer. Consensus between the co-authors and interviewer was 97%.

RESULTS

Background Information

Age. The adults with LD were significantly younger ($M = 33.79$, $SD = 5.47$) ($t = -2.78$, $df = 66.10$, $p < .01$) than the NLD adults ($M = 38.02$, $SD = 8.41$). When we grouped the participants by decade, we found that there was a higher proportion of individuals in the LD group in their 30s (62% versus 53%) and fewer in their 40s (6% versus 17%) than in the NLD group. One factor influencing age difference was that this college attracted a large proportion of non-traditional age students (defined as 25 years or older at entrance) who chose to return to college studies after their children were of school-age. A higher percentage of participants with LD were often of traditional age (18–24) eight to fifteen years ago when they entered the college than the population of this college as a whole (see table I).

Years since exit from college or highest degree. Since responses to questions regarding personal, financial, and social independence are heavily influenced by the number of years in the workforce or profession (rather than age per se), we compared the groups on the number of years that had elapsed since exiting from college (if they had

Table I. Age of Participants

| Age Range | LD[a] | | NLD[b] | |
	N	%	N	%
20–30	16	32	8	20
31–35	23	46	12	29
36–40	8	16	10	24
41–45	1	2	2	5
46–50	2	4	5	12
51–55	0	0	3	7
56–60	0	0	1	2

[a]$N = 50$, $M = 33.79$, $SD = 5.47$
[b]$N = 41$, $M = 38.02$, $SD = 8.41$
$p < .01$

not completed their bachelor's degree) or the number of years since completing their highest degree. The mean number of years for both groups was almost identical (8 years). We, therefore, concluded that there were no significant differences between the groups on years since exit from college of completion of highest degree. Therefore, we have confidence that years since exit or highest degree completion were not going to have an impact on the group comparisons.

Gender.   The gender ratio in both groups was 4:1 females with LD to males, the reverse of the expected ratio because this college had been a college for women until 1982 and still attracted more females than males.

Ethnicity.   Forty-three (86%) were Caucasian among the LD group (1 African American, 3 Hispanic American, and 2 multi-racial), compared to 37 (90%) Caucasian in the NLD group (3 African American and 1 Asian American).

Marital status and parenting.   Given the tendency for women born around 1970 and later to marry in their 30s and to delay marriage and child bearing until after they were established in their careers, it was not unexpected to find that 21 (42%) in the LD group were single, which is slightly more than twice the proportion who were single in the NLD group (8[20%]). Because more of those in the NLD were married (27 [66%]) versus 25 [50%]), the divorce rate was also higher in the NLD group (10% as compared to 4%). Lastly, it follows logically that many more among the NLD group were parents (61%) as compared to those in the LD group (40%) because the NLD group was significantly older and more were married. (For an overview of the demographic variables, see table II.)

INDEPENDENCE

Living Arrangements

Because we were interested in whether the adults with LD were more dependent on their families, we first asked about their living arrangements. There was no significant difference in the number of LD and NLD living alone. Thirty-two percent of adults with LD versus 22% of the NLD reported living alone. Since more of the NLD were married, it was expected that more of them were living with spouses (85% versus 67% of the adults with LD). Although there was no significant difference, it is noteworthy that 11% of LD reported living with parents, siblings, and relatives as compared to 6% of the NLD adults (see table III).

There was no significant difference in the number of years that the LD and NLD had lived in their present arrangement. Over 50% of both groups were living in the same place for over five years. Sixty per-

Table II.   Demographic Variables

Variable	LD[a]		NLD[b]	
	N	%	N	%
Gender Distribution				
Male	13	26	10	24
Female	37	74	31	76
Ethnicity				
Caucasian	43	86	37	90
African-American	1	2	3	7
Asian	0	0	1	2
Hispanic-American	3	6	0	0
Multi-racial	2	4	0	0
Preferred not to answer	1	2	0	0
Marital Status				
Single	21	42	8	20
Married	25	50	27	66
Separated	1	2	1	2
Divorced	2	4	4	10
Widowed	1	2	1	2
Parenting				
Yes	20	40	25	61
No	30	60	16	39

[a]N = 50
[b]N = 41

Table III.   Individuals with whom LD and NLD Participants are Living

Variable	LD[a]		NLD[b]	
	N	%	N	%
Parents	1	3	1	3
Siblings	1	3	1	3
Relatives	2	5	0	0
Spouses	24	67	28	85
Friends	3	8	0	0
Significant Other	5	14	3	9

[a]N = 36
[b]N = 33

cent of the LD and 80% of the NLD lived in their own home or condominium. Thirty-two percent of the LD group rented, as compared to only 17% of the NLD. The fact that more NLD owned either a home or condominium was also expected, since NLD adults were older, more were married and had children. Only one participant in each group reported living in his or her parent's home (see tables IV and V).

Responsibility for Others

Fifty-six percent of NLD adults versus 39% of adults with LD responded that they had responsibility for others. Of those who had

Table IV.   Number of Years in the Present Arrangement

Number of Years	LDª		NLDᵇ	
	N	%	N	%
1 Year	6	12	2	5
1–2 Years	8	16	6	15
3–5 Years	9	18	10	24
5+ Years	27	54	23	56

　　ªN = 50
　　ᵇN = 41

Table V.   Where LD and NLD Presently Live

Variable	LDª		NLDᵇ	
	N	%	N	%
Parent's Home	1	2	1	2
Relative's Home	2	4	0	0
Friend's Home	1	2	0	0
Rental	16	32	7	17
Own Home/Condo	30	60	33	81

　　ªN = 50
　　ᵇN = 41

responsibility for others, most participants in both groups were caring for children (90% for adults with LD versus 96% of the NLD). This finding was not surprising since more of the NLD were older, married, and had children. Two of the adults with LD and three of the NLD also cared for either parents or other relatives.

Financial Independence

We were interested in finding out if participants with LD were more dependent financially. There was no significant difference in financial independence between the two groups (70% for LD compared to 74% for NLD). However, there were some interesting differences regarding the individuals who provided support to those who were not financially independent. Whereas ten of the eleven NLD who received support indicated that they received it from their spouses, only seven of the 15 in the LD group received support from their spouses. Six continued to receive support from their parents, a seventh reported receiving support from a friend, and an eighth from a sister.

Driving

Prior research indicated that a high percentage of adults with LD either did not apply or were not eligible for a driver's license and had orientation problems that inhibited mobility (Blalock 1981; Fafard and Haubrich 1981). Given these earlier findings, we asked participants if they had a driver's license. All participants in the NLD group and all but one person in the LD group had a license.

We then asked the participants with LD if they thought their LD affected their driving. Eleven (22%) of the LD responded that it did affect their driving and negatively rather than positively. The most frequently reported problem was directionality (32%). Twenty percent of the comments indicated that difficulties with visual functioning affected driving, including problems with depth perception, reaction time, and judging spatial relationships. Another 20% of the comments noted difficulty with reading maps. Three comments (12%) pointed to poor attention as affecting driving. Two respondents (8%) indicated that the LD caused anxiety about driving, and another two responses noted that deficient academic skills affected driving. One participant had difficulty reading road signs and another reported trouble with passing a written driving test.

Those attributing difficulties with driving to their LD were asked if they thought their LD may have contributed to accidents. Three participants responded that they believe that accidents they had were related to their LD. For example, one responded that problems with spatial relations resulted in rear ending someone.

EFFECT OF LD ON PERSONAL LIFE

In spite of the independence that most adults with LD reported with respect to their living arrangements, financial status, and mobility, almost half (23 of 50) responded in the affirmative to our question, "Does your learning disability affect your personal life?" Twenty-three participants with LD (46%) reported that their LD affected their personal lives. Thirty-nine percent of the comments describing the effect of their LD on their personal lives indicated that they experienced emotional problems as a result of their LD. Wishing to be someone else, low self-esteem and self-confidence, feeling embarrassed, insecure, and overwhelmed were among the emotional effects of having LD. Other responses mentioned a lack of friends and/or a preference for being alone because they were afraid others would find out about their LD. Problems with executive functioning, specifically time management and organization, accounted for 18% of the comments. Ongoing difficulty with language skills was cited almost as frequently as executive functioning (16% versus 18%). Participants reported difficulties with both oral and written language. Nine percent of the comments centered on academic skills. One parent mentioned how her language-based LD affected her ability to help her child with homework.

Comments indicted that problems with information processing, poor motor coordination, and inappropriate interpersonal skills affected their personal lives. One comment expressed the global impact the LD had on the participant's personal life, when she reported: "It affects everything I do."

However, not all comments described a negative impact of LD. Some participants viewed their LD very positively. Ten percent of the comments were categorized as positive and included statements, such as, "makes me more creative" and "I love it about me." One participant said it made her a better parent because she has a better understanding of her children.

SOCIAL LIFE

Leisure Time and Vacations

We were interested in social life and friendship patterns. When asked with whom the individuals with LD spent their leisure time and with whom they took vacations, participants with LD indicated that they spent slightly more time with parents than did NLD individuals. This difference was insignificant and could be attributed at least in part to marital status, since more individuals with LD were single. Marital status may also explain why more NLD spent both leisure time and vacations with spouses and children, whereas more participants with LD reported spending this time with significant others.

Because feelings of social isolation were often expressed, because participants with LD feared being found out or because they had difficulty communicating with others, we examined very closely the responses of those individuals who indicated that they spend leisure time and vacation time alone. We realized that many people spent some time alone, so we differentiated between those who spent some of the time alone versus those who spent all of the time alone. For both leisure time and vacations, there were more individuals with LD who spent some time alone than individuals in the NLD group (leisure time 18% versus 7%; vacation time 14% versus 5%). Nine participants with LD responded "alone" as one of the choices in response to the question, "With whom do you spend your leisure time?" Seven of the nine also spent time with other people. Seven participants with LD said "alone" in response to the question, "With whom do you take vacations?" Four also responded that they also took vacations with other people. For both questions, two participants only responded "alone;" one participant's spouse had recently died, and the other reported being depressed and very lonely. Only one of the NLD reported spending leisure time only alone (see table VI).

Leisure Activities

Because earlier research indicated the limitations in scope of leisure activities that adults with LD might participate in as a result of their

Table VI.   With whom do you spend your leisure time and vacations?

	Leisure Time				Vacations			
	LD[a]		NLD[b]		LD[c]		NLD[d]	
Individual	N	%	N	%	N	%	N	%
Parents	21	42	12	29	18	36	8	20
Siblings	15	30	11	27	12	24	7	17
Other relatives	5	10	12	29	3	6	4	10
Friends	19	38	22	54	15	30	12	29
Children	25	50	27	66	14	28	19	46
Spouse	36	72	31	76	25	50	27	66
Significant other	10	20	5	12	11	22	4	10
Alone	9	18	3	7	7	14	2	5

[a]$N = 140$ responses   [c]$N = 105$ responses
[b]$N = 123$ responses   [d]$N = 83$ responses

specific learning disabilities, we asked participants, "In which leisure activities do you participate?" From responses, it was evident that both groups participated in numerous activities during their leisure time. Participants with LD mentioned a total of 502 activities ($M =10$) as compared to 420 ($M = 10.2$) reported by the NLD group. In terms of differences in the types of activities, there was very little variation. Even the leisure activity of reading, which was so difficult for the individuals with LD, was reported with approximately the same frequency for both groups (8% LD versus 9% NLD, respectively). (See table VII for a complete list of leisure activities.)

Effect of LD on Participation in Leisure and Community Activities

Despite the number of leisure activities in which individuals with LD participated, 27 reported that their LD affected them negatively during leisure activities and six said it also had a negative impact on involvement in community activities. The most frequent category describing how one's LD affected leisure activities was emotional problems (37%). Emotional problems included low self-confidence and anxiety. One participant reported that anxiety prevents her from participating in activities. She "won't try." Depression and "painful loneliness" were also reported. Two comments described how difficulties with interpersonal relationships and self-esteem affected involvement in leisure activities. For example, one participant explained that it is very hard for her to introduce herself to new people because of oral communication problems and because she is fearful of rejection.

Information processing deficits (15%) cited as affecting participation in leisure activities included memory (e.g., affected their ability to play games) and auditory figure ground difficulties (e.g., inability to speak on the phone when the TV is on). Ongoing problems with academic skills (15% of the comments) also affected leisure activities. For example, one participant explained that homework takes longer, and

Table VII.   In which leisure activities do you participate?

Leisure Activities	LD[a]		NLD[b]	
	N	%	N	%
Watching Television	44	9	39	9
Going to the Movies	40	8	37	9
Participating in Religious Activities	25	5	25	6
Attending Sports Events	27	5	22	5
Attending Plays	38	8	28	7
Attending Concerts	32	6	25	6
Physical Activity	49	10	43	10
Regular Exercising	34	7	28	7
Shopping	39	8	29	7
"Hanging Out"	54	11	36	9
Talking on the Phone	42	8	29	7
Reading	40	8	38	9
Travel	2	.3	10	2
Games	2	.3	2	.5
Computers	3	.5	1	.2
Hobbies	13	3	14	3
Participation in the Arts	6	1	11	3
Participation in Organizations	3	.5	0	0
Volunteering	2	.3	1	.2
Going to Amusement Parks	1	.1	1	.2
Museums/Lectures	5	1	1	.2
Other	1	.1	0	0

[a]N = 502 Leisure activities; M = 210
[b]N = 420 Leisure activities; M = 10.2

therefore, reduces the amount of time for leisure activities. Reading was cited as having an impact, particularly if required to read in front of others.

Though by far the exception, one participant described the positive impact of her LD on leisure activities in that it gave her more energy and resulted in her ability to be more active. (See table VIII for the entire list of ways in which the LD affected participation in leisure activities.)

Table VIII.   Effect of LD on Leisure Activities

Effect	LD[a]	
	N	%
Emotional Reactions	10	37
Academic Skills	4	15
Motor Abilities	4	15
Information Processing	4	15
Attention	1	4
Time Management	1	4
Distorted Self-image	1	4
Positive Impact	1	4
Global	1	4

[a]N = 27

There were only five comments in response to the question, "Has your LD affected your participation in community activities?" Two comments involved emotional difficulties (i.e., anger control and lack of self-confidence), one noted problems with time management, and another reported that oral expression difficulties affected participation, and, as a result, this respondent did not want to speak in front of groups of people. Once again, there was a positive comment: "Made me want to help others more and reach out."

Social Life

We asked participants to rate their satisfaction with their social lives. There were no significant differences in how the LD and NLD groups rated their social lives. On a likert scale ranging from 1 (not very satisfying) to 5 (very satisfying), 60% of the adults with LD rated their social life as highly satisfying compared to 71% of the NLD group. Although there were no significant differences, it is important to note that 18% of the adults with LD versus 10% of the NLD found their social lives not very satisfying. This finding is not surprising given the number of responses from participants with LD who feared "being found out" and mentioned feeling of loneliness and social isolation (see table IX).

EMOTIONAL AND PHYSICAL HEALTH

Counseling

As a result of the debilitating psychosocial effects of LD reported in the literature, we were interested in whether participants were receiving counseling, and if so, the duration and type of counseling. Fifty-six percent of the LD group compared to 34% of the NLD were receiving counseling at the time of the interview, and 46% of the LD group versus 21% of the NLD had received counseling for over five years.

Of those receiving counseling, both groups reported that the individual they saw most frequently for counseling was either a

Table IX. Rating of Social Life

Satisfying	LD[a]		NLD[b]	
	N	%	N	%
1 (Not very)	2	4	2	5
2	7	14	2	5
3	11	22	8	20
4	15	30	16	39
5 (Very	15	30	13	32

[a]N = 50
[b]N = 41

psychologist or a psychiatrist. Counselors and social workers were the next most frequently seen (see table X).

We were also interested in the type of counseling received. Of those receiving counseling, both LD (96%) and NLD (86%) reported that personal counseling was the most frequent type. Marital counseling was the next most frequent type of counseling (32% LD versus 21% NLD), followed by career counseling (29% LD versus 14% NLD) (see table XI).

Support Groups

There was no significant difference in the number of respondents who participated in support groups (21% of the LD versus 12% of the NLD). Of particular interest were the types of support groups in which the LD and NLD participated. The NLD adults attended parenting groups, women's groups, Bible study, and play groups. One participant went to Alanon, a support group for families of individuals addicted to alcohol. One participant with LD also attended a women's group and another also attended Alanon. Otherwise, the support groups were quite different. Other support groups in which the adults with LD participated were: ADD/ADHD, assistance in quitting smoking, weight control, domestic violence, grieving, job search, teacher support, and cancer.

Table X.   Individuals Seen for Counseling

Individuals	LD[a]		NLD[b]	
	N	%	N	%
Psychologist	17	61	5	36
Counselor	6	21	3	21
Social Worker	10	36	3	21
Psychiatrist	14	50	5	36
Priest/Minister	5	18	1	7
Nurse	0	0	1	7

[a]N = 52 responses
[b]N = 18 responses

Table XI.   Type of Counseling

Type	LD[a]		NLD[b]	
	N	%	N	%
Marital	9	32	3	21
Family	7	25	6	43
Personal	27	96	12	86
Career	8	29	2	14
ADD/ADHD	4	14	0	0

[a]N = 55 responses
[b]N = 23 responses

Other Disabilities and Medication

We were interested in finding out if the participants with LD were more susceptible to other disabilities and/or to chronic illnesses. Thirty percent of the LD group said they had another disability, including ADD, ADHD, manic depression, depression, phobia, epilepsy, visual impairment, and chronic illness. The onset of the disability was in adulthood for 17 of the 20 disabilities reported. Only three members of the NLD group reported a disability, including depression, visual impairment, and multiple sclerosis.

Although many more LD respondents reported other disabilities than those in the NLD group, 43% of the NLD versus 36% of the LD took medication regularly. Although fewer of the adults with LD reported taking medication regularly, only one NLD reported taking an anti-depressant, whereas four of the adults with LD regularly took medication for depression.

Effect of LD on Emotional and Physical Health

Whereas 51% reported that their LD affected their emotional health, only 12% reported that it affected their physical health. We were interested in understanding how the LD affected the participants' emotional health. A total of 43 comments were made, and the two most common responses indicated low self-esteem (49%) and feelings of anxiety (21%) (see table XII).

With respect to low self-esteem, some participants knew the terminology and said that their LD caused them to have low self-esteem. Others described how they were "too afraid to try" or how their younger years "destroyed them." A particularly poignant comment was made by the individual who described the negative effect of having been told that she was not smart when she said that the pain elicited by this comment doesn't go away quickly. Feelings of anxiety were expressed, as well as frustration with problems due to disorganization, making mistakes, or having to take longer to complete tasks. One

Table XII.   Effect of LD on Emotional Health

Effect	LD[a]	
	N	%
Self-esteem	21	49
Anxiety	9	21
Depression	4	9
Stress	4	9
Anger Management	2	5
Positive Impact	3	7

[a]N = 43 comments

young mother said that she gets frustrated over getting lost so often. Even when she leaves an hour early, she still gets lost and arrives late.

An equal number of comments (9%) referred to depression and stress. Problems with anger management were also mentioned (5%). One individual described her anger when she had difficulty retrieving information. It "comes out different from planned—escalates emotions until a volcano explodes."

Yet, just as we found with other questions that explored the impact of a learning disability, a few participants gave positive comments (7%): Two participants felt that their LD made them more sensitive individuals and a third said, "Has made me a very strong individual."

We were also interested in whether the LD affected one's physical health. In response to this question, only five responses were made. The effects on physical health included sleep problems, colds, backaches, shoulder pain, and serious illness.

OVERALL IMPACT ON QUALITY OF LIFE

We wanted to know what factors in their lives were perceived as causing them the most problems. The factors we included were: low income, job-related problems, health, loneliness, social/emotional support, intimate relationships, and lack of skills. Participants were asked to rate the degree to which these factors were causing problems from "not at all" to "a lot." The majority of both the LD and NLD groups did not consider any of the factors as causing problems in their lives. However, in all areas there were more participants with LD (albeit a small number) who reported these problems. Low income and job-related problems were identified with the most frequency (24% LD versus 8% NLD and 28% LD versus 15% NLD, respectively). The next highest area perceived to be causing problems were intimate relationships (21% for LD versus 10% for NLD). More of the LD group also cited loneliness and the need for social/emotional support (14% LD versus 8% NLD and 14% LD versus 5% NLD, respectively. Sixteen percent of the individuals with LD as compared to 11% of the NLD responded that lack of skills caused problems. Health was also more of a concern for individuals with LD (10% versus 7%) (see table XIII).

After asking participants the factors they thought caused them the most problems, we then asked them what would improve their quality of life. (See table XIV for the complete list.) With the exception of transportation, more participants with LD indicated that they would benefit from all of those items listed. More education (68%), retirement benefits (61%) and friends/social group (60%) were rated the highest. Fifty-

Table XIII. Factors Causing Problems

Factors	Not at all 1				2				3				4				A lot 5			
	LD N	LD %	NLD N	NLD %	LD N	LD %	NLD N	NLD %	LD N	LD %	NLD N	NLD %	LD N	LD %	NLD N	NLD %	LD N	LD %	NLD N	NLD %
[a]Low Income	27	54	25	66	4	8	4	11	7	14	6	16	6	12	0	0	6	12	3	8
[b]Job-related problems	19	39	16	40	8	16	8	20	8	16	10	25	8	16	4	10	6	12	2	5
[c]Health	32	64	23	59	4	8	8	21	9	18	5	13	1	2	1	3	4	8	2	4
[d]Loneliness	29	59	27	71	6	12	6	16	7	14	2	5	2	4	2	5	5	10	1	3
[e]Social/ emotional support	33	67	27	71	7	14	6	16	2	4	3	8	5	10	2	5	2	4	0	0
[f]Intimate relationships	29	62	27	71	6	13	3	8	2	4	4	11	4	9	2	5	6	13	2	5
[g]Lack of skills	25	51	26	72	6	12	5	14	10	20	1	3	3	6	3	8	5	10	1	3

[a]LD = 50; NLD = 38
[b]LD = 49; NLD = 40
[c]LD = 50; NLD = 39
[d]LD = 49; NLD = 38
[e]LD = 49; NLD = 38
[f]LD = 47; NLD = 38
[g]LD = 49; NLD = 36

Table XIV.   Factors Needed to Improve Quality of Life

Factors	Not at all 1				2				3				4				A lot 5			
	LD N	LD %	NLD N	NLD %	LD N	LD %	NLD N	NLD %	LD N	LD %	NLD N	NLD %	LD N	LD %	NLD N	NLD %	LD N	LD %	NLD N	NLD %
aBetter Employment	2	7	12	39	1	3	5	16	9	30	6	19	9	30	0	0	9	30	8	26
bHealth Benefits	4	17	15	55	3	13	2	7	3	13	3	11	5	22	2	7	8	35	5	19
cRetirement Benefits	4	13	8	28	3	10	5	17	5	17	5	17	8	27	4	14	10	34	7	24
dMore Education	1	3	2	6	4	11	10	30	7	19	11	33	10	27	4	12	15	41	6	18
eCounseling	4	13	17	63	6	20	3	11	13	43	4	15	6	20	3	11	1	3	0	0
fSupport Group	5	26	17	65	1	5	2	8	6	32	6	23	6	32	1	4	1	5	0	0
gFriends/Social Group	4	13	10	33	3	10	10	33	5	17	1	3	14	47	4	13	4	13	5	17
hTransportation	5	29	16	55	2	11	5	17	5	29	3	10	1	6	2	7	4	24	3	10
iSpecial Medical Delivery	5	31	19	73	2	13	1	4	4	25	3	12	3	19	0	0	2	13	3	12

aLD = 30; NLD = 31
bLD = 23; NLD = 27
cLD = 30; NLD = 29
dLD = 37; NLD = 33
eLD = 30; NLD = 27
fLD = 19; NLD = 26
gLD = 30; NLD = 30
hLD = 17; NLD = 29
iLD = 16; NLD = 26

seven percent responded that health benefits were needed, and 60% reported that they felt better employment would improve their lives.

In addition to factors listed in table XIII, ten participants with LD and six NLD responded that more money would improve the quality of their lives. Those in the LD group also added more education (4%) and more and better relationships (10%). Isolated comments included: more time, improved appearance, and improved living arrangements. Singular comments for the NLD participants included: good marriage, more time, their child's choices, mental health insurance, improved living arrangements, traveling more often, and stricter laws for criminals.

DISCUSSION

The participants in this study with learning disabilities demonstrated independence in several ways. Only 12% reported living with parents, siblings, and/or relatives, which is significantly less than the 44.1% who reported living with parents in the National Longitudinal Transition Study and 32% in the survey conducted by the Learning Disabilities Association of America. However, the number is still higher than the control group in which 6% reported living with parents. As noted throughout the paper, this small difference, as well as differences in where participants lived (i.e., own home versus rental), is most likely due to the NLD group being older, and so more were married and had children.

Financial independence has been an issue for individuals with learning disabilities. Only 30% of the participants with LD reported receiving financial help as compared to those in the Greenbaum study (60%), and of those receiving help, approximately one-half received support from their spouses. Parents, a friend, and a sister provided support to the others. Most individuals with learning disabilities in this study were not only living independently, they were able to support themselves financially. In an earlier report (see chapter 14), there were no significant differences on mean income of full-time employed adults with and without LD ($38,500 LD versus $39,018 NLD).

Another indication of independence is mobility. In prior studies, some adults with LD have not been eligible for a driving license, or they did not apply due to orientation problems. In our study, all but one had a driving license; however, eleven participants shared ways in which they felt their LD affected their driving, and three attributed having accidents to their LD.

This group of adults with LD reportedly had social lives that were not unlike their non-learning disabled peers. The participants with LD spent slightly more time with parents, which may also be due to being younger and fewer being married. There were no differences in the number and scope of leisure activities, and 60% of the LD group versus 71% of the NLD group rated their social lives highly satisfying.

Despite these very encouraging results regarding independence and social lives, 46% of participants with LD reported that their LD affected their personal lives, 54% said it affected their participation in leisure activities, and 10% reported that it affected participation in community activities. In all of these areas, emotional problems were cited as the main way in which their LD affected them. They reported low self-esteem and self-confidence, and feelings of embarrassment, anger, and insecurity. Others suffered from social isolation due to concern that their learning disability would be apparent, something they did not want to reveal.

From their responses, it was also evident that their specific learning disabilities continued to affect their lives as adults very much like they impacted them as children and in school. Ongoing problems with processing information, executive functioning, and academic skills were reported. A few described the positive impact, which included being more sensitive, more understanding, and more creative.

We feel that the most important finding was the impact their learning disability was having on their emotional health. Fifty-one percent reported that their LD affected their emotional health. Given this impact, it was not surprising that 56% of the LD group were receiving some sort of counseling, and 46% of those receiving counseling had done so for over five years. Whereas only 12% of participants with LD reported that their learning disabilities affected their physical health, the types of problems reported were stress related. Several other disabilities diagnosed in adulthood included depression and phobia. Also, four of the adults with LD said that they took medication for depression.

There was evidence that loneliness and social isolation was an issue for some of the adults with LD. Some mentioned problems with meeting new people and the fear of their LD being apparent. Fifteen percent of the participants with LD rated social/emotional support and loneliness as problems, and intimate relationships were rated as a problem by 22%.

In spite of their success in living independently, in educational attainment, proportion employed full-time, in occupational status, longevity on the job, and annual salary (see chapter 14), it was evident that the stress of competing, the fear of disclosure, and the impact of their learning disabilities on every aspect of their lives are taking a toll emotionally. This was also evident when more of the participants with LD than NLD cited problems with intimate relationships, loneliness, and the need for social/emotional support as causing them the most problems.

The fact that over 50% of the individuals with LD were receiving some type of counseling is both good and bad news. While the emotional impact this successful group of adults with LD was experiencing is distressing, it was heartening that they were employing the appropriate coping strategy of participation in counseling and support groups. Although it is understandable that more NLD would be receiving family counseling (43% versus 25%) because more were married and had children, we did not expect that more participants with LD (32% versus 21%) would be receiving marital counseling.

Because Vogel and Adelman (see chapter 14) found that the participants with LD held more part-time jobs which may have resulted in spending more time looking for the right environment or "social ecology" (Gerber, Ginsberg, and Reiff 1992), it is understandable that a higher percentage of the LD group would seek career counseling. It appears that while the NLD support groups pertained to normal developmental issues, the adults with LD attended support groups related to their disabilities (LD and/or ADD/ADHD) and to stress (e.g., eating disorders, domestic violence, illness).

These findings point to the importance of counseling, psychological support, and/or psychotherapy intermittently for individuals with LD throughout their lives. Early on, parents need to recognize the necessity of academic support being accompanied by support for social/emotional issues. During transitions and/or periods of extreme stress, individual therapy might be necessary; at other times, it may be helpful for the individuals with LD to participate in therapy with peers, family members, and/or spouses. Support groups can be beneficial in addressing issues of social isolation, adjustment, and overcoming the feelings of fear and inadequacy that new situations tend to generate.

FUTURE RESEARCH

There are several topics that need to be explored in depth in future research. For example, the emotional impact of a learning disability needs to be addressed from the social and medical perspectives. Just as disclosure of an individual's learning disability needs further exploration as it relates to education and employment, these findings indicate that disclosure in one's personal life also needs to be further explored. Further research is also needed on the issue of loneliness. Throughout this study, there were indications of problems with establishing and maintaining intimate relationships, as well as friendships.

Although this may be a problem for society-at-large, it appears to be exacerbated by the problems inherent in having a learning disability. In-depth interviews with individuals who do not express loneliness and have experienced their LD as positive may shed light on factors that result in a happier and more successful personal life for individuals with learning disabilities.

Further longitudinal studies with this population may provide insight into the impact of an LD as one ages, as well as the impact on children and grandchildren.

ACKNOWLEDGEMENTS

This research was supported by a grant from the Thorn River Foundation.

The authors wish to express appreciation to the participants and interviewers who assisted in conducting this study. Special thanks to Ms. Alexa Darby who assisted in the development of the interview strategies, and to Dr. Peter Abrams for his able assistance in data analysis.

REFERENCES

Adelman, P. B. 1988. An approach to meeting the needs of the learning disabled student in a four-year college. In *College and the Learning Disabled College Student: Program Development, Implementation, and Selection*, eds. C. T. Mangrum II and S. S. Strichart. Philadelphia: Grune & Stratton.

Adelman, P. B., and Vogel, S. A. 1990. College graduates with learning disabilities: Employment attainment and career patterns. *Learning Disability Quarterly* 13(3):154–66.

Adelman, P. B., and Vogel, S. A. 1993. Adults with learning disabilities. In *Learning about Learning Disabilities*, ed. B. Wong. New York: Academic Press.

Blackorby, J., and Wagner, M. 1996 Longitudinal postschool outcomes of youth with disabilities: Findings from the National Longitudinal Transition Study. *Exceptional Children* 62:399–413.

Blalock, J. W. 1981. Persistent problems and concerns of young adults with learning disabilities. In *Bridges to Tomorrow*, eds. W. Cruickshank and A. Silber. Syracuse: Syracuse University Press.

Brown, D. 1984. Employment considerations for learning disabled adults. *Journal of Rehabilitation* 74:77–88.

Bruck, M. 1985. The adult functioning of children with specific learning disabilities: A follow-up study. In *Advances in Applied Developmental Psychology*, ed. I. E. Sigel. Norwood, NJ: Ablex Publishing Corporation.

Cohen, J. 1985. Learning disabilities and adolescence: Developmental considerations. In *Adolescent Psychiatry: Developmental and Clinical Studies*, eds. M. Sugar, A. Esman, J. Looney, A. Schwartzberg and A. Sorosky. Chicago: The University of Chicago.

Darby, A., Vogel, S. A., and Adelman, P. B. 2001. Telephone interview strategies in conducting follow-up studies with adults with learning disabilities. *Thalamus* 19(1):41–48.

Fafard, M. B., and Haubrich, P. A. 1981. Vocational and social adjustment of learning disabled young adults: A follow-up study. *Learning Disability Quarterly* 4:122–130.

Gerber, P. 1992. At first glance: Employment for people with learning disabilities at the beginning of the Americans-with-disabilities-act ERA. *Learning Disabilities Quarterly* 15:330–32.

Gerber, P. J., Ginsberg, R., and Reiff, H. B. 1992. Identifying alterable patterns in employment success for highly successful adults with learning disabilities. *Journal of Learning Disabilities* 25(8):475–87.

Greenbaum, B. 1993. A follow-up survey of students with learning disabilities after exiting a postsecondary institution. (Doctoral dissertation, University of Maryland, 1993). Dissertation Abstracts International, 54-08, Section A, 2981.

Haring, K. A., Lovett, D. L., and Smith, D. D. 1990. A follow-up study of recent special education graduates of learning disabilities programs. *Journal of Postsecondary Education and Disability* 9(1 & 2):219–26.

Menkes, M. M., Rowe, J. S., and Menkes, J. H. 1967. A twenty-five year follow-up on the hyperactive child with MED. *Pediatrics* 39:393–99.

Reder, S., and Vogel, S. A. 1997. Life-span employment and economic outcomes for adults with self-reported learning disabilities. In *Learning Disabilities and Employment*, eds. P. Gerber and D. Brown. Austin: PRO-ED.

Rogan, L. L., and Hartman, L. D. 1990. Adult outcomes of learning disabled students 10 years after initial follow-up. *Learning Disabilities Focus* 5(2): 91–102.

Scuccimarra, D. J., and Speece, D. L. 1990. Employment outcomes and social integration of students with mild handicaps: The quality of life two years after high school. *Journal of Learning Disabilities* 23(4):213–18.

Spekman, N. J., Oi, M. T., Goldberg, R. J., and Herman, K. 1989. LD Children grow up; What can we expect for education, employment, and adjustment? Presented at the 40th Conference of The Orton Dyslexia Society, Dallas, TX.

They Speak for Themselves: A Survey of Adults with Learning Disabilities. 1996. Learning Disabilities Association of America, Pittsburgh, PA.

Vogel, S. A. 1982. On developing LD college programs. *Journal of Learning Disabilities* 15:518–28.

Vogel, S. A. 1996. Adults with learning disabilities: Research questions and methodological issues in planning a research agenda for 2000 and beyond. *The Canadian Journal of Special Education* 11(2):33–54.

Vogel, S. A. 1997. *College Students with Learning Disabilities: A Handbook for Students with Learning Disabilities, Faculty, Administrators, and Admissions Counselors* (6th edition). Learning Disabilities Association of America, Pittsburgh, PA.

Vogel, S. A., and Adelman, P. B. 1990. Extrinsic and intrinsic factors in graduation and academic failure among LD college students. *Annals of Dyslexia* 40:119–37.

Vogel, S. A., Hruby, P. J., and Adelman, P. B. 1993. Educational and psychological factors in successful and unsuccessful college students with learning disabilities. *Learning Disabilities Research and Practice* 8(1):59–65.

Werner, E. E., and Smith, R. S. 1992. *Overcoming the Odds: High Risk Children from Birth to Adulthood.* Ithaca, NY: Cornell University Press.

Chapter • 16

Mastery of Literacy and Life:
Individual Interests and Literacy Development in Successful Adults with Dyslexia

Rosalie P. Fink

Many Americans do not read well, leaving a large proportion of the population marginalized "on the outside looking in" (Purcell-Gates 1995, 1991). This chapter is about adults with learning disabilities, a group at high risk for being excluded from the mainstream. In the chapter, I analyze the development of literacy in individuals with dyslexia or reading disability (RD), who are frequently at the fringes of U.S, society due to problems learning basic literacy.

Studies have shown that students with learning disabilities (LD) score significantly lower than control peers in reading (e.g., F = 7.83; p = .007). And, students with disabilities drop out of high school at significantly higher rates than control peers (e.g., 47% compared to 36%) (Zigmond and Thornton 1989). Of youth who were followed 3 to 5 years after high school, only 27% of those with disabilities had attended postsecondary school, compared with 68% of nondisabled youth (p < .001) (Blackorby and Wagner 1996). In addition, the rate of competitive employment for youth with disabilities lagged significantly behind that of youth in the general population 3 to 5 years after high school (57% vs. 69%, p < .001) (Blackorby and Wagner 1996).

Despite these dour statistics, however, studies have shown that some individuals with LD do well academically and professionally in adulthood (Fink 1993, 1995/1996, 1998, 2000; Vogel and Reder 2000). In this chapter, I analyze results of a study of adults with RD who have succeeded in professions that require a high level of literacy and education. The chapter explores the following questions: How, and when in development do highly successful individuals with dyslexia develop literacy? And, how does individual interest motivate and activate their literacy development?

Discussion of the powerful role of interest in learning and development dates back to Dewey (1913). More recently, Renninger and other researchers have found that the influence of interest "is particularly salient when students are in the process of developing their reading skills" (e. g., Renninger 1992, p. 391). This chapter reports on a study that used Schiefele's (1990) definition of the term "individual or topic interest" to refer to a relatively enduring orientation of an individual toward a topic, a domain of knowledge, or materials and activities related to a particular topic or domain. The study, which focused primarily on the development of literacy, compared literacy development in 60 highly successful adults with dyslexia and a group of equally successful adults without dyslexia. Participants with dyslexia included a Nobel laureate, a member of the National Academy of Sciences, and others in diverse fields that required extensive reading (i.e., medicine, law, business, biology, chemistry, education, psychology, anthropology, theatre, art, interior design, and literature). My rationale for studying literacy development in highly successful men and women with dyslexia was that they might have devised novel strategies that could prove useful in the education of others at risk for reading failure, The study included equal numbers of males and females, moving away from the previous tendency of dyslexia research to focus disproportionately on males.

Until recently, instructional research on dyslexia focused primarily on the effectiveness of highly structured skills-based teaching approaches (Foorman et al. 1998; Griesbach 1993; Lyon 1994; Lyon and Moats 1988; O'Conner and Wilson 1995; Snow, Burns, and Griffin 1998). These approaches included systematic phonics instruction and multisensory methods (i.e., simultaneous instruction in the use and association of three sensory channels—visual, auditory, and kinesthetic). These methods have been used at all levels of instruction. In addition, bypass approaches, such as the use of audio- and videotapes and other devices that circumvent and/or support reading, have also been integral components of dyslexia instruction, especially at middle school, secondary, and postsecondary levels (Knight 1986; Morris 1983; Vogel 1987). In recent years, computer assisted programs have been used at various developmental levels with increasing frequency (Anderson-Inman and Horney 1996/1997; Meyer, Pisha, and Rose 1991; Rose and Meyer 1994; Rose and Meyer 1996).

Recently there has been increasing interest in research on adults with learning disabilities (Blalock 1981; Bruck 1990; Felton, Naylor, and Woods 1990; Fink 1992, 1993, 1995/1996, 1998, 2000; Finucci,

Gottfredson, and Childs 1985; Fowler and Scarborough 1993; Gerber, Ginsberg, and Reiff 1992; Gerber and Reiff 1992; Rawson 1968; Roffman 2000; Scarborough 1984; Vogel and Reder 2000). Studies overall have reported both successful adult outcomes and specific continuing difficulties. Fowler and Scarborough found that, while the reading disability persists in adulthood, "there is considerable variability in the severity of the ultimate deficit and its impact on overall functioning" (Fowler and Scarborough 1993, p. 62). Blalock (1981) reported that adults with dyslexia were "amazingly adept" at using context clues to enhance their reading ability; similarly, Bruck (1990) found that the use of context by adults with dyslexia simultaneously improved their reading speed and accuracy. In a study of 25 adults with dyslexia, Lefly and Pennington (1991) found that adults with dyslexia decoded unfamiliar words nearly as accurately as nondyslexic controls, albeit more slowly, confirming and extending results from research on learning disabled children (Meyer et al. 1997; Wolf 2000). Few studies have investigated the adult reading abilities, habits, attitudes, and experiences of highly successful adults with dyslexia (Feldman et al. 1993; Rawson 1968); therefore, the current study focused on these areas.

METHOD

Participant recruitment, selection, and assessment

The goal of recruitment was to find individuals who would inspire and motivate others who currently struggle with dyslexia. All but one of the 60 participants with dyslexia agreed to be identified by name, education, and profession (see appendix 1).

Successful professionals

Recruitment methods were designed to identify participants with dyslexia who had achieved high levels of success in diverse professions that require reading and demand extensive training, skill, and responsibility. Therefore, the sample was not random or representative, but rather was selected on the basis of level of educational and career achievement, field of professional expertise, gender, age, and socioeconomic level. Participants were considered "successful" if they demonstrated professional competence recognized by peers in an area of expertise and supported themselves financially.

Individuals with dyslexia

The choice of selection criteria was guided by the International Dyslexia Association (IDA) research definition of dyslexia. Despite ongoing controversies (e.g., Aaron 1997; Stanovich 1991), this definition maintains the classic notion of an "unexpected" reading problem or "discrepancy" between the person's potential (often measured by the Full Scale IQ) and his or her actual reading achievement (often measured by standardized diagnostic reading tests). The IDA conceptualizes dyslexia as:

> ". . . a specific language-based disorder of constitutional origin characterized by difficulties in single word decoding, usually reflecting insufficient phonological processing abilities. These difficulties . . . are often unexpected in relation to age and other cognitive and academic abilities. . . . Dyslexia is manifest by variable difficulty with different forms of language, often including, in addition to problems reading, a conspicuous problem with acquiring proficiency in writing and spelling" (Orton Dyslexia Society Research Committee 1994, p.4).

Participants were included in the present study and were considered to have dyslexia if they reported having had difficulties learning to decode single words and/or learn adequate reading and spelling skills, beginning by first grade and continuing at least until third grade. Individuals between ages 26 and 50 had been diagnosed with dyslexia by learning disabilities professionals using established assessment instruments. For those older than 50 (educated when documentation was less common), a case history of early and continuing difficulties in reading unfamiliar words, spelling, and writing constituted the "diagnostic signature" of dyslexia (Shaywitz, Fletcher, and Shaywitz 1994, p. 7).

I initially located participants through professional referrals, word of mouth, and notices distributed at professional conferences. In preliminary telephone interviews, I screened prospective participants for exclusionary criteria such as a history of inadequate schooling or poor vision. Profiles of language-based difficulties were recorded and analyzed based on retrospective face-to-face interviews that I conducted individually with each participant. A case history was conducted and included family history of reading disability, personal history of diagnosis/remedial assistance for reading difficulties, and early and/or persistent difficulties with letter identification, word recognition, spelling, writing, slow speed of reading and writing, memory (e.g., difficulty memorizing multiplication tables), laterality (i.e., difficulty making left-right distinctions in speech/action), fine motor control, or second language learning. Males and females were matched for concomitant problems and severity of dyslexia, as shown in table I.

Academic degrees

Despite histories of serious reading problems, 59 of the 60 individuals with dyslexia had graduated from four year colleges or universities.

Table I.   Self-reported problems of the 60 participants with dyslexia*

Problem**	# Males	# Females	Total
Single word decoding	29	30	59
Spelling	30	29	59
Discrepancy	26	27	53
Diagnosis/Remediation	25	25	50
Letter identification	23	23	46
Writing	25	24	49
Slow reading and/or writing	28	26	54
Memory	26	26	52
Laterality (left-right distinction)	16	22	38
Second language	27	28	55
Fine motor (i.e., illegible handwriting)	19	17	36
Familial dyslexia	22	26	48

*Mean Number of Problems Per Participant:

	Males	Females
Mean # of Problems (*SD*)	9.9 (1.3)	10.0 (1.3)
Range	6–12	8–12

**There were no significant differences between males and females ($t = 0.30$, $p = .767$).

One man with dyslexia had attended but did not complete college. Of the 60 men and women with dyslexia, 6 had M.D.s, 17 had Ph.D.s, 4 had J.D.s, 19 had master's degrees, and 12 had bachelor's degrees.

A comparison group was matched on all criteria except dyslexia and included individuals without dyslexia whose high professional and educational achievements were comparable to those of the participants with dyslexia. The comparison group consisted of 5 men and 5 women, including I M.D., 5 Ph.D.s, 1 J.D., and 3 individuals with master's degrees. The comparison group was limited to 10 participants due to the study's limited resources. Like those with dyslexia, participants without dyslexia were active professionals in fields that demand extensive reading. On average, both participants with dyslexia and the comparison group in this study exceeded Gerber and Reiff's notion of "high success, " which Gerber determined by income and other standard indicators of adult well-being (Paul Gerber, personal communication; Gerber and Reiff 1991, p. 34). In contrast, many members of both groups in the present study are professionals who hold positions in prestigious institutions. Many are outstanding professionals who have written major books and are movers and shakers in the top echelons of their fields.

Diversity by geographic region, SES, and race

The majority of participants were white middle class U.S. citizens who came from all regions of the country, including 18 states and the District of Columbia. Most had been raised in middle- to upper-middle class families, although a few came from working class origins. A small number of African-Americans and Hispanics participated, but their numbers were not proportionately representative of minorities in the U.S. population. I tried to locate more minorities; however, finding them proved difficult, presumably because minorities are still not proportionately successful in our society due to ongoing discrimination (Gadsden 1991; Ladson-Billings 1994). At the time of the study, participants earned salaries indicating middle to high socioeconomic categories.

Use of self-report

Recent literature indicates that self-report of childhood reading difficulties by learning disabled adults is valid and reliable (Decker, Vogel, and De Fries 1989; Finucci et al. 1984; Gilger 1992; Lefly 1997; Lefly and Pennington in review). Apparently, accuracy and reliability of self-reported reading difficulties are higher for middle-aged, normally achieving, or high-achieving individuals (Gilger 1992). The mean age of the highly successful adults with dyslexia in the present study was 45 years (age range: 26–75). The mean age of the comparison group was 51 years (age range: 33–62).

PROCEDURES AND INSTRUMENTS

Clinical interviews

Using Gilligan's clinical interview methodology (see Attanucci 1988), I conducted in-depth retrospective interviews (3–9 hours long) in person with each participant. Interviews were guided by 20 interview questions conducted in a semi-structured, open-ended format (see Fink, 1995/1996 for interview protocol). Care was taken to avoid asking questions in a manner likely to influence participants' responses. When possible, I conducted interviews in the naturalistic setting of each person's home or workplace, where individuals recollected their literacy and learning history in a developmental framework, school grade by school grade, content area by content area. Typical questions asked included: "What is your earliest memory of learning differently from other children?" and "What specific strategies did you use for reading, writing, spelling, learning multiplication tables, history, science, and so forth, in first grade, second grade, etc.?" Each interview was audiotaped and transcribed in its entirety by a trained transcriber in order to preserve descriptive detail and ensure accuracy. Interview transcripts were coded according to multiple dimensions of cognitive and affective development, including experiences of humiliation and frustration with learning, experiences of jubilation and joy in learning, topic(s) and type(s) of first books read, ages and circumstances of early memories regarding reading, and relationships with important people. To check for reliability, data were also coded and analyzed by an independent psychologist, who analyzed one quarter of the transcripts for topics of self-selected reading and one third for ages of development of basic fluency. Intercoder reliability for the topic variable was 90%; intercoder reliability for the age variable was 100%.

Additional background information

To verify interview information, I collected additional biographical data from various sources. These included a detailed *curriculum vita* from each participant, diagnostic, school, and clinical reports, when available, information from parents and spouses, when available, information from public sources such as *Who's Who in America* and journal articles, book chapters, full-length books, and works of art created and/or published by each participant.

Literacy measures

I individually administered formal and informal literacy tests to each participant. Assessment instruments included:

(1) *The Diagnostic Assessments of Reading with Trial Teaching Strategies* (DARTTS) (Roswell and Chall 1992), an untimed, nationally normed instrument that spans beginning-through advanced-literacy levels (ceiling = 12th grade). This instrument assesses a person's relative strengths and weaknesses in reading and was selected to help ascertain whether each participant's literacy profile was "jagged" or smooth.

(2) *The Nelson-Denny Reading Test of Vocabulary, Reading Comprehension, and Reading Rate, Form H* (ND) (Brown, Fischco, and Hanna 1993), a college reading test that measures reading ability through postgraduate levels. It is a timed, nationally normed test designed to provide an objective ranking of student ability in vocabulary development, silent reading comprehension, and reading rate.

(3) *The Pig Latin Test* (adapted by Fink from Lefly 1997), an informal instrument containing 48 items administered in an untimed format. It assesses awareness of phonemic elements and ability to manipulate phonemes and syllables, along with other phonological skills.

(4) *The Florida Nonsense Passages* (adapted from Finucci 1974 by Gross-Glenn et al. 1990), an informal instrument that entails reading nonsense words embedded in otherwise meaningful paragraphs. It assesses decoding, oral reading speed, and oral reading accuracy.

(5) *The Graded Nonword Reading and Spelling Test* (Snowling, Stothard, and McLean 1996), an untimed measure of the ability to read and spell novel letter strings. Initially designed for use with children, it is considered suitable for adults with reading difficulties.

Questionnaire

I administered The Adult Reading History Questionnaire, or ARHQ, (Lefly 1997; Lefly and Pennington in review) to assess the existence of dyslexia and gain insight regarding literacy development, habits, and attitudes. The ARHQ has been found to be highly correlated with adult diagnostic criteria in Pennington's familial dyslexic sample ($r = .61 - .73; p < .001$); these correlations are higher than those of other adult self-report validity studies (Lefly and Pennington in review, pp. 9–10). Lefly and Pennington used a cutoff point of .30 to determine the existence of dyslexia. All 60 participants with dyslexia in the present study had ARHQ scores well above .30, as shown in table II. (Mean for total individuals with dyslexia = .60, SD = .09, range = .38 –.82).

Research questions

The following questions guided the present study: (1) How, when in development, and under what conditions do highly successful men and women with dyslexia develop literacy? (2) What literacy levels do they achieve? (3) As adults, do successful individuals with dyslexia show jagged profiles of literacy strengths and weaknesses in word recognition, oral reading, silent reading comprehension, spelling, vocabulary knowledge, and oral and silent reading rate? (4) How do the adult reading abilities, habits, and attitudes of successful individuals with dyslexia compare with those of a nondyslexic comparison group? (5) How do the experiences of males and females with dyslexia differ? (6) What are the implications of the results of this study for theory, research, and educational and clinical practice?

RESULTS

Interview results

When did basic fluency develop?   The 60 successful men and women with dyslexia developed basic fluency, or relative smoothness

Table II. Results of literacy tests and assessments and adult reading history questionnaire*

		Individuals with Dyslexia			Contrasts**	
	Non-dyslexic Controls (N = 10)	Fully Compensated (N = 17)	Partially Compensated (N = 43)	Total Dyslexics (N = 60)	Controls v. Total Dyslexia	Full v Partial
DARTT (%GE < 112)*						
Word Recognition	0	0	30.2	21.7	.103	.010
Oral Reading Acc.	0	0	55.8	40.0	.014	.001
Silent Comp.	10	0	6.9	5.0	.528	.264
Spelling	40	0	79.0	57.0	.327	< .001
Word Meaning	0	0	6.9	5.0	.470	.264
Nelson-Denny (raw score)						
Vocabulary M (SD)	79 (.6)	75.9 (4.4)7	3.9 (5.0)	73.5 (6.3)	.008	.155
GE mean	18.9	17.5	16.9	16.9		
GE range	18.9–18.9	14.6–18.9	11.6–18.9	11.6–18.9		
Comp. M (SD)	75.2 (4.4)	70.5 (3.9)	67.7 (5.6)	68.7 (6.7)	.004	.056
GE mean	18.9	18.6	17.1	17.1		
GE range	16.4–18.9	1113.2–18.9	9.6–18.9	9.6–18.9		
Rate (%SS < 180)	0	0	33.0	23.3	.088	.007
% using extended time	0	53	60	58	.001	.594
ARHQ						
Total Score M (SD)	.07 (.04)	.57 (.09)	.61 (.09)	.60 (.09)	.0001	.126
range	.01–.15	.38–.75	.38–.82	.38–.82		
Florida Passages						
# seconds M (SD)	25.3 (8.4)	78.5 (17.8)	106.7 (38.9)	98.7 (36.5)	.0001	.0060
range	17–50	51–112	51–225	51–225		
# errors M (SD)	1.5 (1.0)	8.8 (3.0)	14.5 (6.0)	12.9 (5.9(	.0001	.0004

Table II.   *continued*

| | Non-dyslexic Controls (N = 10) | Individuals with Dyslexia | | | Contrasts** | |
		Fully Compensated (N = 17)	Partially Compensated (N = 43)	Total Dyslexics (N = 60)	Controls v. Total Dyslexia	Full v Partial
Pig Latin Test						
# correct M (SD)	44.2 (5.6)	40.4 (7.5)3	0.0 (11.9)	33.0 (11.8)	.005	.002
range	30–48	24–48	1–47	1–48		
Graded Nonwords						
Reading M (SD)	19.8 (.4)	17.1 (1.9)	15.0 (3.5)	15.6 (3.3)	.0002	.0231
range	19–20	13–20	6–20	6–20		
Spelling M (SD)	18.8 (1.3)	16 (2.4)	13.0 (4.6)	13.8 (4.3)	.0007	.0136
range	16–20	11–20	2–19	2–20		

*Full data set available upon request (participants' identities withheld)

**Observed probability levels from the statistical contrasts; the first column of contrasts shows comparisons between the nondyslexic control group and the total number of individuals with dyslexia; the second column of contrasts shows comparisons between fully compensated and partially compensated individuals with dyslexia.

***GE = grade equivalent; maximum performance on the DARTT is twelfth grade level.

in reading connected text, between ages 10 and 11 (on average, three to three-and-one-half years later than the nondyslexic comparison group). There were no significant gender differences regarding this variable.

Development of basic fluency represented a memorable turning point for many, following years of intense personal frustration and public humiliation. Consequently, development of basic fluency, of finally "getting it," was an "Ahaa!" experience for many, recalled with vivid emotions and clear memories of a key person at a poignant time. For example, memories of Mrs. Orenberg stood out for Lori Boskin.

> *Lori Boskin (alumni developer):*
> Well, I didn't finally start to learn to read until fourth grade.
> With Mrs. Orenberg. I remember so clearly sitting there with
> Mrs. Orenberg.

How did literacy develop?

Of the 60 successful men and women with dyslexia, many read avidly as children. Despite ongoing struggles with basic, lower level skills (i.e., letter identification, word recognition, and decoding strategies), neither males nor females circumvented reading overall; rather, they sought out books in order to learn. Once they "got into reading" there seemed to be no stopping them, as Dr. Florence Hazeltine recalled.

> *Florence Hazeltine (gynecologist):*
> When I was almost 11, I started to read. . . . And from then on I
> read all the time. (Age 11 and up)

Reading was extremely difficult, laborious, and effortful for these men and women. So why did they read avidly? And, how did they do it?

Literacy development in these individuals was motivated by a strong desire to know more about a content area of passionate personal interest. Consequently, they read every book and magazine they could find in order to satisfy their curiosity about a particular topic. They exemplified the essence of what Chall has called "reading to learn" (1983); their reasons for reading were to explore interesting subjects and learn specific information.

> *H. Girard Ebert (interior designer):*
> I've always been attracted to books and anything that has to do with
> history, decorative arts, architecture. . . . So I took reading, which was a
> problem, and turned it around, because it was the only way that I could
> explore what I was interested in.

> *Ronald Davis (biochemist):*
> You read science for—how things are put together. . . .

Passionate interest in a topic provided the scaffolding necessary to develop literacy skills. A pattern in their reading histories showed that they engaged in a great deal of personal interest reading. Although topics and genres of personal interest varied, fascination with a topic was a common theme.

> *Ronald Davis (biochemist):*
> I became fascinated with nitrogen chemistry. So the way to understand that was to start reading chemistry books. So I got organic chemistry books and read as many as I could find.

Through avid reading in a content area of high interest, these individuals with dyslexia developed knowledge of the specialized vocabulary, concepts, themes, questions, typical text structures, and critical issues of a particular field. Extensive reading about a favorite subject enhanced their depth of background knowledge and enabled them to gain practice, which fostered fluency and development of increasingly sophisticated skills. With practice they developed deep schema knowledge, which supported their literacy development (Anderson 1983). They relied extensively on contextual facilitation to derive meaning from a new text, foraging for context clues in a hunt for new information. And, these context clues proved relatively reliable in a restricted content area. Through unsolicited remarks explaining how they coped, the men and women with dyslexia reported their use of context as an important aid to reading.

> *Alexander Goldowsky (museum coordinator):*
> I tended to be fairly, you know, context-driven. So I made assumptions very quickly based on context and usually substituted a reasonable word.

> *Barbara Bidofsky (special educator):*
> I used context a lot to guess at new words.

> *Baruj Benacerraf (immunologist):*
> Even today, when I can't figure out a word, I guess from context.

Because their ability to decode was often unreliable, they used decoding strategies along with context clues, but not necessarily effectively. Many felt that, in spite of explicit phonics instruction, their ability to decode through the use of phonological strategies remained poor.

> *Charlann Simon (speech pathologist):*
> To this day, I can't sound out a word.

> *Charles Bean (neurologist):*
> Phonics doesn't always work. Even though I'll read phonetically, my phonetic sounds don't always fit with everybody else's.

> *Florence Hazeltine (gynecologist):*
> I can't sound out anything.

> *Annette Jenner (biologist):*
> I had phonics training in the resource room, but it never got into my head.

Even in cases where they had mastered most of the sound-symbol relationships of English, many seemed to have difficulty using this knowledge due to ongoing problems with the blending and sequencing of sounds.

> *Marlene Hirschberg (arts administrator):*
> I could look at the letter and tell you what the sound was, but I couldn't put it together into a word.

Contextual guessing strategies were more reliable than phonological decoding strategies for many of these men and women with dyslexia.

> *Susan Marlett (artist):*
> I cannot figure out how to pronounce a word based on its letters; I always guess it wrong. But I can figure out what words mean from the words around them.

It was easier to guess and correctly predict a word when the schema of a particular topic was familiar. Schema knowledge provided the conceptual scaffolds that supported optimal reading skills in a topic of interest. By focusing on a single domain of knowledge, many of the individuals with dyslexia became virtual "little experts" about their favorite topic, sometimes beginning at an early age. For some, early reading interests later developed into high-powered careers; for others, early reading interests developed into lifelong hobbies.

How did experiences of males and females differ?

Personal interests played a pivotal role in the literacy development of both the men and women with dyslexia. There were clear gender differences in personal reading interests. As children, they chose both fiction and nonfiction that embraced their specific interests. Of the 30 women with dyslexia, 23 preferred fiction, whereas 7 preferred non-fiction. Of the 30 men with dyslexia, 14 preferred fiction, whereas 16 preferred non-fiction. Gender differences in topics of personal interest reading were statistically significant (chi square = 5.71, p = .017). Table III summarizes findings related to gender and topics of high interest reading.

Table III. Early reading interests*

Women $n=30$		Men $n = 30$	
Novels	23	Novels	14
Biographies	2	Biographies	2
Science	2	Science	5
Social Studies	1	Social Studies	6
Cooking	1	Automechanics	1
No Data	1	Sailing	1
		Poetry	1

*Gender differences in topics of high interest reading were statistically significant (chi square = 5.71, p = .017).

Women, more often than men, noted the "pull" of reading materials related to developmental self-identity and relational issues provided in novels. Men, more often than women, were drawn into factual information-loaded materials provided by nonfiction texts. Twenty percent of males with dyslexia, but only three percent of females, read avidly during childhood about social studies. The same pattern emerged with regard to scientific reading. As children, seventeen percent of males with dyslexia, compared to only seven percent of females, were avid science readers. These results, while based on small numbers, mirror the reading interests of nondyslexic children (Whitehead and Maddren 1974, pp. 24–25).

Most important for both males and females with dyslexia in this study was the specificity of their interest-driven reading. Through highly focused avid childhood reading in specialized disciplines and genres, they developed deep background knowledge, becoming conversant with domain-specific vocabulary, concepts, themes, questions, and typical text structures. Repetition and practice within a content domain facilitated optimal skill development.

CURRENT LITERACY ASSESSMENT RESULTS

What literacy levels did they develop?

As adults, the men and women with dyslexia demonstrated most of the salient characteristics of Chall's Stage 5, the highest level of literacy development (Chall 1983). This was demonstrated in their high performance on the DARTT, shown in table II. In 95% of cases, their knowledge of word meanings and silent reading comprehension levels reached ceiling (GE = 12th grade level), as high as the DARTT measures. Only 5% of the individuals with dyslexia did not reach ceiling in these skills. Their scores were similar to those of the nondyslexic control participants. Moreover, according to their strong performance on the ND, the men and women with dyslexia also demonstrated the ability to read silently and comprehend text at high collegiate and postgraduate levels that were only slightly lower than those of the nondyslexic comparison group (see table II).

The solid performance of the adults with dyslexia on both the vocabulary and silent reading comprehension subtests of the DARTT and ND demonstrates their ability as adults to read, understand, make inferences and create meaning from text. These are all Stage 5 skills. Furthermore, their current utilization and application of reading skills demonstrates Stage 5 performance. Stage 5 entails reading materials that are "highly difficult, specialized, technical, and abstract" (Chall 1983, p. 100). Sylvia Law explained how she reads huge amounts of highly technical legal materials today.

Sylvia Law (attorney):
When you're immersed in a field, you kind of know what the forest looks like, and you're looking to see if there's a particular tree in here. So it's easy to just skim and zero in on the important stuff in the law. You know, the most important sentence in a 100 page document, where it says, 'The court says. . . .' So there are a lot of techniques and filtering devices that I use to get through lengthy legal documents.

As Chall points out, the sophisticated Stage 5 reader uses reading for his or her own professional and personal purposes; ". . . reading serves to integrate one's own knowledge with that of others, to synthesize it and to create new knowledge" (Chall 1983 p. 87). The men and women with dyslexia in this study demonstrate all the salient characteristics of Stage 5 except for speed and efficiency, which many of them still lack. All of them read materials that are technical, specialized, and abstract. They do a substantial amount of daily writing in their professions. Moreover, they integrate and synthesize knowledge from other experts with their own knowledge and create and contribute significantly to the canon of new knowledge in their fields of expertise. Their books and scholarly articles number in the hundreds. The impressive scholarly publications and other creative writings of these men and women with dyslexia provide evidence of their creation of new knowledge, a hallmark of Stage 5[1]

As adults, did they show jagged literacy profiles?

The 60 adults with dyslexia showed strengths in components of literacy that Chall (1994) has called higher level "meaning aspects." Higher level "meaning aspects" include vocabulary knowledge and silent reading comprehension. All but six participants with dyslexia scored at ceiling (12th grade level) on the DARTT in these skills, as shown in figure 1. However, despite the congruence of positive results on vocabulary and reading comprehension subtests of both the DARTT and ND, a distinct subset of individuals with dyslexia showed a pattern of ongoing weaknesses in what Chall (1994) has called lower level, "print aspects" of literacy. Their ongoing weaknesses in "print" components were documented in results from the word recognition, oral reading accuracy, and spelling subtests of the DARTT, shown in table II.

---

[1]Among the men and women with RD are Dr. Baruj Benaccerraf, 1980 Nobel laureate in Immunology and Pathology; Lora Brody, TV/radio personality and author of *Cooking with Memories*; Dr. Donald Francis, AIDS researcher activist and protagonist of the movie "And the Band Played On;" Dr. Florence Haseltine, author of *Woman Doctor* and *Women's Health Research*; Dr. Robert Knapp, Harvard oncologist and author of *Gynecological Oncology*; Professor Ronald W. Davis, genomics researcher and biochemistry textbook author; George Deem, New York City artist, Susan Brown, New York City filmmaker; and Professor Sylvia Law, N.Y.U. legal scholar and author of books on poverty, health care, welfare, and the law.

Distinct groups of highly successful adults with dyslexia emerged from this study. One, a compensated group, revealed few, if any, ongoing weaknesses among the subcomponents of reading in adulthood. The compensated group's performance was high across all literacy measures. Seventeen individuals met this criterion, as shown in figure 1. In addition to their ability to comprehend sophisticated text, they demonstrated strong compensation in word recognition, oral reading accuracy, and spelling.

Another group, those with partially compensated dyslexia, showed jagged profiles of literacy strengths and weaknesses. This group consisted of 43 participants. With the exception of six individuals, the partially compensated group also met the criteria on the DARTT of scoring at ceiling in knowledge of word meanings and silent reading comprehension. However, the partially compensated group showed lags in other subskills. They lagged behind individuals with compensated dyslexia and the nondyslexic comparison group in word recognition, oral reading accuracy, and spelling. As table II documents, for each of these subskills, the compensated and partially compensated groups differed significantly based on the results of chi square tests, (word recognition, $p = .01$; oral reading accuracy, $p = .001$; spelling, $p = < .001$). Thus, differences in profiles shown in figure 1 were corroborated by statistical tests.

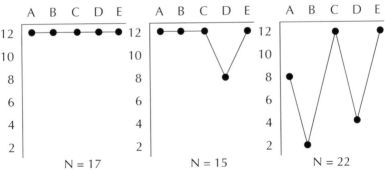

The numbers on the vertical axis represent the grade equivalent score. Maximum performance on this test is 12th grade level.
> A = word recognition
> B = oral reading
> C = silent reading comprehension
> D = spelling
> E = knowledge of word meanings

Six individuals did not fit into these types.

Figure 1.   Profiles of compensated and partially compensated dyslexics.

Partially compensated individuals with dyslexia fell into two categories: one category contained those who lagged behind individuals with compensated dyslexia and the nondyslexic comparison group in spelling alone; another category contained those who lagged behind in spelling, word recognition, and oral reading. Figure 1 illustrates the two types of partially compensated jagged profiles. One dips only in spelling (15 individuals); the other dips in word recognition and oral reading as well as spelling (22 individuals). The six remaining individuals with partially compensated dyslexia showed similar jagged profiles of strengths and weaknesses; however, their strengths did not reach ceiling, and their weaknesses dipped slightly lower than those of the other partially compensated individuals.

When tested as adults and compared with the nondyslexic comparison participants, individuals with dyslexia performed poorly overall on all measures of phonological and decoding skills, including the Pig Latin Test, the Florida Nonsense Passages Test, and the Graded Nonword Reading and Spelling Tests. An analysis of variance was performed to compare the means for the nondyslexic comparison group and the total group of individuals with dyslexia. Differences between the groups were statistically significant on each of these assessments (see table II). For example, on the Florida Nonsense Passages, differences between the nondyslexic comparison group and the total number of individuals with dyslexia were highly significant, both for speed and accuracy, ($p = .0001$). On the Pig Latin Test, differences were also significant. Out of 48 items, the mean number correct for the nondyslexic comparison group was 44.2 ($SD=5.6$); in contrast, the mean for the total individuals with dyslexia was only 33.0 ($SD=11.8$), p = .005. These results, taken together, attest to ongoing difficulties of the individuals with dyslexia with phonological skills such as blending, sequencing, and manipulating language sounds and symbols.

Table II summarizes the results of all the literacy tests administered and shows three main findings: (1) on every measure of literacy, nondyslexic participants outperformed individuals with dyslexia, (2) the fully compensated group consistently outperformed both of the partially compensated groups, and (3) for individuals with partially compensated dyslexia, ongoing jagged profiles of literacy strengths and weaknesses persisted in adulthood.

Did reading rate distinguish compensated from partially compensated readers?

I told participants that I would record the number of questions they had completed on the ND at the end of the standard test time. If they had not completed the test at the end of the standard time, I told them that they could continue under an extended time condition. All nondyslexic participants completed the ND within the standard time. In contrast, 58% of the total individuals with dyslexia used extended time. These differences, shown in table II, were highly significant, ($p = .001$).

Furthermore, on the one-minute reading rate subtest of the ND, 33% of partially compensated individuals had scaled scores less than 180, indicating reading rates that were slower than those of both compensated individuals and the nondyslexic comparison group (see table II). A chi square test comparing compensated and partially compensated individuals' reading rates showed that differences in rate were highly significant, ($p = .007$). Thus, in many cases, rate further distinguished compensated from partially compensated readers. Comparisons of test scores of those who took the ND with standard versus extended time showed that those who took the test with extended time performed well overall, but not as well as those who took the test within the standard time. Based on comparisons of individuals' scores with standard versus extended time conditions, it was apparent that, without the accommodation of extended time, many individuals with dyslexia would have scored lower on the ND.

QUESTIONNAIRE RESULTS

How did the adult reading habits and attitudes of the groups compare?

By adulthood, 25 men and 26 women with dyslexia reported positive reading attitudes, asserting that they valued and enjoyed reading a great deal. All nondyslexic comparison participants reported having a strong positive attitude. Thus, overall reading attitudes of individuals with dyslexia and nondyslexic participants were similar.

When questioned about the extent of their current reading, there was a slight trend for individuals with dyslexia of both types, compensated and partially compensated, to report less reading overall than the nondyslexic comparison group. Participants in all categories reported doing a great deal of work-related reading and, specifically, more reading for work than reading for pleasure. All nondyslexic participants reported doing a great deal of work-related reading. In comparison, 88% of fully compensated individuals and 67% of partially compensated individuals reported doing a great deal of work-related reading (see table IV).

When questioned about the extent of their current reading for pleasure, there were significant differences among the groups. Eighty percent of the nondyslexic comparison group said they engaged in a great deal of reading for pleasure. This compared with only 53% of the fully compensated group and 37% of the partially compensated group.

Table IV. Adult self-reported reading habits, using scale of 0 to 4 from the adult reading history questionnaire*

| | Non-dyslexic Controls (N = 10) | Individuals with Dyslexia | | | Contrasts** | |
		Fully Compensated (N = 17)	Partially Compensated (N = 43)	Total Dyslexics (N = 60)	Controls v. Total Dyslexia***	Full v. Partial***
Work-related Reading						
(% reporting a great deal)	100%	88%	67%	73%	.063	.101
Mean response (SD)	3.7 (.5)	3.5 (1.0)	3.0 (.9)	3.1 (.9)	.0683	.0652
Range	3–4	0–4	1–4	0–4		
Pleasure Reading						
(% reporting a great deal)	80%	53%	37%	42%	.025	.265
Mean response (SD)	3.4 (.8)	2.5 (1.1)	2.2 (1.3)	2.3 (1.2)	.0081	.4049
Range	2–4	0–4	0–4	0–4		
Book Reading						
Mean response (SD)	3.7 (.6)	2.5 (1.2)	2.4 (1.4)	2.4 (1.3)	.0046	.7966
Range	2–4	0–4	0–4	0–4		
Magazine Reading						
Mean response (SD)	3.2 (1.2)	2.0 (1.3)	2.0 (1.4)	2.0 (1.4)	.0113	1.0
Range	0–4	0–4	0–4	0–4		
Daily News Reading						
Mean response (SD)	3.8 (1.2)	2.9 (1.4)	2.7 (1.4)	2.8 (1.4)	.1142	.6199
Range	1–4	0–4	0–4	0–4		
Sunday News Reading						
Mean response (SD)	3.8 (.4)	2.9 (1.0)	2.7 (1.0)	2.8 (1.0)	.0019	.4879
Range	0–1	1–4	0–4	0–4		

*(4 = a great deal; 0 = none, or not at all)

**Full data set available upon request (participants' identities withheld)

***Observed probability levels from the statistical contrasts; the first column of contrasts shows comparisons between the nondyslexic comparison group and the total number of individuals with dyslexia; the second column of contrasts shows comparisons between fully compensated and partially compensated individuals with dyslexia.

Table IV shows that the nondyslexic comparison group and both groups of individuals with dyslexia read numerous books, magazines, and newspapers regularly. However, on average, nondyslexic participants do more of each type of reading than individuals with dyslexia. Nevertheless, of the 30 men and 30 women with dyslexia, 21 men and 20 women read a Sunday newspaper regularly, and 21 men and 16 women read a daily newspaper regularly. These results confirm findings by Finucci and her colleagues regarding the reading habits of men with dyslexia (Finucci, Gottfredsen, and Childs 1985); and, these results extend research to include women. Interestingly, there were gender differences in the extent of book reading among adults with dyslexia. Sixteen women with dyslexia, compared to only six men, read more than ten books per year for pleasure. While the numbers are small, these results fit with results regarding the reading habits of nondyslexic individuals; females overall engage in more extensive book reading than males (Finucci, Gottfredsen, and Childs 1985).

CONCLUSIONS AND DISCUSSION

Stage 5 literacy

Results from this study revealed distinct groups of highly successful adults with dyslexia: a fully compensated group and two partially compensated groups. On average, members of each group developed fluency at a basic level three or more years later than normally developing peers. Literacy development in all groups was augmented by avid reading in a content area of passionate personal interest. And, members of each group currently comprehend complex text at Stage 5, the highest level of reading development. Moreover, they create and write sophisticated, provocative texts of their own, as demonstrated by their publication of important books and scholarly articles.

Despite these noteworthy strengths and accomplishments, the partially compensated men and women with dyslexia manifest persistent ongoing weaknesses in phonological abilities and processing speed, as shown by their lags in word recognition, oral reading accuracy, spelling, and reading rate. Although they show these ongoing deficits, they have mastered the ultimate goal of reading—the ability to make meaning from complex text. This finding is consistent with Weaver's synthesis of a large body of reading research framed by "a theory of reading that puts meaning at the heart of reading from the very beginning" (Weaver 1998, p. 14).

Gender differences

A second finding from this study was that females with dyslexia preferred fiction, whereas males with dyslexia preferred nonfiction. This result fits with findings in the literature on the reading preferences and interests of nondyslexics. It is possible that the finding of gender differences in preferred topics of reading could have greater consequences for adults with RD. The finding of gender differences in reading interests raises an important question for practice: How might teachers engage adults with dyslexia in reading through their preferred interests and genres without promoting gender stereotypes? This issue, which merits further discussion, is beyond the scope of this chapter. However, the issue is discussed in detail elsewhere (see Fink 2000 for further analysis and discussion of issues on gender and dyslexia).

A model of dyslexia

The study reported here confirmed and extended results of previous research on the role of personal interests (Fink 1992, 1993, 1995/96, 1998; Renninger 1992; Schiefele and Krapp 1996) to a larger sample that included a comparison group and equal numbers of men and women with dyslexia. An outcome of the study is a model of dyslexia that explains how individuals with dyslexia, who in adulthood may continue to lack strong integration of basic, lower level "print" skills, construct higher order "meaning" skills. Key elements of the model include four main components: (1) passionate personal interest in a content area that requires reading, (2) avid, highly focused reading, (3) deep schema knowledge, and (4) contextual strategies.

The finding of domain-specific contextual strategies for reading confirms and extends results from previous research by Blalock and Bruck, who independently found that adults with dyslexia are extremely skilled at using contextual cues (Blalock 1981), and that use of context improved their reading speed and accuracy (Bruck 1990). The 60 successful men and women with dyslexia in this study used domain-specific context and developed Stage 5 skills through scaffolding provided by avid reading in a content area of passionate personal interest. In many cases this occurred in conjunction with systematic instruction in phonological decoding strategies. This analysis emphasizes the need for a balanced approach to teaching that simultaneously includes both "print" and "meaning" literacy components in a thoughtful, theoretically sound, integrated program of instruction.

The double deficit hypothesis

This study's finding of three groups of individuals with dyslexia (one compensated and two partially compensated) is consistent with the Double Deficit Hypothesis, in which phonological deficits and processing speed deficits are "depicted as separable concurrent sources of reading disability whose combined presence leads to the most profound forms of reading impairment" (Bowers and Wolf 1993; Wolf 2000). The partially compensated individuals with the most jagged profiles fit the Double Deficit pattern of profound reading impairment. As adults, these individuals are slower in reading speed and weaker in phonological skills, as their weak word recognition, oral reading, spelling, and reading rate scores attest. Instructional techniques that have been suggested for ameliorating literacy difficulties in the most severely affected "double deficit" readers include increased emphasis on instruction that stresses fluency training to promote automaticity. And, theoretical models of reading acquisition have long suggested that development of fluency and automaticity are central components of skilled reading (Adams 1996; LaBerge and Samuels 1974; Perfetti 1977; Stanovich 1980). However, few commercial programs currently provide fluency training (Meyer et al. 1997).

Implications for instruction

I propose here that interest-driven instruction be used to help develop fluency and automaticity. The results of this study suggest that interest-based teaching approaches can provide some of the practice and exposure to print required for fluency development. Moreover, the results suggest that both systematic decoding instruction and literature- and other text-based approaches need to be included simultaneously. This conclusion fits with Pressley's (1998) finding that concurrent skills-based and content-based instruction provides the basis for optimal motivation, desire, and skill in reading. It is also consistent with the conceptualization of reading in *Preventing Reading Difficulties in Young Children* in which "frequent and intensive opportunities to read" and "continued interest and motivation to read. . . ." constitute part of an adequate instructional program (Snow, Burns, and Griffin 1998, pp. 3–4). Strucker and Snow argue that many conclusions from studies of children are applicable to instruction for adults experiencing literacy difficulties, regardless whether adults' difficulties are due to learning disabilities or other factors (Strucker and Snow 2000). The results of this study suggest that interest-based teaching approaches can provide the necessary practice and exposure to print required for fluency development in adults who struggle with literacy. The positive outcomes of these 60 highly successful men and women with dyslexia who developed Stage 5 skills, argue for integrating solid interest-based approaches as a centerpiece of instruction.

These results indicate a need for teachers to provide reading materials based on adults' passionate interests. How can teachers ascertain adults' interests? One way is by using individual reading interest inventories; these questionnaires are easy to administer and modify to fit each adult's age and developmental stage (Fink 1995/1996, 1998, 2000). Another way to ascertain interests is to conduct interviews, inquiring about adults' current and former jobs and careers, hobbies, favorite books, movies, television programs, videos, computer games and activities, and internet websites. After interviewing each adult, gather materials accordingly based on each person's individual interests.

It is never too late to learn to read well. I hope that the results of this study inspire others and empower educators, clinicians, and families to encourage adults who struggle with literacy to capitalize on their passionate personal interests.

ACKNOWLEDGEMENTS

This research was supported by a Spencer Postdoctoral Research Fellowship through the National Academy of Education. The author is grateful to the Spencer Foundation and the National Academy of Education for their generous support. The author would like to thank Dr. Susan Vogel for helping to make this book a reality. Finally, thanks to the men and women who participated in the study; without their courage, candor, and generosity, the study described in this chapter would not have been possible.

REFERENCES

Aaron, P. G. 1997. The impending demise of the discrepancy formula. *Review of Educational Research* 67(4):461–502.

Adams, M. J. 1996. *Beginning to Read: Thinking and Learning about Print.* Cambridge, MA: Massachusetts Institute of Technology.

Anderson, J. R. 1983. *The Architecture of Cognition.* Cambridge, MA: Harvard University Press.

Anderson-lnman, L., and Horney, M. 1996/1997. Computer-based concept mapping: Enhancing literacy with tools for visual thinking. *Journal of Adolescent and Adult Literacy* 40(4):302–306.

Attanucci, J. 1988. In whose terms: A new perspective on self, role, and relationship. In *Mapping the Moral Domain,* eds. C. Gilligan, J. V. Ward, and J. M. Taylor, pp. 201–24. Cambridge, MA: Harvard University.

Blackorby, J., and Wagner, M. 1996. Longitudinal postschool outcomes of youth with disabilities: Findings from the National Longitudinal Transition Study. *Exceptional Children* 62(5):399–413.

Blalock, J. W. 1981. Persistent problems and concerns of young adults with learning disabilities. In *Bridges to Tomorrow: The Best of ACDL,* eds. W. M. Cruickshank and A. A. Silver, pp. 35–55. Syracuse, NY: Syracuse University Press.

Bowers, P. G., and Wolf, M. 1993. *A "Double Deficit Hypothesis for Developmental Reading Disorders.* Paper presented at the Society for Research in Child Development. New Orleans: LA.

Brown, J. I. , Fischco, V. V., and Hanna, G. 1993. *Nelson-Denny Reading Test, Form H.* Chicago: Riverside.

Bruck, M. 1990. Word recognition skills of adults with childhood diagnoses of dyslexia. *Developmental Psychology* 26(3):439–54.

Chall, J. S. 1983. *Stages of Reading Development.* New York: McGraw-Hill.

Chall, J. S. 1994. Patterns of adult reading. *Learning Disabilities* 5(1):29–33.

Decker, S. N., Vogler, G. P., and DeFries, J. C. 1989. Validity of self-reported reading disability by parents of reading disabled and control children. *Reading and Writing* 1(4):327–31.

Dewey, J. 1913. *Interest and Effort in Education.* Boston: Riverside Press.

Feldman, E., Levin, B. E., Lubs, H., Rabin, M., Lubs, M. L., Jallad, B., and Kushch, A. 1993. Adult familial dyslexia: A retrospective developmental and psychosocial profile. *Journal of Neuropsychiatry and Clinical Neuroscience* 5:195–99.

Felton, R. H., Naylor, C. E., and Wood, F. B. 1990. Neuropsychological profile of adult dyslexics. *Brain and Language* 39:485-97.

Fink, R. P. 2000. Gender and imagination: Gender conceptualization and literacy development in successful adults with reading disabilities. *Learning Disabilities: A Multidisciplinary Journal* 10(3):183–96.

Fink, R. P. 1998, Literacy development in successful men and women with dyslexia. *Annals of Dyslexia* 48:311–46.

Fink, R. P. 1995/1996. Successful dyslexics: A constructivist study of passionate interest reading. *Journal of Adolescent and Adult Literacy* 39(4):268–80.

Fink, R. P. 1993. How successful dyslexics learn to read. *Teaching Thinking and Problem Solving* 15(5):1–6.

Fink, R. P. 1992. Successful dyslexics' alternative pathways for reading: A developmental study (Doctoral dissertation, Harvard Graduate School of Education, 1992). *Dissertation Abstracts International* F4965.

Finucci, J. M., Gottfredson, L. S., and Childs, B. 1985. A follow-up study of dyslexic boys. *Annals of Dyslexia* 35:117–36.

Finucci, J. M., Whitehouse, C. C., lsaacs, S. D., and Childs, B. 1984. Derivation and validation of a quantitative definition of specific reading disability for adults. *Developmental Medicine and Child Neurology* 26(2):143–53.

Foorman, B. R., Francis, D. J., Fletcher, J. M., Schatschneider, C., and Mehta, P. 1998. The role of instruction in learning to read: Preventing reading failure in at-risk children. *Journal of Educational Psychology* 90(37):37–55.

Fowler, A. E., and Scarborough, H. S. 1993. Should reading-disabled adults be distinguished from other adults seeking literacy instruction? A review of theory and research (Technical Report #TR9S-7). Philadelphia, PA: National Center on Adult Literacy.

Gadsden, V. 1991. Literacy and the African-American learner. *Theory into Practice* 31(4):270–78.

Gerber, P. J., Ginsberg, R., & Reiff, H. B. 1992. Identifying alterable patterns in employment success for highly successful adults with learning disabilities, *Journal of Learning Disabilities* 25:475–87.

Gerber, P. J., and Reiff, H. B. 1992. *Speaking for Themselves: Ethnographic Interviews with Adults with Learning Disabilities.* Ann Arbor, MI: University of Michigan.

Gilger, J. W. 1992. Using self-report and parental-report survey data to assess past and present academic achievement of adults and children. *Journal of Applied Developmental Psychology* 13:235–56.

Griesbach, G. 1993. Dyslexia: Its history etiology, and treatment. (Report No. CS011300). West Bend, WI: ERIC Document Reproduction Service.

Gross-Glenn, K., Jallad, B. J., Novoa, L., Helgren-Lempesis, V., and Lubs, H. A. 1990. Nonsense passage reading as a diagnostic aid in the study of adult familial dyslexia, *Reading and Writing An Interdisciplinary Journal* 2:161–73.

Kirsch, I. S., Jungeblut, A., Jenkins, L., and Kolstad, A. 1993. *Adult Literacy in America: A First Look at the Results of the National Adult Literacy Survey.* Washington, DC: National Center for Education Statistics, U.S. Department of Education.

Knight, J. 1986. The adult dyslexic in remediation: The ABCs and much more. *Churchill Forum* 8:1–4.

LaBerge, D., and Samuels, S. J. 1974. Toward a theory of automatic information processing in reading. *Cognitive Psychology* 6:293–323.

Ladson-Billings, G. 1994. *The Dreamkeepers.* San Francisco: Jossey-Bass.

Lefly, D. L. 1997. Risk status and phonological processing. (Ph.D. diss., University of Denver, Denver, CO).

Lefly, D. L., and Pennington, B. F. 1991. Spelling errors and reading fluency in compensated adult dyslexics. *Annals of Dyslexia* 41:143–62.

Lefly, D. L., and Pennington, B. F. in review. Reliability and validity study of the adult reading history questionnaire.

Lyon, G. R. (Ed.). 1994. *Frames of Reference for the Assessment of Learning Disabilities: New Views on Measurement Issue.* Baltimore: Paul H. Brookes Publishing Company.

Lyon, G. R., and Moats, L. 1988. Critical issues in the instruction of the learning disabled. *Journal of Consulting and Clinical Psychology* 56:830–35.

Meyer, M. S., Wood, F. B., Hart, L. A., and Felton, R. H. 1997, November. *Selective Predictive Value of Rapid Automatized Naming within Poor Readers.* Poster session presented at the annual meeting of the International Dyslexia Association, Minneapolis, Minnesota.

Meyer, A., Pisha, B., and Rose, D. 1991. Process and product in writing: Computer as Enabler. In *Written Language Disorders; Theory into Practice*, eds. A. M. Bain, L. L. Ballet, and L. C. Moats. Austin, TX: PRO-ED.

Morris, G. H. 1983. Adapting a college preparatory curriculum for dyslexic adolescents: Confronting the problems of what to teach. *Annals of Dyslexia* 33:243–50.

O'Connor, J., and Wilson, B. 1995. Effectiveness of the Wilson Reading System used in public school training. In *Clinical Studies of Multisensory Structured Language Education*, eds. C. McIntyre and J. Pickering. Salem, OR: International Multisensory Structured Language Education Council.

Orton Dyslexia Society Research Committee. 1994. Operational definition of dyslexia. In *Perspectives*, ed. C. Scruggs. 20(5):4.

Perfetti, C. A. 1977. Language comprehension and fast decoding: Some psycholinguistic prerequisites for skilled reading comprehension. In *Cognition Curriculum and Comprehension*, ed. J. Guthrie. Newark, DE: International Reading Association.

Pressley, M. 1998. *Reading Instruction That Works: The Case for Balanced Teaching*, New York: Guilford.

Purcell-Gates, V. 1995. *Other People's Words: The Cycle of Low Literacy.* Cambridge, MA: Harvard University Press.

Rawson, M. 1968. *Developmental Language Disability; Adult Accomplishments of Dyslexic Boys.* Baltimore: Johns Hopkins University Press.

Renninger, K. A. 1992. Individual interest and development: Implications for theory and practice. In *The Role of Interest in Learning and Development*, eds. K. A. Renninger, S. Hidi, and A. Krapp, Hillsdale, NJ: Lawrence Erlbaum Associates.

Roffman, A. 2000. *Adults with Learning Disabilities: Life-long Struggles.* Baltimore: Paul H. Brookes Publishing Company.

Rose, D. H., and Meyer, A. 1996. Expanding the literacy toolbox: Why we must broaden our definition of literacy and incorporate new media in the classroom (Literacy Paper 11): Scholastic, Inc.

Rose, D. H., and Meyer, A. 1994. The role of technology in language arts instruction. *Language Arts* 71(4):290–94.

Roswell, F. G., and Chall, J. S. 1992. *Diagnostic Assessments of Reading with Trial Teaching Strategies*. Chicago: Riverside.

Scarborough, H. S. 1984. Continuity between childhood dyslexia and adult reading. *British Journal of Psychology* 75:329–48.

Schiefele, U. 1990. The influence of topic interest, prior knowledge, and cognitive capabilities on text comprehension. In *Learning Environments*, eds. J. M. Pieters, K. Breuer, and P. R. J. Simons, pp. 323–38. Heidelberg: Springer.

Shaywitz, B., Fletcher, J., and Shaywitz, S. 1994. The conceptual framework for learning disabilities and attention deficit/hyperactivity disorder. *Canadian Journal of Special Education* 9(3):1–32.

Snow, C. E., Burns, M. S., and Griffin, P. (Eds.). 1998. *Preventing Reading Difficulties in Young Children*. Washington, DC: National Academy Press.

Snowling, M., Stothard, S., and McLean, J. 1996. *Graded Nonword Reading Test*. Edmunds, England: Thames Valley Test Publishers.

Stanovich, K. E. 1991. Discrepancy definitions of reading disability: Has intelligence led us astray? *Reading Research Quarterly* 26(7):7–29.

Stanovich, K. E. 1980. Toward an interactive-compensatory model of individual differences in the development of reading fluency. *Reading Research Quarterly* 16:32–71.

Strucker, J., and Snow, C. E. 2000. Lessons of preventing reading difficulties in young children for the study of adult learning and literacy. *Annual Review of Adult Learning and Literacy* 1(1):25–73.

Vogel, S. 1987. Issues and concerns in LID college programming. In *Adults with Learning Disabilities: Clinical Studies,* eds. D. Johnson and J. Blalock, pp. 239–75. Orlando, FL: Grune & Stratton.

Vogel, S. A., and Reder, S. 2000. Literacy proficiency among adults with self-reported learning disabilities. In *Literacy for the 21st Century: Research, Policy, and Practice,* ed. M. C. Smith. Westport, CT: Greenwood Publishing (Praeger).

Vogel, S. A., and Reder, S. 1998. Educational attainment of adults with learning disabilities. In *Learning Disabilities Literacy, and Adult Education*, eds. S. A. Vogel and S. Reder. Baltimore: Paul H. Brookes Publishing Company.

Weaver, C. 1998. *A Balanced Approach to Reading Instruction*. Urbana, Illinois: National Council of Teachers of English.

Whitehead, F., and Maddren, W. 1974. Children's reading interests (Schools Council Working Paper No. 52). London, England: University of Sheffield Institute of Education, Schools Council Research Project into Children's Reading Habits.

Wolf, M. 2000. A provisional, integrative account of phonological and naming-speed deficits in dyslexia: Implications for diagnosis and intervention. In *Cognitive and Linguistic Foundations of Reading Acquisition: Implications for Intervention Research*, ed. B. Blachman. Hillsdale, NJ: Lawrence Erlbaum Associates.

Zigmond, N., and Thornton, H. 1989. Follow-up of postsecondary age learning disabled graduates and dropouts. *Learning Disabilities Research* 1(1): 50–55.

APPENDIX 1

Professionally successful men and women with dyslexia

Men

1. J. William Adams — Headmaster
The Gow School
South Wales, New York

2. S. Charles Bean — Neurologist
Clinical Associate Professor
Jefferson Hospital
Philadelphia, Pennsylvania

3. Baruj Benacerraf — Immunologist
Professor of Immunology
Chair, Department of
Pathology
Harvard Medical School
Boston, Massachusetts

4. William Brewer — Psychologist
Professor of Psychology
University of Illinois
Champaign, Illinois

5. Michael L. Commons — Psychometrician
Lecturer/Research Associate
Department of Psychiatry
Harvard Medical School
Boston, Massachusetts

6. Heriberto Cresto — Social Worker
Latino Health Institute
Boston, Massachusetts

7. Ronald W. Davis — Biochemist
Director, Stanford DNA
Sequencing/Technology
Center
Professor, Stanford University
School of Medicine
Stanford, California

8. George Deem — Graphic Artist
New York, New York
Adjunct Professor of Art
University of Pennsylvania
Philadelphia, Pennsylvania

9. C. Emerson Dickman

Attorney at Law
Maywood, New Jersey

10. H. Girard Ebert

Interior Designer and CEO
H. Girard Ebert, Inc.
Baltimore, Maryland

11. Donald Francis

Virologist/AIDS Researcher
Genentech, Inc.
Founder and President
VaxGen, Inc.
San Francisco, California

12. Miles Gerety

Attorney at Law
Connecticut Public Defender
Bridgeport, Connecticut

13. Daniel Gillette

Learning Specialist and
    Coordinator of Advising
Boston Architectural Center
Boston, Massachusetts

14. Alexander Goldowsky

Program Developer
New England Aquarium
Boston, Massachusetts

15. David Gordon

Marketing Consultant
Adaptive Computing
Beverly, Massachusetts

16. Philip Hulbig

Tutor
Walpole, Massachussetts

17. Robert Knapp

Gynecologist
Professor and Chair
Department of Gynecology
Harvard Medical School
Boston, Massachusetts

18. John Moore

Social Worker
Boston, Massachusetts

19. Jonathan Pazer

Attorney at Law
Law Offices of Pazer and
    Epstein
New York, New York

20. Bart Pisha   Computer Specialist
Director of Research Center
  for Applied Special
  Technology (CAST)
Peabody, Massachusetts

21. Cruz Sanabria   Early Childhood Educator
Boston, Massachusetts

22. Michael Schweitzer   General and Vascular Surgeon
Virginia Surgical Specialists
Richmond, Virginia

23. David Selib   Sales Manager
Reebok International
Medfield, Massachusetts

24. Larry B. Silver   Psychiatrist and Writer
Clinical Professor of
  Psychiatry
Georgetown University
  School of Medicine
Washington, DC

25. James Soberman   Dentist
Clinical Assistant Professor
  of Prosthodontics
New York University
New York, New York

26. Michael Spock   Co-Director/Researcher
Chapin Hall
Center for Children
University of Chicago
Chicago, Illinois

27. A. McDonald Vaz   Writer
Miami Beach, Florida

28. Michael Van Zandt   Research Scientist
Institute for Diabetes
  Discovery
Branford, Connecticut

29. Thomas C. West   Writer
Visualization Research
  Institute
Washington, DC

30. Glenn Young

Learning Disabilities
  Program Specialist
Washington State Department.
  of Social and Health Services
Seattle, Washington

Women

1. Hannah Adams

Elementary Teacher
Cambridge, Massachusetts

2. Tania Baker

Biochemist;
Professor
Massachusetts Institute
  of Technology (MIT)
Boston, Massachusetts

3. Barbara Bikofsky

Special Educator
Adjunct Instructor
Lesley University
Cambridge, Massachusetts

4. Lori Boskin

Director of Alumni Relations,
  Special Projects, and
  Promotions
UCLA School of Law
Los Angeles, California

5. Lora Brody

Cookbook Author
TV and Radio Personality
Newton, Massachusetts

6. Terry Bromfield

Senior Lecturer
Adjunct Assistant Professor
Lesley University
Cambridge, Massachusetts

7. Ann L. Brown

Researcher/ Educator
Professor of Education
University of California
Berkeley, California

8. Susan E. Brown

Filmmaker
New York, New York

9. Jane Buchbinder

Fiction Writer
Boston, Massachusetts

10. Susan Cobin   Administrator/Principal
Talmud Torah Day School
Saint Paul, Minnesota

11. Ellen Gorman   Social Worker
New Haven Adult Education
New Haven, Connecticut

12. Stacey Harris   Attorney at Law
Brookline, Massachusetts

13. Florence Haseltine   Gynecologist/Director
Center for Population
  Research
National Institutes of Health
Washington, DC

14. Marlene Hirschberg   Arts Administrator/Director
Jewish Community Center
Milwaukee, Wisconsin

15. Melissa Holt   Head Teacher
South Shore Day Care
Quincy, Massachusetts

16. Annette Jenner   Neurobiologist
Biology Teaching Fellow
Harvard University
Boston, Massachusetts

17. Anita Landa   Educator
Associate Professor
Lesley University
Cambridge, Massachusetts

18. Sylvia Law   Attorney at Law
Professor of Law, Medicine,
  and Psychiatry
New York University
  School of Law
New York, New York

19. Nancy Lelewer   Writer
Research Associate in
  Neurology
Harvard Medical School
Boston, Massachusetts

20. Joanne Lense

Social Worker
Bronx Lebanon Hospital and
  Knight Education
New York, New York

21. Susan Marlett

Artist
Clearway Technologies
Fort Lee, New Jersey

22. Robin Mello

Storyteller/Actress
Adjunct Instructor
Tufts University
Medford, Massachusetts

23. Fiona Moore

Social Worker
Human Resource Institute
Brookline, Massachusetts

24. Tania Phillips

Elementary Teacher
Northampton, Massachusetts

25. Priscilla Sariville

Arts Educator
Assistant Professor
Lesley University
Cambridge, Massachusetts

26. Marla Silver

Social Worker
Easton Hospital
Easton, Pennsylvania

27. Charlann Simon

Author and Program
  Developer
Speech/Language and
  Learning Specialist
Tempe, Arizona

28. Jane Smith

Anthropologist
American University
Washington, DC

29. Beth Steucek

Manager
Executive Vice President
New England Innkeepers
Rye, New Hampshire

30. Lezli Whitehouse

Language Clinician
Boston, Massachusetts

Chapter • 17

Forward Thinking:
Adults with Learning Disabilities/Dyslexia in the New Millennium

Susan A. Vogel

The overarching purpose of this book is to provide a rich compendium of information regarding adults with learning disabilities/dyslexia (LD/D) in higher education (HE) and beyond so that we can learn how to assist them more effectively and thereby enhance their chances for success in every aspect of their lives. This volume includes contributors from those countries where the needs of adults with LD in HE are presently being addressed, namely, Canada, Israel, the United Kingdom, and the United States. The contributors are psychologists, counselors, diagnosticians, service providers, attorneys, civil rights advocates, researchers, and adults with LD themselves. By sharing their groundbreaking work, we hope to enrich our understanding of the legislation, to enhance the HE environment, and to better prepare adults with LD for success beyond HE on an international scale. In this final chapter, we provide some of the cutting edge developments that have occurred in the recent past and then close with some universal specific recommendations that are the result of what we have learned to date.

THE SCOPE OF THE PROBLEM TO DATE

Researchers in the countries providing support services have contributed the most recent statistical reports regarding the incidence of LD among students in higher education. The American Council of

Education has been monitoring the incidence of self-reported disabilities in HE among first-year students since 1978. In their most recent statistical report, Henderson (2001) reported that 3.6% of first-year students self-reported a learning disability. In the UK, The Higher Education Statistics Agency (1999) reported an almost identical incidence rate of 3.8% of first-year students with LD. Israel has only just begun to report such data. The first such data appeared in an unpublished report submitted to the Israel Council on Higher Education in which Margalet, Breznitz, and Aharoni (1998) reported that between 1.5% and 3% of Israeli students in HE had a learning disability. In fact, the range of incidence is no doubt much broader than reported in Israel. For example, Heiman and Precel (2003) found that 4.98% of students enrolled in the Open University reported having a learning disability, almost double the incidence reported five years earlier. The reasons for the perceived variation in incidence at different colleges and universities in the US were investigated by Vogel, et al. (1998) using a complex model of institutional and programmatic factors. They reported that the range was from ?% to 10% depending on the type of institution (e.g., open admissions versus highly competitive admissions criteria; type of degrees offered including associate, bachelors; graduate degrees such as doctorate; and professional degrees), and the size of the student body (i.e., smaller institutions had a higher incidence of students with LD). Regardless of the incidence at a specific institution, the number of students with LD/D in HE represents a significant number of students and they are the focus of this volume on HE and beyond.

A CASE STUDY REGARDING AN ALTERNATIVE MECHANISM TO LEGISLATION FOR PROVISION OF COLLEGE/UNIVERSITY SUPPORT SERVICES FOR ADULTS WITH LD/D

In the last 20 years, we have witnessed a dramatic increase in the number of students with LD/D attending colleges and universities in the four countries that were the focus of this book. One of the outcomes that we are hoping will be achieved in the next decade is legislation that mandates access to higher education for qualified students with L/D/D in many more countries. Israel provides an alternative model in provision of support services and accommodations in the absence of legislative mandates that may prove helpful to other nations. In that country, a small group of professionals banded together under the umbrella organization called LESHEM (Hebrew for the flame of a candle), founded by a powerful parent advocate, Ms. Ruth Kaplan, and began lobbying for support services and accommodations in HE. Ms. Kaplan, a high-ranking civil servant in the Israeli government, initially raised money through private corporations and foundations. At the same time, she brought together experts from Canada, the United States, and Israel. A series of events funded and organized by LESHEM made the needs of highly capable college and university students with LD/D known including: (1) Susan Vogel's Handbook regarding college/ university students with LD/D and the necessary support services and accommodations was translated into Hebrew and distributed to every college/university President and the highest academic officers throughout the country; (2) An international conference was organized that included over 40 speakers from Canada, Israel, the United Kingdom, and the United States and over 300 participants; (3) The US Ambassador to Israel hosted a reception in his home where government representatives and leading professionals spoke to an invitation-only audience; (4) Professionals gave expert testimony before important government committees and enlisted their support; and (5) LESHEM funded the initial efforts of professionals in a few institutions in the country to provide different aspects of the needed support services including an ambitious comprehensive summer program, personal counseling support groups, and accommodations.

All of these efforts resulted in significant support in spite of the fact that formal legislation has not yet been implemented. The Planning and Finance Committee of the Israel Institute for Higher Education has now allocated financial support to approximately 40 institutions of HE to operate support centers under the supervision of LESHEM. The amount of the allocation to these institutions is based on the number of students with LD/D who receive support services. Although not all services are provided on each of the 40 campuses, they include assistance in the admissions process; diagnostic testing; academic counseling; provision of accommodations; training for service providers; special courses for students with LD/D on study skills, test taking strategies, time management, and computer technology; provision of workshops for faculty, administrators, and Supportive Professional Staff (SPS); and consultation services for faculty, administration, SPS, and students. A second initiative funded by the Institute provides half tuition for subject matter tutors to students with LD/D. Lastly, those students who are eligible for National Disability Insurance can receive up to full tuition and assistance with living expenses. Although threatened by economic shortfalls, the government has thus far continued to provide support through the Planning and Finance Committee of the Institute of Higher Education.

ELIGIBILITY FOR ACCOMMODATIONS IN COLLEGE, GRADUATE SCHOOL, AND PROFESSIONAL LICENSURE

In Chapter One, Sid Wolinsky and colleagues provided an in-depth history of the legislation and challenges brought by adults with LD/D that reached the courts. One such challenge (see Bartlett versus the New York State Board of Bar Examiners) confirmed the importance of a qualified clinician's interpretation of the diagnostic test results in relation to the individual's peers of equal cognitive abilities and educational attainment (rather than comparing the individual to national norms based on their age mates). This case made a strong statement in support of accommodations for gifted adults enrolled in elite institutions or taking licensure examinations such as teaching, law, and medicine throughout the world who, without accommodations, will not be able to by-pass the negative impact of their disability and achieve their goals.

FLAGGING TEST SCORES OF STUDENTS WITH LD/D

Another factor that may indirectly result in an increase in access to a larger than ever number of students with LD/D is the recent decision of the Educational Testing Services (ETS), the largest testing company in the US (possibly in the world) to discontinue the practice of flagging test scores when the individual takes the examination with accommodations (see chapter 1). College/university applicants who before were reluctant to request needed accommodations for fear of biasing the admissions decision against them when the test score report disclosed that they had some sort of disability, may very well be more likely to request accommodations, score higher than they would have without accommodations, and be accepted as a result of this groundbreaking settlement. This change in the practice of flagging by ETS resulted in The American College Testing Company and the College Board also discontinuing the practice of flagging on the tests they administer. Battles are still to be waged, however, against the National Board of Medical Examiners and the Law School Admissions Council who still refuse to discontinue the practice of flagging. However, the US ¤goliaths¤ in the testing arena headed up by ETS should serve as models to other countries to discontinue the practice of flagging transcripts, high school exit examinations, matriculation examinations, university admissions tests, and licensure tests for entrance into professions such as teaching, nursing, medicine, and law.

CREATING A MORE WELCOMING CAMPUS ENVIRONMENT

Important directions have emerged in the new millennium regarding factors that contribute to university students' academic success in addition to faculty attitude, knowledge, and practices (see chapter 11). The focus has been broadened to include administrators and supportive professional staff (SPS) who may be the first college/university personnel with whom the students have contact when they make inquiries and/or disclose their disability during the application or registration process.

Other factors that are being explored that make a campus more welcoming are policies and procedures including, for instance, those that mandate that electronic-based communication be accessible to screen reading technology for those with severe reading disabilities or visual impairments. Other institutional policies provide for priority registration, a petition process for course substitutions, and an appeal process for denial of accommodations.

My colleagues and I launched a three-year project to enhance campus climate and thereby academic success for students with LD/D. The project team began by assessing the campus climate and knowledge and practices of faculty, administration, and SPS as the first step in a three-year project. Following this self-study, instruments were developed that addressed the specific informational needs of faculty, administrators, and SPS, taking into consideration the differences in how each of the constituents wanted to acquire the information, e.g., web-based information, workshops, speakers, film/video, one-to-one consultation, etc. Following implementation and provision of workshops, courses, web-based alternatives, etc. the campus climate is then re-assessed.

LONG-TERM RETROSPECTIVE AND FOLLOW-UP STUDIES

Retrospective and prospective follow-up studies are described in Chapters 13, 14, and 15. We need to conduct more such studies regarding the accomplishments and continuing challenges that college-able adults with LD/D face. Pamela Adelman and I have joined forces with Christopher Murray and Carol Wren of DePaul University to launch a 20-year follow-up study of college-able adults with LD/D compared to their non-disabled peers. In addition to educational attainment, employment and occupational status, the impact of LD/D in their personal lives and on the job, and the use of compensatory strategies and/or accommodations, we are pursuing in-depth, the emotional impact of LD/D, the quality of the adults' interpersonal relationships, and issues related to parenting children with LD/D.

LOOKING AHEAD

The recommendations below are offered in order to improve access and academic success for students with LD/D. They are based on the recommendations made by the Association on Higher Education and Disability (AHEAD) organization on the occasion of the reauthorization of the Higher Education Act. AHEAD represents almost 2,000 professionals (about one-third are from outside the U.S.) We have learned from the preceding chapters that there are more similarities than differences about our concerns. We are in many respects a global community. Although enrollment of students with LD/D has increased dramatically in the last five years, tuition and fees have increased as well, state support for public institutions has decreased , and the needs of students with LD/D have increased as a result of reductions in vocational rehabilitation support. We therefore make the following recommendations knowing that they are appropriate for all of us engaged in helping adults with LD/D achieve their highest goals.

RECOMMENDATIONS

1. Financial aid in the form of scholarships rather than loans or work-study contracts should be considered on the basis of work load, not the number of credit hours carried. Students with disabilities enrolled half time often spend the same amount of time studying as class mates enrolled full time. Students who have severe LD/D may receive poorer or even failing grades if forced to take a full-time load. They need to spend time on their course work while at the same time they may need to learn to use new adaptive technology to meet the demands of university courses. Often using this essential technology, such as screen readers to access printed material, takes a great deal of time. At the same time, living expenses remain constant whether students study part time or full time.

2. Year round study should not only be supported financially, but encouraged, allowing students to keep pace and make up for taking less than a full load during the year. If year round support is unavailable, students are faced with the difficult decision of carrying a heavier load than advisable and getting poorer grades than they would otherwise.

3. The maximum level of support should be increased for student assistance in the early stages of their educational experience when the adjustment to the demands of college/university is the most challenging. Moreover, if students flounder in their early course work, they carry the burden of these poor grades throughout their educational career and their grade point average will be affected negatively for the duration of their educational career at that institution.

4. Institutions should provide training for faculty, administration, and supportive professional staff and establish institutional policies and monitoring procedures to insure that

electronic-based information including Distance Education courses are accessible to screen reader technology.

5. Workshops, web-based instruction, and one-to-one consultation should be made available to faculty to familiarize them with the principles of Universal Design for Learning and Assessment. Use of these principles has been found to maximize learning for all students and minimize the need for accommodations for students with disabilities.

6. Funding for innovative initiatives, model programs, and long-term follow-up studies regarding adult outcomes should be provided as well as conferences and publications to disseminate these projects.

CONCLUSIONS

We have learned that different legislation can generate postsecondary support services and accommodations for adults with LD/D. Moreover, these adults can attain similar levels of educational, occupational and financial status as their non-disabled peers when given the opportunities. They can also achieve international recognition in spite of dyslexia. Legislation and challenges to the law vary by nation and decade, but we share the desire to create environments that nurture success. Through an international collaboration, we can continue learning from one another and fostering and monitoring success not only for adults with LD/D, but for their children and grandchildren.

REFERENCES

Fink, R. 2002. Successful careers: The secrets of adults with dyslexia. *Career Planning and Adult Development* 18:118–35.

Heiman, T., and Precel. K. 2003. Students with learning disabilities in higher education: Academic strategies profile. *Journal of Learning Disabilities* 36(3):248–58.

Higher Education Statistics Agency. 1999. *Students in universities: 1997/1998.* Reference Volume. Cheltenham, UK: Author.

Margalit, Breznitz and Aharoni, M. 1998. B'dicat hatipul b'studentim im likuyi limeda b'mosdot le'haskala geyoha (Students with learning disabilities in higher education institutions). Unpublished report. Israel: The Council for Higher Education.

Vogel, S. A., Leonard, F., Scales, W., Hayslip, E., Hermanson, J., and Donnells, L. 1998. The National Learning Disabilities Postsecondary Data Bank: An overview. *Journal of Learning Disabilities* 31(3):234–47.

Index

(Page numbers in italics indicate material in tables or figures.)